THE
COOK'S
BOOK
CONCISE EDITION

THE COOK'S BOOK

CONCISE EDITION

EDITOR-IN-CHIEF
JILL NORMAN

LONDON • NEW YORK • MELBOURNE
MUNICH • DELHI

Senior Project Editors
Annelise Evans, Michael Fullalove, Pippa Rubinstein

Consulting Editor
Norma MacMillan

Senior Art Editors
Susan Downing, with Alison Donovan

Editors
Lucy Heaver, Caroline Reed, Frank Ritter

Designer
Alison Shackleton

Art Director
Carole Ash

Publishing Director
Mary-Clare Jerram

Publishing Manager
Gillian Roberts

DTP Designer
Sonia Charbonnier

Production Controller
Joanna Bull

Photographers
Steve Baxter, Martin Brigdale, Francesco Guillamet, Jeff Kauck,
David Munns, William Reavell

First American Edition 2007
07 08 09 10 9 8 7 6 5 4 3 2

First published as *The Cook's Book* in 2005

Published in the United States by DK Publishing, Inc., 375 Hudson Street
New York, New York 10014

Published as *The Cook's Book Concise Edition* in 2007 by Dorling Kindersley Limited
Project Manager and Editor Claire Tennant-Scull
Project Designer Elaine Hewson

DK books are available at special discounts for bulk purchases for sales promotions, premiums,
fund-raising, or educational use. For details, contact: DK Publishing Special Markets, 375 Hudson
Street, New York, NY 10014. SpecialSales@dk.com

A catalog record for this book is available
from the Library of Congress
ISBN 978-0-7566-3231-1

Color reproduction by GRB, Italy
Printed and bound by Star Standard, Singapore

Discover more at **www.dk.com**

CONTENTS

FOREWORD

THIS BOOK IS BASED ON THE BELIEF THAT HOME COOKS CAN BENEFIT FROM UNDERSTANDING CHEFS'
TECHNIQUES. CHEFS PRACTICE AND PERFECT THEIR SKILLS DAILY; THEY DEVELOP SHORTCUTS WHERE POSSIBLE,
BUT ALSO ACCEPT THAT A SLOW PROCESS, PERFORMED WELL, MAY BE NECESSARY FOR A GOOD RESULT.

WHILE MANY TECHNIQUES REMAIN ROOTED IN THE CLASSIC FRENCH TRADITION, MAINSTREAM WESTERN
COOKING IS CONSTANTLY EVOLVING AS CHEFS EMBRACE IDEAS FROM OTHER CUISINES OR INVENT WHOLLY
NEW PRACTICES.

THE TALENTED CHEFS FROM MANY COUNTRIES WHO HAVE CONTRIBUTED TO THIS BOOK ARE ALL AT THE TOP OF
THEIR PROFESSION AND AT THE FOREFRONT OF CULINARY DEVELOPMENT. THEY SHARE THEIR EXPERTISE AND
DEMONSTRATE THE BEST METHODS FOR PREPARING ALL KINDS OF FOOD THROUGH HUNDREDS OF PRECISE STEP-
BY-STEP PHOTOGRAPHS AND EXPLANATORY NOTES. THESE ENABLE YOU TO FOLLOW CLOSELY HOW A CHEF
FILLETS A FISH OR CLARIFIES A CONSOMMÉ; A BAKER ACHIEVES THE RIGHT TEXTURE IN A DOUGH OR THE PERFECT
CRUST ON A LOAF; OR A PASTRY CHEF CREATES A SUMPTUOUS TART OR A STUNNING DESSERT. THE TECHNIQUES
ARE FOLLOWED BY SIMPLE RECIPES BASED ON THE INGREDIENTS PREPARED, AND SIGNATURE DISHES FROM
EACH CHEF'S REPERTOIRE.

THE PRINCIPAL CHAPTERS ARE DEVOTED TO PREPARATIONS SUCH AS SAUCES, CAKES, OR DESSERTS, OR TO
INGREDIENTS SUCH AS EGGS, VEGETABLES, OR MEAT. THESE ARE INTERSPERSED WITH CHAPTERS THAT GIVE
AN INSIGHT INTO THE TECHNIQUES, TOOLS, AND FOODS OF SOME OF THE WORLD'S FAVORITE CUISINES. HERE
EACH CHEF DEMONSTRATES THE KITCHEN SKILLS AND RECIPES THAT TOGETHER WILL CREATE AN AUTHENTIC
MEAL, INVITING YOU TO NEW CULINARY ADVENTURES, BE THEY THAI OR INDIAN. SOME CONCENTRATE
ON CLASSIC PREPARATIONS; OTHERS SHOW HOW TRADITIONAL TECHNIQUES ARE NOW BEING APPLIED
TO NEW INGREDIENTS.

ASIAN INFLUENCES HAVE BEEN ABSORBED INTO WESTERN COOKING IN RECENT DECADES: SHAUN HILL ADOPTS
A CHINESE METHOD OF STEAMING DUCK TO RID IT OF EXCESS FAT, AND THEN FRYING IT UNTIL THE SKIN IS CRISP.
NEW TECHNIQUES HAVE BEEN DEVELOPED TO CREATE A NEW STYLE OF COOKING: PAUL GAYLER DEMONSTRATES
LIGHTER AND LESS TIME-CONSUMING JUS-BASED CLASSIC SAUCES, AS WELL AS MANY SIMPLE, FRESH-TASTING
VEGETABLE SAUCES. CHARLIE TROTTER INTRODUCES THE CONCEPT OF "RAW" AND THE USE OF A DEHYDRATOR
TO KEEP VEGETABLES CLOSE TO THEIR NATURAL STATE, THUS PRESERVING FLAVOR AND TEXTURE.

TECHNIQUES ARE THE KEY TO GOOD COOKING. *THE COOK'S BOOK* PROVIDES THE MOST COMPREHENSIVE GUIDE
TO ALL YOU MAY EVER NEED IN THE KITCHEN.

JILL NORMAN

INTRODUCING THE CHEFS

WHEN THE IDEA FOR THIS BOOK WAS FIRST PUT FORWARD, IT SEEMED OBVIOUS THAT CHEFS FROM DIFFERENT PARTS OF THE WORLD SHOULD BE INVITED TO PARTICIPATE. THE GLOBAL KITCHEN IS INCREASINGLY A REALITY. CHEFS TRAVEL FROM ONE CONTINENT TO ANOTHER TO TALK AND WORK TOGETHER, TO DEMONSTRATE THEIR SKILLS, TO DEVELOP THEIR EXPERTISE, AND TO CREATE NEW IDEAS.

THE FIRST PERSON I APPROACHED WAS THE INFLUENTIAL CHARLIE TROTTER IN CHICAGO; HIS IMMEDIATE ENTHUSIASM MADE THE PROJECT SEEM POSSIBLE, RATHER THAN ABSURDLY AMBITIOUS. HIS ENCOURAGEMENT AND SUGGESTIONS ABOUT OTHER CHEFS HAVE BEEN INVALUABLE. THROUGH CHARLIE I MET TOP PARISIAN PÂTISSIER PIERRE HERMÉ, WHOSE CREATIONS SPARKLE LIKE JEWELS IN THE WINDOWS OF HIS BOUTIQUES. IN PARIS, I ALSO TRACKED DOWN AN OLD FRIEND, KEN HOM, WHO AGREED TO WRITE THE CHINESE CHAPTER. THE ITALIAN ROOTS AND MODERN AMERICAN APPROACH OF NEW YORK CHEF MICHAEL ROMANO MADE HIM THE NATURAL CHOICE TO WRITE ON PASTA.

IN THE U.K., SHAUN HILL, PAUL GAYLER, AND MARCUS WAREING BROUGHT THEIR MANY TALENTS TO THE BOOK, FOLLOWED BY SKILLED BAKER DAN LEPARD AND INVENTIVE YOUNG INDIAN CHEF, ATUL KOCHHAR. NEW ZEALANDER, PETER GORDON, LONG A RESTAURATEUR IN LONDON, DREW ON HIS ECLECTIC FUSION FOOD TO ILLUSTRATE THE TECHNIQUES OF FLAVORING. HAMBURG PÂTISSIER, STEPHAN FRANZ'S KNOWLEDGE OF DIFFERENT TRADITIONS ENABLED HIM TO WRITE ON GERMAN, FRENCH, AND AMERICAN CAKEMAKING.

SOME OF THE MOST INTERESTING FOOD TODAY IS AUSTRALIAN AND I WAS DELIGHTED WHEN TWO AUSTRALIAN CHEFS AGREED TO JOIN US: CHRISTINE MANFIELD, WHO HAS AN INSTINCTIVE FEELING FOR WORKING WITH ASIAN INGREDIENTS; AND DAVID THOMPSON, MASTER OF CLASSIC THAI COOKING, WHO TEACHES EVEN THE THAIS. THE CHEFS HAVE COLLABORATED, EXCHANGED IDEAS, AND ALWAYS BEEN MUTUALLY SUPPORTIVE. WORKING WITH SUCH TALENTED AND CREATIVE PEOPLE HAS BEEN VERY REWARDING. I AM VERY GRATEFUL TO THEM ALL FOR THEIR UNSTINTING COMMITMENT TO MAKING *THE COOK'S BOOK* A REALITY.

Jill Norman

JILL NORMAN

MARCUS WAREING

INSPIRATION FOR A DISH CAN COME FROM CONVERSATION, A BOOK, A FLAVOR — ANY OF THESE CAN PLANT A SEED.

Marcus Wareing's culinary training began at Southport College in England. At the age of 18, he moved to the Savoy Hotel in London, then worked at the Michelin-three-star restaurant, Le Gavroche, under Albert Roux and Michel Roux Jr. Marcus next worked at the Point, a luxury resort in upstate New York; at the Grand Hotel in Amsterdam, Holland; and at Gravetye Manor in England. On his return to London, Marcus was part of the starting brigade at Aubergine, working beside Gordon Ramsay from 1993 to 1995. He was proud to be named Young Chef of the Year by the Restaurant Association in 1995.

After working under Daniel Boulud in New York and Guy Savoy in Paris, Marcus became head chef at L'Oranger in London, gaining his first Michelin star at the age of 25. In 1999, he opened Pétrus with Gordon Ramsay in St. James's, London, regaining his Michelin star, and in 2007 Pétrus gained a second. Pétrus relocated to the Berkeley Hotel in 2003, and Marcus returned to the starting point of his career with the relaunch of the Savoy Grill and Banquette at the Savoy Hotel. In 2003, the Savoy Grill earned a Michelin star.

In 2006 Marcus cooked for the Queen as part of the Great British Menu television series. His first book, *Cook the Perfect …* is published by Dorling Kindersley.

USEFUL INFORMATION

The following reminders will help you to make the most of this unique guide to cooking, drawn from some of the top restaurant kitchens of the world. Specific terms, unfamiliar techniques, and less common ingredients are explained in the glossary on p482.

USING THE RECIPES

Recipe introductions provide background to the dish, its origins and preparation, and serving suggestions. Read through the recipe to ensure you have all the necessary ingredients and equipment.

■ Each recipe serves four unless otherwise stated.

■ Measurements are provided in cups and spoons, and (where appropriate) in both stardard and metric weights. In baking recipes, metric weights are given in addition to cups, for those cooks who prefer to measure ingredients by weight instead of volume. Note that standard and metric weights—and volume and weight measures—for the same ingredient are not exact equivalents.

■ Ovens should be preheated to the temperature specified in the recipe. Both Fahrenheit and Celsius temperatures are given.

■ Cooking times are only intended to be a guide. They can vary according to the ingredients (for example, ripeness or thickness), the heat, or the equipment, such as type of pan. Check cooking progress where it is suggested in the recipe.

■ When a recipe can be partially or fully prepared in advance, instructions are included at the appropriate stage. Follow the instructions for chilling, storing, and finishing as appropriate.

■ When preparing recipes that have to be frozen, if necessary, turn the freezer to the appropriate setting in advance, following the manufacturer's directions.

Accurate measuring

■ All cup and spoon measures are level, unless heaping or scant are specified in a recipe.

■ Use a clear measuring cup for liquids and stand it on a level surface, then check the quantity at eye level.

■ Do not pour ingredients into a measuring spoon or cup over the food you are preparing in case excess overflows into the mixture.

■ Weighing ingredients using kitchen scales is a very accurate means of measuring, particularly for baking recipes.

Ingredients

The quality of the ingredients is reflected in the finished dish, so all foods should be in the best condition. Fresh produce, fish, meat, and poultry should be just that—fresh. Frozen ingredients should be good quality and adequately packed so as not to have deteriorated during storage because of freezer burn, which dries out the surface of food. They should not be beyond their sell-by or expiration date. Dried or pantry ingredients, such as flour, grains, nuts, and seeds, should be in good condition; discard items that are stale or beyond their expiration date. Oils and vinegars deteriorate in flavor when stored in very warm or light conditions.

Follow recipe instructions and tips on choice of ingredients, for example, on the size and ripeness of fruit. Essential preparation or cutting instructions are given in the ingredients list. When preparation is mentioned before the ingredient, this should be completed before measuring the quantity.

■ Unless otherwise stated, all vegetables and fruit are assumed to be medium in size. They should be washed, scrubbed, or peeled as usual, unless alternative instructions are given.

■ Ingredients that discolor or deteriorate once prepared should be cut at the appropriate stage in the recipe.

■ Use the type of flour specified—all-purpose, bread, cake, or pastry—because substitution may affect the recipe result.

■ Use granulated sugar, unless otherwise stated.

■ Use fresh herbs, unless dried herbs are specified.

■ Use the type of oil specified in the recipe.

■ Vinegars have different flavors and preservation qualities, so use the one listed.

■ Use the type of milk specified, for example, whole milk.

■ Use large eggs, unless otherwise stated. Eggs vary, so in some recipes weights are also given for greater accuracy and success.

Note It is recommended that young children or the vulnerable should avoid recipes made with raw or undercooked eggs.

EQUIPMENT

A well-equipped kitchen should have a small selection of good-quality, basic equipment, which is well cared for and kept in good condition. As a general rule, the simpler the tool and the more frequently it is to be used, then the better quality it should be. Knives and pots and pans are used often and, with care, those that are of good quality will last for many years. Less expensive items, such as whisks, spatulas, spoons, strainers, and mixing bowls, usually do not have as long a working life.

Personal choice is important so that you have implements that are comfortable and practical for your requirements, skills, everyday quantities, and style. Equipment should work well together: Pots and pans, ovenware, and bakeware should be right for your stove in type, size, and shape. Check manufacturer's guidelines when planning your selection of pots and pans—some materials do not work on certain types of heat. Select one or two small electrical appliances for a range of tasks, rather than having several items that could be used for the same jobs. If you are equipping a kitchen from scratch, start with a few essential, high-quality items and build on these as your cooking repertoire develops.

Note Some types of plastic wrap and resealable plastic bags are unsuitable for use with heat. Check manufacturers' directions before use in any recipe that calls for these items.

Pots and pans

Cast iron This conducts heat well and heats up quickly. It also retains heat well, which can be an advantage for long, slow cooking. However, cast-iron pans are heavy and, if not enameled, will rust unless they are oiled or "seasoned" after washing.

Copper Although an excellent heat-conductor, pots and pans made from this reactive metal need to be lined. Tin and silver were the traditional linings, but stainless steel is preferred nowadays. Copper pots and pans are beautiful but expensive.

Enameled iron and steel When a glassy enamel finish is applied to metal pots and pans, it makes them more durable and hard-wearing, and excellent for both stovetop and oven cooking. The pots and pans need to be cleaned without scrubbing, however, and are vulnerable to chipping when hot.

Earthenware and ceramics Porcelain, glazed earthenware, and stoneware do not conduct heat particularly well but withstand high temperatures, so are normally reserved for ovenware. Some surfaces are more tough than others; all are prone to chipping.

Ovenproof glass Glass is not as good a heat-conductor as metal, but glass bakeware is practical, durable, versatile, and inexpensive, and it is available in many styles.

Stainless steel Because this is not the best conductor of heat, pots and pans for stovetop use have a layer of another metal in the base. This may be copper, copper and silver alloy, or aluminum or aluminum alloy. Stainless steel does not react with acid or alkaline ingredients, making it suitable for cooking all types of foods. High-quality, sandwich-base stainless-steel pots and pans are very durable and, with care, will have a long life.

Nonstick cookware There is a wide choice of varying quality. As a general rule, nonstick coatings do not withstand high heat well, so most manufacturers recommend that nonstick pans be used over low or medium heat. Their advantages are that little or no fat is needed for cooking and they are easy to clean.

Knives

From the vast choice available, select a small number of knives according to quality, material, and the tasks to be performed. The best knives are made from one piece of metal that can be seen to go right through the length of the handle. A large cook's or chef's knife with a blade at least 8in (20cm) long; a paring knife; a small to medium serrated knife (good for tomatoes and thin-skinned fruit); and a bread knife make a good basic kit. A sharpening steel or whetstone is essential: The safest knife is a sharp knife. A blunt one is far more dangerous, as well as being frustrating to use. It is also important to have a wooden block or rack for storing knives so they cannot knock together and damage and dull each other.

Carbon steel Knives can be honed to razor sharpness and are durable. However, they will stain if used to prepare acidic foods, such as lemons and tomatoes, and are prone to rusting.

Stainless steel This is nonreactive, but it does not sharpen well.

Carbon-stainless This combines the best of carbon and stainless steel—knives can be sharpened, are durable, and do not stain or rust. High-quality knives are expensive, but they will last for years

Other utensils and electrical appliances

Select other kitchen tools according to the cooking you want to do. Thermometers give accurate temperature readings when deep-frying and candymaking, as well as testing meat and poultry for doneness. Zesters and graters are invaluable for citrus fruit and cheese, and a siphon is essential for making foams.

Food processor This machine will chop, purée, knead, grind, and combine foods, but does not whip or cream well. Blades for slicing, shredding, grating, and cutting julienne are optional, along with a wide variety of attachments for many purposes, including juicing. Among the many features, a pulse setting is very useful.

Electric mixer A hand-held mixer will beat air into ingredients (most usefully when the bowl is set over a pan of hot water), cream fats, and combine mixtures. A heavy-duty stand mixer, being more powerful, beats cake batters and kneads bread doughs with ease.

Blender This produces smoother purées than a food processor, so is preferred for soupmaking. Hand-held immersion blenders can purée the food directly in its pan or bowl, and can also be used to whip cream and make mayonnaise.

Ice-cream maker There are several types of machine that will churn and freeze mixtures to make smooth ice cream and sorbet.

HYGIENE

Cutting boards, knives, and other utensils used in the preparation of raw poultry, meat, or fish must be washed thoroughly with hot soapy water before being used again. Many professional kitchens color-code their boards to avoid the risk of cross-contamination.

SAUCES & DRESSINGS

PAUL GAYLER

Most home cooks appear to regard saucemaking as some secret or mystical exercise, exclusively reserved for temperamental chefs in posh restaurants. During my many years in top kitchens I have often been asked, "How do you know what goes with what?" and "How do you make sauces?" Admittedly, at first sight the saucemaking aspect of cooking is enough to send any cook into despair; the repertoire of classic sauces alone is so vast that a mere listing of their names can baffle a beginner. However, saucemaking is not rocket science, and learning a few of the basic sauces (called mother sauces) will give you the ability, freedom, and confidence to produce many more. For any cook, saucemaking can become one of the most rewarding branches of cookery.

What is a sauce? A sauce is best described as a flavorful liquid, made from a variety of bases that have been lightly thickened. Stocks of all flavors should be made with the utmost care and attention, as they ultimately form the base flavor, quality, and success of your sauce. Ideally, I suggest making your own stocks, whether meat, fish, or vegetable. Although a little time-consuming, they are well worth the effort. If your time is limited, use a bouillon powder or consommé. Instructions for making stocks are in the chapter Stocks & Soups, p54.

Sauces can be thickened by a simple reduction (rapidly boiling to evaporate excess liquid) or by the addition of a little starch. The majority of the classic sauces are made with one form of starch or another, but sauces are also thickened by other means. Hollandaise or mayonnaise sauces are emulsified with eggs; butter sauces with butter; cream sauces are finished with cream; and vegetable sauces are thickened with puréed vegetables. There are even some sauces thickened with animal blood, although these are somewhat rare nowadays. Complex sauces are the basis of great French cuisine and the glory of any dinner party or special occasion. They may be time-consuming, but in terms of flavor they really pay dividends in the finished dish.

The variety of sauces The term sauce covers a very wide range of accompaniments. There are the many classic French sauces, such as white béchamel, blond velouté, brown veal and chicken jus sauces, warm white butter sauces (beurre blanc and beurre fondu), and cold savory butter sauces. There are the salsas of Mexico and Spain, and the hot and spicy sauces of the Far East. Also included are light vinaigrettes (French dressings) for salads or fish dishes, and the relishes and chutneys synonymous with old England.

Over the last decade or so our eating patterns have changed dramatically. Our knowledge of world cuisines has increased, with many of us traveling and eating out more often than ever before. Today's chefs are responding to demands for lighter sauces that are simpler, less rich, and more easily prepared than those of the past, whether they are for everyday use or for special occasions.

Marrying sauces with foods Whatever sauce you choose to make, it is extremely important that it complements, highlights, and enhances the flavor of the dish it accompanies, whether it be eggs, fish, vegetables, meat, poultry or game, salad, or a dessert. The sauce should never overpower the food or be overpowered by it. Generally, a sauce must have a clear flavor, good texture, and a glossy appearance. In this chapter you will find the basics of cooking a good sauce, suggestions for sauce variations, and some sauces in new styles for your enjoyment.

Today, supermarkets offer an increasing range of ready-prepared sauces, but nothing can compare to the flavors of fresh sauces made in your own kitchen. One last thought: I always teach my cooks that the refinement of flavor of any sauce, or dish for that matter, depends on the seasoning, which in turn depends entirely on the tastebuds of the cook. A good sauce always can be achieved if it is frequently and appreciatively tasted during its making. I wish you "Bon appetit!" as you go forward and improve your knowledge and appreciation of great sauces.

BASIC SAUCEMAKING TECHNIQUES

Successful saucemaking relies on one or more of the following professional techniques, according to the type of sauce you want to prepare. The techniques are not difficult and they will ensure that you achieve superb results. Equipment such as whisks, spatulas, skimmers, and fine strainers will prove invaluable to the process. I have found it vitally important to use the right piece and size of equipment for the job or task in hand—it certainly makes cooking, and in particular saucemaking, much easier.

Whisking

Rapid whisking will emulsify and blend ingredients, aerate and add lightness to sauces containing egg yolks or cream, and make white sauces smooth and glossy. You can either use a supple, slim balloon whisk or a flat coil whisk.

To incorporate the maximum air, whisk from the bottom of the bowl or pan up, working around the sides and across the middle.

Cooked sauces that contain egg yolks are usually whisked in a bowl set over a pan of simmering water to prevent them from curdling.

Skimming

One of the most important and often overlooked steps in sauce-making, skimming removes fat, foam, and other impurities, which would otherwise spoil the flavor and appearance of a sauce.

Skim regularly during the cooking process, using a shallow perforated skimmer to remove any foam or other impurities as they rise to the surface of the sauce.

Brown sauces made in advance can be chilled and any excess fat that solidifies on the surface can be skimmed off with a spoon.

Straining & sieving

Straining removes solid ingredients and sieving helps emulsify liquids to make elegantly smooth sauces.

To sieve, hold a fine-mesh strainer over a pan or bowl and pour in the sauce. Using the back of a ladle, press the sauce through the strainer. Discard solids left in the strainer.

Reducing

Reducing a sauce will decrease its volume through evaporation and thus intensify its flavor. To reduce, cook in an uncovered pan over high heat, stirring occasionally.

Deglazing

Pan sauces and gravies are made from the deglazed caramelized juices released from roasted or fried meat, poultry, and vegetables.

To make a pan sauce, remove the food from the pan and spoon off excess fat, then deglaze the caramelized juices by adding stock, water, or wine and stirring to loosen the particles and incorporate them into the liquid. Reduce and finish as required. Making a sauce like this gives a richness and depth of flavor that cannot be achieved just by simmering ingredients.

Clarifying butter

When butter is heated gently, the milk solids will separate from the butterfat and the clear liquid fat—clarified butter—can be poured off. Unsalted butter is better for clarifying than salted butter.

Clarified butter can be heated to higher temperatures than ordinary butter, so is often used for sautéing. I also like to use clarified butter for hollandaise and béarnaise sauces.

1 Cut butter into cubes, put into a pan, and heat gently just until the milk solids have separated from the fat (left). Do not let the butter get too dark or its fresh taste will be destroyed. Skim off any froth.

2 Carefully pour the clear liquid butter into a bowl (right). Discard the milk solids in the pan. Skim off any impurities on the surface of the clarified butter.

WAYS TO THICKEN A SAUCE

Most sauces are given body and consistency by combining a flavorsome liquid with one or more thickening agents. Some are added at the beginning of the saucemaking process, while others are added at the last minute. In addition to the thickeners below, sauces can also be thickened with blood (for poultry and game dishes) and colorful fruit or vegetable purées.

Blending

Many sauces can be quickly made in a blender. Hollandaise and pesto are examples. Blenders—goblet or immersion—are also great for blending purées and liquids together for light, last-minute sauces.

Seasoning

Salt and pepper are necessary to enhance the flavors in a sauce, but they should be used in moderation. Before serving, taste the sauce and adjust the seasoning, if necessary. White pepper is preferable to black in pale sauces.

FLAVORINGS

■ Always use fresh herbs in sauces. Soft herbs, such as chives, tarragon, and basil, should be chopped and stirred in at the last moment. Hardy herbs, such as rosemary and thyme, can be cooked in the sauce.
■ Freshly crush or grind spices and add sparingly at the start of cooking. Taste and add more later, as needed.

Roux

This cooked mixture of butter and flour is used to thicken white sauces such as béchamel. Melt butter in a pan until foaming, stir in an equal amount of flour, and cook, stirring, for about 40 seconds. Stir in milk and simmer until thickened.

Butter

Chilled butter whisked into a hot sauce gives body and shine. Be sure the butter does not get too hot, or it will separate.

Take the finished sauce off the heat and gradually whisk in small cubes of well-chilled unsalted butter.

Bread

Bread is sometimes used to thicken sauces—bread sauce is a good example. Around the Mediterranean, bread is widely used with nuts in sauces such as Turkish tarator, Italian salsa di noci, and Spanish romesco (p44).

Beurre manié

Beurre manié (or kneaded butter) is a paste of butter and flour added at the end of cooking. To make it, use a fork to mix soft butter with all-purpose flour in a ratio of two to one. Gradually whisk small pieces into the hot sauce until it thickens.

Arrowroot, potato flour & cornstarch

These forms of starch are always mixed with a little cold liquid first before being added to a sauce at the end of cooking. They will thicken the sauce immediately.

Arrowroot and potato flour (fécule) are used in brown sauces and to thicken rich reduced broths, while cornstarch is the normal thickener in some Chinese dishes and sweet sauces.

In general, 1½ tsp arrowroot or cornstarch will thicken 1 cup of sauce. Mix the starch with liquid, then whisk into the sauce and simmer gently for 2 minutes to thicken. Do not cook longer or the sauce will tend to become thin again. Finish the sauce as required.

Eggs & cream

Eggs, particularly the yolks, are the thickening base of many emulsion sauces. Hot emulsified sauces such as hollandaise are cooked in a bowl over a pan of simmering water to prevent the yolks from overheating.

Egg yolks mixed with cream (to make what is called a liaison) are sometimes used to enrich and thicken classic velouté sauces. A liaison is always added at the end of cooking.

To thicken with a liaison, put the egg yolks and cream in a bowl and whisk in a spoonful of the hot sauce. Add this mixture to the rest of the sauce in the pan, off the heat. Return to very low heat and cook, stirring constantly, until the sauce coats the back of the spoon. Do not allow the sauce to boil or it will curdle. Serve immediately.

EMULSIFIED SAUCES

Chief among emulsified sauces are mayonnaise, hollandaise, and beurre blanc. They are made by forming an emulsion of droplets of fat such as oil or melted butter in a liquid such as water, vinegar, or lemon juice. Egg yolk is often present to hold the emulsion stable.

Emulsified sauces have a certain notoriety for separating and curdling. The key is to create—and maintain—the emulsion correctly: The speed at which the fat is added and sustaining the right temperature throughout the process are important.

MAYONNAISE

A smooth and delicious sauce made from egg yolks, oil, vinegar, and mustard, mayonnaise is perhaps the most popular of all cold sauces and forms the basis of numerous variations. It is especially good with poached and deep-fried fish, cold fish and shellfish, and cold meats.

Olive oil can be rather overpowering in mayonnaise, so I recommend the use of an unflavored oil such as sunflower or canola.

Being a bit of a traditionalist, I prefer to make mayonnaise using a whisk and bowl, but—for those keen on saving labor—I have also included a method using a blender or food processor.

Before you start, make sure all ingredients, especially eggs and oil, are at room temperature, since they are difficult to emulsify when cold. To establish the emulsion right from the beginning, add the oil literally drop by drop to start with.

Makes 1¼ cups

2 egg yolks
1 tsp Dijon mustard
1 tsp white wine vinegar
1 cup sunflower or canola oil
2 tsp lemon juice

BLENDER MAYONNAISE

Mayonnaise can be made successfully in a blender or a food processor, but always make at least 1¼ cups. I have learned from experience that a small amount does not blend properly.

Place the egg yolks, mustard, vinegar, and a pinch of salt in a blender or food processor. With the machine switched to the lowest speed, blend these ingredients together. With the machine still running, trickle in the oil in a steady, slow stream through the hole in the lid until the mayonnaise is thick and emulsified. Add the lemon juice and blend briefly, then adjust the seasoning to taste.

1 Place the egg yolks, mustard, and vinegar in a mixing bowl. Add a pinch each of salt and pepper (for preference, white pepper).

2 Steady the bowl on a dampened kitchen towel and pour in the oil—drop by drop to begin with, then a drizzle—whisking all the time.

3 Add the oil in a steady stream as the sauce begins to thicken, whisking continuously to keep the emulsion stable.

4 When all the oil has been incorporated and the mayonnaise is thick, stir in the lemon juice and adjust the seasoning to taste.

Classic mayonnaise-based sauces

Aïoli (garlic mayonnaise)
Add 4 crushed garlic cloves to the egg yolks, then continue as for the master recipe. Perfect with hot or cold fish and as a dip for vegetables.

Rouille (chili mayonnaise)
Add a pinch of saffron and ¼ tsp cayenne pepper to aïoli (above). Traditionally served with the Mediterranean fish soup bouillabaisse.

Tartar sauce
Add 2½ tbsp finely chopped gherkins, 2 tbsp rinsed and chopped capers, 2 tbsp chopped parsley, 2 tbsp chopped chervil, and 2 chopped shallots to the finished mayonnaise. Good with deep-fried and pan-fried fish.

Rémoulade
Add 1 finely chopped anchovy fillet and 2 tbsp chopped tarragon to tartar sauce (left). Serve with cold meats, cold fish, and fried fish.

Truffle mayonnaise
Replace 1 tbsp of the sunflower or canola oil with truffle oil, then add a little finely shaved truffle to the finished mayonnaise. Great with fish, vegetables, and cold meats.

Thick, glossy, and unctuous—perfect mayonnaise

Rescuing curdled mayonnaise

When mayonnaise separates into coagulated flecks of egg and oil, it has curdled. (In the trade this is also known as splitting.) Curdling can happen for several reasons. Here are the most likely causes of curdling:

- The egg yolks or oil were too cold.
- The oil was added too rapidly to begin with.
- Too much oil was added.

Happily, curdled mayonnaise is easy to rescue.

1 Place 1 egg yolk or 1 tsp Dijon mustard (this will affect the flavor slightly) in a bowl, then trickle in the curdled mayonnaise, whisking.

2 Continue whisking in the curdled mixture until it is all incorporated and smooth.

HOLLANDAISE SAUCE

For me, hollandaise is the best of all sauces—wonderfully smooth, light, and delicate. A good, well-made hollandaise has a rich yellow color, a slightly tart flavor, and a fluffy texture—somewhat like a warm mayonnaise in consistency. It is the perfect match for poached fish or vegetables and egg dishes. Hollandaise is sometimes made using simple melted butter, but I find that clarified butter gives a richer, smoother flavor.

A curdled hollandaise can be returned to respectability by placing a fresh egg yolk in a clean bowl and whisking in the curdled sauce a little at a time.

Makes 2½ cups

2 tbsp white wine vinegar
2 tbsp water
1 tsp lightly crushed white peppercorns
4 egg yolks
1 cup (2 sticks) unsalted butter, clarified (p26)
juice of ½ lemon
pinch of cayenne pepper

IN A BLENDER

If you are short of time, you can make hollandaise in a blender.

Follow step 1, then leave the vinegar reduction until cold. Strain the mixture and add a pinch each of salt and pepper. Place with the egg yolks in a blender and blend for a few seconds. Heat the clarified butter. With the machine switched to its highest setting, trickle in the hot butter and blend until thick and fluffy. Add the lemon juice and adjust the seasoning.

1 Place the vinegar, water, and peppercorns in a small, heavy-based pan and bring to a boil. Lower the heat and simmer for 1 minute, or until reduced by one-third (to about 2½ tbsp).

2 Remove from the heat and leave until cold, then strain the liquid into a heatproof bowl. Add the egg yolks to the liquid and whisk together.

3 Set the bowl over a pan of simmering water: The base should be just above the water. Whisk the mixture until it thickens and is ribbonlike, creamy, and smooth in texture, 5–6 minutes.

Hollandaise sauce—a warm emulsion of butter and egg yolks

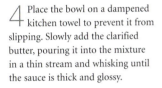

4 Place the bowl on a dampened kitchen towel to prevent it from slipping. Slowly add the clarified butter, pouring it into the mixture in a thin stream and whisking until the sauce is thick and glossy.

5 Add the lemon juice, then season with salt, white pepper, and cayenne pepper. Serve at once. If you need to keep the hollandaise warm, use a water bath (p33) or transfer it to a vacuum flask.

BÉARNAISE SAUCE

Made in exactly the same way as hollandaise, béarnaise sauce has the addition of tarragon and shallots infused in the vinegar. It is one of France's best-loved sauces, enduring the test of time, even in these days of modern sauces. It is usually served, in its simplest form, as an accompaniment to grilled or broiled steaks and fish.

To make béarnaise sauce, at step 1 of the basic hollandaise recipe, add 2 tbsp roughly chopped tarragon and 2 chopped shallots to the vinegar reduction. Then stir 1 tbsp chopped tarragon and 1 tbsp chopped chervil into the finished sauce before serving.

Hollandaise-based sauces

A hollandaise can be flavored with a variety of ingredients.

Foyot sauce
Boil ⅔ cup dry sherry to reduce by half. Let cool, then add to the finished sauce. Serve this with grilled meats, fish, and vegetables.

Maltaise sauce
When blood oranges are in season, there is no better sauce than maltaise to accompany vegetables, particularly asparagus. Simply add the grated zest and strained juice of 2 small blood oranges to the finished sauce instead of the lemon juice.

Mousseline sauce
Fold in ⅓ cup semi-whipped cream just before serving. This is good with steamed asparagus or poached fish. Try adding 1 tbsp chopped herbs too, such as chives, chervil, or tarragon.

Mustard sauce
Stir 1 tbsp Dijon mustard into the finished sauce. Serve with grilled or broiled fish or chicken.

Noisette sauce
Add ¼ cup beurre noisette (p31) to the finished sauce. The nutty flavor goes well with fish.

Olive sauce
Add 1 heaped tbsp chopped good-quality black olives to the finished sauce. This is great with asparagus and egg dishes.

Saffron sauce
Crumble ½ tsp saffron threads into the vinegar and water mixture when you start to make the hollandaise sauce.

Watercress sauce
Add 1 heaped cup chopped watercress leaves to the finished sauce and stir to mix.

Béarnaise-based sauces

Like hollandaise, béarnaise sauce has many variations. The following are some of my favorites.

Balsamic sauce
Replace half the white wine vinegar with balsamic vinegar, then stir 1 tsp balsamic vinegar into the finished sauce in place of the lemon juice. Balsamic sauce is ideal with grilled or roasted meats or fish.

Choron sauce
Add 2 tbsp well-reduced tomato sauce (p40) to the basic recipe. The tomato sauce must be thick, otherwise it will thin the basic béarnaise sauce too much. A well-reduced tomato purée could also be used. Choron sauce is good with grilled or broiled steaks, lamb, chicken, or fish.

Horseradish sauce
For the classic accompaniment to roast rib of beef, stir 1 tbsp white horseradish into the basic sauce. This is also good with grilled or broiled fish, especially salmon.

Paloise sauce
Replace the chopped tarragon with chopped mint. Paloise goes very well with lamb.

BEURRE BLANC

Beurre blanc—also known as white butter sauce—was one of the first sauces I made when I became a professional cook many years ago, and it still stands the test of time. It is another classic emulsified butter sauce, rich in flavor and simple to prepare. Beurre blanc is great with poached and broiled fish. Lightly salted butter makes a slightly thicker sauce than unsalted butter. It is a matter of taste.

Makes 1¼ cups

2 shallots, finely chopped

3 tbsp white wine vinegar

4 tbsp dry white wine

2 tbsp cold water

14 tbsp unsalted or slightly salted butter, chilled and diced

squeeze of lemon juice

1 Place the shallots, wine vinegar, and wine in a small pan and bring to a boil.

2 Lower the heat and reduce the contents until only 1 tbsp liquid remains, about 2 minutes. It should have a light syrupy consistency.

3 Over gentle heat, add the water, then whisk in the butter a little at a time until completely emulsified. Season with salt, white pepper, and lemon juice.

Variations

The flavor of beurre blanc can be varied by changing the type of vinegar or wine and by including other ingredients.

Beurre rouge

For a red butter sauce, replace the white wine with 6 tbsp good-quality red wine and the white wine vinegar with 1 tbsp red wine vinegar.

Herb beurre blanc

Add 1 tbsp finely chopped herbs, such as basil, tarragon, or rosemary, with the shallots.

Saffron beurre blanc

Add a pinch of saffron threads to the vinegar and wine reduction, then proceed as for the basic recipe.

Usually served unstrained, beurre blanc can be strained for a smoother sauce

OTHER BUTTER SAUCES

Compound butters—beurres composés in French—are simple to prepare and very versatile. After blending in the flavorings, roll the butter in wax or parchment paper into a cylindrical shape and chill in the refrigerator or freezer until ready to serve. Enjoy compound butters with grilled or broiled meats, poultry, and fish. Simple sauces like beurre noisette or beurre noir for fish or vegetables are made by heating butter on its own or, in the case of beurre fondu, by adding a little water and lemon juice.

CAFÉ DE PARIS BUTTER

This compound butter is particularly good with grilled or broiled steak and fish.

Makes 1¼ cups

2 tbsp ketchup

1 tsp Dijon mustard

½ tsp chopped capers

1 shallot, finely chopped

1 tsp snipped chives

1 tsp chopped tarragon

2 anchovy fillets, rinsed and chopped

1 tsp Cognac

1 tsp Madeira

1 tsp Worcestershire sauce

pinch of paprika

10 tbsp unsalted butter, softened

1 Place all the ingredients, except the paprika and butter, in a bowl and mix together well. Season with the paprika, and some salt and pepper. Let stand for 24 hours in a warm place so the flavors can infuse.

2 Using a wooden spoon, beat the infused mixture into the softened butter. Roll the butter in wax or parchment paper into a sausage shape, secure the ends, and chill until required.

3 To serve, place a slice of the butter on the meat or fish. The butter will slowly melt over the food and add a wonderful flavor.

BEURRE NOISETTE

For beurre noisette (brown butter sauce), heat 4–5 tbsp salted butter in a pan over medium-high heat until it foams and turns nutty brown, about 2 minutes. Add a squeeze of lemon juice. Serve with vegetables or pan-fried fish.

BEURRE NOIR

Beurre noir (black butter sauce) is cooked in the same way as a beurre noisette, but for 20–30 seconds longer. Traditional with pan-fried skate.

BEURRE FONDU

Bring 4 tbsp water to a boil in a small pan. Off the heat, whisk in 10 tbsp cubed, lightly salted butter until emulsified. Add a squeeze of lemon juice. Serve with asparagus or other vegetables, alongside or instead of hollandaise.

WHITE SAUCES

Easy to prepare and endlessly adaptable, white sauces have been the base of classic European cooking for many years. Béchamel and velouté—the two basic white sauces—are made by combining flour and melted butter to make a roux, then adding differing quantities and combinations of milk, cream, and stock. There are countless variations of these basic sauces, as well as modern adaptations and quicker versions for time-pressed cooks. Here, I give the recipe for a classic béchamel sauce, followed by a modern version of velouté sauce, which is made without a roux. The white sauce in its many guises is here to stay.

BÉCHAMEL SAUCE

Béchamel is the king of white sauces and the one from which many others derive. Contrary to general opinion, it is better to add the milk all at once, rather than little by little, to avoid a lumpy sauce. This recipe gives a medium béchamel, which can be enriched with cream before serving.

Makes 2½ cups

4 whole cloves
1 small onion, halved
2½ cups whole milk
1 small bay leaf
4 tbsp unsalted butter
4 tbsp all-purpose flour
freshly grated nutmeg
½ cup heavy cream (optional)

1 Stick the cloves into the onion. Place in a saucepan with the milk and bay leaf. Bring almost to a boil, then simmer gently for 4–5 minutes. Let cool and infuse.

2 In another pan, melt the butter over low heat. Add the flour and cook gently, stirring frequently with a wooden spoon, until the roux is pale yellow, 30–40 seconds.

3 Remove the pan from the heat. Strain the cooled milk into the roux and whisk vigorously to mix it in smoothly.

ALL-IN-ONE

For a quicker version of béchamel, use this all-in-one method, which omits the stages of infusing the milk and making a roux. The result is still good, although less refined.

  Melt 4 tbsp unsalted butter in a pan. Mix together 2½ cups whole milk and 4 tbsp all-purpose flour. Add to the melted butter, whisking until the sauce thickens. Bring to a boil, then reduce the heat and simmer for 5–6 minutes, whisking frequently. Season with salt, pepper, and nutmeg. Strain before use. Makes 2½ cups.

4 Return the pan to medium heat and continue whisking until the sauce thickens and comes to a boil, 4–5 minutes. Reduce the heat and let simmer gently for 20–25 minutes. When the sauce is smooth and glossy, season with salt, white pepper, and nutmeg.

The ideal coating consistency for a béchamel sauce. Enrich with the cream before serving, if desired

The right consistency

The correct consistency for a béchamel sauce—whether thin, medium, or thick—depends on how you intend to use it:

■ A thin béchamel is ideal for lightly coating vegetables, fish, and meat and for adding body to soups.

■ A medium béchamel is also used for coating vegetables, particularly in a mornay sauce for cauliflower. And it is the one for gratins and pasta dishes like lasagna.

■ Thicker béchamel sauces are used to bind ingredients for fillings and stuffings and for soufflé bases.

The quantities of flour and butter you use to make the sauce largely determine its consistency, although a béchamel that is too thick can ultimately be thinned with a little more milk and a sauce that is too thin can be thickened by whisking in beurre manié (p25).

No matter what consistency of béchamel you are aiming for, if it goes lumpy, whisk vigorously or transfer the mixture to a blender and blitz until smooth.

Thin béchamel
For a thin béchamel, reduce the quantity of butter and flour in the master recipe to 2 tbsp each. The sauce should have the consistency of pourable light cream and only just coat the back of a spoon. If the finished sauce is too thin, whisk in a little beurre manié, in a few small pieces, to thicken it.

Medium béchamel
The sauce produced by using the 4 tbsp each of butter and flour specified in the master recipe has a consistency that will coat the back of a spoon well but still flow easily. Adjust as necessary with a little beurre manié, to thicken, or more milk, to thin.

Thick béchamel
By increasing the amount of butter and flour to 6 tbsp each, the sauce becomes thick enough to bind a mixture but still flow when a spoonful is knocked against the side of the pan. Thin down a sauce that is too thick by stirring in a little extra milk.

Variations

Medium béchamel is the basis of three classic sauces.

Mornay sauce
Add ¾ cup finely grated Cheddar or Gruyère cheese and 1 tsp Dijon mustard to the sauce off the heat. Stir in 2 egg yolks mixed with 4 tbsp heavy cream. Good with cauliflower.

Parsley sauce
Add 3 tbsp chopped parsley and a squeeze of lemon juice to the sauce.

Soubise sauce
Blanch 2 large chopped onions, then sauté them in 4 tbsp butter. Add the béchamel and a pinch of sugar. Cook for 10 minutes, then blend to a purée. Stir in 2 tbsp heavy cream. Serve with lamb or pork.

 KEEPING SAUCES WARM IN A WATER BATH

To keep sauces warm until ready to use, a water bath (bain-marie) is ideal, especially for warm emulsified sauces such as hollandaise and beurre blanc, which are less stable than white and brown sauces.

Place the pan or bowl of sauce in a saucepan or roasting pan of barely simmering water (the water bath). The temperature of the sauce must remain below boiling point. A double boiler (right) serves the same purpose.

To prevent a skin from forming on the surface of the sauce while it is being kept warm, cover with a piece of lightly buttered parchment paper before placing it in the water bath.

VELOUTÉ SAUCE: a modern interpretation

The classic velouté sauce is based on a roux, like a béchamel. However, chefs nowadays prefer a richer, creamier sauce, made without a roux and derived simply from natural-flavor reductions.

The liquid required for a velouté is fish, chicken, or veal stock (as appropriate) plus wine and cream. When I'm making a velouté with chicken stock, I like to add a little delicacy to the sauce by sweating some thyme with the shallots.

Makes 2 cups

4 shallots, finely chopped
sprig of fresh thyme (for chicken velouté only)
1 tbsp unsalted butter
1¼ cups dry white wine
⅓ cup vermouth
1¾ cups well-flavored chicken, fish, or veal stock
1¾ cups heavy cream

1 In a covered saucepan, sweat the shallots and thyme, if using, in the butter over a low heat until softened. Add the wine and vermouth. Increase the heat and bring to a boil, stirring.

2 Reduce the heat and simmer, uncovered, until the liquid has reduced by two-thirds and is syrupy in consistency, about 25 minutes. Stir occasionally during simmering.

INCREASING THE FLAVOR

■ For a sauce lacking in flavor, add a splash of wine or champagne to a velouté made with fish stock, or port or Madeira to a velouté made with chicken or veal stock.

■ If the sauce lacks piquancy, whisk in a squeeze of lemon juice at the end.

5 After reduction, the sauce should be thick enough to coat the back of a spoon. If it is too runny, reduce for a further 5 minutes.

6 Before serving, press the sauce through a fine-mesh strainer into a clean pan. If the sauce is not to be used immediately, keep it warm in a water bath or double boiler (p33).

3 Add the stock and stir to combine, then bring back to a boil. Cook, uncovered, over high heat until reduced by half, about 20 minutes.

4 Add the cream and stir to combine. Bring back to a boil, then reduce the heat and simmer, uncovered, until the sauce has reduced by over half and has thickened.

The rich creaminess of velouté sauce

Velouté-based sauces

Here are some of my favorite variations on velouté sauce. Use chicken, fish, or veal stock for the basic velouté, according to the dish with which you are serving the sauce.

Aurore sauce

Add ½ cup fresh tomato sauce (p40) or tomato purée to the finished velouté. Serve with poached chicken or veal.

Caper velouté

Make the basic velouté with the stock used for poaching ham or lamb. Stir in 2 tbsp rinsed, drained capers and 4 tbsp heavy cream, and simmer gently for 5 minutes. Serve with the ham or lamb.

Champagne velouté

Add 4 tbsp champagne with the wine and vermouth. Serve with turbot and sole.

Curry velouté

Five minutes before completion, stir ½ tbsp curry paste into the velouté. The curry flavor should be mild and delicate.

Mushroom velouté

Add 1½ cups sliced button mushrooms to the cream and simmer for 5–6 minutes before adding to the reduced stock. Serve with chicken, pork, veal, eggs, or pasta.

Mustard velouté

Add 2 tsp Dijon mustard to the sauce at step 5. Do not re-boil, because this can make the sauce slightly buttery. For extra flavor and color, stir 1 tsp chopped herbs, such as parsley or tarragon, into the finished sauce. Serve with salmon, mackerel, and herring.

Saffron & tomato velouté

Add a large pinch of saffron strands to the stock and simmer to infuse, then make the velouté as normal. Add 2 peeled, seeded, and chopped tomatoes plus, if desired, 1 tbsp chopped basil, to the finished sauce. This goes wonderfully with white fish and shellfish.

Tarragon velouté

Stir 1 tbsp finely chopped tarragon into the finished sauce. This is especially good with broiled fish or white meat dishes.

BROWN SAUCES

The original brown sauce—the espagnole—was the fundamental sauce in French haute cuisine. Made from rich brown stock thickened with a brown roux, it took two to three days to make and was the base for countless other classic sauces—chasseur and bordelaise among them.

Today, most cooks and many professional kitchens consider the espagnole too time-consuming and uneconomical to prepare. They prefer in its place a simple jus lié (usually shortened to jus), such as light veal jus or chicken jus. The product of the slow reduction of a well-flavored stock enlivened with meat trimmings, a jus is thickened with a starch such as arrowroot, potato flour, or cornstarch toward the end of cooking. Although lighter than the classic espagnole, the modern-day jus is developed into brown sauces in exactly the same way—by the addition of flavorings, such as mushrooms, mustard, shallots, or Madeira, and by mounting them with butter.

As a general rule, light veal jus is best suited to meat-based dishes and chicken jus to poultry and fish-based dishes. When a jus for lamb or duck is required, replace the base stock accordingly. A vegetarian jus uses vegetable stock.

LIGHT VEAL JUS

The jus most favored by professional cooks— rich, refined, and glossy, it forms the base of many excellent brown sauces for meat.

Makes 2½ cups

3 tbsp vegetable oil
12oz (340g) veal trimmings, cut into small pieces
5oz (150g) chicken wings or carcasses, chopped into small pieces
2 shallots or 1 onion, chopped
1½ cups chopped mushrooms or mushroom trimmings
1 medium carrot, chopped
1 garlic clove, chopped
½ tbsp tomato paste
sprig of thyme
1 bay leaf
1¼ cups dry white wine
2½ cups water
6 cups veal or dark chicken stock
1 tbsp arrowroot, mixed with a little water

BROWNING BONES

When browning the meat bones and trimmings, it is important that they are cooked until deep golden brown. This, together with the caramelizing of the vegetables, will achieve the correct color for the finished jus. Insufficient browning gives a pale jus.

1 Heat the oil in a large pan. When smoking, add the veal and chicken, and fry over high heat, moving the pieces around, until they are golden brown all over, about 20 minutes.

2 Add the vegetables and garlic, and fry until they are golden and caramelized, about 10 minutes. Add the tomato paste, thyme, and bay leaf, and cook for 2–3 minutes longer.

3 Pour in the wine and water, and bring to a boil, scraping the sediment from the bottom of the pan with a wooden spoon to release the caramelized juices.

4 Boil, uncovered, until the liquid is reduced by two-thirds, about 25 minutes.

5 Add the stock. Bring back to a boil, then boil, uncovered, for about 20 minutes to reduce again by half, regularly skimming off any impurities. When reduced by half, stir in the arrowroot mixture to thicken the liquid.

6 Cook for 2 minutes longer, then press through a fine-mesh strainer set into a clean pan. The resulting jus should be thick enough to coat the back of a spoon lightly.

Light veal jus—
the professionals'
basic brown sauce

LIGHT CHICKEN JUS

The delicate flavor of this jus makes it ideal for chicken or pan-roasted fish or for braising vegetables like celery and Jerusalem artichokes.

Makes 2½ cups

3 tbsp vegetable oil
2¼lb (1kg) chicken wings or carcasses, chopped into small pieces
2 shallots, chopped
1½ cups chopped mushrooms or mushroom trimmings
1 garlic clove, chopped
3 tomatoes, quartered
1 tsp tomato paste
sprig of thyme
1 bay leaf
1¼ cups dry white wine
2½ cups water
6 cups dark chicken stock
1 tbsp arrowroot, mixed with a little water

1 Heat the oil in a large pan. When smoking, add the chicken and fry over high heat until golden brown all over, about 20 minutes.

2 Add the shallots, mushrooms, and garlic, and fry until golden and caramelized. Add the tomatoes, tomato paste, thyme, and bay leaf, and cook for 6–8 minutes longer.

3 Pour the wine and water into the pan and bring to a boil, scraping the sediment from the bottom of the pan with a wooden spoon to release the caramelized juices. Boil, uncovered, until the liquid is reduced by two-thirds, about 25 minutes.

4 Add the stock. Bring back to a boil, then boil, uncovered, to reduce again by half, about 20 minutes, regularly skimming off any impurities that rise to the surface.

5 Stir in the arrowroot mixture to thicken the jus and cook for 2 minutes, then press through a fine-mesh strainer into a clean pan. The resulting jus should be thick enough to coat the back of a spoon lightly.

Mounting with butter

In professional kitchens, brown sauces are always finished with butter, just before serving. This important technique is called "monter au beurre" (mounting with butter). The butter acts as an emulsifier and serves to make the sauce richer and smoother, as well as adding sheen. It can also be used to correct a finished sauce that is too sharp in flavor.

To mount with butter, add small pieces of chilled, unsalted butter to the finished sauce and whisk them in. Once the butter has been added, the sauce should never be re-boiled because this will cause the butter to separate and float to the surface, thus making the sauce greasy. To correct a sauce if this does happen, remove the surface layer of fat with a small ladle.

1 Cut a chilled piece of butter into cubes. Take the pan of sauce off the heat and whisk in each cube of butter before adding the next.

2 When all the butter has been whisked in, the sauce will be glossy and smooth.

PAN SAUCES

Pan sauces are generally made at the last moment, while the meat is resting. Once the meat or poultry has been roasted or pan-fried, it is removed and any excess fat in the pan is skimmed off. Liquid, such as a simple stock, jus, or wine, is then added to the hot pan and stirred into the caramelized juices. This is known as deglazing. These juices are then reduced, and wine, cream, or butter is stirred in to finish the sauce. Shown below are the steps in making a pan sauce after roasting a chicken.

Gravies made from simple roasts are also prepared in this way and may be thickened with flour or another form of starch or by reduction of the pan liquid.

1 Remove the chicken from the pan and skim off most of the fat. Put the pan over medium heat and add 1 cup white wine. Scrape up the juices and boil until syrupy.

2 Add 1 cup chicken or vegetable stock and boil until syrupy again. Add about 1 tsp beurre manié (p25) and stir until the mixture thickens, then cook for 1–2 minutes.

3 Stir in 1 tsp Dijon mustard and 2 tbsp light cream. The sauce can be strained at this point, if preferred. Season to taste and add chopped soft herbs, such as tarragon, if desired.

Venison with cherries, cinnamon & walnuts

Ever since I discovered dried cherries I have been experimenting with them in different dishes. They are great with poultry and game, as here in one of my favorite recipes for a sauce for sautéed venison medallions.

2 tbsp vegetable oil

4 medallions of venison loin, about 6oz (175g) each, seasoned

3 tbsp sherry vinegar

4 tbsp cherry brandy

½ cup full-bodied red wine

½in (1cm) cinnamon stick

⅔ cup game or veal jus

⅓ cup dried cherries

1 tbsp red-currant jelly

4 tbsp port wine

2 tbsp broken walnut pieces

2 tsp unsalted butter, chilled and cut into small pieces

Heat the oil in a large pan. Add the medallions and sauté until golden all over, 3–5 minutes. Remove from the pan and keep warm.

Drain excess oil from the pan. Add the sherry vinegar and deglaze the pan. Bring to a boil and cook until the vinegar has evaporated.

Add the cherry brandy, red wine, and cinnamon stick, and cook until the wine has reduced by half, 3–4 minutes.

Pour in the jus and add the dried cherries, then simmer for 5 minutes.

Remove the cinnamon stick and add the red-currant jelly, port, and walnuts. Whisk in the butter, piece by piece, then season to taste. Pour the hot sauce over the venison and serve.

Scrape up the caramelized juices to deglaze the pan

VEGETABLE & HERB SAUCES

With just a few simple processes, you can create colorful, fresh-tasting sauces based on vegetable and herb purées. Vegetables can be cooked or used raw and you can purée in a blender or food mill, press through a strainer, or pound with a mortar and pestle.

The addition of a little cream and/or butter will smooth the texture and add richness. Sauces like this are superb served with anything from pasta and fish to meat and poultry dishes. Here are a few of my favorite vegetable and herb sauces.

TOMATO SAUCE

This simple yet versatile sauce is perfect with fish, meat, poultry, and vegetables. Rather than puréeing the sauce in a blender, I sieve it. This keeps the rich color and removes the tomato skins. If the sauce is a little bitter, add more sugar.

Makes 2½ cups

2 tbsp unsalted butter
1 tbsp olive oil
2 shallots, chopped
sprig of thyme
1 small bay leaf
3 garlic cloves, crushed
2¼lb (1kg) fresh, over-ripe plum tomatoes, seeded and chopped
2 tbsp tomato paste
1 tbsp sugar
1 cup water
½ cup tomato juice (optional)

1 Place the butter, oil, shallots, thyme, bay leaf, and garlic in a saucepan. Cover and sweat over low heat until the shallots are soft but not browned, 5–6 minutes.

2 Stir in the tomatoes, tomato paste, and sugar. Cook over low heat, uncovered, for 5 minutes. Add the water and tomato juice, if using, and bring to a boil.

3 Reduce the heat and simmer, uncovered, for 30 minutes. Season, then use a ladle to press the sauce through a strainer. Return to the pan and reheat before serving.

VARIATIONS

Rustic style
For a more robust tomato sauce, do not sieve it, and remove the bay leaf and thyme just before serving.

Italian style
To produce a simple Italian-style sauce, add 1 tbsp chopped basil or oregano just before serving.

Spicy
For a fiery kick, chop a fresh, hot chili and add with the tomatoes.

Slow-simmered tomato sauce, smooth and rich

WATERCRESS SAUCE

Here's a good example of a sauce created simply by mixing cream and butter with a vegetable purée. Variations are limitless—instead of blanched watercress, try 1lb (450g) asparagus, broccoli, Jerusalem artichokes, or leeks, chopped into 1in (2.5cm) pieces. The watercress sauce is superb with poached salmon or turbot.

Makes about 2 cups

1lb (450g) watercress, stems removed
1 cup vegetable or light chicken stock
1 cup heavy cream
2 tbsp unsalted butter

1 Plunge the watercress into a pan of boiling water to blanch for 30 seconds. Drain in a colander, then refresh in a bowl of ice water. Squeeze the watercress in a piece of cheesecloth or a dish towel to remove all excess water.

2 Put the watercress in a medium-sized saucepan with the stock and cream. Bring to a boil, then reduce the heat and simmer for 10 minutes, stirring occasionally. Transfer to a blender and process to a smooth purée.

3 Press the purée through a fine-mesh strainer back into the pan. Bring to a boil, stirring, then remove from the heat and whisk in the butter and seasoning to taste. Serve hot.

BELL PEPPER SAUCE

This sauce is great with fish, vegetables, and pasta.

Makes about 2 cups

2 red bell peppers, seeded and chopped
3 tbsp unsalted butter
1 cup water or vegetable stock
sprig of thyme
½ cup heavy cream

1 Put the peppers in a saucepan with 1 tbsp of the butter. Cover and sweat over low heat until the peppers are slightly softened. Add the water or stock and thyme. Bring to a boil. Reduce the heat and simmer gently, uncovered, for 15–20 minutes. Discard the thyme.

2 Transfer the mixture to a blender and process to a purée. Press through a strainer back into the pan. Reheat, then whisk in the cream, remaining butter, and seasoning to taste.

MOREL SAUCE

The perfect choice with steaks and veal chops.

Makes 1¼ cups

¼oz (10g) dried morels
1¼ cups hot chicken stock
2 shallots, chopped
2 tbsp unsalted butter
splash of Cognac
½ cup dry white wine
4 tbsp heavy cream
6 tbsp Madeira

1 Soak the morels in the stock for 30 minutes. Remove them. Strain and reserve the liquid.

2 Put the shallots in a saucepan with 2 tsp of the butter. Cover and sweat over low heat until soft. Stir in the morels and sweat for 2 minutes, then add the Cognac, wine, and liquid from the morels. Simmer, uncovered, until reduced by half, about 15 minutes.

3 Transfer to a blender and process to a purée. Return to the pan. Reheat, then add the cream, Madeira, remaining butter, and seasoning.

PESTO ALLA GENOVESE

In addition to pasta dishes, pesto sauce is good with fish, meat, and vegetables. The version here is quick, but if you prefer you can make it more traditionally using a mortar and pestle.

Makes ⅔ cup

2½oz (75g) basil leaves (about 2 cups)

2 garlic cloves, crushed

1 tbsp roughly chopped pine nuts

2 tbsp freshly grated Parmesan

7 tbsp extra virgin olive oil

1 Place the basil, garlic, pine nuts, and cheese in a blender. With the motor running, pour in the oil in a slow stream through the feed tube.

2 Process until a smooth sauce is formed, then season with salt and pepper. Alternatively, pound the basil, garlic, pine nuts, and cheese in a mortar with a pestle, then slowly work in the oil. Pesto can be kept in the refrigerator for up to 1 week, although it will lose flavor and color.

CHIMICHURRI

One of my favorite steak sauces is chimichurri from Argentina, which is made just like pesto sauce. Process or pound together 2 cups flat-leaf parsley leaves, 2 crushed garlic cloves, 2 seeded and minced hot red chilies, 2 tbsp wine vinegar, 1 tsp chopped oregano, and 7 tbsp olive oil.

HORSERADISH SAUCE

This piquant sauce is the classic accompaniment for hot or cold roast beef, steak, and smoked fish.

Makes about 2 cups

3 cups fresh white bread crumbs

½ cup milk

2in (5cm) piece of fresh horseradish root

2 tbsp white wine vinegar

½ tsp prepared English mustard

½ cup heavy cream

1 Place the bread crumbs in a bowl, pour in the milk, and let soak for 20 minutes.

2 Scrub and peel the horseradish. Finely grate it into a bowl. Add the vinegar and mustard.

3 Squeeze excess milk from the bread crumbs, then add them to the horseradish mixture.

4 Whip the cream until slightly peaked and fold into the horseradish mixture. Season to taste with salt and pepper.

MINT SAUCE

The traditional partner for roast or grilled lamb, mint sauce is incomparable when freshly made from mint leaves just picked from the summer garden. The amount of vinegar you add will depend on the consistency preferred for the final sauce. If you can't find malt vinegar, use rice vinegar or a mild white wine vinegar instead. Mint sauce will keep, chilled, for several days.

Makes ⅔ cup

4oz (115g) mint
1 tbsp sugar
2 tbsp malt vinegar, or to taste

1 Remove the leaves from the mint stems. Place the leaves in a mortar with the sugar and crush to a pulp with the pestle.

2 Leave for 30 minutes, by which time the sugar will have extracted the juice from the mint. Give the sauce a final pounding, then add malt vinegar to taste and stir to combine.

RAW TOMATO SAUCE

Light, fresh, and slightly tangy, this uncooked tomato sauce is the essence of summer. Do not be tempted to boil the sauce and serve it hot—raw tomato sauce is completely different in make-up from the cooked version. It is good with grilled fish and marinated vegetables.

Instead of using a food mill, you can purée the sauce in a blender and then press the purée through a strainer to remove skin and seeds.

Makes about 2 cups

1lb (450g) very ripe, soft tomatoes, chopped
1 tbsp tomato paste
10 basil leaves
1 tbsp sugar
2 tbsp sherry or raspberry vinegar
7 tbsp olive oil

1 Combine the tomatoes, tomato paste, basil, sugar, and vinegar in a bowl. Cover and leave for 2 hours at room temperature. Purée the mixture by working it through a food mill.

2 Slowly add the oil to the tomato mixture, whisking constantly. Season to taste with salt and pepper. Serve at room temperature. The sauce can be kept in the refrigerator for up to 3 days.

Raw tomato sauce— the fresh taste of summer

NUT SAUCES

Sauces based on nuts can be found all over the world, with each region having its own favorites—peanut sauces in Southeast Asia, for example, almond sauces in regions of India, walnut sauces in some parts of Africa, and coconut sauces in the Caribbean.

In Europe, all kinds of nuts are used, often blended or pounded with bread and garlic to make wonderful smooth sauces that are served with pasta, fish, and simple grilled dishes. Three of the most popular and simply made nut sauces are described here.

SALSA DI NOCI

In Liguria, a region of northwest Italy, this sauce of pounded walnuts is traditionally served with pansotti, a pasta stuffed with local wild herbs, but it goes well with other types of pasta, too.

Makes 1¼ cups

2 garlic cloves, crushed
4½oz (125g) walnut halves, blanched and skinned (1 heaped cup)
3 tbsp fresh white bread crumbs
4 tbsp olive oil
¼ cup freshly grated Parmesan
4 tbsp sour cream or plain yogurt
milk to thin, if needed

1 Place the garlic, walnuts, and bread crumbs in a mortar. Add the oil and, using the pestle, pound to a rough purée.

2 Mix in the Parmesan, sour cream or yogurt, and seasoning to taste. If the sauce is too thick, thin it by stirring in a little milk.

ALMOND TARATOR

This Turkish sauce is great with grilled and deep-fried foods.

Makes 1¼ cups

3 slices white bread, crusts removed
4 tbsp milk
1¼ cups whole blanched almonds
3 garlic cloves, crushed
½ cup olive oil
juice of 1 lemon

Sprinkle the bread with the milk and leave for 30 minutes. Purée with the almonds, garlic, oil, and lemon juice in a blender. Season.

ROMESCO SAUCE

This spicy red sauce from Catalonia is wonderful with grilled shellfish, oily fish, and meats. If you prefer a milder sauce, remove the chili seeds.

Makes 1¼ cups

2 small, dried, hot red chilies
⅔ cup olive oil
3 garlic cloves, crushed
4 tbsp roughly chopped blanched almonds
3 tbsp roughly chopped, blanched and skinned hazelnuts
2 slices white bread, crusts removed and cubed
7 tbsp tomato juice or tomato purée
2 tbsp white wine vinegar
pinch of smoked paprika

1 Soak the chilies in boiling water for 10–15 minutes. Drain and chop, removing the seeds, if desired. Heat 3 tbsp of the oil in a frying pan, add the garlic and all the nuts, and fry until golden. Remove with a slotted spoon to drain.

2 Add another 3 tbsp oil to the pan. When hot, add the bread cubes and fry until golden. Remove with a slotted spoon and drain on paper towels. Pour the tomato juice or purée and the remaining oil into the pan to warm through.

3 Put the fried garlic, nuts, and bread cubes in a blender. Add the white wine vinegar, warmed tomato juice and oil, and chopped chilies, and blend to a purée. Season with the smoked paprika and salt to taste.

Pan-grilled mackerel with orange romesco

Mackerel is one of the unsung heroes of our seas. It has never really been renowned as a delicacy, which I feel is a great pity and far less than it deserves, because it is cheap and nutritious and has a wonderful flavor. Mackerel is best grilled and in this recipe the spiciness of romesco sauce beautifully cuts the richness of the fish.

1 bulb of fennel, trimmed and cut into 8 slices or wedges

4 tbsp extra virgin olive oil plus extra for brushing

4 mackerel fillets, about 6oz (175g) each

juice of 1 orange

grated zest of ½ orange

⅔ cup romesco sauce (see opposite)

12 red cherry tomatoes, halved

12 black olives, pitted and quartered

Blanch the fennel in boiling salted water for 2–3 minutes, then remove with a slotted spoon to drain.

Heat 2 tbsp olive oil in a large, ridged, cast-iron grill pan over medium heat. Season the fennel slices and place on one side of the pan. Cook, turning regularly, until tender and golden.

At the same time, season the mackerel and brush all over with oil. Place in the pan alongside the fennel and grill until cooked and lightly charred all over, 3–4 minutes on each side.

Meanwhile, combine the orange juice, zest, and romesco sauce in a bowl.

Heat the remaining 2 tbsp oil in a small pan and gently warm the cherry tomatoes and olives for 1 minute. Season to taste.

To serve, arrange the fennel, olives, and tomatoes on four warmed serving plates, top with the pan-grilled mackerel, and spoon the orange romesco sauce over all.

SAVORY FRUIT SAUCES

We have long enjoyed fruit-based sauces with savory food, to add a contrast in flavor and texture. Traditional partners for simply roasted meat and poultry, served hot or cold, include apple sauce with pork or duck, and Cumberland sauce with goose or ham.

Many of these fruit sauces are simply made by simmering fruit with flavorings and sugar, and are eaten immediately. Chutneys and relishes, however, are usually left to mature for a month or more, which improves their flavor.

AUTUMN FRUIT CHUTNEY

For the best flavor, leave in a cool, dark, dry place for 1–2 months before serving.

Makes 4½lb (2kg)

2lb (900g) tart apples, peeled, cored, and chopped

1lb (450g) pears, peeled, cored, and chopped

1lb (450g) onions, chopped

1 garlic clove, crushed

1⅔ cups raisins

4 cups cider vinegar or white wine vinegar

1 tbsp ground ginger

1 tbsp ground cinnamon

2 tsp ground turmeric

1½ tbsp salt

2 cups packed dark brown sugar

1 Place the apples, pears, onions, garlic, raisins, and vinegar in a nonreactive kettle. Bring to a boil. Simmer until the apples and pears are soft but still keeping their shape, about 20 minutes.

2 Add the spices, salt, and sugar, and stir until the sugar has dissolved. Reduce the heat and simmer until most of the liquid has evaporated and the chutney is thick, 45–60 minutes.

3 Ladle the boiling-hot chutney into sterilized jars and seal. For long storage, process in a boiling water bath.

OLD-FASHIONED APPLE SAUCE

One must never contemplate eating roast pork without apple sauce. Here is a favorite recipe of mine, dating back to the early 18th century.

Makes 1¼ cups

1lb (450g) tart apples, peeled, cored, and thickly sliced
strip of lemon peel
⅓ cup cold water
2 tbsp sugar
1 tbsp unsalted butter, chilled and diced

1 Place the apples in a medium-sized saucepan with the lemon peel and water. Cover and simmer gently until the apples have softened, 10–12 minutes. Stir in the sugar, then remove from the heat and let cool.

2 Remove the lemon peel. Press the apples through a strainer or purée them in a blender. Return to the pan and reheat gently, then stir in the butter. Serve the sauce warm.

GOOSEBERRY & MINT SAUCE

This tart sauce is wonderful with roast pork and goose. I also like to serve it with oily fish.

Makes about 2 cups

1lb (450g) under-ripe or thawed, frozen gooseberries, ends trimmed
4 tbsp cold water
7 tbsp sugar, or to taste
½ cup sweet muscat wine
small bunch of mint, chopped

1 Put the gooseberries in a heavy-based saucepan with the water, half the sugar, and the wine. Bring to a boil, then reduce the heat and simmer, uncovered, until the fruit has softened, about 10 minutes.

2 Transfer to a blender and process to a purée. Add the remaining sugar, or more to taste. Let cool. Before serving, stir the mint into the sauce and season to taste.

CUMBERLAND SAUCE

The most refined of all savory fruit sauces, Cumberland is a particular favorite at Christmas time, served with cold meats such as ham, duck, or goose. The sauce can be kept in the refrigerator for 2–3 days. When in season, use a blood orange for an even richer color.

Makes 1¼ cups

1 small orange	¾ cup red-currant jelly
1 lemon	1 tsp Dijon mustard
1 shallot, finely chopped	5 tbsp port wine
	½ tsp ground ginger

1 Using a zester or vegetable peeler, take the zest off the orange and lemon. Cut the zest into julienne strips. Put the strips and shallot in a small saucepan of boiling water and blanch for 2 minutes, then drain in a strainer and set aside.

2 Combine the red-currant jelly, mustard, port, and ginger in the saucepan and stir over low heat until the jelly melts. Do not boil. Add the juices of the orange and lemon, the zest, and shallot. Season. Serve at room temperature.

Cumberland sauce—the perfect accompaniment to cold meats

HOT & SPICY SAUCES

These kinds of sauces will delight the adventurous, heat-seeking cook because they add zip and intensity to the culinary repertoire. In the realm of hot ingredients, it is undoubtedly the chili pepper that wears the crown, but other interesting hot flavorings, such as mustard seeds, horseradish root, and fresh ginger, also have an important part to play in spicing up sauces.

SPICY TOMATO & HORSERADISH KETCHUP

Make this ketchup during the summer when ripe, juicy tomatoes are at their peak. Unlike other ketchups, it can be used immediately. Stored in a cool, dry place, it will keep for up to 6 months. Once opened, refrigerate it.

Makes about 3 cups

4½lb (2kg) ripe plum tomatoes, cut into large pieces
1 tbsp tomato paste
1 cup finely chopped onions
2 cups peeled, cored, and chopped tart apples
6 whole cloves
1 tsp mustard seeds
1 cinnamon stick, broken into pieces
½ tsp celery seeds
1 cup distilled white vinegar
3 tbsp coarse sea salt
1 cup packed light brown sugar
3in (7.5cm) piece of fresh horseradish root, peeled and grated

Spicy tomato and horseradish ketchup is superb with fried fish, grilled steaks, and hamburgers

1 Put the tomatoes, tomato paste, onions, and apples in a nonreactive kettle with the cloves, mustard seeds, cinnamon stick, celery seeds, half of the vinegar, and the salt. Slowly bring to a boil, then reduce the heat to a simmer.

2 Simmer, stirring occasionally, until the tomatoes are soft and pulpy and the mixture has reduced by one-third, 1–1½ hours. Using the back of a ladle, press the mixture through a fine sieve into a clean pan.

3 Add the remaining vinegar, the sugar, and horseradish. Cook over low heat until the sugar dissolves, then simmer until the ketchup is thick, 30–40 minutes. Pour into sterilized jars and seal. Let cool before using.

BERBERE

Add a spoonful of this fiery-hot sauce from Ethiopia to beef stews and lentil dishes. Berbere will keep for 3 months in the refrigerator.

Makes 1¼ cups

6 dried ancho chilies

3 tbsp peanut oil plus extra for brushing

2 tsp cumin seeds

1 tsp black peppercorns

2 tbsp smoked paprika

1 tsp ground cardamom

½ tsp ground allspice

½ tsp ground cinnamon

½ tsp ground coriander seed

½ tsp ground ginger

1 onion, grated

2 garlic cloves, crushed

1 Preheat the oven to 450°F (230°C). Place the ancho chilies on a baking sheet, brush with oil, and roast until charred all over, 6–8 minutes. Peel the chilies while warm, then place in a bowl and cover with boiling water. Let soak for 30 minutes.

2 Dry-roast the cumin seeds and peppercorns in a frying pan.

3 Drain the chilies, reserving the soaking liquid. Put them in a blender with the whole and ground spices, the onion, and garlic. Add 5 tbsp soaking liquid and the oil, and process to a smooth sauce.

4 Transfer the sauce to a small pan and cook over low heat until thick, about 10 minutes. Let cool before serving.

SMOKY YELLOW PEPPER SALSA

Scotch bonnet chilies are extremely hot. If you prefer a milder salsa, use another variety of chili instead.

Makes 1¼ cups

3 tbsp olive oil

2 yellow bell peppers, seeded and quartered

½ Scotch bonnet chili, seeded and chopped

3 tbsp chopped cilantro

2 tbsp lemon juice

½ small onion, finely chopped

1 tbsp maple syrup

1 Heat 1 tbsp oil in a ridged, cast-iron grill pan. Add the peppers and cook until tender and slightly charred, 5–6 minutes. Let cool.

2 Coarsely chop the peppers. Put in a bowl with the remaining ingredients, mix, and season.

DIPPING SAUCES

Middle Eastern hummus, Indian raita, Mexican guacamole, and Mediterranean tapenade are just a few examples of sauces designed to be dipped into using bread, crisp breadsticks, or pieces of raw vegetables and fruit. Dipping sauces can also be spooned onto canapé toasts to eat with drinks before a meal or served as side dishes with grilled meats and fish and with curries. They are great for picnics, too. To allow the flavors to develop, make dipping sauces in advance and keep them in the refrigerator.

RAITA

A cooling, yogurt-based dipping sauce, this is traditionally served with most Indian meals.

Makes 1¼ cups

1 English cucumber, peeled
½ tsp salt
½ tsp cumin seeds, dry-roasted
½ cup plain whole-milk yogurt
½ tsp sugar
1 garlic clove, crushed
1 tbsp chopped mint
1 tbsp chopped cilantro

1 Finely grate the cucumber. Toss with the salt and leave for 1 hour.

2 Squeeze out as much liquid from the cucumber as you can.

3 Crush the cumin seeds to a fine powder in a mortar with a pestle. Add to the cucumber with the remaining ingredients, mix, and chill.

TOMATO TAPENADE

This vegetarian-friendly, flavor-packed dipping sauce, served with a basket of warm breads, has been on my menu at The Lanesborough for over five years. It is also excellent with grilled fish and lamb.

Makes 1 cup

3½oz (100g) oil-packed sun-dried tomatoes, drained and roughly chopped (about ½ cup)
1 tsp Dijon mustard
2½ tbsp capers, rinsed and drained
3 tbsp pitted green olives
2 garlic cloves, crushed
1 tsp chopped rosemary
1 tsp lemon juice
6 tbsp extra virgin olive oil

1 Put all the ingredients in a food processor. Using the on-off pulse button, process to a coarse purée, but not until smooth.

2 Season the tapenade with salt and pepper to taste. Serve at room temperature.

VINAIGRETTES

In broad terms, a dressing is a sauce for salad, and much of the success of a salad lies in the harmony and balance of its dressing, which should flavor and complement, never dominate. The most common salad dressing is vinaigrette, which at its simplest is a blend of good-quality vinegar and a non-scented oil. Over the past decade, chefs have begun using all manner of vinaigrettes, both to dress exciting salads and as an alternative to the heavier sauces of classic French cuisine. Some ideas are given here.

CLASSIC VINAIGRETTE

Vinegars can vary in acidity, but I find a ratio of three or four parts oil to one part vinegar will produce a pleasing dressing, suitable for most uses. If it is to be served over fish or meat and vegetables, six parts oil to one part vinegar is better. Be sure to have all ingredients at room temperature. Larger quantities of vinaigrette can be made in advance and stored in a sealed jar at room temperature. Shake well before use.

Makes about ⅔ cup

2 tsp Dijon mustard
2 tbsp good-quality vinegar (champagne or white wine)
4½ tbsp vegetable oil
4½ tbsp olive oil

1 Combine the mustard, vinegar, and a little salt and pepper in a bowl.

2 Gradually add the oils in a thin stream, whisking constantly. Check the seasoning.

CRUSHED TOMATO VINAIGRETTE

This tasty dressing is a perfect partner for grilled fish or vegetable salads.

Makes about 1 cup

1 quantity classic vinaigrette (left)
4oz (115g) ripe cherry tomatoes
pinch of sugar
1 garlic clove, crushed

Place all the ingredients in a blender and process to a smooth purée. Thin slightly with a little warm water, if necessary.

Vinaigrette variations

Classic vinaigrette can be transformed into a host of other dressings by adding a few simple flavorings. Here are three.

Orange & rosemary

Add the grated zest and juice of 1 orange and 1 tsp chopped rosemary to classic vinaigrette. Let infuse overnight before using.

Honey & ginger

Add 1 tbsp mild, liquid honey and 1 tsp grated fresh ginger to classic vinaigrette. Let infuse overnight before using.

Truffle & Madeira

Place ½ cup Madeira and 1 chopped shallot in a small pan. Bring to a boil and boil to reduce until thick and syrupy. Let cool, then add to classic vinaigrette with 1 tsp truffle oil. Set aside to infuse for 1 hour, then strain. For a real treat, add ½ tsp chopped fresh truffles to the dressing just before serving.

WARM & CREAMY DRESSINGS

During the colder months, it makes a change to prepare a salad with a warm dressing or to use a warm dressing to sauce fish, shellfish, or meat. Warm dressings can be made in advance or at the last minute with the pan juices from cooking fish or meat.

Creamy-textured dressings, made with light, heavy, or sour cream or mayonnaise and cheeses of all kinds, are quick and simple to prepare. They are ideal for dressing crisp salad leaves or as a sauce for cold shellfish and poached fish.

SAUCE VIERGE

Toss this version of vinaigrette with warm vegetables or serve it with grilled fish or shellfish.

Makes 1¼ cups

1 garlic clove, crushed
1 shallot, finely chopped

7 tbsp olive oil
½ cup peeled, seeded, and finely diced tomatoes
juice of ½ lemon or 1 tbsp balsamic vinegar
pinch of sugar
2 tbsp chopped basil

1 Put the garlic and shallot in a small pan with the oil. Warm gently until soft, but do not fry.

2 Add the tomatoes and cook on low heat for 4–5 minutes. Add the lemon juice or vinegar.

3 Add the sugar and the chopped basil to the sauce and stir to mix. Season to taste with salt and pepper. Keep the sauce warm until ready to use.

A PAN DRESSING

Remove sautéed fish or meat from the pan and keep warm. Heat 1 tbsp olive oil in the pan. Add 2½oz (75g) fresh wild mushrooms and sauté until golden. Add 1 crushed garlic clove and 2 finely chopped shallots and cook for 1 minute. Pour in 4 tsp champagne vinegar and 2 tsp balsamic vinegar, and cook for 1 minute. Remove from the heat. Swirl in 2 tbsp chopped flat-leaf parsley, 3 tbsp olive oil, 2 tbsp walnut oil, and seasoning to taste. Pour over the fish or meat or use to dress salad leaves to serve alongside.

ROQUEFORT DRESSING

Use this to dress salad leaves, with crisp bacon crumbled over.

Makes 1¼ cups

2½oz (75g) Roquefort cheese
6 tbsp heavy cream
2 tbsp sherry vinegar
4 tbsp olive oil
1 tbsp warm water

Purée the cheese in a blender. Add the cream, vinegar, oil, and water, and process again briefly to mix. Season to taste and serve.

Bresaola with soft goat cheese dressing

Creamy dressings based on blue cheese have always been popular, but other cheeses are now being widely used. My creamy goat cheese dressing is a good example, here served with the Italian cured beef, bresaola.

3½oz (100g) soft goat cheese, crumbled (about 1 cup)

1 tbsp sherry vinegar

4 tbsp light cream

5 tbsp olive oil

1 tsp Dijon mustard

12oz (350g) bresaola

2 handfuls of arugula leaves

2 handfuls of small watercress sprigs

2 tbsp white truffle oil

Put three-quarters of the goat cheese in a blender. Add the vinegar, cream, olive oil, and mustard, and process until smooth and creamy. Season with salt and pepper.

Arrange the bresaola on four serving plates. Place a small bouquet of arugula and watercress in the center of each plate and drizzle with the creamy dressing.

Sprinkle the remaining crumbled goat cheese on top of each salad. Drizzle with the truffle oil and serve immediately.

STOCKS & SOUPS

SHAUN HILL

A well-made stock is the basis of a good sauce or soup—without it, most lack power or finesse. Depending on the type of sauce or soup being made, the cook may need good butter, cream, olive oil, and vinegar, but in most cases the heart of a good sauce or soup is a clear stock that sings out the taste of its principle ingredient, as well as those of the other ingredients with which it was made. Stocks have an indispensable role, especially in the restaurant kitchen. Restaurants tend to use prime cuts of meat and fish—such as tenderloin and chops, Dover sole and sea bass—that are cooked only briefly. Anything only just cooked or, in the case of red meat, undercooked, preserves its tenderness and fine texture. The element lacking in this luxurious, last-minute cuisine is any intensity or depth of flavor from the meat or fish being used. Strong flavors come only from prolonged and thorough cooking. In cooking, the considerations of texture and flavor must always be balanced. A lightly boiled carrot retains its crunchy texture, but lacks flavor when compared to one that has been cooked to a mush but strongly tastes of itself. The trick is to aim for the best of both worlds.

Depth and intensity of flavor In the classic French kitchen, compensation for the shortfall in depth of flavor in briefly cooked prime cuts, such as a grilled chicken breast or turbot fillet, is provided in the form of the gravy or sauce that partners it. All the bones and scraps are used to make good, strongly flavored basic stocks for this purpose, as well as to give a layer of complexity to soups that may otherwise be made largely from starch and vegetables.

The humble ingredients that go into the stockpot belie its vital importance in cooking. The cook should resist any tendency to use it as a swill bin for whatever needs tidying away. Meat bones need to be roasted carefully to prevent blackened tips from imparting bitterness to the stock; fish bones should be gently sweated in oil or butter so that some deepening of color can take place. This sweating process, technically known as the Maillard reaction, alters the surface proteins, caramelizing them for a more pronounced and significantly altered flavor. It accounts for the difference, say, between a boiled chicken and a roasted bird, or a poached and grilled sole.

Some characteristics are true of all stocks, irrespective of their main ingredient. They should be clear and relatively fat-free, because fat boiling in a stock will emulsify, creating a cloudy texture and a muddy taste. However, meat and fish stocks should become gelatinous enough to set when cooled, so that the sauces and soups made with them have a more substantial and sticky feel in the mouth. No salt should be added at any stage—stocks are building blocks rather than finished dishes. Stocks are usually reduced at some stage, concentrating any saltiness they may have, and they may be added to ingredients with their own salty properties, such as cheese.

Soupmaking While saucemaking, with veal stock as its cornerstone, is viewed as the apex of cooking expertise, soupmaking is often seen as basic, as though its preparation represents a lesser skill. Perhaps people have become too accustomed to the bland offerings of commercial soup companies. Soup also has an image as a vehicle for recycling leftovers, being at best a rustic rather than a refined dish. This poor reputation is entirely undeserved, for the craftsmanship needed to make a superb soup is exactly the same as that needed to create a subtle sauce. The cook has to draw on both skill and personal taste to decide on balance, seasoning, texture, and even the optimum cooking temperature as the flavors are blended into a liquid.

As this chapter will illustrate, there are four main styles of soup. There are those in which the ingredients are turned into purée; those in which meat or vegetables are suspended in broth; those thickened by egg yolks and cream; and, finally, consommé, which is the celebration of the stock as the star of the show. For many of these soups, chicken stock is the main player, and a clear and well-made stock is a great start in making a classic, well-flavored, mouth-satisfying soup.

CHICKEN, VEAL & FISH STOCKS

Chicken stock is easily achievable for the home cook. There are two styles, and the initial choice is whether to make a dark stock, which I simply call chicken stock, or a lighter version, which I call white stock. They are ready in hours (rather than the days needed for veal stock). They do not, however, keep well, so must be made when needed. Otherwise, once cooled they have to be frozen or regularly reboiled. Either type, or veal stock, serves as the base for a fine soup. Use fish or chicken stock for fish soup.

CHICKEN STOCK

Roasting the bones gives dark chicken stock an intense flavor. It is particularly good for gravy and for consommé. The stock is clear and concentrated, because most of the chicken fat is rendered away during roasting.

There is a school of thought that likes the vegetables as well as the bones to be roasted until light brown, but I have found this to be unnecessary. How much the bones are darkened has an impact on the finished stock in much the same way as the degree to which coffee beans are roasted affects the beverage produced. Darker means stronger, but perhaps slightly bitter, too.

The ratio of bones to water in the recipe is a guideline and the general rule is the more bones the better, especially if you want a powerful stock. Prolonged cooking will produce little improvement in the depth or concentration of the stock. If you want to strengthen it, either use more bones or strain the finished stock into a clean pot, skim away as much fat as possible, then simmer until the liquid has reduced by whatever margin you feel appropriate.

There is little strength or flavor in a stock made with skin and backbones. Whole carcasses, raw or cooked, cut up, or wing tips are best. Raw carcasses may be supplied free of charge by butchers who sell chicken separately as boneless breast halves and legs. You can buy stewing hens very cheaply if no bones are available. These are generally older birds. The meat is not much good, but use it and cook the carcasses to the point of disintegration for the extra body and flavor they give to stock.

Makes about 6 cups
2¼lb (1kg) raw or cooked chicken bones
3 quarts (3 liters) water
1 onion, quartered
1 leek, coarsely chopped
1 carrot, coarsely chopped

1 Preheat the oven to 400°F (200°C). Place the bones in a roasting pan and roast for about 20 minutes. Transfer to a stockpot.

2 Pour any fat from the roasting pan, then add 2 cups of the water. Bring to a boil, scraping up any burned-on residues.

3 Pour this deglazing liquid over the roasted bones in the stockpot. Add the remaining water and bring to a boil.

4 Skim off any foam from the surface, then add the vegetables. Let simmer until the bones begin to disintegrate, about 3 hours. If the water level drops below the bones, replenish it.

5 Drain the stock into a pitcher or bowl, then leave the pot and contents for a minute or so. Any stock held in the bones will fall to the bottom of the pot, to be ladled out.

SOUPS WITH SOLID INGREDIENTS

Soups with solid ingredients suspended in a stock base can be a meal in themselves rather than a prelude. Minestrone is a hearty Italian classic; Scotland's cock-a-leekie, a chicken broth spiked with prunes and leeks, is in the same chunky style. Asian soups tend to be delicate and quick to prepare and cook. Fish soups may be close to a stew or more like consommé with a substantial garnish.

SHRIMP & SEA BASS SOUP

This clear seafood soup uses dashi as its base. It is flavored with soy sauce, which should be the genuine Japanese article, brewed and then aged. Many firms make cheaper products in Singapore for the foreign market. Tamari can be substituted for those avoiding gluten in their diet.

Ingredients
1 cup spinach leaves, blanched (p482)
4 cups dashi (p61)
3½oz (100g) sea bass fillet, cut into 4 cubes
4 large raw shrimp, peeled and deveined
1 tsp soy sauce
½ small, hot red chili
1 scallion, chopped
1 tbsp arrowroot
few drops of lemon juice

1 Squeeze out as much water as possible from the blanched spinach, then cut into strips.

2 Bring the dashi to a boil in a saucepan, and add the fish and shrimp. Cook for just a few moments and then add the soy sauce, chili, and scallion.

3 Whisk the arrowroot and 1 tbsp cold water in a bowl. Stir into the soup and bring to a boil, then remove the chili. Add the lemon juice and spinach, and serve.

THICKER SOUP

Adding arrowroot, cornstarch, rice flour, or the Japanese thickening agent kuzu will give a soup body. Arrowroot is not an authentic Asian ingredient like kuzu, but is easier to find. It acts rather like a hot liquid counterpart of gelatin, giving body to a clear stock. Cornstarch and kuzu are used in much the same way as arrowroot, diluted in a little cold water and then whisked into the hot soup at the end of cooking.

4 Once the stock reaches boiling point, turn the heat right down and let simmer gently until a white crust forms, at least 1 hour. When the crust is hard, poke a gap though it to check on the clarity.

FOR CLARITY

■ Chill the clarification mixture so that the cold egg whites shrink onto the other ingredients and help bind them. Some chefs add ice cubes to the mix to chill it effectively.

■ Before it boils, gently stir the stock while heating it so that the ingredients stay evenly distributed and the egg white does not burn on the bottom of the pot. But once boiling, do not stir, or the consommé will be cloudy. Leave it at a bare simmer.

■ Cheesecloth is very fine. Carefully straining the consommé through a strainer lined with cheesecloth ensures a totally clear result.

THAI CHICKEN SOUP

Thai and Vietnamese ingredients are so widespread that even my rural grocery store stocks galangal and lemon-grass. This recipe uses coconut milk as its base, with key Thai flavorings, but makes no pretence at authenticity. Bruise the herbs with the flat of a heavy knife to help release their juices. They have fibrous textures but wonderful flavor, and I strain them out before serving. Nam pla, a sauce made from fermented fish, is salty, so there is little need to add salt to the soup.

4 stalks of lemon-grass, cut into ½in (1cm) lengths and bruised

7oz (200g) galangal, peeled and diced

5 kaffir lime leaves, bruised

1 chicken leg

2 cups water

2 small, hot chilies

4 cups coconut milk

1 tbsp nam pla

juice of 3 limes

3 scallions, minced

2 tbsp chopped cilantro

1 Place the herbs, chicken, and water in a medium saucepan and bring to a boil. Simmer until the chicken is cooked, about 30 minutes. Remove the chicken and dice the meat. Add the chilies to the soup.

2 Bring the soup back to a boil. Pour in the coconut milk and heat slowly. You want the soup to become hot enough for the flavors to infuse the coconut milk, but do not let it boil.

3 Strain the soup into a clean pan or tureen, then add the nam pla, lime juice, scallions, cilantro, and diced chicken. Taste for seasoning. Cut the strained-out chili into slivers and use as a garnish, if desired.

COCONUT MILK

■ It is best to use the dried or block form, which is always unsweetened. The wrapper will advise dilution, according to whether thin or thick coconut milk is required. It is the thin version that's needed here, but make allowance for any reduction of water when cooking the main ingredients.

■ Coconut milk separates if heated too much or too long and will rise to the top of the soup if cooled. If this happens, pour it into a blender with some of the chicken and blend it back to a more homogeneous state.

MINESTRONE

One of the world's great soups, minestrone is found in many versions, most of which are probably authentic to some region of Italy. The consensus is that the soup should be thick, an almost solid mass of ingredients rather than garnish swimming in clear broth. It should contain pasta, cabbage, and tomato, and many more vegetables besides. Use whatever is in season and keep to the spirit of the recipe rather than the precise list here. Asparagus or zucchini make fine additions in spring or summer, as do basil leaves instead of parsley. This recipe calls for bacon—combined with green cabbage, it lends a satisfying background to the other ingredients. Vegetarians can keep the dish meatless by omitting the bacon and substituting water or vegetable stock for the chicken stock.

2 tbsp olive oil

2 slices of bacon, cut into ¾in (2cm) strips

1 small onion, minced

1 leek, minced

1 celery stalk, minced

1 carrot, minced

¼ head of Savoy cabbage, coarsely chopped

1 small potato, peeled and coarsely chopped

2 tbsp dried white beans, soaked overnight in cold water, then boiled until tender, about 1 hour

3 tbsp tomato purée

6 cups chicken stock

3 tbsp dried pasta (short or stubby shapes or others broken into small lengths)

1 tbsp coarsely chopped flat-leaf parsley

freshly grated Parmesan for serving

1 Heat the oil in a large saucepan and gently fry the bacon and vegetables (except the cabbage and potato). When the vegetables start to soften, stir in the cabbage, potato, beans, and tomato purée.

2 Season with salt and pepper, then continue cooking on a low heat for 10 minutes, stirring from time to time. Add the stock and bring to a boil.

3 Add the pasta and bring back to a boil. Simmer until the pasta is just cooked, 7–8 minutes. Add the parsley and check the seasoning. Serve with Parmesan on the side.

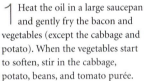

COCK-A-LEEKIE

This is a substantial soup—enough for a full lunch. It's Scottish in origin, and its essence, in contrast to anywhere else's chicken soup, lies in the use of prunes to flavor the broth. This is not such a bizarre idea when you think of the successful pairing of rabbit or pork with prunes. Its other singular aspect is the inclusion of beef or beef stock. The soup may be likened to pot au feu, with the meat—here beef and chicken—either eaten along with the broth or as a separate course after it.

This recipe feeds six or eight people, and it is hardly worth making the soup for fewer. If you do not have a pot large enough to hold the whole chicken and beef as they cook, dismantle the chicken into legs and breasts. Add them 15 minutes later because they will cook more quickly.

Remember that the cooking liquid is to be drunk, so don't be tempted to oversalt. Add whatever extra may be needed at the end of cooking.

1lb 2oz (500g) piece of beef brisket
6 cups chicken stock or water
1 small roaster chicken, about 2¾lb (1.25kg)
2¼lb (1kg) leeks, cut into 1¼in (3cm) lengths
8oz (250g) moist prunes, pitted

1 Place the beef and stock or water in a large pot. Bring to a boil, then simmer for 30 minutes. Add the chicken to the pot and simmer for 30 minutes longer. Use a large spoon to skim off any froth that rises to the surface. Replenish the liquid levels with water, if necessary, to keep the chicken covered.

2 Add the leeks and prunes. Simmer for 10 minutes longer. Taste the soup for seasoning and add salt and pepper, if needed.

3 Lift out the chicken and cut into small pieces. Place these in deep bowls with the leeks and prunes, and ladle in the broth.

THICKENED SOUPS

Success in soups thickened by a liaison of whole eggs or egg yolk and cream lies in restraint, especially with the cream. Use no more than equal volumes of egg to cream, and add a little at a time to the hot broth. Do it away from direct heat in case the egg cooks into omeletlike threads before you have a chance to incorporate it.

The objective is to make a slightly thicker, smoother soup. Once this is achieved, more cream and egg will only make the soup too rich to be consumed by the bowlful. Avoid prolonged reheating after adding the liaison. The silky texture isn't stable enough to withstand boiling—this is a last-minute technique before serving.

AVGOLEMONE (BEID BI LAMOUN)

This lemon, chicken, and rice soup is claimed by countries across the eastern Mediterranean, but is most famous as a Greek dish. It is thickened with eggs and lemon juice, and makes a refreshing, sharp, and tangy summer soup. The soup sounds deceptively simple, but has two major aspects, both of which need care. The stock must be well flavored, made with plenty of chicken, or it will not withstand the lemon juice. And the broth

must not boil once the eggs and lemon are added. They must be gently and briefly cooked at a temperature safely below boiling point.

| ¼ cup long-grain rice |
| 6 cups well-flavored chicken stock |
| 3 eggs |
| juice of 1 large lemon |

1 Put the rice and stock in a saucepan and bring to a boil. Simmer until the rice is completely cooked, about 15 minutes.

2 Whisk the eggs and lemon juice in a bowl until the mixture becomes frothy. Add a ladleful of hot stock and continue to whisk.

3 Remove the soup from direct heat. Whisk the egg, lemon, and stock mixture into it. Continue to whisk until the texture is velvety. Season and serve with lemon wedges.

NORTH SEA FISH SOUP

The fragile nature of this soup comes from the egg and cream liaison and is part of its appeal. The freshness and texture of the seafood are central, so it must all be just cooked and no more. Not all fish cook at the same speed: Cut denser-fleshed species into smaller pieces or add them earlier.

The choice of fish is a guideline. Buy what is freshest and best value on the day. Three different fish and one shellfish make an interesting soup. Use only fillets of fish and remove pin bones—the line of little bones head to tail along the center of fish such as salmon or bass.

1lb (500g) fish fillets and shellfish— a selection from red mullet or bass, haddock or cod, salmon or turbot, peeled raw shrimp or scallops

1 tbsp lemon juice
2½ cups fish or chicken stock
¼ cup white wine
2 shallots, chopped
1 egg yolk
1 tbsp heavy cream
1 tomato, peeled, seeded, and chopped
1 tbsp chopped parsley
croûtons for serving

1 Skin the fish, if necessary, and cut into 1¼in (3cm) pieces. Season with salt, pepper, and lemon juice. Bring the stock, wine, and shallots to a boil in a large saucepan.

2 Add the fish in the order it takes to cook—red mullet or bass first; 2 minutes later the turbot, if using; then the haddock, cod, or salmon; and, finally, the shrimp or scallops.

3 Simmer the soup for up to 10 minutes (cooking times may vary slightly). As soon as the fish is cooked, the soup is ready to be finished and served.

4 Stir the egg yolk and cream together in a bowl. Take the soup from direct heat and stir the mixture in, then add the tomato and parsley. Serve with croûtons.

MAKING CROÛTONS

These are small dice of white, crustless bread fried until crisp. Fry in whatever is appropriate to the soup—here, a mixture of sunflower oil and butter is best. Or, you can use clarified butter, which does not burn as quickly as whole butter. Heat the oil and butter in a small frying pan and add small, neat dice cut from 2 slices of crustless white bread. Shake the pan so the croûtons color and cook evenly. Spoon them out onto paper towels and pat dry.

PURÉED SOUPS

Soups that are blended to a thick, smooth purée are the easiest to make. Most use dried legumes or other carbohydrate to give body, taste, and texture. Any soup that is thickened with potato is best if blended as soon as the potato is done and before it becomes overcooked and glutinous. So the size of the potato pieces and the timing of their addition to the stock are important.

SAFFRON SOUP

This soup is an advance on leek and potato soup. It was a regular menu item at Robert Carrier's London restaurant when I worked there in the early 1970s. It has not dated and can be jazzed up with lobster or shrimp, or served with sippets (see below).

1 tbsp olive oil
1 large onion, sliced
7oz (200g) leeks, cut into 1¼in (3cm) lengths
1 cup peeled, diced potatoes
1 tsp saffron threads
1 tsp ground cumin
4 cups chicken stock
2 tbsp white wine
2 tbsp heavy cream
1 tbsp lemon juice
snipped chives for garnish

SIPPETS

For these toasts, use the thin French loaf known as a "ficelle" (string) rather than a baguette. Preheat the oven to 350°F (180°C). Cut the bread into thin slices and spread out on a baking sheet. Bake for 20 minutes, turning the slices over once the upper sides have dried. When you turn them, you can rub the other sides with peeled garlic, pounded anchovies, or an herb paste (pound any mixture of thyme, chives, parsley, basil, and tarragon with olive oil and a little salt). At the end of cooking, the sippets should be dry, not soggy.

1 Heat the oil in a heavy-based pan and gently fry the onion until soft. Add the leek, potatoes, saffron, cumin, and stock. Season with a little salt and pepper, then cover so that the soup cooks without too much reduction.

2 When the potato is soft the soup is ready—check after about 10 minutes. How long it takes to cook varies according to the type of potato and the size of the dice. Do not let the potato disintegrate into the soup.

3 Purée the soup with the white wine in a blender. Add the cream and lemon juice, and check for seasoning. If the soup is too thick, dilute it with more stock or water; if too thin, add more olive oil. Garnish with snipped chives.

Chickpea & langoustine soup

I first came across this soup in Tuscany years ago, and it has appeared regularly on my menu ever since. The earthiness of the background chickpea blend is a good foil for the sweetness and extravagance of the shellfish. Dried chickpeas need a lot of soaking. If preferred, use canned chickpeas—replace the water with stock and just bring the chickpeas to a boil, then blend with the onion and garlic mixture.

1 cup dried chickpeas

4 cups water

1 onion, chopped

2 garlic cloves, chopped

4 tbsp olive oil

1 tsp coriander seeds, crushed

4 raw langoustine (scampi) or crayfish tails, or large whole shrimp

1 cup white wine

1 tbsp lemon juice

1 tbsp snipped chives

Soak the chickpeas overnight in plenty of cold water. Drain and rinse, then put into a pot with the 4 cups water and bring to a boil. Do not add salt. Skim away any foam that rises to the surface as the water comes to a boil. Turn the heat down to low, cover, and simmer until the chickpeas are tender, 30–40 minutes.

Fry the onion and garlic in half the oil in a frying pan until soft but not brown. Add the coriander seeds and langoustines. Cook gently for 3–4 minutes longer, then add the wine. Remove the langoustines and peel them.

Add the cooked onion and garlic mixture to the chickpeas and their cooking liquid. Purée in a blender, in batches if necessary. If the soup is too thick, add more water or stock to thin it. Reheat if necessary, then season with salt, pepper, and the lemon juice.

Serve the soup in warmed bowls, with a langoustine, a scattering of snipped chives, and a drizzle of olive oil on top.

FLAVORINGS

Peter Gordon

PETER GORDON

What is flavor? Is it a physical or an intellectual thing? Is it defined by region, or purely by individual taste? How do we learn to like a flavor, and can we learn to dislike a flavor? At what point in a child's life does the taste of Gorgonzola cheese become more appealing than that of applesauce?

Flavor is generally defined as the sensation experienced when food comes into contact with the tastebuds on the tongue. Four basic tastes—sweet, salty, sour, and bitter—are detected and identified by groups of specialized tastebuds located on different parts of the tongue. Another sensation, called unami, has arisen from Japanese cuisine, a flavor coming from naturally occurring monosodium glutamate in some mushrooms, seaweeds, and other foods.

In my opinion, flavor is the combination of physical and cerebral sensations derived from anything we put in our mouths. A chunk of mango gives a slightly differing flavor to a purée of the same mango, which I put down to the textures and sensations the fruit in these two forms gives to the tongue. While the flavor of mango can be recreated in a laboratory from chemicals called ketones, nothing but a real mango can give the sensation of a mango in the mouth.

Regional preferences I am intrigued as to why people living in certain areas have a liking for one type of flavor over another. Why, for example, are lime juice and tamarind used so often in the salads, soups, and curries throughout Southeast Asia? Why is it that Thai people enjoy sour flavors usually tempered by sugar or sweet ingredients, while followers of French haute cuisine choose delicate buttery sauces? Spices have been traveling into Europe for many centuries, yet few European cuisines utilize these in anything other than baked goods. In India and the Middle East, cinnamon and cloves are as at home in a savory stew as they are in a dessert. Is it simply that ingredients producing these flavors are available regionally, or are there genetic or practical reasons for such preferences? I cannot provide a definitive explanation, but I have observed over many years of cooking in restaurants that flavors can strongly evoke early episodes in people's lives.

Many customers have brought elderly parents to the restaurants where I have been cooking, to give them the opportunity to sample different kinds of foods. In the past I expected such clients to offer some resistance to my culinary ideas, but that has not proved to be the case. Instead, I have shaken the hands of many appreciative men and women who were transported back to their youth, serving in foreign offices in Asia or the Middle East. One dish of braised pork cheeks with star anise and black cardamom had a gentleman reminiscing about his time in Burma (Myanmar). He had never eaten pork cheeks during his time there, but the flavors reminded him strongly of living in the country. Even more than visual reminders, flavor seems to have the ability to recall a bygone time. Somehow the brain keeps a record of a flavor locked away, and a mouthful of a sauce with tamarind and chili can bring back all the memories associated with tasting the flavor in the distant past.

Flavors for the occasion Visiting a new, unfamiliar environment can have a powerful influence on our appreciation of flavor. When I set off on my Asian travels in 1985, I was no great fan of the chili or the raw banana. But after two weeks in Bali I would often have a couple of bananas for breakfast, and at intervals during my morning letterwriting I would dip a chili into a bowl of sugar and munch it, washing it down with my kopi Bali. Arriving back in the U.K. a year later, I lost my appetite for raw bananas (I still love them cooked into a cake or fritter) but retained a love of chili. I can only put down these changes to eating "the right food in the right place." Take away the palm trees, the heat, and the sense of being on vacation, and you can also diminish the pleasure of the flavor. Likewise, a bratwurst and sauerkraut in a bun might seem the best thing ever in a snowy Berlin winter, but try eating it on a sunny beach in New Zealand and the flavors could not seem more wrong.

HERBS

Herbs are the leaves and stems of edible aromatic plants; essential oils in these leaves and stems give each herb its distinctive flavor.

I divide herbs into two groups—hard and soft. Hard herbs can withstand cooking for reasonable periods without losing impact. In fact, some benefit from cooking to mellow their flavor. In this group I include rosemary, sage, thyme (once the stems are woody),

bay leaves, kaffir lime leaves, curry leaves, screwpine leaves (daun pandan), lemon-grass, and the larger leaves from older oregano.

Soft herbs are best used raw in a dish or added in the last few minutes, or seconds, of cooking. They include chives, the basil and mint families, chervil, parsley, cilantro, tarragon, and young thyme, marjoram, and oregano.

Chopping herbs

When herbs are chopped they release their flavor more readily than if they are used whole. For some herbs, the leaves are stripped (see right), while for others—such as chervil, basil, and dill, which have tender and flavorsome stems—the whole herb is chopped. If chopping whole herbs, gather up the sprigs into a bunch, then chop with a rocking motion, rotating the knife and pushing the herbs back into a pile. For herbs such as chives, rather than chopping just snip them with scissors.

Once chopped, herbs deteriorate quickly, so try to chop them at the last minute, or keep in a covered jar in the refrigerator until needed.

1 To chop herb leaves (a mixture or a single variety, such as the basil leaves shown in the photographs), gather them together and then roll them up tightly.

2 With one hand, hold the rolled herb leaves on a board. Using a large knife, slice across the roll to cut the herbs into shreds (this is called a chiffonade). Gather into a pile.

3 Using either the knife or a mezzaluna, chop the herbs using a steady rocking motion, turning the pile 90° halfway through, until you have the size you want.

Stripping leaves

Stripping is a quick way to remove herb leaves from the stems. It is particularly suited to herbs with woody stems, such as rosemary (shown here). Hold the stem 2in (5cm) from the end and run the thumb and index finger of your other hand along the stem to rip off the leaves. Then pick the leaves from the softer stem at the tip.

Pounding herbs

Herbs are often pounded in a mortar with a pestle when making marinades, pestos, and some sauces. The pounding action forces the flavor of the herbs into the other ingredients. Good examples of pounded mixtures are pesto sauce (with basil) and Thai-inspired marinades (lemon-grass and chilies).

Drying herbs

Some herbs dry better than others, retaining their taste and scent. For hard herbs, rinse and pat dry, then gather and tie the stems together with string. Hang up in a cool to warm (not hot) room with plenty of airflow. Once dry, leave in bundles or strip off the leaves.

For softer herbs, lay them on paper towels on trays. Leave in a cool to warm room (if hot or humid, the herbs might go moldy).

Store in airtight containers and use within 4 months of drying, or while they still smell fragrant. Dried herbs are more concentrated than fresh, so use sparingly. A good rule of thumb is that for every 1 tsp of fresh herbs you can substitute—where appropriate—½ tsp dried.

Freezing herbs

Frozen herbs can be preferable to dried herbs, depending on what you're planning to do with them. For example, if I didn't have fresh basil I'd rather use frozen basil in my tomato linguine than dried.

You can either buy frozen herbs (keep an eye on expiration dates) or freeze them yourself. Wash the herbs and spread on paper towels to dry, then place on a tray lined with plastic wrap. Freeze them, uncovered, for about 3 hours. Once frozen, strip the leaves from the stems and pack in freezer bags. Herbs can be kept in the freezer for up to 6 months.

HERB MIXTURES

Herbs are an intrinsic part of any cuisine. They can add a fresh and cleansing quality or a deep earthy flavor to many different meals. Herbs are also often used together to create a rounded flavor and complexity. They are great team players that are well worth experimenting with.

BOUQUET GARNI

A bouquet garni is a bundle of herbs used to flavor "wet" dishes, such as soups and stews, where you want to remove the herbs after the dish has finished cooking. The classic combination of herbs is bay leaf, thyme, and parsley, although bouquet garnis can also contain sage and rosemary, plus spices such as whole cloves or allspice berries.

To make a bouquet garni, you can either tie the herbs together with string, using bay leaves as the outer wrapper, or tie everything up in a small cheesecloth bag.

GREMOLATA

This Italian salsa is traditionally sprinkled over cooked dishes such as osso bucco as they are served. I also like it on scrambled eggs and salmon at a weekend brunch, and with poached chicken and veal.

1 tightly packed cup flat-leaf parsley leaves

1 garlic clove, crushed

finely grated zest of 1 large lemon

Finely chop the parsley, then add the garlic and chop together. Mix in the lemon zest. Store, covered, in the refrigerator for no more than a few hours before using.

SALSA VERDE

This sauce is traditionally served with poached or grilled meats and fish. You can either make it by hand, chopping with a knife, or use a small food processor, blitzing the herb leaves with the oil first. Substitute other soft herbs in place of any of those suggested, if you prefer.

½ cup flat-leaf parsley leaves	1 tbsp small capers, rinsed
½ cup basil leaves	¼ cup snipped chives
½ cup mint leaves	1 scallion, finely sliced
¼ cup chervil leaves	½ cup extra virgin olive oil
⅛ cup tarragon leaves	1 tsp grain mustard
3 cornichons, rinsed	grated zest and juice of ½ lemon

WASHING HERBS

Herbs bought from a supermarket will already be washed, but bunches from the local farmers' market will probably contain the odd twig, leaf, or insect. Fill a deep bowl with cool water and plunge in the herbs, holding by the stems. Shake around a bit, then drain in a colander or give them a few good swings outdoors. Gently pat them dry in a dish towel before chopping.

1 Chop the parsley, basil, mint, chervil, and tarragon. Roughly chop the cornichons and capers, or, if the capers are very small, leave them whole. Put in a bowl with the chives, green onion, oil, mustard, and lemon zest, and mix together. Finally, stir in the lemon juice and season to taste.

2 Let the salsa sit at room temperature for at least 30 minutes so that the flavors can develop. Stir before serving.

THAI BASIL & CILANTRO-MARINATED SQUID

This appetizer is quick to make on two counts: The marinade is assembled in seconds, and the squid needs only brief marinating and cooking. White pepper is used for its distinctive flavor, so don't replace it with black. You can also use the marinade on sliced chicken or turkey breast or fish fillets.

1½ heaped tsp white peppercorns
½ tsp salt
1 garlic clove
handful of Thai basil
handful of cilantro, including roots, stems, and leaves
14oz (400g) squid, cleaned, then body finely sliced into rings and tentacles separated
2 tbsp peanut oil
1 tsp nam pla (fish sauce)
2 tsp finely chopped or grated pale palm sugar

1 Lightly pound the peppercorns, salt, and garlic in a mortar with a pestle until combined. Add the basil and cilantro, and work into a chunky paste. Put the squid into a bowl and coat with the paste. Leave at room temperature for 15 minutes.

2 Heat a wok until smoking. Add half the oil and swirl it around. Add half the squid and cook over high heat for 30 seconds, tossing it a little. Tip the squid into a bowl. Wipe the wok clean, then cook the remaining squid in the same way.

3 Return the first batch of squid to the wok and add the fish sauce and palm sugar. Toss together and cook for 20 seconds longer.

Serve the squid immediately, with chunks of peeled cucumber and lime wedges

GREEN HERB OIL

This vibrant green oil, fragrant with herbs, is great to drizzle over grilled swordfish, goat cheese salad, or poached chicken breast. My favorite herbs to use are oregano, basil, mint, and tarragon, but a combination of several can be inspiring. Store the oil in the refrigerator or a cool, dark place. It stays fragrant for a week.

You can use the sediment to brush on grilled fish when almost cooked, or mix it into mashed potatoes for color and a subtle flavor.

Makes 1 cup

1½ cups tightly packed herbs of your choice

⅔ cup light-tasting oil (grapeseed, sunflower, or light olive oil)

½ cup extra virgin olive oil

1 Bring a large pan of water to a boil. Plunge the herbs into the boiling water and stir gently, then leave for 5 seconds.

2 Drain the herbs in a strainer, then tip them into a bowl of ice water. Let them cool for 20 seconds, stirring gently once.

3 Remove the herbs from the ice water and drain well in the strainer, then pat dry with a dish towel or paper towels.

4 Place the herbs in a blender and add the light-tasting oil. Blend for 20 seconds, then set aside for 10 minutes.

5 Pour the oil through a fine strainer and funnel into a clean bottle or jar. If desired, reserve the sediment for later use (see above).

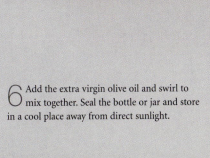

6 Add the extra virgin olive oil and swirl to mix together. Seal the bottle or jar and store in a cool place away from direct sunlight.

SPICES

Spices are the highly aromatic and scented parts of tropical plants —the seeds and fruit, bark, and root. The number of edible fragrant seeds is vast, and includes caraway, cardamom, coriander, cumin, fennel, peppercorns, poppy, star anise, sumac, and wattleseed. Barks include cinnamon and cassia. Roots include ginger, galangal, and sassafras, when dried and ground.

Spices can be used whole—often dry-roasted to enhance flavor —or ground. They play a huge part in giving all kinds of dishes another dimension. For example, they can be added to breads, cakes, and pastries; rubbed into meats and fish before cooking; braised with onions and potatoes for aromatic Indian dishes; and fried in coconut oil with shrimp paste to make heady Thai curries.

Bruising spices

Spices added whole to a dish are often bruised first so that their flavors will be released more easily. Those commonly bruised include fresh ginger, galangal, and lemon-grass (see left). To bruise, trim or peel the spice, then place on a board. Lay a heavy knife flat on the spice and, using the heel of your hand, press down to crush and break open—do not smash.

Grating spices

It is often easier and quicker to grate fresh root and rhizome spices, such as ginger (see right), galangal, wasabi, and horseradish, rather than to chop them finely. Peel them before grating. Once grated, fresh ginger flesh can be squeezed to extract the juice, which is used in many Asian dishes. Whole dried nutmegs are also grated, using a grater with very fine holes.

LEMON-GRASS & TOMATO ROASTED SARDINES

Sardines fresh from a Portuguese or Moroccan port, served on fresh white bread with a juicy lemon wedge, are the food of memories. Replacing the lemon with lemon-grass and adding lightly acidic tomatoes is the fusion effect. The oiliness of the fish benefits from the hit of citrus.

3 lemon-grass stalks

4 garlic cloves, finely sliced

½ cup olive oil

2 very ripe tomatoes, chopped into smallish chunks

few sprigs of thyme, chopped

8–12 sardines, about 4½–5½oz (125–150g) each, gutted and scaled

4 slices of good-quality, crusty white bread

1 Preheat the oven to 400°F (200°C). Place a nonreactive baking dish, large enough to hold the sardines comfortably in one layer, in the oven to heat. Preheat the broiler, too.

2 Cut off the top half of each lemon-grass stalk and bruise it (see above). Put into the baking dish with half the garlic, half the oil, and the tomatoes. Roast for 12 minutes. Remove from the oven and mix well.

3 Trim the base off the other half of the lemon-grass stalks and peel off the three outer layers. (Discard these or use to flavor soups or stock.) Mince the peeled lemon-grass. Mix with the remaining garlic, the thyme, and some sea salt and pepper.

4 Lay the sardines on a board and stuff the stomach cavities with the minced lemon-grass mixture. Brush thoroughly on both sides with the remaining oil.

5 Put the sardines in the baking dish. Return to the oven and roast for 5 minutes. Turn the sardines over and transfer to the broiler. Broil to color the fish and finish cooking, 2–4 minutes. They are cooked when the flesh is opaque and will pull off the bone easily.

6 Toast the bread (or use untoasted) and spread with the tomato mixture from the baking dish. Top with the sardines and lemon-grass stalks, and serve piping hot with extra salt and pepper. Make sure you chew on the lemon-grass stalks as you eat the sardines.

Dry-roasting spices

The flavor of spices is greatly enhanced when they are roasted, which can be done in the oven or on the stovetop. The oven method will give a more even roasting and is good for large or irregular-shaped spices such as star anise, cinnamon, and cloves. Whichever method you use, keep an eye on the spices as their color darkens and the aroma increases—burned spice will just add bitterness to a dish. Once roasted, leave spices to cool before crushing or grinding to use in spice blends, rubs, and marinades.

To dry-roast in the oven, preheat the oven to 325°F (160°C). Spread out the spices in a baking pan and roast until they are aromatic and lightly colored. If you are dry-roasting a selection of different spices (as shown right), be aware that they may take different times—a cinnamon stick, snapped into a few pieces, benefits from about 8 minutes of roasting; cumin seeds need about 7 minutes; and cloves, just 4 minutes. Transfer to a plate to cool.

To dry-roast on the stovetop, heat a heavy frying pan over medium heat. Put the spices in the pan and cook, shaking the pan constantly to keep the spices moving, until they darken and their aroma increases. Transfer the spices to a bowl or plate to cool.

Frying spices in oil

This is a good method to use when you have both oil and small, whole spices, such as caraway, coriander, cumin, and sesame seeds, in a recipe. By frying the spices in the oil, their flavor gets trapped in the oil.

Heat a pan until quite hot. Add 2–3 tbsp oil and then 1 tbsp spice seeds. The oil should not be too hot when you add the spice. Reduce the heat to medium-low and fry until the spices are lightly colored. Immediately remove from the heat.

Crushing spices

As well as helping to release aroma, crushing spices in a mortar with a pestle (see right) allows more of their surface area to be exposed to the food they are flavoring. As a result, you will need to use less of a crushed spice than if you use it whole. Crushing also makes spices more digestible—biting into a whole clove in a cake is much less appealing than enjoying the flavor imparted by a finely crushed clove.

Grinding spices

At work, I frequently use a domestic coffee grinder for grinding spices, as do many other professional chefs. Others prefer special spice grinders. The effect of these machines is much the same as using a mortar and pestle to crush spices finely. However, when using a grinder it is harder to control the degree to which the spices are ground, and overheating from overgrinding can cause the essential oils to dissipate if the ground spices are not used quickly.

SPICE BLENDS

Spice blends come primarily, but not exclusively, from Asia and North Africa, where the spice trails wove their ways in days of old. These blends are generally used to "sprinkle on flavor" after a dish is cooked, although you can also stir them into soups, stews, and other dishes for a more subtle approach. You can buy prepared spice blends, but making your own with freshly ground spices allows you to vary the blend according to the dish. Store spice blends in airtight containers and use within one month of making.

GARAM MASALA

This spice blend is one of the basics in any Indian kitchen, and variations on the mixture are endless. Usually added toward the end of the cooking process, it can also be sprinkled onto prime cuts of meat and fish to infuse them with spice flavor before cooking.

Makes enough to flavor up to 4½lb (2kg) of meat, fish, or lentil stew

1½ tbsp green cardamom pods, lightly dry-roasted
1 tbsp fennel seeds, lightly dry-roasted
1 tbsp cumin seeds, lightly dry-roasted
1 tbsp coriander seeds, lightly dry-roasted
1 tbsp black or white peppercorns
¼ cinnamon stick, lightly dry-roasted
½ tsp dried red pepper flakes
½ tsp ground ginger
large pinch of grated nutmeg

Grind the cardamom pods, fennel, cumin, and coriander seeds, peppercorns, and cinnamon. Pass through a strainer. Mix with the remaining ingredients and store in an airtight container.

PISTACHIO DUKKA

This Egyptian spice blend has been served in Antipodean restaurants and cafés for the past 10 years. It is now beginning to appear in restaurants in Europe and North America, alongside extra virgin olive oil as a dip for bread.

Serves 10 as a dip

¼ cup shelled pistachio nuts
¼ cup sesame seeds
2 tbsp cumin seeds
1 tbsp coriander seeds
1½ tsp fine sea salt
1 tsp freshly ground black pepper

1 Preheat the oven to 325°F (160°C). Spread the pistachio nuts evenly in a small baking pan and roast until they are fragrant but still retain their green color, about 15 minutes. Remove from the pan and let cool.

2 Lightly dry-roast the sesame, cumin, and coriander seeds in the oven (p79). Let cool, then roughly crush the coriander seeds.

3 Coarsely chop the pistachio nuts, then mix with the other ingredients. Store the dukka in an airtight container.

SPICE RUBS

The purpose of a spice rub is to impart flavor to the outside of food before it is cooked—in contrast to a marinade, where you want the flavor to seep a little deeper into the food. Spice rubs work really well in dishes where the food is wrapped before cooking (for example, in banana leaves, foil, or a roasting bag). Rubs are equally good for small cuts of meat or fish just before they are cooked very briefly as they are for larger items, such as a leg of lamb or a whole duck to be left overnight before cooking.

SALMON WITH CAJUN BLACKENING SPICES

The spices for this rub are not dry-roasted first, since the fierce heat used to sear the salmon will roast them during cooking. You don't want the spices to burn, but they should "eat" into the fish. I like to serve this with thick yogurt, lemon wedges, and a tomato and cucumber salad. The spice mix makes enough for eight pieces of salmon fillet, so keep the excess for next time.

1 tbsp ground cumin

1 tbsp coriander seeds, crushed

1 tbsp dried ground garlic

2 tbsp paprika or pimenton (smoked Spanish paprika)

1 tbsp coarsely ground white or black pepper

1 tbsp dried thyme

1 tsp dried oregano

2 tbsp fine salt

4 salmon fillets, about 6oz (170g) each, skinned

vegetable oil

1 Mix together all the spices, herbs, and salt. Using half of the mixture, rub into both sides of the pieces of salmon and lay them on a tray. Cover and leave at room temperature for up to 30 minutes.

2 Heat a heavy-based frying pan over high heat until very hot. Brush the pan with oil, then place the fillets in the pan. Let cook for 2 minutes without moving them. Turn the fish over, cover the pan, and cook for 2 more minutes. The spices will have blackened and the fish will be barely cooked inside. Transfer the salmon to warm plates and serve.

SPICE MARINADES

The purpose of a marinade is to add flavor as well as to help tenderize protein foods. Simply adding liquid, such as yogurt or oil, will turn a spice rub into a marinade. If based on yogurt, the marinade will tenderize tough meat and make fish and prime meat cuts firm yet delicate. Alternatively, fruits (papaya, pineapple, and kiwi fruit, for example), chilies, or citrus juices can contribute the tenderizing enzymes. A marinade can be used for basting during cooking, as the liquid in a braised dish or stew, and to make a sauce (if used to marinate raw meat it must be boiled first). If you want to brown food that has been marinated, drain and dry it well.

CUMIN, NIGELLA & PEPPER MARINADE

This yogurt-based spice marinade works very well with monkfish (as described here), making the flesh a bit firmer and adding wonderful flavor. You can also use the marinade for kabobs of boned shoulder or leg of lamb (leave these to marinate for 24 hours) and for chicken legs or pork chops. I like to serve the monkfish with chunks of icy cold watermelon, lemon wedges, and some thick plain yogurt.

4 tbsp olive oil
1 tbsp cumin seeds
1 tbsp freshly ground black pepper
1½ tbsp nigella seeds
1 tsp salt
1 tbsp dried mint
⅔ cup plain yogurt
4 monkfish tails, on the bone, about 7oz (200g) each, skinned
large handful of mint

1 Put 2 tbsp of the oil in a small frying pan and add the cumin seeds and black pepper. Set the pan over medium heat and cook until the seeds are fizzing and becoming aromatic. Add the nigella seeds and salt and count to 15, then tip the mixture into a large mixing bowl. Add the dried mint and stir to mix. Let cool, then mix in the yogurt.

2 Add the monkfish to the bowl and rub the marinade onto the flesh, mixing well. Cover the bowl with plastic wrap and put into the refrigerator. Let marinate for 4–6 hours.

3 Preheat the oven to 400°F (200°C) and put a ceramic baking dish in the oven to warm. Remove the monkfish from the bowl and wipe off and discard excess marinade. Drizzle 1 tbsp oil into the baking dish and add the fish. Roast until the fish is cooked, 15–18 minutes. To test for doneness, use a sharp knife to separate the flesh from the bone at the thickest end—it should come away easily.

4 Just before serving, strip the mint leaves from the stems. Scatter the mint leaves over the monkfish, drizzle with the remaining 1 tbsp oil, and serve immediately.

MACE & CHILI MARINADE

Lip-smacking, sweet, and spicy, this marinade works well with pork chops (as here), and with pork tenderloin, chicken, or duck legs, whether grilled, broiled, or roasted. The chops are great with potato salad and green beans.

7 tbsp maple syrup	1 tbsp fennel seeds, dry-roasted and coarsely ground
5 tbsp tomato paste	3 blades of mace, lightly dry-roasted and coarsely ground
3½ tbsp unsalted butter	
1 small red onion, finely chopped	1½ tsp sea salt
2 garlic cloves, finely chopped	4 pork chops, about 7oz (200g) each
2 tsp dried red pepper flakes	½ cup water

1 Place all the ingredients, except the pork and water, in a pan. Bring slowly to a boil, stirring. Reduce the heat and let simmer, stirring frequently, until thickened, 12–15 minutes.

2 Transfer to a bowl and let cool completely. Then add the pork chops and rub the marinade into the meat. Cover the bowl with plastic wrap and let marinate in the refrigerator overnight.

3 Preheat the broiler. Wipe excess marinade from the chops (reserve the marinade), then broil for 6–8 minutes on each side. Or, roast in a preheated 400°F (200°C) oven for 15–20 minutes. Meanwhile, place the marinade in a pan with the water and bring to a boil, stirring. Taste for seasoning. Pour this sauce over the chops before serving.

CHILIES

All chilies have a characteristic flavor and not just heat. A fresh green chili is an immature red chili—leave it long enough and it will turn red. I like the flavor of fresh green chilies when I'm making a refreshing crunchy salsa with, say, cucumber, apples, mint, or melon. Red chilies have a deeper, more mature flavor and work well with almost anything. When chilies are dried they develop different characteristics, and fresh and dried chilies are usually not interchangeable in a recipe.

As a rule of thumb, a large, smooth chili will be far less hot than a small wrinkly one. But whatever the size, it is the seeds and ribs in a chili that contain the heat. If you are not used to cooking with chilies, start with half the quantity given in a recipe.

Seeding fresh chilies

To lessen the heat of a chili, cut it in half lengthwise, then scrape out the seeds and ribs with a spoon or knife. An alkaloid in chilies, called capsaicin, can irritate your skin, so you might want to wear plastic or rubber gloves when preparing chilies. Otherwise, avoid putting your fingers to eyes or lips, and thoroughly wash your hands.

Roasting dried chilies

Dry-roasting chilies gives them a light smoky flavor. Heat a heavy-based frying pan over high heat, add the chilies, and roast until they start to darken in color and blister; do not let them burn. Alternatively, spread the chilies on a baking sheet and roast in a preheated 400°F (200°C) oven until they puff up, 5–10 minutes.

Grinding dried chilies

Once dry-roasted, chilies can be soaked and the flesh pushed through a strainer (p84), or they can be cooled and then ground to a fine powder. You can also grind dried chilies without first dry-roasting them. Use a mortar and pestle for grinding or an electric spice or coffee grinder. Store ground chili in an airtight jar in a cool, dark place.

SOAKING & SIEVING DRIED CHILIES

This process enables you to use dried chili flesh in a dressing, paste, or stew without the papery skins. If you do not want too fierce a heat, first break open the chilies and shake out the seeds.

1 Put the chilies in a bowl of warm, lightly salted water and set a small plate on top to keep them submerged. Soak until they are malleable, 15–30 minutes, depending on size.

2 Drain the chilies and put them in a strainer. Using a ladle or the back of a spoon, press the flesh through the strainer into a bowl. Or, if the chilies are large enough, scrape the flesh from the skin. Discard the skin and seeds.

CHILI OIL

Drizzle this oil over a shellfish risotto or over roasted or grilled meats or fish, or mix it into salad dressings, marinades, and salsas. The heat of the oil will depend on the chilies you use. It will keep for up to 6 months.

Remove the stems from 6 fresh, unblemished chilies, about 1oz (20–30g) in total, and cut lengthwise in half. Put the chilies and ⅔ cup light olive oil in a small pan over medium heat. When the mixture starts to bubble, stir it a little. Once the bubbling slows down, but before the chilies wilt completely and darken too much, remove from the heat and pour into a bowl. Let cool completely, then decant the oil and chilies into a clean jar or bottle and pour in another ⅔ cup oil. Leave for a few days before using. Keep in the refrigerator, or in a cool, dark place.

RED CURRY PASTE

This dense-tasting, sweetish paste is delicious spread over grilled meats or fried fish, but it is most useful when making a coconut-based curry. Use whatever chilies you prefer—the amount and type will determine the heat of the finished paste. It will keep in the refrigerator for 2 weeks.

Makes enough for 12 portions of curry	
vegetable oil for deep-frying	3½oz (100g) fresh ginger, thinly sliced
2 large red onions, sliced into ½in (1cm) thick rings	scant 2oz (50g) galangal, thinly sliced
2 red bell peppers, quartered and seeded	20 garlic cloves, quartered
5 moderately hot red chilies, halved lengthwise	3½ tbsp tomato paste
	½ tbsp salt

1 Heat oil for deep-frying to 325°F (160°C). Add the onions and fry, stirring occasionally, until they are lightly blackened and shriveled, 10–15 minutes. Using a slotted spoon, remove the onions and drain on paper towels. Deep-fry the bell peppers for 7–8 minutes, then drain.

2 Add the chilies to the hot oil and deep-fry until they are tinged black and shriveled, 4–5 minutes. Remove and drain. Deep-fry the ginger with the galangal for 5 minutes. Fry the garlic, which will cook quite quickly.

3 Put all the deep-fried ingredients in a food processor and process to a fine paste. Add the tomato paste and salt, and process again briefly to combine the ingredients.

4 Transfer the paste to a clean jar or plastic container and cover the surface with parchment paper. Let cool. (The frying oil can be used to baste foods on the grill or to fry fish. Cool in the pan, then decant into a jar.)

Tomato chili jam

This jam is indispensable in my kitchens at home and at work. It is great on toast with a fried egg on top, dolloped onto roast lamb or pork, used to glaze a fillet of fish under the broiler, or in a sandwich of goat cheese, arugula, and avocado. The chilies you use will affect the final taste—I prefer finger-sized serrano chilies. The jam will keep for 2 months.

Simmer until the jam is thick and glossy

Makes about 1lb 2oz (500g)

1lb 2oz (500g) very ripe tomatoes

2 thumbs of fresh ginger, roughly chopped

3 tbsp nam pla (fish sauce)

4 fresh serrano or other red chilies, finely sliced

4 garlic cloves, finely sliced

1½ cups sugar

½ cup red wine or cider vinegar

Put half the tomatoes, the ginger, and fish sauce in a blender and purée until smooth. (Although some people have an aversion to tomato seeds, they provide the pectin that makes this jam set, so I don't suggest passing the puréed tomatoes through a strainer.) Chop the remaining tomatoes into ½in (1cm) dice (you can peel them if you want, but I don't).

Put the puréed tomatoes, chopped tomatoes, and all the remaining ingredients into a deep pot and slowly bring to a boil, stirring frequently. Once the mixture boils, reduce the heat to a gentle simmer.

Skim off any foam that rises to the surface, then simmer for 30–40 minutes, stirring every few minutes to release the solids that will settle on the bottom of the pot. Be sure to scrape the sides of the pot from time to time so that the jam cooks evenly. The jam is ready when it thickens and becomes glossy.

Pour the jam into sterilized glass jars, seal, and label. Let cool to room temperature before storing in the refrigerator.

SALTY FLAVORINGS

Salt has two major roles in the kitchen, which are to flavor food and to preserve it. Refrigeration and freezing have mostly replaced the role of salt as a preservative, although there are still many foods that depend almost entirely on salt for their production. Among them are capers, olives, and anchovies. These, with salt itself, are used to add savor and to heighten the flavor of other foods. In the Asian kitchen, several flavoring ingredients are used to add saltiness, including soy sauce, fish sauce (nam pla or nuoc nam), miso (a savory paste made from soybeans), gomasio (toasted sesame seeds mixed with salt), and salted black beans.

Preparing salted anchovies

Salted anchovies are far superior to anchovies in brine. Rinse excess salt from the anchovies and pat them dry with paper towels. Using your thumbnail, split an anchovy open, then separate the flesh from the spine. The fillet should come off easily. Remove the second fillet in the same way. Pull off any remaining small bones.

Pitting olives

Pitting olives can be a tedious job, but it is often essential. The simplest and quickest method is to squash the olives, one at a time, with a flat knife blade, then squeeze or pull out the pit. Alternatively, you can use a tool, such as a cherry pitter, that pushes a hole all the way through the olive and extracts the pit.

TAPENADE

Made from many of the salty products of the Mediterranean, tapenade has a surprisingly light taste. Use it as a crostini topping, dollop it onto grilled tuna and swordfish, or drizzle it over spring lamb with roasted tomatoes. It will keep in the refrigerator for up to a week.

Makes 10oz (300g)

1 heaped cup roughly chopped black olives
1 salted anchovy, rinsed, filleted (see left), and roughly chopped
2 tsp capers, lightly rinsed
1 garlic clove, minced or crushed
few leaves of flat-leaf parsley, roughly chopped
⅓ cup extra virgin olive oil

1 Put the olives, anchovy fillets, capers, garlic, and parsley into a mortar and pound with a pestle until amalgamated.

2 Slowly drizzle in the olive oil and pound to a smooth, thick paste. Alternatively, blitz all the ingredients together in a food processor, making sure not to overwork until too fine.

ANCHOVY BUTTER

I love this butter melted into pasta that has been tossed with broccoli. It's also great dolloped onto grilled fish or lamb chops, substituted for regular butter in a chicken sandwich, or spread on toast with very sweet tomatoes and chives. Store in the refrigerator for up to 2 weeks.

Makes 10oz (300g)

5 salted anchovies, rinsed and filleted (see left)
¾ cup + 2 tbsp unsalted butter, at room temperature
2 scallions, finely sliced
⅓ cup olive oil

Put all the ingredients into a food processor and process for about 15 seconds to a paste, scraping down the sides of the processor bowl once or twice. Alternatively, mince the anchovy fillets and beat them into the butter, along with the scallions, then whisk in the olive oil. Use at room temperature.

CAPER DRESSING

Almost a runny salsa, this dressing is perfect spooned over grilled snapper or tuna, or lightly steamed asparagus. Make it just before you need it, otherwise the cilantro leaves will discolor.

Serves 6 as a dressing

2 tsp coriander seeds, lightly dry-roasted

small bunch of cilantro

grated zest and juice of 1 large, juicy orange

2 tbsp small capers in brine, drained

⅔ cup extra virgin olive oil

2 tbsp light soy sauce

stems, add to the mortar, and pound into the seeds. Add the orange zest and pound in, then add the capers and smash them roughly, keeping them chunky.

1 Finely grind the coriander seeds in a mortar with a pestle. Remove the leaves from the cilantro and set aside. Chop the cilantro

2 Mix in the olive oil, then the orange juice and soy sauce, and finally the cilantro leaves. Let the dressing infuse for a few minutes before serving.

BLACK BEAN, LIME & CHILI DRESSING

Salted (or fermented) Chinese black beans have a delicious musty taste—full on the tongue and quite rich. In this chunky dressing, they add texture and color contrast to the other ingredients, working as a foil for the acidity of the limes and the chilies (use more or less chili, according to your taste).

Spoon the dressing generously over fish such as salmon, mahi mahi, or swordfish, or on grilled chicken legs, duck breasts, or pork chops. The dressing can be kept in a covered jar at room temperature for up to a day.

Serves 6 as a dressing

1 small red onion, finely sliced or diced

grated zest and juice of 3 limes

½ fresh red chili, finely chopped

½ fresh green chili, finely chopped

¼ cup grated pale palm sugar or Demerara sugar

2 tsp nam pla (fish sauce)

3 tbsp black beans, rinsed and roughly chopped

2 tsp toasted sesame oil

⅔ cup peanut or grapeseed oil

1 Put the onion, lime zest, and lime juice into a bowl and mix together. Leave for 20 minutes.

2 Add the chilies, palm sugar, and fish sauce. Stir to dissolve the sugar. Add the black beans, the toasted sesame oil, and peanut or grapeseed oil, and mix well. Let the dressing infuse for 30 minutes before using.

CITRUS & SOUR FLAVORINGS

Citrus and sour flavors play an important balancing role in cooking. In dishes of pork belly, duck, or sardines, for example, a little zing from citrus fruit or a sour hint from tamarind is a good way to offset the richness. These flavors are not commonly used in North America or Europe, where vinegar traditionally provides the souring agent, but elsewhere in the world many types of citrus and sour flavors are considered essential—for example, preserved lemons, sumac, and tamarind in the Middle East; limes and ground dried mango in Southeast Asia and India; yuzu in China and Japan; and lemon myrtle and bush and finger limes in the Pacific and Australasia.

SALTED, SPICED, PRESERVED LEMONS

Traditionally used in Moroccan tagines (stews), preserved lemon peel now flavors all kinds of dishes—from salads and dressings to stewed fruits and simple cakes. You need a sterilized canning jar that will hold 10 lemons (they should be a little squashed). To use, take a lemon from the jar, rinse briefly, quarter, and scrape the flesh from the peel—the peel is the part you want. You can add the flesh to marinades and to chickpea or lentil soups. It will be salty and sour.

Makes 10 lemons

14 medium to large unwaxed, ripe lemons
1½ cups coarse sea salt
1 cinnamon stick, snapped into 4
1 tbsp fennel seeds, lightly dry-roasted (p79)
2 thumbs of fresh ginger, thinly sliced

1 Wash the 10 plumpest lemons in tepid water and dry thoroughly. Hold each lemon, pointed end up, on a board and cut lengthwise into quarters, not cutting all the way through the base so the quarters stay connected.

2 Stuff each lemon with as much salt as it will hold, then put it into the jar. Sprinkle the spices in as you pack in the lemons. Add any remaining salt to the jar, then seal and leave in a cool place for 3 days.

3 Squeeze the juice from the remaining lemons. Press the lemons in the jar to compress them further, then pour the juice into the jar. The lemons should be completely covered (you may need extra juice). Seal the jar and leave for at least 8 weeks before using.

Dried limes

Usually added whole to stews and soups, dried limes give a sharp and bitter background flavor that works well with sweet spices. Dried limes can also be crushed and soaked to use in marinades or put under a roasting leg of lamb.

Dried mangoes

Dried unripe mango, in strips or ground into a brown powder, gives a tart, fruity background taste to vegetarian dishes. It is also good mixed into a chicken broth or used to flavor poached fish. It can be the tenderizer in a marinade, too.

Kaffir lime

The zest is added to salad dressings and fish cakes, the juice (what there is) adds an edge to sour dressings, and the leaf (which freezes well) is essential in many Thai and Malaysian dishes.

Pomegranate molasses

The flavor varies from sweet, with a hint of tartness and sourness, to very sour. Add to soda water for a refreshing beverage, drizzle over drupe fruit and berries, or brush over roast chicken 10 minutes before the end of cooking.

Sumac

A coarse powder ground from berries, sumac has a sour taste. Use in spice mixtures, such as zatar, or sprinkle over cooked foods.

Tamarind

Available sour or sweet, tamarind can be bought in the pod; in jars of dark, sour, resinous paste; and in blocks of compressed pulp and seeds.

Yuzu

This citrus fruit has a sweet, pungent aroma and an agreeable sour taste. The grated zest is much used in Japanese cooking; the bottled salted juice is added to dressings, dips, and marinades.

CHOCOLATE

Its use in sweet dishes is well known, but chocolate can be added to savory dishes, too. One example is the moles of Mexico, famous for their complex flavors—a good mole is thickened with bread and nuts, flavored with a startling array of spices, and finished with the richness of chocolate and the aroma of oranges. The recipe below is inspired by moles, but chocolate is used altogether differently.

BLACK BEAN, CHOCOLATE & PEANUT PURÉE

Serve this as a spread for breads or as a garnish for roast venison or duck. It will keep in the refrigerator for up to 2 days.

Serves 6–8 as a spread

⅔ cup dried black beans, soaked overnight and drained

2 red onions, thinly sliced

⅔ cup olive oil

6 garlic cloves, chopped

1 tsp pimenton (smoked paprika)

⅓ cup sherry vinegar

½ cup roughly chopped, roasted peanuts

1½oz (40g) bittersweet chocolate (55–65% cocoa solids), roughly chopped

2 tbsp soy sauce

1 Put the soaked beans into a pan of cold water. Bring to a boil, skimming off any foam, then partly cover and simmer until tender, about 1 hour. When the beans are done, drain them in a colander.

2 Meanwhile, sauté the onions in half the olive oil until they are caramelized, stirring occasionally. Add the garlic and pimenton, and cook for a few more minutes. Add the vinegar and peanuts, and cook for another minute, stirring well.

3 Put the hot beans and onion mixture into a food processor with the chocolate, soy sauce, and remaining olive oil. Process to a chunky paste. Taste and add more soy sauce or salt, if needed. Cool.

VANILLA

The first time I had vanilla in anything other than a dessert was in 1996: It was teamed with duck and kumara (New Zealand's native sweet potato) in a samosa. Since then I have experimented using vanilla in lots of savory dishes—for example, in an oil to drizzle over a shrimp dish; stewed with cannellini beans to serve with duck; and, with saffron, for flavoring braised onions to serve with halibut.

EXTRACTING VANILLA SEEDS

Vanilla beans (which are the cured unripe fruit of a climbing orchid) are used whole or split open, or the seeds alone may be used. After infusing a dish with a split vanilla bean, the seeds can be scraped out and added back—they look great in creamy desserts. Use the empty pod to flavor vodka or sugar syrups, if you don't want to use it in cooking. If a vanilla bean is kept whole, it can be rinsed, dried, and used again to flavor another dish.

1 Lay the vanilla bean on a cutting board and, using the tip of a sharp knife, carefully cut the bean in half lengthwise.

2 Using a teaspoon or the back of a small knife, scrape off the sticky seeds along the length of the bean, pressing firmly.

 **VANILLA EXTRACT**

Pure vanilla extract is made by crushing the cured beans and extracting the vanillin (the chemical compound that gives vanilla its aroma and flavor) with alcohol. Cheaper vanilla flavoring is made from synthesized vanillin aldehyde.

EGGS & DAIRY PRODUCTS

MICHAEL ROMANO

Of all our foodstuffs, the egg is perhaps the most versatile, and certainly one of the most nutritious. Used as an ingredient, the egg is prized for its ability to bind, lighten, emulsify, and enrich. Cooked and eaten on their own, eggs lend themselves to dozens of preparations. Egg yolks and whites have very diverse properties and are at times used separately to achieve different effects.

The protein and fat properties of egg yolks allow them to enrich, emulsify, or otherwise bind ingredients such as fats and liquids, which do not normally combine. Hollandaise and mayonnaise are sauces that owe their rich, creamy texture to that ability. Yolks are also used in cakes and some bread-baking and pastamaking; as the basis of certain sauces like sabayon; and in drinks like eggnog. As a wash they help baked foods brown and, when hard-cooked and sliced or chopped, they are used as a garnish. Egg whites can increase to about eight times their shell volume when air is beaten into them, and therefore help create the airy lightness of some cakes as well as giving us meringues and soufflés. Whites are also useful in the clarification of liquids, such as consommé and wine, because the albumin they contain can attract and entrap particulate matter.

Products from milk and cream Left to stand, unhomogenized milk separates into two layers— the thinner body of milk, and the milk fat, or cream, at the top. Today, most cream is produced by centrifugal extraction, and is usually pasteurized or ultrapasteurized, a heating process that extends its shelf life but compromises its flavor and ability to whip.

Yogurt is made by mixing milk with helpful bacteria to ferment and thicken it. Unlike cream, yogurt cannot be boiled and reduced. It is heated by tempering—a little hot liquid is added to bring the yogurt slowly to temperature before it is incorporated in a dish. However, if the dish subsequently boils during cooking, there is a chance that the yogurt will coagulate and separate from the sauce.

Crème fraîche is a fermented, thickened cream with a tangy, bracing flavor. In France, it is made from unpasteurized milk and thickens naturally. Elsewhere, it is produced by adding sour cream or buttermilk to pasteurized heavy cream, but the flavor is not as good as that of the French original.

Butter is cream's apotheosis. It is made by churning cream long enough to cause the fat to separate from the cream's liquid, or whey. Unsalted butter, sometimes called sweet butter (although all butter is made from sweet cream), contains no added salt. It is, I think, best used in baking and pastrymaking. Unsalted butter is more vulnerable to spoilage than salted—salt acts a preservative.

Cheese Derived from various animal milks—most typically the milk of cows, goats, and sheep— cheese is an ancient product. Cheeses can be mild or pungent, soft or hard. They can weigh as little as 1oz (30g), or as much as 300lb (135kg), as do some Swiss cheeses. Most cheeses can be enjoyed the day they are made, and some are wonderful after years of attentive aging.

How you store cheese depends to a great extent on the cheese type and its state when you buy it. The freshest cheeses, most of which are packed in food storage containers, should be kept tightly covered and refrigerated for no more than a week. Use a container also for storing whole young goat cheeses or other small whole cheeses. Put these in the coldest part of your refrigerator. Soft-ripened and other soft-textured or creamy cheeses should be similarly stored, wrapped in plastic wrap, but not for too long or rinds will become slimy and the interior hard. Firm cheeses are best stored in a plastic bag in the refrigerator door or the warmest part of the refrigerator.

Check stored cheese before eating for bad odors, cracking rinds, or discoloration, all of which indicate that the cheese should be discarded. Some cheese, however, can mold superficially without affecting its quality. If you notice mold on a semi-soft cheese, such as Emmental or Fontina, or a firmer cheese, cut it away together with some of the cheese surrounding it. However, throw away a moldy soft-ripened cheese, such as Brie or Camembert.

BASIC EGG PREPARATION

Aside from cooking eggs whole, both in their shells (hard-cooked, soft-boiled, and coddled) and out (poached, fried, and au plat), most preparations that utilize eggs will require either beating yolks and whites together, or separating the yolk and white and beating them separately. Here are some notes on the best methods to use when performing these basic but essential tasks.

SEPARATING EGGS

Many recipes call for eggs that have been separated, which means they are divided into yolks and whites. It's a good idea to give the eggs a sniff test before you start—a bad egg will be obviously smelly. One bad egg will spoil all the rest.

1 Have two nonreactive bowls ready. Tap each egg in turn against a hard surface (the lip of the bowl is good for this) to break its shell. Insert your fingers in the break and halve the shell roughly along its "equator," keeping the egg's contents in one shell half.

2 While shifting the contents back and forth between the shell halves, allow as much white as possible to fall into one bowl. Finish by dropping the yolk into the second bowl and discarding the shells.

REMOVING ANY STRAY YOLK

For egg whites to be beaten successfully, it's important that they be free from even the smallest speck of yolk. This is because yolks are fatty, and fat inhibits air incorporation. If, when separating the eggs, some yolk has fallen into your whites, remove it either by scooping it out using a bit of broken shell, or by touching the yolk with the corner of a damp paper towel (the yolk should adhere to the towel). In some cases, too much yolk will have landed in the whites. If that happens, you'll need to discard the whites and start again.

BEATING WHOLE EGGS

Break the eggs into a nonreactive bowl. Beat with a fork, whisk, or mechanical or electric beater until the yolks and whites are completely combined, about 45 seconds. Once beaten, the eggs are ready to be used to make an omelet (p102) or in any other recipe that calls for beaten eggs in the ingredients.

BEATING EGG YOLKS

Separate the eggs into two bowls. Beat the yolks with a whisk and a figure-eight motion. This breaks them up and gives them volume. Once lightly aerated, they're ready to receive other ingredients, such as oil (to make mayonnaise, for example) or sugar (for cakes and other desserts). In many cases, the ingredients to be beaten in with the yolks can be added right from the beginning, as is the case with zabaglione (see opposite).

CHILLED MOSCATO-PINEAPPLE ZABAGLIONE

This light and citrussy zabaglione differs from
the traditional dessert in two ways. One is that
instead of Marsala, it uses Moscato d'Asti, the
extraordinary Italian dessert wine. It is also
chilled, which makes it very refreshing indeed.
This is excellent on its own, or you can dollop
it over fruit. Accompany the dessert with the
Moscato d'Asti remaining in the bottle.

Serves 4–6

4 egg yolks
½ cup sugar
½ cup frozen unsweetened pineapple juice concentrate, thawed
¼ cup Moscato d'Asti wine
1 cup heavy cream

1 In a large, metal mixing bowl, combine the
egg yolks, sugar, pineapple concentrate, and
wine. Beat with a balloon whisk to combine.
Set the bowl over a saucepan one-third full of
simmering water (the base of the bowl should
not touch the water) and whisk constantly until
the mixture has thickened and coats the back of
a spoon, about 10 minutes.

2 Transfer the zabaglione to the bowl of an
electric mixer and beat on low speed until
cool. Refrigerate to chill the zabaglione
thoroughly, at least 1 hour.

3 Just before serving, whip the cream in a
bowl set over ice until soft peaks form. Fold
it gently into the chilled zabaglione. Spoon into
dessert glasses over tropical fruit—such as thinly
sliced carambola, sticks of pineapple, and mango
chunks—or berries, or serve it plain.

BEATING EGG WHITES

To beat—or more properly whip—egg whites, the type of bowl you use is of greater importance than it is for whole eggs or egg yolks. Avoid plastic bowls, which, despite washing, can retain a grease film that will inhibit the "mounting." Unlined copper bowls are best for turning out stable, voluminous whites, due to a positive reaction that occurs between the whites and the metal. If beating whites in a glass or stainless steel bowl, you can help stabilize them by adding a pinch of cream of tartar.

I think that whites are best beaten with a balloon whisk, which should be large enough to keep a maximum amount of white moving and aerated as you whip. A whisk gives you a bigger stroke than any other kind of beater, and therefore more volume. Here are more tips for success:

■ Make sure the interior of the bowl is spotlessly clean and free of grease. Especially if using copper, you may want to wipe the interior of the bowl with lemon juice or vinegar, then rinse and dry thoroughly.
■ Whites will "mount" more easily if they're at room temperature.
■ When separating the eggs, take care to prevent any yolk from falling into and contaminating the whites (p94).
■ Use a large balloon whisk that is perfectly clean.
■ Beat just until the whites are stiff but not dry.
■ Use beaten whites as soon as possible to preserve their volume.

1 Separate the eggs, putting the whites in a large, perfectly clean bowl (see above). Begin beating the whites slowly, using a small range of motion to break up their viscosity.

2 Continue to beat steadily, using larger strokes, until the whites have lost their translucency and begin to foam. If you relax your shoulders and work from the wrist, the job will be much easier.

3 Now increase your speed and use an even larger range of motion, to incorporate as much air as possible. Continue to beat until the whites have mounted to the desired degree.

Beating egg whites with an electric mixer

You can beat whites using a standard or hand-held electric mixer (but never a blender or food processor, which don't incorporate enough air). If using a standard mixer, start on low speed and gradually increase as the whites stiffen. Pay attention, because this method leads more easily to overbeating than any other. Follow the same speed progression if using a hand-held mixer, but move the beaters through the whites for maximum aeration.

4 In most cases, the whites should be stiff but not dry. Test by lifting some of the whites out of the bowl; the peaks that form should be firm but glossy, with tips that droop gently.

 OVERBEATEN EGG WHITES

If you overbeat egg whites they will be stretched to capacity, so they can't expand farther in baking to leaven foods. Overbeaten whites are grainy and, because water leaches from them, they will slide around in the bowl if you tilt it. If you have overbeaten whites, they will have to be discarded.

FOLDING EGG WHITES

This is the process by which beaten egg whites are incorporated into other, usually heavier, mixtures. The aim is to deflate the whites as little as possible as you fold, to retain maximum volume. Folding is always done using a large rubber spatula, and the whites are added in two batches.

1 Gently drop half of the beaten egg whites onto the surface of the heavier mixture—never the reverse, which could deflate the whites. With your spatula, cut down through the center of the whites and gently bring some of the heavier mixture up and over them.

2 Turn the bowl, continuing the cut, lift, and sweep process just until no whites are visible. Drop the rest of the whites on top and fold in, this time working more delicately. At the end of the folding process, no egg whites should be visible, unless the recipe directs you to leave some traces of white.

BITTERSWEET CHOCOLATE MOUSSE

Serves 4–6

10oz (280g) bittersweet chocolate, broken into pieces
3 tbsp unsalted butter
5 eggs, separated
4 tbsp sugar
½ pint heavy cream
1 tsp vanilla extract

1 Combine the chocolate and butter in a bowl and set over a pot of simmering water to melt. Set aside to cool slightly.

2 Put the egg yolks and 2 tbsp of the sugar in another bowl and set over the pot of simmering water (the base of the bowl should not be in contact with the water). Whisk until warm to the touch.

3 Transfer the egg yolk mixture to the bowl of an electric mixer and beat at high speed until fluffy and pale in color. Fold the yolk mixture into the chocolate mixture.

4 In a clean bowl, beat the egg whites with the remaining sugar until they hold firm peaks. Fold the egg whites, in two batches, into the chocolate-yolk mixture (see left).

5 In a bowl set over ice, whip the cream with the vanilla until it holds soft peaks, then fold into the chocolate mixture.

6 Transfer the mousse to individual serving cups or a large bowl. Cover and chill until set, at least 2 hours. To complete, just before serving, sprinkle shavings of bittersweet chocolate on top, if desired.

BASIC EGG COOKING

Egg cooking, to my mind, is characterized by two concepts: diversity and simplicity. There are so many different ways to cook eggs, yet most remain quite simple in execution. One thing is for certain, however: All egg cooking requires attention, because the threshold between done and overdone is quite narrow. Here is how to guarantee successful results.

BOILING EGGS

This cooking method is thought to be so simple, it's become a standard for kitchen competence, as in, "He can't even boil an egg!" In fact, there are some important guidelines worth following:
■ Despite the description, eggs must never be boiled, just simmered. This is because boiling can toughen whites and lead to overcooking.
■ The unsightly green ring around the yolk is caused by a reaction between the iron in the yolk and the sulfur in the egg's albumen. The main reason for a ring to appear is overcooking, although using older eggs can also cause a ring. You can help to prevent a ring from forming by putting just-cooked eggs immediately under cold running water to stop any further heat penetration overcooking them.
■ Older eggs are easier to peel, because their lower acidity discourages the whites and the shells from sticking together.
■ Eggs straight from the refrigerator will take a few minutes longer to reach desired "doneness" than will those at room temperature.

1 Put the eggs in a pot that is large enough for them to remain in a single layer at the bottom. Cover them by at least 2in (5cm) with cold water. Bring the water to a boil over high heat, then immediately lower the heat so that the water simmers.

2 For soft-boiled eggs (see left), which have a set white and a runny yolk, simmer them gently for 2–3 minutes.

3 If you want hard-cooked eggs (see left below), when both the yolk and white will be set, continue to simmer, allowing about 10 minutes in total.

4 At the end of the cooking time, place the pot in the sink under the tap and run cold water into it to displace the hot water and stop the cooking process. Continue until the eggs are cool enough to handle.

5 To peel boiled eggs, crack the shell at the rounded end and, using the sides of your thumbs, push the shell and thin inner membrane away from the cooked egg, trying not to dig into the egg white too much.

soft-boiled egg

hard-cooked egg

BLUE SMOKE DEVILED EGGS

These curry-flavored stuffed eggs were developed at Blue Smoke, our barbecue and jazz restaurant in New York City.

Serves 5–6

10 eggs, hard-cooked (see left)
7 tbsp mayonnaise, homemade or store-bought
1 tsp Champagne or white wine vinegar
¼ tsp dry mustard
2 tsp Dijon mustard
¼ tsp cayenne pepper
¼ tsp curry powder

1 Peel the eggs. To enable the egg halves to stand upright, cut a small sliver from both ends of each egg. Halve the eggs widthwise, making sure both halves are the same size.

2 Set the egg-white cups aside and transfer the yolks to the bowl of a food processor. Add the mayonnaise, vinegar, mustards, cayenne, and curry powder, and process until smooth. Season to taste with salt and pepper.

3 Pipe the mixture into the egg-white cups, making rosettes, or spoon it in neatly. Serve immediately, or cover lightly with plastic wrap and keep refrigerated.

CODDLING EGGS

A softly coddled egg is gently cooked to produce a result not dissimilar to soft-boiled—the differences being that for coddling, eggs are added to the boiling water and then cooked off the heat, so needing less active watching time. Perhaps it is the cook being coddled? It takes 30 minutes to hard-cook a coddled egg, so if that is the stage of cooking desired, it is probably a much better idea to boil the egg instead.

1 Put enough water into a pot to cover the eggs by 1½–2in (4–5cm) when they are added. Bring to a boil. Using a large perforated spoon, gently lower the eggs into the boiling water one by one. Immediately remove from the heat and cover the pot.

2 Leave for 6 minutes for softly coddled eggs (i.e. just set white and a very runny yolk) or allow 8–10 minutes for more firmly cooked. To ensure that the egg yolk is centered in the white, at the beginning of the cooking time turn the eggs over gently in the pan several times using the perforated spoon. Stop the cooking process by running cold water over the eggs.

POACHING IN ADVANCE

To poach eggs ahead of time for later use, skip the salt-water bath after cooking and instead plunge them into a bowl of plain chilled water to arrest the cooking. Then refrigerate the eggs in the water. When you're ready to serve them, transfer the eggs to a pot of simmering, salted water to heat through for 1 minute. Do not cook them further.

POACHING EGGS

For poaching, choose the freshest eggs you can find because their whites will be thicker and less likely to disperse when cooking. To help the egg white coagulate rather than form streamers in the water, add white vinegar in the proportion of about 1 tsp to 1 quart (1 liter) water. Do not add any salt, because it discourages coagulation. Unless you are a poaching pro, you will probably want to do no more than 4 eggs at a time. For this amount, I use a large saucepan with about 6 cups of water.

In professional kitchens, when serving the eggs immediately, we often plunge them into another pot of hot water, salted but without vinegar, to season them and remove any vinegary taste.

1 Bring a pan of water to a gentle boil and add a little vinegar (see above). Have ready another pan of simmering salted water. One at a time, crack the eggs onto a small plate, without breaking the yolk, then slide carefully into the pan of vinegared water.

2 Using a basting motion, work to envelop the yolk with the white, "shaping" the egg just until the white is set, about 20 seconds. Repeat with the remaining eggs. Adjust the heat so the water is at a gentle boil. Poach until the whites appear completely set, 3–5 minutes.

3 Using a slotted spoon, carefully lift the eggs from the water and dip them into the simmering salted water for 30 seconds. Then place them on a clean dish towel to drain briefly. They are now ready to be served, on hot, buttered, toasted English muffins, for example.

SCRAMBLING EGGS

There's more than one way to make great scrambled eggs. The method you choose depends on how you like your scrambled egg curds—large, small, or, in the French manner, totally blended to make a luscious cream.

If you like traditional scrambled eggs, what you're aiming for is what a friend of mine calls "concupiscent curds"—soft and billowing, no matter the size. To get these, keep the egg mass moving slowly and over gentle heat, and don't overcook. The last-minute addition of cream enriches the eggs deliciously and stops the cooking so that they stay creamy.

Serves 2

4 eggs

1–2 tbsp butter

4 tsp light or heavy cream

1 Beat the eggs well, then season them with salt and pepper. Heat a nonstick or well-seasoned frying pan or skillet over medium heat, then add the butter and melt it. Pour in the beaten eggs. If you want large curds, allow the eggs to set for a bit before you start to scramble them.

Sprinkle scrambled eggs with some snipped chives and serve with buttered toast

SCRAMBLING EGGS: The French method

The French method produces eggs that are rich and super-creamy. It's a bit more laborious and time-consuming than the traditional method, but once you try it, you'll probably be hooked. The eggs are cooked in a double boiler, which should be placed over hot but not boiling water.

2 Using a wooden spoon or heat-resistant rubber spatula, pull the mass of setting egg to the center of the pan, so uncooked egg can come into contact with the hot pan. Continue this process, stirring slowly and gently, for about 2 minutes, breaking up the curds somewhat. For smaller, "tighter" curds, don't wait as long to start scrambling, and stir more vigorously.

1 Beat the eggs well, then season with salt and pepper. For extra creaminess, add some butter cut in pieces (2 tbsp butter for 3–4 eggs).

2 Melt 1 tbsp or so of butter in the top of a double boiler. Add the eggs and start stirring with a wooden spoon or whisk. Stir constantly until the eggs have thickened into a creamy mass, 10–15 minutes.

 TIPS FOR SUCCESS WHEN SCRAMBLING EGGS

■ The eggs should be well beaten so that whites and yolks are completely combined.
■ Season with salt and pepper only after the eggs are beaten and you're ready to cook them, because salt can thin them out, thus inhibiting a fluffy result.
■ Butter is the usual fat of choice for cooking eggs by the traditional method, although some people prefer to use oil for various reasons.
■ For the traditional method, a nonstick pan is easiest to use, but if you choose not to, your pan should be well seasoned to prevent the eggs from sticking. The pan should be preheated before butter is added—it should be hot enough to melt the butter within a few seconds, but not so hot that the butter browns before the eggs go in. I suggest that you experiment with this, starting with medium heat and adjusting the heat as necessary.
■ For the French method the eggs are best made in a double boiler filled with hot water.

3 Just before you think the eggs are done to your satisfaction, remove the pan from the heat and add the cream. Stir to mix the cream quickly into the eggs, then serve.

3 Add 1–2 tbsp of light or heavy cream to the eggs to stop their cooking. Stir to mix, then turn them onto serving plates.

MAKING A CLASSIC FOLDED OMELET

A classic omelet is without a doubt one of the most glorious egg dishes. It isn't hard to make once you get the knack, which shouldn't take long at all. What you're aiming for is a soft, oval "egg-pillow," firm on the outside and runny to almost moist within—like scrambled eggs encased in a thin cooked-egg layer.

■ A 3-egg omelet is probably easiest to manage; never use more than 6 eggs per omelet.

■ You'll need a nonstick or well-seasoned pan. The egg mass should not come more than ¼in (5mm) up the side of the pan.
■ The pan should be hot enough to begin setting the beaten eggs as soon as they're added, but not so hot that some of the egg mass fries or colors before the rest can cook.
■ You'll need to work quickly—an omelet takes less than 2 minutes to cook.

Serves 1

3 eggs

1–2 tbsp butter

1 Beat the eggs, then season with salt and pepper. Melt the butter in a 6–8in (15–20cm) omelet or frying pan over medium-high heat. When the butter begins to foam, add the eggs and shake the pan gently to distribute evenly.

2 Start stirring with a table fork, keeping the rounded side of the fork as parallel as possible to the pan's bottom while continuing to shake it. As soon as the eggs are set but still soft, in 20–30 seconds, stop stirring.

3 With the help of the fork, fold the side of the omelet nearest you halfway over itself, as if folding a letter. Grasp the handle of the pan from underneath, with your palm facing upward, and lift the pan to a 45° angle.

4 With your free hand, sharply tap the top of the handle closest to the pan, which will encourage the other side of the omelet to curl over the folded portion. Use the fork to fully "close the letter."

5 Bring the serving plate to the omelet, then tilt the pan so the omelet falls onto the plate, seam-side down. Serve immediately.

Adding a filling to a classic folded omelet

Fillings for classic folded omelets may be savory—shredded cheese, cooked vegetables, such as zucchini, mushrooms, artichokes, and asparagus, and mixtures such as sautéed chicken livers and onions—or sweet, such as jams, jellies, or various fruit compotes.

You'll need about 1 cup of filling for a 3-egg omelet. If using a cooked filling, it should be hot. Before making the first fold (step 3), place the filling across the center of the omelet, then fold as shown to enclose the filling.

Distribute shredded cheese and sautéed halved asparagus spears down the center of the omelet, then fold it into three

OTHER OMELETS

In addition to the classic folded omelet, there are also thick, flat omelets, which are cut in wedges for serving hot, warm, or at room temperature, and fluffy soufflé omelets.

Flat omelets

For unfolded omelets, filling ingredients such as cheese, vegetables, and herbs are mixed with the beaten eggs at some point during the cooking process. The omelet is most often cooked in oil or a combination of oil and butter in a frying pan or skillet until set and browned on one side. Then the omelet is turned over to color the other side, or transferred to the oven or broiler for the final browning. In Italy, flat omelets are called frittatas (see the recipe for sweet onion frittata with balsamic vinegar on p104). They are known as tortillas in Spain, where they traditionally contain potatoes and onions, and as eggah in the Middle East.

Soufflé omelets

Fluffy omelets are made by separating the eggs, then beating the whites until stiff and folding them into the yolks. They can be either sweet or savory. In the former case, the yolks are beaten with sugar (4–5 tbsp for 4 eggs, or to your taste) until light, and the beaten whites folded in. The cooked omelet is commonly sprinkled with confectioners' sugar, or may be served with jam or jelly. For savory soufflé omelets, garnishes such as finely grated cheese, minced herbs, or sautéed, thinly sliced mushrooms can either be mixed in with the yolks before folding in the whites, or sprinkled atop the cooked omelet. In both cases, cooking starts on the stovetop in a pan with melted butter, and is finished in the oven or under the broiler.

Egg white omelets

A low-fat version of the classic folded omelet is made just with egg whites. You will need to use a nonstick pan, which eliminates the need for fat. To color and enrich the omelet you could add baked mashed sweet potato or butternut squash, in the proportion of 1–2 tbsp per egg white. Mix in the vegetable after the whites are beaten and carefully mix them together.

SWEET ONION FRITTATA WITH BALSAMIC VINEGAR

This oniony frittata was inspired by a dish served at a trattoria that my partner Danny Meyer and I visited and loved. Located in Nonantola, in the heart of Emilia-Romagna's balsamic vinegar region, the Osteria di Rubbiara serves a small wedge of the frittata to accompany its famous chicken stewed in Lambrusco wine. Of course the frittata is excellent on its own, drizzled with a few precious drops of aged balsamico tradizionale.

Serves 4–6

2 tbsp olive oil

4 large onions, about 2½lb (1.1kg) in total, thinly sliced (about 8 cups)

1 tsp minced garlic

2 tsp minced oregano

1¼ tsp kosher salt

⅛ tsp freshly ground black pepper

2 tbsp balsamic vinegar

2 tbsp water

10 eggs

3 tbsp finely grated Parmesan (Parmigiano Reggiano)

2 tbsp minced parsley

1 Heat the olive oil in a 10in (25cm) nonstick skillet over medium heat. Add the onions, garlic, and oregano, and season with half the salt and pepper. Cook, stirring occasionally, until the onions are tender and browned, 25–30 minutes.

2 Add the balsamic vinegar and water, and stir well to incorporate any browned bits. Continue cooking to reduce the liquid and coat the onions. (The onions can be prepared up to a day ahead to this point and kept, covered, in the refrigerator.)

3 Put the eggs in a large bowl and beat until combined and frothy. Add the Parmesan, parsley, and remaining salt and pepper. Pour the egg mixture into the skillet and mix with the onions.

4 Over medium-high heat, stir while shaking the pan back and forth. The eggs will begin to form small curds. When the eggs are set but still somewhat soft on top, stop stirring and shaking the pan to let the frittata set.

5 Loosen the frittata from the skillet with a rubber spatula and slide it onto a large dinner plate. Cover the frittata with another dinner plate and, holding them together, invert the plates.

6 Slide the frittata back into the skillet and continue cooking over high heat to brown the other side, about 2 minutes. Carefully transfer the frittata to a large dinner plate. Cut into wedges and serve hot or at room temperature.

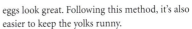

FRYING EGGS

Eggs can be fried over relatively high heat, and the cooking can be accelerated by covering the pan. Doing that requires some vigilance to avoid overcooking the yolks, however. There is also the option of flipping the nearly set eggs over for a short time to create eggs "over easy," rather than leaving them unturned "sunny side up."

FRENCH FRYING EGGS

I learned this unusual method in France while working with three-star chef, Michel Guérard. Madame Guérard had a fondness for eggs cooked in this manner. It is quite different from what we think of as fried eggs, and resembles a poached egg cooked in hot fat. The frying produces a delicious caramelized taste, and the eggs look great. Following this method, it's also easier to keep the yolks runny.

Be sure you have your utensils ready, because the eggs cook very quickly. The wooden spoon for basting must be absolutely dry, otherwise the egg white will stick to it. To remove any moisture, first dip the spoon briefly in the hot oil.

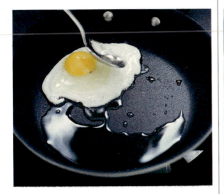

1 For 4 eggs, heat 1–2 tbsp butter, oil, or lard in a skillet. Break each egg into a saucer, then slide it into the hot pan. Baste the egg with the hot fat to help cook the yolk, and season with salt and pepper as it begins to set.

2 Cook until the egg white is set and the yolk runny or set, according to your preference. For a firm egg white, cook with the pan covered.

1 In a heavy-bottomed large saucepan, heat 3 cups of vegetable or olive oil over high heat until the oil reaches a temperature of about 375°F (190°C). Crack an egg into a small cup, without breaking the yolk, then transfer it to a ladle. Tilt the pan slightly, then gently lower in the ladle to slide the egg into the hot oil.

2 With a dry wooden spoon, gently and quickly baste the egg with the oil until the egg has taken on an oval shape, and the yolk is completely concealed by the white. Continue with the process for 1 minute. The egg should be set and lightly colored.

3 Using a slotted spoon, lift the egg from the oil and drain it on paper towels. Before eating, season the egg with salt and pepper.

FRIED EGGS & BACON

This is my favorite Sunday breakfast. For 2 servings, brown 6 slices of good-quality bacon, preferably regular or thick-cut, then drain off most of the fat. Spread out the bacon slices in a single layer. Slide 4 eggs into the pan on top of the bacon. Season the eggs as they start to set, then cover the pan and cook until they are done to your liking, basting them with the bacon fat occasionally. Sprinkle with Tabasco or your favorite sauce for eggs, then serve with plenty of hot toast.

CHEESE SOUFFLÉ

Surely one of the most sublime achievements of egg cooking is the soufflé. Fragrant, feather-light, and golden crowned, few dishes capture the diner's imagination like a perfect soufflé. Soufflés are remarkably versatile and can be served as appetizers, light main courses, or spectacular desserts. And contrary to popular belief, a soufflé is not difficult to make—it simply requires focus and attention to detail to obtain great results.

| 4 tbsp butter |
| 1 small white onion, minced |
| 2 whole cloves |
| 1 small bay leaf |
| ½ tsp anchovy purée (optional) |
| ¼ tsp Aleppo pepper or paprika |
| 3 tbsp all-purpose flour |
| 1 cup milk |
| 5 tbsp freshly grated Parmesan (Parmigiano Reggiano) |
| 2 tbsp finely diced Gruyère or Montasio cheese |
| 3 egg yolks |
| 4 egg whites |

1 Preheat the oven to 350°F (180°C). Using 1 tbsp of the butter, coat a 6in (15cm) soufflé dish, or four 3in (7.5cm) individual dishes. Do this by brushing the soft, not melted, butter over the bottom of the dish in a circular motion, then up the sides. Refrigerate to set the butter.

2 Melt the remaining butter in a heavy-bottomed saucepan and add the onion, cloves, bay leaf, anchovy purée (if using), and Aleppo pepper or paprika. Cook gently until the onion is softened but not at all colored.

3 Stir in the flour and cook gently for 4–5 minutes. Slowly add the milk, using a small whisk to incorporate it into the butter and flour roux. Bring to a very slow simmer and cook, stirring often, for 10–15 minutes. The sauce should be thicker than heavy cream and smooth.

4 Strain the sauce into a bowl, pressing well on the solids. Discard the solids. Stir the cheeses into the hot sauce until completely melted and smooth, then mix in the egg yolks.

FLAVORING SOUFFLÉS

With all soufflés, there are three basic elements: The flavor base, egg yolks to enrich and bind, and beaten egg whites to lighten. In the case of savory soufflés, the flavor base can be béchamel or velouté sauce, or a vegetable purée, either on its own or in combination with the sauce. Minced meats, such as ham or sweetbreads, chopped vegetables and mushrooms, and grated cheese are frequently used to flavor savory soufflés. For dessert soufflés, the flavor base can be a crème pâtissière (p418), or simply a very reduced fruit compote enhanced, perhaps, by an eau-de-vie or liqueur. In all cases, the important thing is to have the correct proportions and to combine the ingredients properly.

BAKING EGGS SUR LE PLAT

It has been said that French chefs will test the mettle of a new cook by requiring him or her to prepare this deceptively simple dish. The challenge lies in regulating both the cooking procedure and temperature so that the eggs are cooked to just the right point.

5 Beat the egg whites until they hold soft peaks. Pile half of the whites on top of the cheese mixture and fold them in thoroughly, using a rubber spatula.

6 Spoon the remaining whites on top and fold them in more lightly and delicately. Pour the mixture into the prepared soufflé dish.

1 Preheat the oven to 400°F (200°C). Place ½ tbsp melted butter in a small enameled cast-iron gratin dish. Season the bottom of the dish with salt and pepper (this prevents the salt from marring the appearance of the eggs).

2 Place the dish on medium heat and slide in 2 eggs, without breaking the yolks. Cover the eggs with another ½ tbsp melted butter.

3 Transfer to the oven and bake just until the whites are set and milky and the yolks have a shiny, glazed appearance, 6–8 minutes. Serve the eggs immediately.

Once baked, take the souffle to the table immediately and serve

7 Run your thumb around the edge of the mixture to make a groove (this will cause the soufflé to rise with a high cap). Place in the middle of the oven and bake until set, puffed, and browned, 25–30 minutes.

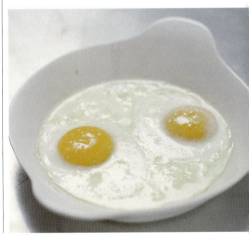

SUR LE PLAT EXTRAS

Although somewhat untraditional, I sometimes like to sprinkle the eggs in step 2 with some finely minced herbs—tarragon and chives being among my favorites —just before cooking.

COOKING WITH CREAM

Things of particular excellence are often called the "cream" of their kind. And cream is an unsurpassed treat. It adds richness and incomparable flavor to a wide range of sweet and savory dishes, and mellows sauces of all kinds. Rich creams can be boiled and reduced and, unless there is too much fat or acidity in the sauce, they usually will not "break" (when fat and liquid separate).

WHIPPING CREAM

Only those creams with a fat content of at least 30 percent will whip. As with beating egg whites, your goal is to whip as much air as possible into cream to make it stiffen. Most recipes call for cream whipped to the light or stiff stage.

■ Light whipping cream, with 30–36 percent fat, can be whipped, but heavy or whipping cream, with a fat content of 36–40 percent, will double in volume when beaten.

■ Have your bowl and beater, as well as the cream, well chilled, because fat droplets in the cream need to stay cold and firm to bond and create a stiff structure. Otherwise, your cream will go from liquid to butter while you keep trying to make it mount.

■ I find hand-beating with a chilled balloon whisk best, but you can use an electric mixer.

■ To maintain the cold, I beat over a bowl of ice.

■ Whipped cream can be stored for several hours in the refrigerator, where it may exude some liquid as it stands. If the cream hasn't been overbeaten, stir this liquid back in or pour it off.

1 Put the chilled cream in a bowl set in a larger bowl of ice. Start beating with a broad circular motion at a leisurely pace, about two strokes per second (or on low speed using a mixer), until the cream begins to thicken.

2 Now beat a bit faster if you like (or at a medium speed if using a mixer) for 2–3 minutes. At this point the cream will probably be softly or lightly whipped—it will barely hold its shape when lifted with your beater.

3 For stiffly whipped cream, which mounts sufficiently to make firm peaks, keep beating. At this point you can fold in other ingredients, such as sugar or vanilla.

OVERWHIPPING CREAM

If you whip cream beyond the stiff peak stage, it will develop a granular texture. If this happens, the cream can be beaten further until it completely separates into butter and whey, and the butter can then be used in cooking or desserts. Discard the whey.

Pumpkin-chocolate chip cheesecake with country cream

"Country cream," our name for a topping we use with lots of desserts, is a tangy and slightly richer alternative to whipped cream. It can also be frozen and scooped like ice cream (try it with a dash of cinnamon). I serve it with a very delicious, seasonal variation on the classic American cheesecake. If you choose to use fresh pumpkin for the cheesecake instead of canned, be sure to cook it down slowly and thoroughly after it has been peeled, boiled, and puréed, so that the water content is reduced.

Serves 6–8

For the crust

1½ cups graham cracker crumbs

4 tbsp confectioners' sugar

6 tbsp butter, melted

For the filling

1lb (450g) cream cheese, at room temperature

½ cup granulated sugar

2 eggs

½ tsp vanilla extract

½ cup canned pumpkin purée

1 tsp ground cinnamon

½ tsp freshly grated nutmeg

½ tsp ground cloves

½ cup semisweet chocolate chips

For the country cream

½ cup sour cream

½ cup mascarpone

½ cup plain, whole-milk yogurt

½ cup granulated sugar

2 tsp vanilla extract

Prepare the crust: In a large mixing bowl, combine the crumbs, sugar, and butter, and knead together until well blended. Press evenly over the bottom and sides of a 9in (23cm) springform pan. Chill until needed.

Preheat the oven to 350°F (180°C). In the bowl of an electric mixer fitted with the paddle attachment, beat the cream cheese and sugar together until smooth. Add the eggs and vanilla, and mix until well blended. Add the pumpkin purée and spices, and continue mixing until thoroughly combined.

Remove the mixing bowl from the machine and fold in the chocolate chips with a rubber spatula. Pour the filling into the chilled crust.

Place in the oven and bake for 30–40 minutes. The center of the cheesecake should feel somewhat firm to the touch. Let the cheesecake cool to room temperature, then refrigerate, covered, for at least 6 hours or overnight.

To make the country cream, place all the ingredients in a deep mixing bowl and set the bowl over a larger bowl filled with ice. Whisk together until the mixture will hold soft, smooth peaks and is the consistency of whipped heavy cream. (This makes 2 cups of country cream. It can be kept, covered, in the refrigerator for up to 3–4 days.)

To serve the cheesecake, remove the sides of the springform pan. Cut the cheesecake into portions and serve topped with the country cream. Alternatively, serve the cheesecake with plain whipped cream, or with chocolate sauce or ice cream.

FISH & SHELLFISH

CHARLIE TROTTER

"When cooking seafood, always have a sensual touch." That is a note I once wrote to myself, and it truly embodies my thoughts about seafood. There is sheer hedonism in eating the unique creatures that reside in the waters of the Earth, with all their delicious textures and flavors. I encourage you to begin a journey of exploration with seafood unlike any you have made before. Try new species. Test new cooking methods. The possibilities are endless.

I work with a variety of purveyors to secure seafood from around the world, and my interest just keeps growing. As with fruits and vegetables, I'm only interested in working with seafood that is in season. This is so important, because it almost guarantees a wonderfully flavorful product. Many people are unaware that fish and shellfish are seasonal, but they certainly are. Everything on Earth has a season, and seafood is no exception.

Protecting fish stocks I certainly respect and appreciate the efforts of aquaculturists, as I have concerns about the overfishing of certain species. Overfishing denies all fish species a fighting chance of maintaining their populations. It is no longer simply the familiar scenario of nets raking the ocean and getting everything. Overfishing has gone beyond that. Some fishing fleets use sonar technology and satellites to direct them into the best areas, where they capture everything there is to be found. I cannot agree with that approach at all. Some parts of the world, such as Australia, have legislated against overfishing, allowing fish species time for regeneration to sustainable levels. That is what I would like to see in force everywhere.

While I'm not a great fan of fish farms, I do believe there is a place for them. Catfish, a "bottom feeder" from the United States' Deep South, is a wonderful example of a fish that, when produced with the necessary care and restrictions, is being farmed very successfully. I would love to see every fish farm across America producing fish of such high quality. My main concern with most farming is that the fish are raised in a restricted area, which makes them more prone to disease. They have to be given antibiotics, and most people would prefer the fish they eat to be antibiotic-free.

Storing and preparing fish and shellfish Purchase fresh fish as close to the day of cooking and serving as possible, since it is highly perishable. However, it can be kept for up to 24 hours, and following a few simple steps will ensure its quality and safety.

Whole fish should be stored whole on crushed ice in the refrigerator. Place crushed ice in a pan to catch drips if melting takes place, and then place the fish on top. Cover the entire fish with more crushed ice and place in the refrigerator. Fillets should be placed in a plastic or metal container, which is then covered with plastic wrap. Set this covered container on crushed ice in the refrigerator. Never store fillets in direct contact with crushed ice because contact with water will cause the fillets to break down. Shellfish, still in their original bags, should be stored in the refrigerator in a bowl covered with wet paper towels. Shellfish should never come in direct contact with ice or cold water. Frozen fish should be stored, in its packaging, in the freezer. Before using, let it thaw in the refrigerator for 24 hours. Never thaw fish by microwaving or by putting it into direct contact with water.

Fish preparation is not as daunting as you might think. The basic techniques for whole fish are cleaning, scaling, gutting, and cutting or filleting, with slightly different methods used for flatfish and round fish. Of course you can buy fish already prepared, but it is unlikely to be as fresh as whole fish you deal with yourself, and you are able to control how it is done.

It is best to avoid handling shellfish until you are ready to prepare them for immediate cooking. When selecting mollusks, pay close attention to the shells. Fresh mollusks, such as mussels, should have hard, well-cupped shells; avoid those that are broken. Before preparing for cooking, gently tap each shell—if it does not close, the mollusk is dead and not safe for consumption.

PREPARING ROUND FISH

Round fish are those "fin fish" that are round in body shape and have eyes on both sides of their heads (the other type of fin fish are flatfish). There are both freshwater and saltwater varieties of round fish. Some of the more popular are salmon, snapper, sea bass, grouper, tuna, and cod. The techniques used to prepare a round fish will vary according to how you are going to cook it, but the most common are gutting, scaling, boning (if you intend to stuff the fish), cutting into steaks, and filleting.

GUTTING THROUGH THE STOMACH

Gutting a fish means to remove all the viscera (everything in the stomach cavity). While most of the fish you buy in the U.S. and Canada have already been gutted, there are instances when you will need to know how to do this yourself. The most common way is to remove the viscera through a cut into the stomach, but fish can also be gutted through the gills (see opposite). A pike is shown in the photographs here.

BUYING FISH

It is easier to assess the quality of whole fish than that of steaks or fillets, so always try to buy fish whole and then ask the person behind the counter to prepare it for you or do this yourself (following the instructions here and on the following pages).

■ When buying whole fish, use your sense of smell as an aid in determining quality. Sniff under the gills and in the stomach cavity—fish should not smell strong or fishy. The skin should be very smooth, not slimy, and eyes should not be cloudy.

■ For fillets and steaks, sniff the flesh—it should smell sweet and of the sea.

1 Hold the fish firmly on its side and, using a fish knife, small chef's knife, or kitchen scissors, make a shallow slit in the underside, cutting from the tail end to the head end.

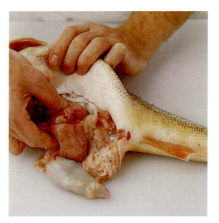

2 Pull out the guts (viscera), then cut off the gills (p119), taking care since they can be sharp. Discard the guts and gills.

3 Rinse the cavity under cold running water to remove any remaining blood and guts. Pat the fish dry with paper towels. It can now be scaled (see opposite) and boned.

GUTTING THROUGH THE GILLS

This technique is often used for fish to be poached whole or cut into steaks, as well as for small flatfish, because it keeps their natural shape. Before gutting this way, scale the fish and trim the fins. A rainbow trout is shown here.

1 First, remove the gills at the base of the head (the gills are sharp, so hook your index finger around them to pull them out).

2 Put your fingers into the hole left by the gills and pull out the viscera.

3 Using kitchen scissors, snip a small slit in the stomach at the ventral (anal) opening near the tail. Insert your fingers and pull out any remaining viscera.

SCALING & TRIMMING

While there are no hard and fast rules about whether or not to scale a fish, there is one important general guideline that should prove helpful. If you plan to eat the skin then it is best to scale the fish. If, on the other hand, you are going to remove the skin before serving the fish, then there is no need to scale it. A salmon is shown here.

1 Lay the fish on a work surface covered with a plastic bag or newspaper. If the fish is small, you can lay it in the bottom of the sink under cold running water. Take hold of the fish by its tail, then begin to scrape off the scales from the top side using a fish scaler. Scrape from the tail toward the head. Turn the fish over and scrape off the scales on the other side.

SCALING WITH A KNIFE

If you don't have a fish scaler, you can use a chef's knife to scale the fish. Scrape off the scales with the back, blunt side of the knife blade.

2 Cut off the back (dorsal) fins and belly fins with kitchen scissors, then trim off the fins on either side of the head. If desired, trim the tail with the scissors to neaten it, perhaps cutting into a "V" shape.

BONING THROUGH THE STOMACH

To bone a whole fish in this way, it is first gutted through the stomach (p114), and then scaled and the fins trimmed. Once boned, it can be stuffed for cooking, most commonly by baking. A sea bass is shown here.

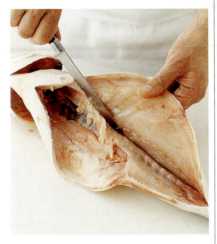

1 Open up the fish. Loosen the ribcage (transverse bones) from the flesh on the top side by sliding a sharp knife along the ribcage. Turn the fish over and repeat, to loosen the transverse bones from the flesh on that side.

2 Snip the backbone at head and tail ends using kitchen scissors. Then, starting at the tail, peel it away from the flesh. The transverse bones will come away with the backbone.

BONING FROM THE BACK

Boning a whole round fish from the back prepares it for stuffing and then baking or cooking en papillote. First scale the fish, then trim off the fins. Do not gut the fish. Use a filleting knife, or other sharp, flexible knife, for boning. A black sea bass is shown here.

1 Cut down the back of the fish, cutting along one side of the backbone from head to tail. Continue cutting into the fish, keeping the knife close on top of the bones. When you reach the belly, don't cut through the skin.

2 Turn the fish over and cut down the back from tail to head along the other side of the backbone. Continue cutting as before, to cut away the flesh from that side of the backbone.

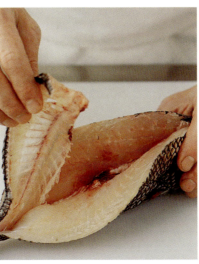

3 Using kitchen scissors, snip the backbone at the head and tail ends, then remove it. Pull out the guts (viscera) and discard. Rinse the cavity under cold running water and pat dry.

4 Pull out any pin bones (the line of tiny bones down each side of the fish) using large tweezers or small needle-nose pliers.

FILLETING

A round fish is typically cut into two fillets after it has been gutted. It is best to use a filleting knife, because the blade is long and more flexible than that of a regular kitchen knife. Once filleted, the fish can be cooked by almost any method. However, it's important to note that if a fillet is small and very thin (such as the red mullet shown here), you will need to be very careful not to overcook it.

1 Depending on the fish you are preparing and whether you are going to leave the skin on the fillets, scale the fish (p115). Using a filleting knife, cut into the fish at the head end, just behind the gills, cutting with the knife at an angle just until you reach the backbone.

2 Starting near the gills, cut the fish down the length of the back, cutting along the top side of the backbone.

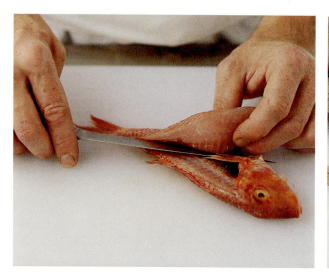

3 Working again from head to tail, continue cutting over the bone, keeping the knife flat and folding the fillet back as you cut. When the fillet has been freed, remove it.

4 Turn the fish over and repeat the process to remove the second fillet, this time cutting from the tail to the head.

SKINNING A FILLET

If you plan to skin fish fillets, there is no need to scale them or the whole fish from which the fillets are cut, unless you want to fry the skin later for use as a garnish. Round fish and flatfish fillets are skinned in the same way. A whole salmon fillet is shown here.

1 With the fillet skin-side down, insert a fish knife into the flesh near the tail end, turning the blade at a slight angle. Cut through the flesh just to the skin.

2 Turn the blade of the knife almost flat and take tight hold of the end of the skin. Holding the knife firmly in place, close to the skin, pull the skin away cutting it off the fillet.

CUTTING STEAKS

Any large round fish can be cut into steaks, but those that are most commonly found in steak form are varieties of tuna, swordfish, and salmon. With the exception of halibut, flatfish are too thin to cut into steaks.

Fish steaks can be cooked in many ways, although thickness may determine the best method. For instance, a thinly cut steak of about ½in (1cm) is better quickly broiled than grilled, while a thicker steak of about 1in (2.5cm) will fare well on a grill. A salmon is shown here.

1 Gut the fish through the stomach (p114). Scale it, then trim off the fins. Using a chef's knife, cut off the head just behind the gills.

2 Holding the fish firmly on its side, cut across to get steaks of the desired thickness.

PREPARING FLATFISH

Flatfish, which with round fish comprise the family of "fin fish," are flat and oval-shaped, with eyes on only one side of the body. They typically have a colored top side, which may be dark brown, black, or dark gray, and a white underside.

Common types of flatfish are halibut, flounder, turbot, and Dover sole. They can be cooked in a variety of ways, including broiling, grilling, steaming, sautéing, baking, and poaching. Flatfish make a very dramatic presentation when served whole.

GUTTING & TRIMMING

If you plan to serve a flatfish whole, this is the first part of the preparation you need to do (the second part is to remove the skin, see opposite). Flatfish are normally gutted as a first step to ensure that there is no viscera to cut into when the fish is being trimmed. Then the fins are trimmed and the fish is scaled, if necessary. A European plaice is shown in the photographs here.

1 With a chef's knife, make a small cut along the stomach so you can reach in to remove the guts (viscera) and any roe. Discard these.

2 Use kitchen scissors to trim away the fins. Leave about ¼in (5mm) of fin still attached to the fish to ensure that you don't cut into the fish body when trimming.

3 Scale the white side of the fish, if necessary (see below), then cut off the gills with scissors and discard them. Rinse the fish inside and out under cold running water.

SCALING FLATFISH

If the skin on the white side of a flatfish feels rough to the touch, scale it after gutting the fish and trimming off the fins (see above).

Lay the fish on paper or a plastic bag. Using a special fish scaler, or the back (blunt) side of a chef's knife, carefully scrape off the scales, working from the tail toward the head.

There is no need to scale the dark side of a flatfish as this skin will be removed before serving.

GUTTING BY TAKING OFF THE HEAD

When you are planning to serve a flatfish whole but without the head, use this easier way to gut the fish. It can also be used to gut a fish prior to cutting it into fillets.

Trim the fins (see above), then, if necessary, scale the skin on the white side of the fish (see left). Lay the fish with the dark side up and make a V-shaped cut all the way around the head. Grasp the head gently but firmly and, with a quick twisting turn, pull the head away. The guts (viscera) and the gills should come out with the head. Rinse the cavity under cold running water to remove any remaining blood and guts.

SKINNING & FILLETING A DOVER SOLE

Dover sole requires special handling, differing from the preparation of other flatfish. Most chefs prefer to skin Dover sole prior to filleting; however, if the sole is being prepared to cook whole, the skin is left on. Note that only the black skin is removed. The delicate white skin remains intact, even when the fish is cut into fillets.

1 Make a small cut through the skin at the tail end, cutting at an angle, to separate a flap of the dark skin from the flesh.

2 Using a towel, take hold of the freed flap of dark skin securely. Holding the tail end of the fish firmly with your other hand, pull the dark skin away from the fish. Fillet the fish to get two fillets.

GRIPPING THE SKIN

To get a good grip on the skin when pulling it from a fish, you can either grasp the flap of skin in a dish towel or dip your fingers in salt first. Pull off the skin sharply, parallel to the flesh and as quickly as possible.

FILLETING A SKATE WING

Skate is a type of ray fish. It is prized for its "wings," which are often filleted to remove the meat from the gelatinous cartilage. Filleted skate wings are most commonly just lightly sautéed, although they are also delicious poached in a light court bouillon (p140).

1 Lay the skate wing on a board dark-side uppermost, with the thickest side nearest to you. Cut into the flesh on the thickest side until you reach the cartilage that is about halfway down.

2 Turn the wing around. Turn the knife flat on the cartilage and cut the flesh away until you reach the outer edge of the wing. Cut along the edge and detach this fillet. Repeat on the other side. Remove the skin from the fillets as for round fish (p118).

PREPARING SHELLFISH

The shellfish family of seafood is made up of two primary categories: crustaceans and mollusks. Crustaceans, such as lobsters, shrimp, and crabs, have an exterior skeleton, segmented bodies, and jointed limbs. Most mollusks have hard shells—univalves (e.g. abalone and conch) have a single shell and bivalves (e.g. scallops, clams, oysters, and mussels) have two shells. The third type of mollusk, cephalopods (e.g. octopus and squid), don't have a hard outer shell.

Shellfish are usually cooked by boiling or steaming. Crustaceans may also be grilled and many mollusks are served raw.

CLEANING & DEBEARDING MUSSELS

Mussels sold live usually have a fibrous attachment (called a "beard") on their shell. This beard needs to be removed and the shells thoroughly scrubbed prior to cooking. Mussels are most commonly steamed to open their shells, and a popular way to serve them is in a wine and chopped tomato liquid. They may also be shucked to grill or to stuff and bake. Unlike clams and oysters, mussels are almost never served raw.

1 Scrub the mussels under cold running water to remove all grit and sand. Scrape off any barnacles using a small, sharp knife.

2 Pinch the stringy dark "beard" between your index finger and thumb, and pull it away from the mussel shell.

MOLLUSK SAFETY

■ When buying oysters and clams, check that the shells are tightly closed. The exception is geoduck clams, which are usually slightly open; however, they should close when tapped lightly. Mussel shells may also gape open slightly; like geoduck clams, they should close immediately if tapped. If this does not happen, do not buy the mollusks, or—if already purchased—discard them.

■ To prepare mollusks for cooking, first discard any with broken shells. Some, such as clams, tend to be sandy so it is a good idea to "purge" them. Put them in a large bowl of cold water with some cornmeal and let soak overnight in the refrigerator. The clams eat the meal and expel the sand.

■ After boiling or steaming mollusks such as clams and mussels, check that all have opened; discard any that are still closed. Also discard oysters that smell "fishy" once shucked open. Seafood should smell fresh.

SHUCKING OYSTERS

For the technique of opening (shucking) oysters, "practice makes perfect." Use a thick dish towel or wear a special wire mesh glove to protect your hand from the sharp edges of the oyster shell. And hold the oyster flat as you work to prevent the delicious briny liquid from spilling out (if you are going to cook them, shuck over a pan to catch the liquid). If you intend to serve oysters raw on the half shell, scrub them well before shucking.

1 Hold the oyster in a thick dish towel, rounded shell down. Insert the tip of an oyster knife into the hinge and twist to open the oyster shell. Carefully cut the muscle, keeping the blade of the knife horizontal and close to the top shell, to release the oyster. Lift off the top shell.

2 Loosen the oyster from the bottom shell by gently sliding the knife underneath the oyster. Take care not to cut the oyster meat, nor to tip the shell and spill out the briny liquid.

SHUCKING CLAMS

There are two types of clams: hard shell (such as littleneck and cherrystone) and soft shell (e.g. longneck steamers). All clams should be scrubbed well and, as they tend to be very sandy, they are best purged (see opposite). Then they can be shucked to eat raw or cooked. Alternatively, they can be boiled or steamed to open the shells. During the shucking process, try to retain the delicious liquid in the shells.

1 Holding the clam rounded shell down in a thick dish towel to protect your fingers, work the tip of the knife between the top and bottom shells, then twist the knife upward to force the shells apart.

2 Slide the knife over the inside of the top shell to sever the muscle and release the clam, then do the same to release the clam from the bottom shell. Take care not to cut into the clam meat. If serving raw on the half shell, snap off the top shell. For soft-shell clams, remove the dark membrane from the clam meat before serving.

SHUCKING SCALLOPS

Although most home cooks will buy scallops already shucked, you will sometimes find them in the shell. Scrub the shells clean before shucking. The scallops can then be served raw, as part of sushi or sashimi meals, or cooked. The red or orange scallop roe (also called the coral) can be sautéed and served alongside the scallop dish, or puréed and added to a sauce.

1 Holding the scallop firmly in your hand, flat shell uppermost, insert a long, thin, flexible knife in between the top and bottom shells, keeping the blade as close to the inside of the top shell as possible to avoid damaging the scallop meat inside. Slide the knife around the top shell to sever the muscle.

3 Pull or cut away the viscera and fringelike membrane from the white scallop and the roe; discard the viscera and membrane. Rinse the scallop and roe before use.

2 When the scallop meat has been released from the top shell, remove the shell. Then detach the scallop from the bottom shell with the help of the knife, again taking care not to cut into the scallop meat.

PREPARING ABALONE & WHELKS

Abalone is a large mollusk consisting of a "foot" covered by a single shell. The foot, which is really a muscle that adheres it firmly to its rock, is the edible part. Harvesting abalone is highly regulated, so you rarely find it for sale alive and in the shell. It is now farmed in California and Hawaii.

To prepare abalone, you need to cut around the inside of the shell to free the foot, which then needs to be trimmed of any dark skin and fringe, and viscera. The flesh of some abalone is tough so it must be tenderized by beating it with a meat pounder. Abalone is most often eaten raw. Alternatively, slice it thinly and sauté quickly—like squid and octopus, it should be cooked briefly, or be given a long, slow simmering, because otherwise it will be tough.

Whelks are sea snails. After scrubbing and purging (p121), they are usually cooked in the shell—by simmering in salted water, stock, or court bouillon (p140)—and then pulled out with a small fork for eating. Alternatively, you can simmer whelks just long enough to be able to remove them from their shells, then use them in soups or stews.

CLEANING A LIVE LOBSTER

Here is how to clean and cut up a live lobster before cooking it. Reserve the tomalley (greenish liver) and any coral (the roe, which will be black) to use in a sauce, flavored butter, or stuffing. The head, body, and legs can be used in a fish stock; they contain incredibly intense lobster flavor.

1 Leave the rubber bands in place around the claws. Lay the lobster flat on a cutting board and hold it firmly. Put the tip of a heavy chef's knife into the lobster's head, then cut straight down and split it in two.

2 Remove the claws by twisting them off the lobster or, if necessary, by cutting them off with the chef's knife.

3 Take hold of the body and head section with one hand and the tail section with the other hand. Twist to separate them.

4 Spoon out the tomalley and any coral from the head and tail sections, and reserve. The tail section and claws are now ready for cooking.

TAKING THE MEAT FROM A COOKED LOBSTER

Rather than cut up a live lobster before cooking, you can cook the lobster whole and then take out the meat to use in a wide variety of dishes. To cook, simply plunge the lobster into a deep pot of boiling water and boil until the shell turns red. For a 1lb (450g) lobster this will take about 6 minutes.

1 Take firm hold of the tail section and twist sharply to separate it from the body and head section.

2 Turn the tail section over and, using kitchen scissors, cut down the center of the flat underside of the shell.

3 With your thumbs, press on both sides of the cut and pull open the tail shell. Remove the meat in one piece.

4 With lobster crackers or a small hammer, crack open the claw shells. Take care not to crush the meat inside.

5 Remove the meat from the claws, in whole pieces if possible. Discard any membrane attached to the meat.

PICKING COOKED CRAYFISH

Crayfish are very similar to lobsters, just much smaller. Since they are farmed, they are available year round. After boiling them in your favorite seafood or crab boil—with some cayenne added for a kick—let them cool, then serve. This is how to get at their sweet meat.

1 Break off the head section (suck out the delicious juices from the head, if you like).

2 Gently squeeze the tail to crack the shell, then carefully remove the meat by pulling off the sides of the shell.

PREPARING SHRIMP

Shrimp contain a small sand line, also known as the intestinal vein. Unless the shrimp are small, this vein is usually removed before cooking (the process is called deveining). This is done because the vein can tend to be a bit gritty on the palate. You can devein shrimp after peeling or while they are still in the shell.

Large shrimp to be stuffed and then broiled or baked are first cut open or "butterflied."

Peeling & deveining

1 Pull off the head, then peel off the shell and legs with your fingers. Sometimes the last tail flange is left on the shrimp. Save heads and shells for use in stock, if desired.

Deveining without cutting

Peel the shrimp, or just pull off the head and leave the shrimp in shell. Use a toothpick to "hook" the vein and remove it. Rinse the shrimp under cold running water and pat dry.

PREPARING LANGOUSTINES

Also called scampi or Dublin Bay prawns, these are small members of the lobster family. Only the tail is eaten. Langoustines are prepared in the same way as shrimp (although their shell is tougher).

2 Run a paring knife lightly along the back of the shrimp to expose the dark intestinal vein. Remove the vein with the tip of the knife or your fingers. Rinse the shrimp under cold running water and pat dry.

Butterflying

Peel the shrimp. Make a cut along the back so that the shrimp can be opened flat, like a book. Do not cut all the way through. Remove the vein, then rinse the shrimp under cold running water and pat dry.

Langoustines with green curry sauce & scallions

Sweet, buttery langoustines contrast with the sharpness of green curry sauce, resulting in a unique flavor. The aroma of kaffir lime leaves adds exotic flair. If you don't have shellfish oil for garnishing, you can mix 2 tsp of the juices from the langoustines with 1 tbsp extra virgin olive oil.

For the green curry sauce

6 scallions, chopped

2 jalapeño chilies, seeded and chopped

2 garlic cloves, chopped

1 tbsp minced fresh ginger

1 tbsp coriander seeds, dry-roasted (p79) and crushed

½ tsp cracked black pepper

4 kaffir lime leaves, torn

2 lemon-grass stalks, chopped

2 cups loosely packed chopped basil

1 cup loosely packed chopped cilantro with stems

3 tbsp olive oil

grated zest and juice of 4 limes

¼ cup coconut milk

For the langoustines

2 shallots, minced

2 tbsp extra virgin olive oil

12 scallions, cut in half

8 baby golden beets, peeled and quartered, or 2 medium golden beets, peeled and cut into 1in (2.5cm) pieces or wedges

8 raw langoustines, peeled

2 cups firmly packed tiny lettuce leaves

For garnish

4 tsp shellfish oil

4 tsp finely shredded basil

To prepare the sauce, purée the scallions, chilies, garlic, ginger, coriander seeds, cracked pepper, lime leaves, lemon-grass, herbs, olive oil, and lime zest and juice in a blender. Press the purée through a fine-mesh strainer into a small saucepan. Add the coconut milk and season to taste with salt and pepper. Set aside.

Before serving warm the sauce over medium to low heat until just hot, about 3 minutes (the sauce will darken).

To prepare the langoustines, heat a sauté pan over medium heat. Add the shallots, olive oil, scallions, and beets. Cook for 2 minutes. Add the langoustines, increase the heat to high, and sauté them for 2–3 minutes on each side, or until just cooked through. Remove the langoustines from the pan and season to taste.

Add the lettuce leaves to the sauté pan and toss to quickly wilt the lettuce. Transfer the lettuce, beets, and scallions to a bowl and season to taste with salt and pepper. Slice each langoustine into two pieces.

Cover the center of each plate with a generous amount of the green curry sauce. Arrange some of the wilted lettuce, langoustines, and vegetables on top of the sauce. Drizzle the shellfish oil around the plate and top with the shredded basil and a grinding of pepper.

CLEANING A LIVE BLUE CRAB

The cleaning process described here will prepare a hard-shell crab for cooking in a soup or sauce. Alternatively, it can be done after the crab has been boiled or steamed (skip step 1).

1 Hold the crab on its back on a cutting board. Insert the tip of a chef's knife into the crab, directly behind the eyes, and quickly bring the knife blade down to the board.

2 Pull and twist off the small, folded tail flap (the apron) from the underside. Female crabs have rounded aprons; male crabs have thin, pointed aprons.

3 Press down on the center and leg section, and pull off the top shell.

4 With kitchen scissors, snip off the gills ("dead man's fingers"). Discard the spongy sand bag that is located behind the eyes.

5 Cut the crab in half or into fourths. It is now ready for cooking.

CLEANING A LIVE SOFT-SHELL CRAB

Soft-shell crabs are blue crabs that have molted their hard shells. The most popular ways to cook soft-shell crabs are deep-frying and sautéing. The entire crab is eaten—the newly formed shell is crunchy and delicious.

1 With kitchen scissors, cut across the front of the crab to remove the eyes and mouth.

2 Fold back the top shell so you can snip away the gills from both sides.

COOKING CRAB

A whole live crab is most commonly cooked by boiling, although it can also be steamed. The cooking time will vary according to the size of the crab. As a general guide, a 1lb (450g) blue crab will take 8–10 minutes to boil. Dungeness crab will take longer—about 15–20 minutes for a 2lb (900g) crab. When cooked, a crab's shell turns red.

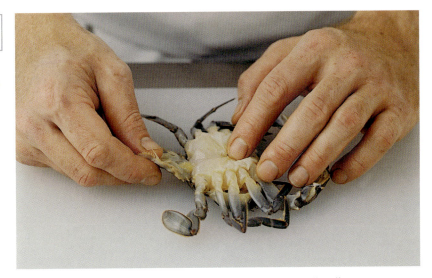

3 Turn the crab over. Unfold the tail flap (the apron) on this side and pull it off. This also removes the guts (viscera).

REMOVING THE MEAT FROM A COOKED CRAB

All large, meaty crabs have the essential parts of claws, legs, and body. Shown here is a common European crab, which contains soft brown meat as well as white meat. Dungeness crab is prepared in much the same way.

1 Set the crab on its back on a cutting board and firmly twist the claws and all the legs to break them from the body.

2 Lift up the triangular tail flap (the apron) on the underside of the body, then twist it off and discard.

5 Crack or cut the central body section into several large pieces. Dig out the white meat using a lobster pick or skewer, discarding small pieces of membrane. Reserve the white meat in a bowl.

6 Spoon out the soft brown meat from the shell and reserve it to serve with the white meat (there is no brown meat in a Dungeness crab). Discard the head sac. If there is any roe, spoon this out too and reserve it.

3 Crack the central section of the shell under the tail. Using your thumbs to start off, prize it apart, then lift off the shell. Remove any white meat from the shell using a teaspoon.

4 Pull off the gills ("dead man's fingers") from the sides of the central body section and discard them. Also discard the intestines, which will either be on each side of the shell or be clinging to the body.

7 With poultry shears or the blunt side of a heavy knife, tap one side of the shell on each leg to crack it. Lift out the meat, in one piece if possible, using a lobster pick to help. Add to the white meat from the body.

8 Crack the claws with special lobster crackers, a nutcracker, or a small hammer and extract the meat. Check all the white meat for bits of membrane and shell before serving.

COOKING SEAFOOD

Seafood is one of the most delicate foods to cook. There are many ways in which it can be prepared, including baking, broiling, grilling, and curing. Shellfish is often prepared by steaming or deep-frying.

Whatever method is chosen, use the suggested cooking times only as a guide, because seafood can be easily overcooked and the wonderful flavor and texture destroyed.

CURING

There are many methods of curing seafood, although most are used more for flavor than for storage of the fish. One of the most popular preparations is gravlax, where salmon is cured in a salt and sugar mixture (see right). Other curing techniques include escabeche, ceviche, salting, and smoking.

WAYS TO CURE

■ For escabeche, popular in South America and the Mediterranean, fish is pan-fried and then marinated with herbs, aromatic vegetables, and an acid such as lemon juice or vinegar.
■ Ceviche, a common technique in Mexico, involves marinating seafood in lime or lemon juice with herbs and aromatic vegetables.
■ Salting, primarily used for cod, is done by covering the fish in salt, which draws out the juices. It may then be dried to preserve it. The fish is always soaked before cooking. Salt cod is the main ingredient in the popular French dish, brandade.
■ Smoking is done in two ways. Hot smoking cooks the seafood so it is ready to eat; as it is only partially preserved it cannot be kept for more than a few days. Cold smoking uses already cured seafood and cool smoke so the seafood dries rather than cooks. You can smoke seafood on a barbecue grill, on the stovetop, or using a smoker, available in most sporting and specialty food stores.

GRAVLAX

For this Swedish specialty, raw salmon is cured in a sweet salt mixture. Dill is the most common flavoring, although peppercorns or slices of orange or lemon are also sometimes used. The salmon is sliced paper-thin for serving.

Serves 8–10

¼ cup coarse salt
¼ cup sugar
1½ tbsp chopped dill
2 tbsp black peppercorns, crushed
2 tbsp Darjeeling tea leaves
2 tbsp vodka (optional)
grated zest of 2 small lemons
1 salmon fillet, skin on, about 2lb (900g)
slices of lemon and orange for garnish (optional)

1 Make the cure by mixing together the salt, sugar, dill, peppercorns, tea leaves, optional vodka, and lemon zest. Spoon half of the cure onto a sheet pan covered with cheesecloth and spread out into an even layer.

2 Place the salmon fillet, skin-side down, on the cure. Sprinkle the remaining cure over the salmon to cover it evenly. Press the cure down onto the flesh of the fish.

3 Wrap the fish tightly in the cheesecloth, then weigh it down with something such as a heavy skillet or cutting board. Refrigerate for 48 hours, turning the fish over every 12 hours.

4 Unwrap the fish and quickly rinse off the cure under cold running water. Pat the fish dry with paper towels.

5 Lay the fillet out flat, flesh-side up, and slice very thinly on the diagonal, cutting away from the skin. Gently lift the slices off the skin and serve, garnished with slices of citrus if desired.

Open-faced tomato tart with gravlax & caper vinaigrette

Gravlax is used in this preparation, but smoked salmon or anchovies would work nicely as well.
These tarts can also be made in bite-sized pieces and used as an appetizer for a dinner party.

Makes 4

For the tart crusts

1 tbsp olive oil

1 tbsp minced garlic

¼ cup minced shallots

1 cup (225g) butter, cubed

2 cups (225g) all-purpose flour

1 cup (225g) cream cheese

1 egg, beaten, for wash

For the filling

1 tbsp plus 2 tsp olive oil

3 garlic cloves, thinly sliced

1 shallot, julienned

3 small tomatoes, cored and cut into eighths

1 tbsp tomato paste

2 tbsp drained capers

For the caper vinaigrette

2 tbsp drained capers, halved

⅓ cup extra virgin olive oil

1½ tbsp freshly squeezed lemon juice

For the topping

2 cups yellow grape tomatoes, or red and yellow cherry tomatoes, cut into thin rings

6oz (175g) gravlax (p132)

2 tbsp chopped flat-leaf parsley

To prepare the dough for the tart crusts, heat the olive oil in a small pan and sauté the garlic and shallots until translucent, about 2 minutes. Let cool to room temperature. Place the butter, flour, and cream cheese in an electric mixer with the shallot mixture. Mix on medium speed until blended into a dough. Form into a ball, wrap, and refrigerate for 1 hour.

Preheat the oven to 350°F (180°C). Divide the dough into fourths and roll out each piece into a 7in (18cm) circle. Place on a sheet pan lined with parchment paper. Pinch or crimp the edges of the dough circles to create a slight rim. Brush the circles with egg wash, then bake until golden brown, about 15 minutes. Let cool while you make the filling and vinaigrette.

To prepare the filling, heat 1 tbsp of the olive oil in a small pan and sauté the garlic and shallot for 1 minute. Add the tomatoes, tomato paste, and capers, and cook over medium-low heat until the liquid from the tomatoes has evaporated. Press 3

tbsp of the filling through a strainer. Whisk the remaining 2 tsp olive oil into the strained pulp to make a tomato oil; set aside for the garnish. Season the remaining tomato filling and set aside.

To prepare the vinaigrette, whisk together the ingredients in a small bowl until emulsified.

Turn the oven up to 400°F (200°C). Spread the tomato filling over the tart crusts and arrange the yellow tomato rings in a pinwheel shape over the filling. Put the tarts into the oven and bake until golden brown, about 10 minutes, or until the tomatoes have softened. Remove from the oven and arrange the gravlax slices over the top.

To serve, place a tart in the center of each plate. Sprinkle with the parsley and spoon the tomato oil around the plate. Drizzle the caper vinaigrette around the plate and finish with some sliced caper berries, and a grinding of black pepper.

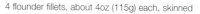

BAKING

Most fish—either whole or in fillets or steaks—can be baked in the oven, as can shellfish such as clams and oysters. Baking is also sometimes used to finish cooking fish that has first been pan-grilled (p145). In addition to the plain baking of fish, there are some special techniques. These include baking a stuffed whole fish, baking en papillote, baking in salt, and baking in pastry. Baking fish in a wrapper—be it parchment paper or foil, banana leaves, salt, or puff pastry—seals in all the flavors and can be a dramatic table presentation.

BAKING TIPS

■ Whole fish that can be baked include sea bass, porgy, trout, red snapper, and tilapia.
■ Fish fillets suitable for baking include skinless bass, flounder, halibut or fluke, sole, grouper, hake, mullet, perch, tilefish, and salmon.
■ Fat or oil-rich whole fish are ideal for baking as they remain beautifully moist. Lean whole fish need to be basted during cooking to prevent them from drying out in the heat of the oven.
■ When baking fish steaks and fillets, coat them with oil or butter, to keep them moist. If the fish is lean, brush it with more oil or butter during baking. You can also add a topping such as chopped herbs, a bread-crumb mixture, slices of lemon, sliced mushrooms, or a sauce.
■ Bake fish at 350–400°F (180–200°C). A whole fish will take about 10 minutes to each 1in (2.5cm) of thickness. Fish fillets need about 6 minutes per ½in (1cm) of thickness and fish steaks about 10 minutes per 1in (2.5cm) of thickness.

BAKED FLOUNDER FILLETS

For this simple method of baking fish fillets, brushing them with melted butter or oil will ensure they remain moist during the cooking process. Other fish fillets that can be cooked this way include bass, snapper, and salmon.

4 flounder fillets, about 4oz (115g) each, skinned
2 tbsp chopped parsley or another herb
4 tbsp melted butter or olive oil plus extra for the baking sheet
lemon slices for garnish

1 Preheat the oven to 350°F (180°C). Place the fillets side by side on a buttered or oiled baking sheet or in a baking dish. Season with salt and freshly ground black pepper, and sprinkle with the chopped parsley. Brush the fish with the melted butter or oil.

2 Put into the oven and bake until done, up to 6 minutes according to thickness. Test for doneness with the tip of a knife. The flesh should just pull apart but still look moist and opaque in the center of the fillet.

3 If necessary, return to the oven to bake for another minute or so. When the fish is ready, remove it from the oven and transfer to hot plates. Garnish with lemon slices and serve.

BAKED WHOLE BASS

This is a simple yet delicious way to bake a whole fish. Instead of bass you could use whole catfish, salmon, or trout.

2 tbsp butter

1 shallot, minced

2 cups morel mushrooms, cut into thirds

¼ cup chicken stock or water

1 tbsp minced thyme plus sprigs for garnish

1 sea or striped bass, about 1½lb (675g), gutted, scaled, and boned through the stomach (p116)

2 tbsp extra virgin olive oil

lemon wedges for serving

1 Preheat the oven to 425°F (220°C). Melt the butter in a sauté pan over medium heat and sweat the shallot, covered, until translucent.

2 Add the mushrooms and cook, uncovered, for 1 minute. Add the stock, increase the heat to medium-high, and sauté until the mushrooms are tender, about 5 minutes. Stir in the minced thyme and season with salt and pepper to taste.

3 Rub the fish all over, inside and out, with the olive oil, then sprinkle with salt and pepper. Spoon the mushroom stuffing into the cavity in the fish (see right).

4 Place the fish on an oiled or foil-lined baking sheet. Bake until just cooked through, about 15 minutes. To test for doneness, gently lift one side of the cavity skin with a paring knife to check that the color of the flesh has changed from dark and translucent to light and opaque. Transfer the fish to a serving plate.

Serve garnished with thyme sprigs and lemon wedges

SERVING WHOLE COOKED FISH

After cooking a whole fish—most commonly by baking, poaching, or braising—the easiest way to serve it is to transfer it from its baking dish or pan to a cutting board and prepare the fish for serving while still in the kitchen. After preparation, transfer the fish to a large heated platter to serve. Alternatively, you can lift the fish from its baking dish or pan directly onto the heated platter, and present it at the table for serving.

Serving whole round fish

Whole round fish, such as the red snapper shown here, are easily served using a fork, large spoon, and knife.

1 Carefully peel away the skin from the top of the fish, cutting it from the head and tail if these are left on. Scrape away any dark flesh, and scrape off the bones that lie along the back of the fish.

2 Cut down the center of the fish with the edge of the spoon, then lift off the top two fillets, one at a time. Snap the backbone at the head and tail ends, and lift it out. Replace the top fillets to reshape the fish. If you have done the preparation in the kitchen, transfer to a hot platter.

Serving whole flatfish

For large flatfish such as Dover sole, as shown here, you can use a table knife and large spoon for serving at the table.

1 Place the fish on a hot serving platter. With the knife and spoon, push away the fin bones from both sides of the fish. With the edge of the spoon, cut along both sides of the backbone, just cutting through the flesh to the bone. Lift off the top two fillets, one at a time.

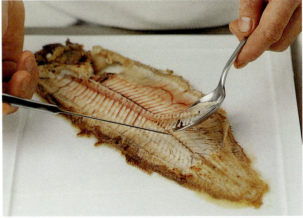

2 Lift out the backbone and set it aside to discard. You can replace the top fillets for an attractive presentation.

BAKED SALMON EN PAPILLOTE

This recipe demonstrates how to cook fish "in a package." While the traditional method uses parchment paper, other wraps such as foil and plantain and banana leaves also work well. Here, salmon is cooked en papillote, but many other types of seafood are suitable for this simple method, including bass, halibut, cod, and scallops.

| olive oil for brushing |
| 8 baby turnips, cut in half |
| 2 celery stalks, thinly sliced on the diagonal |
| 1 cup thinly sliced fennel bulb |
| 8 baby carrots, cut in half |
| 4 tbsp snipped chives |
| 4 pieces of salmon fillet, about 3oz (85g) each |
| sprigs of thyme |

1 Preheat the oven to 425°F (220°C). Cut out four large, heart-shaped pieces of parchment paper. The halves of each heart should be about twice the size of a piece of salmon. Brush one half of each heart with olive oil.

2 Divide the vegetables and chives into four portions. Place one portion in the center of the oiled half of one paper heart. Season a piece of salmon with salt and pepper, and set it on top. Add a few sprigs of thyme.

MICROWAVING

Microwaving is a simple and very quick way to cook seafood, producing tender, moist results. It is also healthy, since it uses little or no fat—just a light brushing of oil, if desired. Moisture can be added by brushing the seafood with stock or water before microwaving. For extra flavor, try using some wine or fresh citrus juice. You could also add some fresh herbs.

Most seafood can be microwaved, including fillets, steaks, fish nuggets, and even shellfish, such as shrimp and scallops. This method is not recommended for whole fish.

MICROWAVED SALMON STEAKS

All kinds of fish steaks and fillets can be cooked in this way. To give your fish a hint of flavor, brush it with an herb-flavored oil before cooking. A mustard oil basting would also be delicious. Just remember not to use too much flavoring when preparing fish, as its delicate sweet taste can easily be masked.

Serves 2

2 salmon steaks

olive oil for brushing

3 Fold over the other half of the heart. Crimp the open edges to seal them by making a series of small folds all around. Fill and seal the remaining packages in the same way. Place the packages on a baking sheet.

1 Place the salmon steaks in a single layer in an oiled microwave-safe dish. Season with salt and pepper, then brush the steaks with olive oil. Cover the dish loosely with plastic wrap.

2 Put the dish into the microwave to cook at 100% power. For salmon steaks about 1in (2.5cm) thick, cooking time will be 2–3 minutes. The cooking time is the same for fillets that are about 1¼in (3cm) thick.

4 Bake until the paper packages are puffed up and lightly browned, 5–7 minutes. To serve, cut open the packages and transfer them to individual serving plates. Alternatively, put the sealed packages on the plates and let each person open his or her own package.

MICROWAVING TIPS

■ Fish and shellfish need to be in pieces of equal thickness to ensure that they cook evenly.

■ Even cooking is also helped by turning the dish several times. A "rotating plate," found in many microwaves, does this automatically.

■ Another way to prevent uneven cooking is to microwave the fish with a little liquid. The steam created in the sealed environment helps to cook the fish gently and evenly.

■ After microwaving, most fish should be allowed to stand for 1–2 minutes. Take care when removing the cover from your microwave container, as the steam inside will be very hot.

■ The wattage times of microwave ovens vary significantly, so it is important to follow your microwave owner's manual for guidelines.

3 Remove the dish from the microwave and let it stand for 1–2 minutes. Then carefully remove the plastic wrap, starting at one corner to let the steam escape. Serve the fish hot.

POACHING

Poaching is a luscious way to cook seafood. It uses a well-seasoned liquid and very low, controlled heat. The classic method poaches seafood in fish fumet (a concentrated fish stock) and wine, and after cooking the liquid is used to make a sauce to serve with the fish. Court bouillon (see below) is also often used as the poaching liquid for seafood, but after cooking it is discarded. Another, lesser-known technique utilizes olive oil for slow poaching. Salmon is particularly wonderful poached in olive oil—it simply melts in the mouth.

POACHED SKATE WING

Skate is one of the best fish to poach in a court bouillon. Here, the wings are filleted and skinned before poaching, but they can also be cooked whole. Then, after poaching, the skin can be peeled away easily and the flesh lifted from the cartilage. Serve the skate hot or cold.

2lb (900g) skate wings, filleted (p120) and skinned (p120)

For the court bouillon
4 cups water
½ cup white wine vinegar or lemon juice
½ cup sliced onion
2 bay leaves
12 sprigs of thyme
12 sprigs of parsley
1 tbsp black peppercorns

1 To prepare the court bouillon, combine the water, vinegar or lemon juice, onions, bay leaves, thyme and parsley sprigs, and black peppercorns in a saucepan and bring to a boil. Reduce the heat and simmer for 10 minutes. Remove from the heat. Let the court bouillon cool until warm before using.

2 Cut the skate into four equal pieces. Place the pieces in a fish poacher or another pan in which they will fit comfortably. Ladle enough of the warm, not hot, court bouillon into the pan to cover the fish.

POACHING TIPS

■ Suitable fish for poaching include cod and halibut (whole or in steaks or thick fillets), whole trout, skate wings, whole striped bass, and salmon (whole or in steaks or thick fillets).
■ Poach fish for 5–7 minutes to each 1in (2.5cm) of thickness, or until the internal temperature of the piece reaches 145°F (63°C).
■ Shellfish that are excellent poached include lobster, crab, shrimp, and crayfish.

SERVING THE SKATE COLD

If you want to serve the skate cold, lift the pieces out of the court bouillon and place them in a shallow dish. Set this in an ice bath—a larger vessel such as a roasting pan filled with ice water—to cool down rapidly. Once cooled, cover the dish and keep the fish in the refrigerator until ready to serve.

3 Bring the court bouillon back to just below a simmer (160–180°F/70–82°C). Do not let the liquid get too hot or to boil.

4 Cook at just below a simmer until done, 10–15 minutes. Use a spoon and fork to test for doneness: the flesh should be flaky.

5 To serve the skate hot, lift it out of the court bouillon and arrange on a hot serving platter with some of the herbs and onion.

STEAMING

Steaming is a gentle way to prepare fish and shellfish. It is very close to poaching and braising except that the fish does not come into direct contact with any liquid. Therefore, the flavors are pure, and the fish retains its shape.

Any fish that is suitable for braising or poaching is also a great candidate for steaming. Some favorites include bass, all flatfish, John Dory, mahimahi, pompano, tilefish, and walleye. Shellfish that are good steamed include clams, mussels, shrimp, lobster, and crab.

STEAMED CLAMS

Other mollusks, such as mussels, are also often cooked in this way.

Serves 2

1 cup white wine
1 tbsp chopped parsley
1 small garlic clove, minced
squeeze of lemon juice
2 dozen small hard-shell clams, scrubbed and purged (p121), if necessary

STEAMING TIPS

■ Steam whole fish and fish steaks and fillets on a rack set above the steaming liquid. For steaming most shellfish, a rack isn't needed.

■ Depending on the liquid used for steaming, it can be served with the seafood. For example, if shrimp are steamed in beer, they can be served in the beer, with plenty of bread to soak it up. The liquid from steaming a fish can be incorporated into a sauce to serve over the fish.

■ Cooking time for fish is about 8 minutes per 1in (2.5cm) of thickness.

1 Combine the wine, parsley, garlic, and lemon juice in a large pot with a tight-fitting lid. Bring to a boil, uncovered, then reduce the heat until the liquid is simmering.

2 Add the clams to the pot. Cover tightly and turn the heat back to high. Steam until all or most of the clams have opened, 2–3 minutes (discard any clams that remain closed). Transfer the clams to wide serving bowls, ladling the cooking liquid over them. Serve immediately.

BRAISING

Braising is a very gentle way to cook seafood in the oven, and produces wonderfully tender and moist results. Both whole fish and fish portions can be braised. Typically the liquid used for braising is water or fish stock, and you can add a variety of flavoring ingredients, including carrots, celery, and herbs such as thyme and parsley. The braising liquid is usually served with the seafood—simply strained or forming the base of a sauce.

BRAISED MONKFISH

Serves 6

1lb (450g) mixed carrots, celery, and onions

6 sprigs of rosemary

2 large monkfish fillets, about 1lb (450g) each, skinned

4 cups fish stock, heated to simmering

BRAISING TIPS

■ Any fish that is appropriate for baking is also fine for braising, but the method is particularly suitable for delicate-flavored fish, such as cod, snapper, porgy, skate, salmon, monkfish, and bass.

■ Strong-flavored oily fish, such as eel or barracuda, should not be braised because their flavor would become even more concentrated.

■ Fish braising times in a 425°F (220°C) oven are about 8 minutes for each 1in (2.5cm) of thickness.

1 Preheat the oven to 425°F (220°C). Roughly chop the vegetables and place in an oiled roasting pan that is deep enough to hold the fish and braising liquid. Add the herbs. Season the monkfish fillets with salt and pepper, then lay them on top of the bed of vegetables and herbs.

2 Ladle enough simmering fish stock into the pan to come halfway up the fish. Cover the pan with a lid or foil and braise in the oven until the fish is cooked, 12–15 minutes. The flesh should be white through the center of the fish.

Spoon the flavorful braising liquid over the fish when serving or use to make a sauce to serve alongside

BROILING

Both broiling and grilling are dry-heat methods of cooking that involve high temperatures. It's therefore important to select the appropriate seafood for these methods, and to ensure that you don't overcook it.

Fat, oil-rich fish such as salmon are best for broiling, although lean fish are good too, as long as you give them some kind of coating to keep them moist. Flouring and then dipping in oil is one idea; another is to dip the fish in oil and then coat it with bread crumbs. Many shellfish are ideal for broiling, including shucked scallops, langoustines, and halved lobsters in shell.

BROILING TIPS

■ Cooking times will vary according to the thickness of the fish or shellfish. Allow about 4 minutes per side for a fillet that is 1in (2.5cm) thick, or a whole fish of this thickness. Thinner fillets, about ½in (1cm) thick, will require only 2 minutes of cooking per side.

■ The distance from the heat source will also vary according to the thickness of the fish. Fillets and whole fish that are 1in (2.5cm) thick should be broiled 4–6in (10–15cm) from the heat source; broil ½in (1cm) fillets at a distance of 2in (5cm).

■ Whole fish, fish steaks, and thick fish fillets will need to be turned over halfway through the cooking time and may need brushing with additional oil or melted butter. Very thin fillets don't need to be turned over, because you can cook them through just by broiling on one side for 4–5 minutes.

■ If broiling fish fillets with the skin on, cook for only three-fourths of the suggested time.

BROILED RED MULLET FILLETS

4 red mullet fillets, about 4oz (115g) each, scaled

melted butter or olive oil for brushing

1 Preheat the broiler. Score the skin of the fish fillets with a sharp knife. Arrange the fillets, skin-side up, on the rack of the broiler pan and brush them with melted butter or olive oil. Season with salt and pepper.

2 Place the pan 2in (5cm) from the heat source and broil until the fish fillets are cooked through, 4–5 minutes. They do not need to be turned over during cooking. Test for doneness with the tip of a knife.

GRILLING

Grilling is a great way to cook fish and shellfish. The smoke imparts wonderful flavor—adding wood chips such as hickory or mesquite to the coals also enhances the flavor—as will marinating the seafood beforehand or basting with a marinade during cooking.

Seafood suitable for grilling include salmon and trout, cod and haddock, sea bass, mahimahi, tuna and swordfish, lobster, tiger shrimp and jumbo shrimp, and baby octopus.

Using a hot ridged, cast-iron grill pan will produce similar results to grilling over hot coals, although it doesn't impart a smoky flavor. When food is cooked on a grill pan it is described as pan-grilled or pan-broiled.

PAN-GRILLED SCALLOPS

Sea scallops are delicious grilled—either on a grill pan, as shown here, or over hot coals. The preparation (marinating and threading onto skewers) is the same for both methods.

¾ cup extra virgin olive oil

1 tbsp chopped parsley or cilantro

12 large sea scallops, shucked

1 Mix together the oil, parsley or cilantro, and salt and pepper to taste in a bowl. Put the scallops in a shallow dish. Spoon the oil mixture over them and turn to coat all sides. Cover and let marinate in the refrigerator for 2 hours.

2 Thread the scallops onto skewers. (If using wooden skewers, soak them in hot water for 30 minutes before using.) Heat a ridged, cast-iron grill pan until thoroughly hot.

GRILLING TIPS

■ Be sure the grill rack is clean and hot before putting on the seafood to cook. This will prevent the food from sticking to it.

■ Leave the skin on whole fish as this helps to hold it together (and also helps prevent it from sticking to the grill rack). If you are going to remove the skin before serving, there is no need to scale the fish.

■ Small whole fish are easy to grill, although they may fall apart. Putting them in a grill basket will prevent this from happening.

■ Fish steaks and fillets need to be at least ½in (1cm) thick so that they don't overcook.

■ For small pieces of seafood, such as cubes of fish, scallops, and shrimp, thread them onto skewers. This will make it easier to turn them during cooking.

■ An interesting idea is to wrap fish in grape leaves before putting it on the grill.

■ To make attractive criss-cross grill marks, re-position the seafood halfway through the cooking time on each side—lift it up and turn it 45°, then replace it on the hot grill or pan.

3 Place the scallops on the hot pan and grill, turning them over once, until they are done, 2–3 minutes. When ready the scallops will have become opaque, but will still feel tender to the touch. Remove from the pan and serve immediately, on or off the skewers.

PAN-FRYING

Pan-frying is an excellent way to cook fish and shellfish. The seafood remains moist and succulent within a crisp, browned exterior. In general, lean fish are the best suited to pan-frying, either whole or in steaks or fillets. Fat, oil-rich fish can be pan-fried, but the quantity of oil or other fat used for cooking may need to be reduced.

Grapeseed and canola oils are the best ones to use when pan-frying or

when sautéing (see below). Olive oil is good too, but you'll need to watch carefully as it has a lower smoke point than grapeseed and canola oils. If you want to use butter, mix it with oil or choose unsalted or clarified butter (p24), to avoid any burning of the fat at high heat.

To achieve a wonderful crisp crust, coat the seafood with flour, cornmeal, or bread crumbs before putting it into the pan.

PAN-FRIED RED MULLET

4 red mullet, gutted, scaled, trimmed, and head removed (p114)

cornmeal for coating

grapeseed oil for frying

lemon juice to finish

SAUTÉING SEAFOOD

This cooking method is very similar to pan-frying. The main differences are the quantity of oil or other fat used (more for pan-frying than sautéing), the heat (higher for sautéing), and the moving of the seafood in the pan (for sautéing the seafood is tossed and turned almost constantly, while for pan-frying it is usually turned once). Sautéing is not a good method to use for fragile fish, since the tossing in the pan will break the fish into pieces. However, it works very well for fish such as skate and for firm shellfish.

Finish with a squeeze of lemon juice

1 Season the fish with salt and pepper, then coat it on both sides with cornmeal. Shake off the excess. Set a nonstick frying pan or cast-iron skillet over medium-high heat and add a small amount of grapeseed oil (use just enough oil to coat the bottom of the pan).

2 Put the prepared fish into the hot oil, presentation side (the side that will be uppermost when serving) down. Pan-fry until the fish is golden brown on the presentation side, about 2 minutes.

3 Turn the fish using tongs and cook until the other side is golden brown. To test for doneness, insert a thin-bladed knife into the center of the fish, then touch the tip of the knife to your thumb. If the knife is warm, the fish is ready. Drain briefly on paper towels.

DEEP-FRYING

Deep-frying is one of the most popular ways to cook seafood. Small, whole, lean fish; pieces of fish; and shellfish, such as shrimp and shucked clams, oysters, and scallops, are all well suited to deep-frying. The seafood is usually coated with flour, crumbs, or batter before frying, which protects it from the heat of the oil as well as providing a crisp, tasty crust.

There are a number of fats and oils you can use when deep-frying. The most common are rendered animal fat (such as bacon and duck), and corn, peanut, canola, and safflower oils. Take care not to put too much fat or oil in the pan—it should not be more than half full.

Frying times will vary according to the size of the fish and on the temperature of the oil (see right). As a general rule, however, fry fish for 7–9 minutes to each 1in (2.5cm) of thickness. Fry shellfish until they turn golden brown and float to the surface of the oil.

FRYING TEMPERATURES

When frying small, whole fish the oil should be at about 350°F (180°C). Shellfish and small pieces of fish should be fried at a slightly higher temperature, around 375°F (190°C).

BREADED & DEEP-FRIED SHRIMP

oil for deep-frying

2lb (900g) raw large shrimp, peeled and deveined

all-purpose flour for coating

2 eggs, beaten with 2 tbsp water

fresh bread crumbs for coating

For serving

lemon wedges

tartar or cocktail sauce

1 Heat oil for deep-frying in a skillet or other pan to 375°F (190°C). Make sure the shrimp are completely dry, then season them with salt and pepper. One at a time, dip them in flour to coat evenly. Shake off excess flour.

2 Next, dip the shrimp in the egg wash (eggs beaten with water). Lift out of the egg wash and let excess drip off, back into the bowl.

3 Finally, dip the shrimp into fine bread crumbs, to cover completely. Press to ensure the crumbs adhere, then shake off excess. As the shrimp are breaded, lay them on a tray.

4 Add the breaded shrimp, in small batches, to the hot oil. Do not crowd the pan. Deep-fry, turning the shrimp so they cook and color evenly, until golden brown, about 2 minutes.

5 When the shrimp are golden brown and crisp, remove with a slotted spoon to drain on paper towels, then serve immediately, with lemon wedges and tartar or cocktail sauce.

POULTRY & GAME BIRDS

SHAUN HILL

Intensive farming has transformed poultry from being an occasional treat, perhaps bought for a special event, to cheap and everyday meat. Today's poultry may seem to have little in common with the well-flavored and well-nurtured products of before. But do not be disheartened—a good butcher will guide you to the best quality. Terms such as "free-range" (or "range") and "natural" may mean only minimal access to daylight—no more than mass-produced birds. And they guarantee nothing regarding the quality or type of feed used. The term "organic" is now more reliable, but having a trusted supplier to advise you is better still.

Buying poultry and game birds Most poultry is available year-round. Choose a large bird for a more developed flavor and a better ratio of meat to bone. The meat should look plump rather than bony and the skin should have no dry patches. With game birds there is quite a difference between young and old. Young birds are tender and suit roasting, whereas older specimens are tougher and need to be braised. A good game bird will be plump and heavy relative to its size.

In Europe, game birds are seasonal. The first grouse appears in August (on "The Glorious Twelfth"), and the majority of game birds follow in late September and October. Of course, it is possible to farm some birds all year round, as is done in North America, so the definition of what constitutes a game bird has changed. Wild birds are more strongly flavored than their farmed counterparts and may have a tougher texture.

Handling and storage Raw poultry carries high levels of bacteria and there are important guidelines in its safe preparation and storage. First, always scrub the board and knives you use to prepare poultry in hot, soapy water before using them again to carve the same bird once cooked. Commercial kitchens use different, color-coded cutting boards to avoid any risk of cross-contamination. Second, store raw poultry at the bottom of the refrigerator as a precaution against juices from the raw meat dripping onto other food, especially foods that will not be cooked further. Cooked and cooled poultry should be stored in the upper part of the refrigerator to prevent contamination from raw meats.

Poultry is best bought fresh and used immediately. Birds stored in the refrigerator dry out quickly, because the meat has little or no fat covering. Game birds are generally smaller than poultry and are even more prone to drying out. However, covering or wrapping the meat in plastic wrap is a good preventive measure. Birds kept for any length of time should be turned and rewrapped regularly. A light brushing with oil also inhibits drying, but the oil can flavor the finished result. Bland oils such as sunflower are better than olive oil, unless you want the flavor of olive oil in the finished dish.

To enjoy frozen poultry at its best, buy it fresh, wrap it carefully, and freeze it yourself. Ready-frozen poultry rarely has any opportunity to develop flavor. I feel there is little point in buying frozen game birds either, because for me part of the pleasure in eating game is the fleeting nature of the hunting season. However, a properly frozen bird will be superior to a fresh bird that was not well handled and will still make a first-rate meal.

Cooking poultry and game birds An important general rule for all cooking methods is to use the right size of container for cooking the bird. If it is a chicken to be poached, find a pot that allows the bird to be covered using the minimum of liquid, so that you end up with a smallish quantity of well-flavored stock. If roasting, use a pan large enough to collect the cooking juices ready for use in a sauce or gravy, but not so large that fat and cooking juices spit over the oven wall.

When cooking, use the method that suits the bird best. Small, young birds are fine roasted, but older, larger ones may well be better braised or poached. Birds should be brought to room temperature before cooking, rather than taken straight from refrigerator to oven. Use cookbooks only as a general guide for cooking times, and always test the meat for doneness before serving.

PREPARING A WHOLE BIRD

A fresh bird should be plump relative to its size and weight and its skin should be unblemished by dry patches or signs of bruising. Patches of dry skin indicate that the bird has been stored badly or frozen, and it will need lots of extra butter or oil during cooking in compensation. Bruising is generally a problem with shot game birds such as wild duck. Look out for red patches in particular, as these will turn dark and unsightly during cooking.

A traditional preparation of any whole bird involves sewing a piece of string through it so that it remains in a tight shape throughout cooking. This technique, known as trussing, has its disadvantages, however. Heat will take longer to penetrate to the center of a trussed bird, and removing the string is a messy business.

Removing the wishbone is important if you want to make carving of the cooked bird or dissection into pieces a great deal easier.

PARTS OF A BIRD

All poultry divides into two main parts: breast and legs. Whether the breasts are halved, the wings are left attached to the breast or served separately, or the legs are further subdivided into thigh and drumstick will be a matter of portioning, cooking time, or convenience rather than any major separation of differing types of meat on the bird.

Leg meat is darker and denser in texture and will take longer to cook than the paler, more delicate breast meat. Swift cooking processes like frying or roasting show the advantages of breast meat, while slow cooking processes like braising and poaching favor the leg meat. In reality, a touch of compromise will produce uniformly acceptable results from the entire bird.

Whole chicken on its back

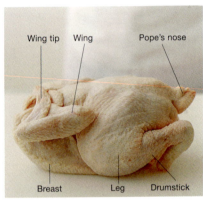

Whole chicken on its breast

REMOVING THE WISHBONE

1 Lay the bird on its back and lift the flap of skin from around the bird's neck. Run your finger around the neck cavity and you will feel the wishbone just in from the edge.

2 Using a small, sharp knife, scrape the meat away from the wishbone so that it is exposed and clearly visible.

3 Run the blade of the knife just behind the bone, then use your fingers to lift and twist the wishbone free. Pull the skin back into place.

ROASTING

White poultry meat needs plenty of oil or butter while roasting, or it will be dry. Only the duck family has enough natural fat to be roasted without help. In all poultry, the breasts tend to cook before the legs, so care is needed for both to be in perfect condition at the same time. This may mean turning the bird on its side or basting frequently.

Oven temperatures are important. A high initial temperature is needed to brown and caramelize the skin, but too much high heat will dry out the delicate breast meat. Possible solutions include covering the bird with buttered paper or foil halfway though cooking, turning the bird on its breast so that the back and legs take most of the heat, or reducing the oven temperature. However, few people roast a bird in isolation—potatoes, stuffings, and suchlike all make demands on oven space and temperature levels. Try to take advantage of differing heat levels in the oven and move the roasting bird to a lower rack.

White meats such as poultry are best cooked right through, but will not withstand prolonged cooking. When testing for doneness, insert a skewer into either the thigh or the thick end of the breast nearest the bone. If the juices run clear, the bird is cooked. Any traces of blood and it is not.

Resting the cooked meat has two functions. First, it allows the heat from the outer part to gently finish cooking the center. It also gives you a chance to decant any fat in the roasting pan, and lets juices blend in with caramelized scraps from the roasting process and start producing the base for a sauce or gravy. The time needed to rest a bird will vary: A turkey will retain heat for 20 minutes, but a partridge may be ready in five. If you feel it has cooled too much, return the bird to the oven for a few moments before serving.

Lastly, there is the gravy. The pan residues contain concentrated flavor to make gravy taste of what has just been cooked and not some all-purpose commercial preparation. You can also tinker with the style of the finished dish by adding herbs such as tarragon or oregano or maybe some chopped garlic or lemon zest.

Roasting whole birds

Ovens vary, so be guided in cooking times by testing the meat for doneness. For convection ovens, follow the manufacturer's directions.

TYPE OF BIRD	TIME (OVEN WEIGHT)	TEMPERATURE	POSITION OF BIRD
Chicken	45 minutes per 2¼lb (1kg) or 20 minutes per 1lb (450g)	First 15 minutes @ 425°F (220°C); remainder of time @ 375°F (190°C)	On back
Goose 5lb (2.25kg)	30 minutes per 2¼lb (1kg) or 15 minutes per 1lb (450g)	400°F (200°C)	1 hour on back, 1 hour on front, 30 minutes on back
Turkey 5lb (2.25kg)	45 minutes per 2¼lb (1kg) or 20 minutes per 1lb (450g) plus 20 minutes	400°F (200°C)	On back
Duck	50 minutes per 2¼lb (1kg) or 25 minutes per 1lb (450g)	350°F (180°C)	On back
Wild duck	First 15 minutes @ 1 hour @	425°F (220°C); 375°F (190°C)	On back
Quail	20–25 minutes	400°F (200°C)	On back
Squab (pigeon)	15–20 minutes on each side	400°F (200°C)	On sides
Woodcock	20 minutes	400°F (200°C)	On back
Mallard crown	20 minutes	400°F (200°C)	On back
Guinea fowl	40 minutes per 2¼lb (1kg) or 20 minutes per 1lb (450g)	400°F (200°C)	On sides
Red legged partridge	25 minutes	400°F (200°C)	On sides
Gray partridge	30 minutes	400°F (200°C)	On sides

ROASTING: CHICKEN

Taking the same level of care and concentration with a simple process such as roasting a chicken as with some complex culinary tour de force will produce surprisingly fine results. Indeed, if the basic roasting of the bird is sloppily executed, any fancy footwork with sauces and garnish will be a waste of effort, for the dish will never excel.

As with all cooking, the enemy is dryness, and this can be avoided by paying attention to detail: The heat of the oven and the chicken's position in it, the amount of butter or oil, and, of course, the length of time allocated to cooking.

Larger chickens are generally better flavored than small, so err on the side of generous and use any leftovers for sandwiches.

1 chicken, about 4lb (1.8kg), wishbone removed (p214)
2 tbsp olive oil
1 tbsp butter
½ cup water

1 Preheat the oven to 425°F (220°C). Paint the oil on the chicken, then rub on the butter and season. Place in a roasting pan that fits, pour in the water, and put into the middle of the oven. After 15 minutes, reduce the heat to 375°F (190°C). Roast for 25 minutes longer.

2 At this point, baste the chicken with the juices in the pan. Turn the bird over onto its breast so that the oven heat—which is greater the higher you are in the oven—can focus on the thighs. Baste the chicken again, then continue roasting for 25 minutes.

CHEF'S TIPS

■ Cooking times given here assume that the oven has been preheated and that a fresh, rather than thawed frozen, chicken is being cooked.

■ The most accurate way to test for doneness is with an instant-read thermometer. Insert it first into the breast (for chicken and turkey, the breast meat will be perfectly cooked at 160°F/71°C) and then insert it into the thigh (the temperature reading should be at least 170°F/76°C). Duck and game birds are cooked more rare than chicken and turkey.

■ A whole lemon pushed into the central cavity of the bird will help to keep the chicken moist and impart a subtle lemon scent.

4 Take the chicken from the oven and tip any juices from its interior back into the pan. Put the chicken on a plate, cover loosely with foil, and let it rest for 10 minutes before carving (p156). Meanwhile, make the gravy (p157).

STUFFING

A stuffing to accompany a roast bird can be cooked in two ways. Either it is pushed under the skin of the bird onto the breast, as with the watercress and apricot stuffing below, or it is wrapped in foil and baked alongside the bird for the last 25 minutes of cooking. The central cavity is not such a good spot for stuffing, because little heat penetrates the bird until it is quite well cooked.

3 Turn the chicken onto its back and test for doneness. Insert a skewer into the part least likely to be cooked through—the thigh or the thick end of the breast. If the juices run clear, the bird is cooked. If there are traces of blood continue cooking and test again after 10 minutes.

This stuffing is cooked in the oven for the last 25 minutes of roasting the bird, when the oven temperature has been reduced to 375°F (190°C). Once all of the stuffing ingredients have been combined, roll into a fat cigar shape, wrap in buttered foil, and secure the ends. At the end of cooking, unwrap the stuffing roll, slice it, and serve with the roast bird.

Sausage stuffing

2 tbsp butter
1 shallot, finely chopped
1 garlic clove, crushed
grated zest of ½ lemon
8oz (250g) fresh pork sausage meat
2 heaping cups fresh white bread crumbs
1 heaping cup parsley, chopped

1 Heat the butter in a small pan and sweat the shallot with the garlic, lemon zest, and some freshly ground black pepper until soft but not colored. Stir in all the remaining ingredients and add salt to taste.

2 Turn the stuffing onto a clean board and knead once or twice to incorporate all the components. Use as described (see left).

Stuffing under the skin

If the stuffing is to be added to the bird, this is better done by placing it under the skin at the neck end, rather than putting it in the central cavity. Stuffing placed inside this cavity does not start cooking until heat reaches it late in the roasting process, and imparts little to the bird's texture or taste, whereas stuffing placed under the skin will not only cook properly, but will help to protect the delicate breast meat during cooking. Any butter or fat involved will help keep the meat moist as it melts or renders down.

1 Lift the flap of skin around the wishbone area, at the neck end, and draw this back until it exposes as much of the breast as needed.

2 Push the stuffing in under the skin onto the breast, then pull back the skin to cover the stuffing neatly. Tuck the ends of the skin under the bird and keep in place with the wing tips.

Watercress & apricot stuffing

This stuffing suits drier white poultry such as chicken or guinea fowl, because the apricots will lend moistness to the texture of the meat, while the watercress gives a peppery contrast.

½ cup dried apricots
⅓ cup skinned hazelnuts (p480)
3 slices of white bread, processed into crumbs
1 small bunch of watercress, roughly chopped

1 Put the apricots into a small pan of water and bring to a boil. Drain.

2 Put the hazelnuts into a food processor and process for a few seconds to chop, then add the apricots, watercress, and bread crumbs. Process for a few more seconds, then scrape the stuffing into a bowl. Use as described (see left).

CARVING CHICKEN & OTHER SMALL BIRDS

All poultry with white flesh—that is, chicken or turkey—is carved in the same way. Ducks, with their denser texture and elongated breasts, are slightly different and will be tackled later (p159). The point of carving is simple—to render the meat easy to eat. Next, and secondary to this, you want it to look as presentable as possible. Thirdly, you want the least waste, with very little meat left on the bone or carcass.

The traditional shape of a carving knife is long and slim, tapering to a point at the top of the blade. This is fine, but not crucial. Sharpness is the essential quality, and while a serrated knife or chopper will not do, a finely honed cook's knife will stand in very well. This is because there are two aspects to carving poultry, one of which is better tackled by the traditional carving knife. This is the slicing of the breast into thin

strips, especially on large birds such as turkey. The other aspect of poultry carving is the division of the bird into pieces or parts—thigh and drumstick, for example—and this is better done with the power given by the shape of a cook's knife than with the finesse of the carving knife. You can use both or either.

The choice of fork, too, is important (see opposite). How you use it is a matter of choice.

1 Once the cooked bird has rested and any juices from it have been collected and added to the sauce or gravy, place the bird on its back on a clean carving board. Hold the bird with a carving fork, then use a carving knife to cut the skin between the leg and the breast. Next, draw the knife down and cut close to the breast.

2 Lift the leg backward to release the bone from the body and enable the cooked meat in crevices on the backbone to be taken off in one slice. Repeat the process for the other leg.

3 Hold the bird steady with the carving fork. Keeping the carving knife as close to the breastbone as possible, slice downward and lengthwise along one side of the bone to release the breast. Repeat on the other side.

PRESENTATION

■ The thicker the slices, the longer they will retain their heat. Thin slices draped into a fan will need to be served immediately, if that is your aesthetic preference.

■ It is a question of personal taste, but I would leave a little meat on the wing when carving chicken, to make a more substantial portion.

4 You now have two legs and two breast halves. In order to serve equal portions of both white and dark meat, you divide these in half. Carve the breast halves at a slight diagonal into equal and elegant pieces.

5 Slice each leg through the joint to separate the thigh and drumstick. Place all the carved meat with the stuffing on a platter and serve with the gravy (see opposite).

MAKING GRAVY

Make the gravy in the roasting pan in which the chicken has just been cooked, so that residues in the pan will dissolve into the gravy. If desired, add some herbs or some chopped garlic or lemon zest. Use tomato purée, sparingly, rather than tomato paste in gravy—paste tends to overpower other ingredients.

1 Using a large spoon, skim off most of the fat from the pan juices. Put the pan on the stovetop over low heat. Mix 1 tbsp all-purpose flour with 1 tbsp of the chicken fat and whisk it into the remaining pan juices.

2 Add 1¼ cups water or stock and 1 tbsp tomato purée, increase the heat, and bring to a boil, whisking constantly.

3 Strain the gravy into a clean container, then pour into a gravy boat.

CARVING FORKS: ANOTHER METHOD

The choice of carving fork is as important as the sharpness of the knife. Forks come in two styles. One is shaped like a tuning fork with two long, straight prongs and a short stem. This type of fork is good for prodding and jabbing things, but not for carving. You need the shape that has a long stem leading to short, curved prongs. When held in reverse—the curved edge downward—these prongs will secure the meat completely without damaging it. Once the meat is held like this, you will have complete control over the carving and slicing.

ROASTING: GOOSE

There is little point in buying a tiny goose to feed four. An 11lb (5kg) goose will feed six, or four with leftovers. The giblets and extra fat will be counted as part of the overall weight, so in fact your 11lb (5kg) goose will weigh more like 9lb (4kg) when you are putting it in the oven.

Prick the skin of goose (and duck), especially at the tail end where most fat lies, to ease its flow from the bird during cooking. Use a trivet or rack to lift the bird above the fat so that it roasts rather than fries, and put 1 tbsp water in the roasting pan to keep the rendered fat in peak condition for reuse later.

Just as with duck, a fruity sauce or stuffing will work well with the rich meat—roast quinces perhaps, or red cabbage braised with red wine and orange juice. Use the giblets (excluding the liver) to make stock for the gravy. The wise cook will use the first harvest of goose fat from the bird during cooking to roast accompanying parsnips or potatoes.

Leftover cooked goose can be shredded and mixed in with a little of its fat and plenty of seasoning to make potted goose or rillettes.

1 Preheat the oven to 400°F (200°C). Using a sharply pointed skewer, prick the goose all over, especially in the fat gland underneath the wing, the pope's nose area, and along the sides of the breasts.

2 Cover the legs with foil and place the bird on its back on a rack in a large, deep roasting pan. Season the skin with salt and pepper. Add 1 tbsp water to the pan and place it in the oven. Roast for 1 hour.

GIBLET STOCK FOR GRAVY

Put the giblets in a pan with 1 diced carrot, 1 diced onion, and 6 cups water. Bring to a boil, then reduce the heat so that the liquid simmers and cover the pan. Once the goose is out of the oven, drain the fat from the roasting pan into a bowl. Deglaze the pan with the strained giblet stock, scraping in any caramelized residues and bringing to a boil.

CARVING GOOSE & DUCK

Both goose and domestic duck are carved pretty much like chicken, whereas the wild duck family is treated differently. The meat will be cooked through and should be tender, so splitting the bird into sections rather than cutting into strips is what is needed.

3 Turn the goose onto its breast (take care not to tip the interior juices into the fat). Decant the fat. Roast for another hour, then turn the goose onto its back. Decant the fat and remove foil from the legs. Roast for 30 minutes longer.

4 Remove the goose from the oven and transfer to a board to rest for 15 minutes. Pour off the remaining fat from the pan and make the gravy (p157), using the giblet stock.

1 With the bird on its back, cut the skin between each leg and breast; lift the leg away from the body so that the thigh bone pops out and cut it away at the base. The leg can now be divided through the joint into drumstick and thigh.

2 Keeping the carving knife as close as possible to the body, slice downward and lengthwise along one side of the breastbone. Each breast will come off as a whole piece that can be subdivided into as many pieces as needed. The larger the piece, the longer it will retain heat.

3 If desired, carve each breast of the bird on the diagonal into several slices.

ROASTING: TURKEY

An 11lb (5kg) turkey will not only feed six hungry diners, it will also delight/plague them with leftovers. The timings are similar to goose: 1 hour on its back in an oven preheated to 400°F (200°C), then 1 hour breast-side down, and a final 30 minutes on its back again. Just as with goose, turkey legs should have a protective foil wrapping for the first 2 hours of cooking. If your oven is small in relation to the size of the bird, you may be well advised to cover the breasts with foil also.

There will not be any quantity of fat rendering down and you will have to spread oil and butter across the bird to keep the flesh moist and tender.

After it has cooked, let the turkey rest for 15–20 minutes so that the meat settles, making it easier to carve, and any cooking juices can seep back into the roasting pan. Make gravy in exactly the same way as for chicken (p157).

SERVING IDEAS

Cold roast turkey is as versatile as chicken and lends itself to excellent salad treatments. Try the following:
■ Sliced turkey brushed with olive oil, served on a bed of cooked brown lentils and bacon in mustard vinaigrette.
■ Cubed turkey and chestnuts tossed in spiced mayonnaise on crisp salad leaves.

CARVING: TURKEY LEGS & BREAST

Remove the legs by cutting the skin between them and the main body. Press back each leg until it disconnects, then cut away the upper edge from the main body. To remove each breast, keep the carving knife very close to the carcass and slice downward and lengthwise along one side of the breastbone to release the breast. The breast will come off in one piece.

Drumstick

To carve the drumstick, hold it upright by the bone and slice the meat downward into strips.

Thigh

If the thigh is very large, cut out the bone first. Slice down the thigh to expose the bone, then cut underneath it and remove. Then slice the dark thigh meat into strips.

Breast

Lay a breast half, or a boneless whole breast roast (as shown above), flat-side down, on the carving board and slice across with a sharp knife in the way you would slice a loaf of bread.

Roast quail with salad leaves & walnut dressing

The contrasts of warm and cold and the use of a sweet and sour dressing add to the interest and complexity of this dish. This was a favorite item on the menu at Gidleigh Park for many years, either as a first course or as a light lunch. It also yielded quail carcasses for the owners' Siamese cats—which was almost as important.

Divide the quail into legs and breasts

4 quail, wishbones removed (p152)

1 tbsp sunflower oil

2 thick-cut slices of bacon, cut into strips

1 tbsp pine nuts

2 tbsp walnut oil

1 tsp sherry vinegar

a selection of salad leaves, such as frisée, radicchio, romaine hearts, and mâche

1 tbsp snipped chives

¼ cup chicken or veal stock or water

Preheat the oven to 400°F (200°C). Smear the quail all over with the oil and season with salt and pepper. Brown the birds quickly on each sides in a frying pan, then put them on their backs into a roasting pan. Roast in the oven until cooked, about 25 minutes.

Meanwhile, broil the bacon until crisp, and dry-roast the pine nuts until browned (p480).

Whisk together the walnut oil and vinegar, and brush the salad leaves with half the dressing. Arrange the leaves on plates and scatter the hot bacon, pine nuts, and chives around.

Lift the quail from the roasting pan and dismantle into legs and breasts. Discard the backs. Put the pan on the stovetop and pour in the stock or water and the remaining dressing. Stir to deglaze the pan, then bring just to a boil. Strain this sauce around the quail and salad, and serve immediately.

SQUABS WITH SPICES

A squab is a young pigeon, specially reared for the table. The meat is pale and tender with a delicate flavor, unlike that of wild pigeons, which is leaner, darker, and more gamy.

There is, in fact, a well-established tradition of rearing pigeons for the table. In 11th-century England, well-to-do Normans liked to keep a dovecote to provide meat for the household. Also, squab pigeons have long been popular in North Africa, and feature in the famous Moroccan sweet pastry dish, bisteeya.

These small birds take longer to cook than you would think, since the meat is firm-fleshed, so allow 35–40 minutes. The pan juices will make a fine sauce.

1 small red bell pepper, cored, seeded, and chopped
1 garlic clove
1 tbsp chopped mint
8 golden raisins, heated in ¼ cup sweet wine until plump
1 tsp ground cinnamon
1 tsp ground cumin
1 tsp saffron threads
2 tbsp olive oil
4 squabs, wishbones removed (p152)
½ cup white wine

1 Put the bell pepper, garlic, mint, raisins, and spices in a mortar and use the pestle to grind them together almost to a pulp. Stir in the olive oil. Rub the mixture all over the squabs. Wrap the birds in plastic wrap and let marinate in the refrigerator for 2 hours.

2 Preheat the oven to 400°F (200°C). The legs take longer to cook, so put the birds on their side in a roasting pan so that the legs take most of the direct heat. Roast for 15–20 minutes, then turn the birds over and continue roasting until done, about 20 minutes longer.

CHEF'S VARIATIONS

■ An alternative way of dealing with squabs is to roast the birds on their backs, then carve the legs off when the breasts are cooked. Return the legs to the oven to finish cooking while the squab breasts are resting.
■ The pan juices make a good addition to a rice pilaf (p312), made with plenty of interesting extras like cubes of eggplant and zucchini.

3 Stir the wine into the pan juices and heat through. Strain into a bowl, skim off the fat, and serve with the squabs.

ROAST WOODCOCK

Woodcocks, and their smaller relative snipe (both of which are hunted, not sold in markets), are distinctive in several ways. Their meat is dark and deeply flavored, and there is the bonus of the brains, which are delicate and delicious.

Neither bird has a spleen, so traditionally they were cooked without being eviscerated; the giblets, once cooked, were spread on toast. You are welcome to do this, but I find it a touch too visceral for good appetite. The head is skinned and left on during cooking, since the brains are a delicacy and are eaten in much the same way as a lollipop. No sauce other than the pan juices made into gravy will be needed. The function of the toast is to soak up these juices.

Some brown lentils braised with chopped bacon and red wine or a sprinkling of dried fruit in the gravy would act as counterpoint to the richness of the meat, but any hint of cream or creamy vegetable accompaniment will be unwelcome. Small roasted potatoes could accompany the woodcocks.

4 woodcocks, wishbones removed (p152)

1 cup unsalted butter

4 slices of French bread

1 Preheat the oven to 400°F (200°C). Make an incision at the base of the neck of each bird and peel back the skin over the top of the head. Wrap the head in foil to stop it from overcooking. Spread the butter generously over the birds and place on their backs in a roasting pan. Roast for 20 minutes, basting with the melted butter.

2 While the birds are roasting, toast the French bread. Take the birds out of the oven. If you haven't eviscerated the woodcocks, use a spoon to do so now.

3 Cut off the head and neck, and split in half through the beak. Carve the birds into legs and breasts, and arrange on the toast. Put the head on the side. Serve with the pan juices.

POACHING

Poaching is the slowest and most delicate cooking method. This makes it perfect for two quite differing kinds of meat—delicate kinds, like fish or chicken breast, or particularly dense or tough meat, like beef brisket. Meat should never be boiled, but always poached. It must come to a boil and then simmer, otherwise the finished texture will be like boiled rags, rather than the clean creaminess that the method can achieve.

The main reason for poaching poultry rather than roasting it is to obtain the cooking liquid. Most recipes that use the method depend heavily on this liquid for the finished dish. And with those

that aren't as dependent on it, there will be the bonus of well-flavored stock for whenever soup or some other sauce is to be made. Poached duck is superb, but you may have difficulty finding a pot large enough for the job. The steaming and poaching of game birds is usually confined to dishes like mousses and terrines.

Two items are essential for success with poaching: patience and a lidded pot—patience, because any attempt to rush will provoke the hard boiling that dries out meat, and a lidded pot, because the steam rising will still cook anything protruding from the water as evaporation reduces the stock levels.

CHICKEN POT AU FEU WITH PARSLEY HOLLANDAISE

The quality of chicken needed for poaching is the same as that needed for roasting. Stewing hens (older birds generally bred for egg production) are good only for stock.

The finished dish has three aspects: the broth; the cooked vegetables and meat; and the sauce that accompanies them. You eat the broth like any other soup, with a spoon, then ladle sauce onto the remainder: Two courses in one, in fact. So serve the dish in a deep plate and have soup spoons as well as knives and forks at the ready.

1 chicken, about 11lb (5kg), wishbone removed (p152)
12 small new potatoes
8 baby artichokes, outer leaves removed, cut into quarters, and brushed with lemon juice
8 baby carrots, trimmed
⅔ cup shelled fresh fava beans, unskinned

For the hollandaise

3 egg yolks
4 tsp white wine
7 tbsp unsalted butter, clarified (p24)
juice of ½ lemon
few drops of hot pepper sauce
1 cup parsley, finely chopped

1 Bring the water to a boil in a large pot (see opposite). Add the chicken, the unpeeled potatoes, and a pinch of salt. Bring the water back to a gentle simmer, then cover the pot and poach for 30 minutes.

2 Add the artichokes and carrots, and cook for 5 minutes, then add the fava beans, plus any other green vegetable you want to include— maybe cabbage strips or green beans. Cook for about 5 minutes longer.

3 To test the chicken for doneness, pierce the thigh to the bone—the juices should run clear, not red. Tip the bird slightly as you lift it out, so that the hot stock in its cavity runs back into the pot.

4 To make the sauce, put the egg yolks and wine in a stainless steel bowl set over a pan of hot water. Whisk until the mixture is thick and falls in a ribbon from the whisk. Slowly whisk in the clarified butter. Add the lemon juice, pepper sauce, parsley, and seasoning.

5 Dismantle the chicken into serving pieces and place in deep bowls. Add the vegetables and pour some of the cooking liquid over. Serve with the parsley hollandaise sauce alongside.

CHEF'S TIPS

■ To calculate how much water is needed, place the chicken in the pot, then pour in enough cold water just to cover it. Remove the chicken and heat the water.

■ Take care when salting the water in which you are going to cook the chicken. If you scatter salt like a sumo wrestler starting a difficult bout, then you will end up with stock that tastes like the Dead Sea. A pinch will suffice. More can be added later, if needed.

CUTTING UP POULTRY

If you intend to cook a bird in any way other than whole, you will need to know how to cut it up into its component parts. All poultry is formed in the same way, so the difference between cutting up, say, a turkey and a pheasant will be more to do with one of size rather than of technique.

Ducks and geese are configured slightly differently. They have long breasts and comparatively short legs, which affects carving, but in essence they, too, are taken apart in the same way.

Cutting a bird into four pieces

1 Remove the wishbone from the bird (p152), then cut down through the skin between one of the legs and the carcass.

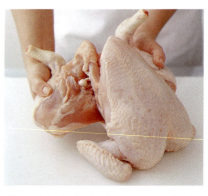

2 Bend the leg back as far as you can. The tip of the leg bone—a ball and cup arrangement with the backbone—will pop free.

3 Cut the leg away from the backbone, then repeat the process with the other leg. Each leg can be divided into thigh and drumstick.

4 Pull a wing out to its fullest extent, then, using poultry shears, cut off the wing tip at the second joint.

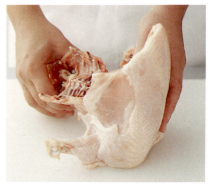

5 If a crown (the whole breast, with wings, on the bone) is wanted, snap the backbone at its halfway point.

6 Using poultry shears, remove the lower end of the backbone, which has no meat attached to it.

7 If the breasts are to be cooked on the bone, cut along the breastbone from neck to tail. Trim away any unwanted sections of backbone.

8 The chicken cut into four pieces: two breast halves with first wing joint ("drumette") attached and two whole legs.

Cutting a bird into eight pieces

1 Using poultry shears, cut through the ribs two-thirds of the way along each breast half and at an acute angle.

2 Each leg can be further divided. Locate the joint above the drumstick that connects it to the thigh and slice through to divide.

3 The chicken after being cut into eight pieces: two whole wings, two breast halves, two thighs, and two drumsticks.

Dividing the crown

The crown consists of the main part of the bird: The legs and pope's nose are removed, leaving the whole breast and wings on the bone. The crown may be cooked whole or divided.

If the breast halves are to be cooked on the bone, run the blade of a sharp knife along the dividing bone, then chop the breastbone in half (see step 7, opposite).

The breast halves can be removed from the whole crown or after chopping it in half (see below). The breastbone will act as a natural brake, so you can press firmly on either side of the central bone and follow its contours.

Cutting chicken wings

The whole wings can be cut from the breasts using a sharp knife or poultry shears, cutting through the ball and socket joint where they are attached to the breast (see right). Chicken wings have sweet, accessible meat and it is a shame not to use them as part of whatever dish is being made with the chicken. If they are not used, they can be cooked separately or added to the carcass and used for making stock.

Taking a breast half from the bone

1 Using poultry shears, cut away the ribs and the backbone. Work from the thickest (wing) end of the breast toward the narrowest part.

2 Using a sharp knife, separate the meat from the bone by following the contours of the breastbone, cutting the breast neatly away.

3 Locate the small inner fillet on the underside of the breast and slice any connecting membrane to remove it.

FRYING

It is only chicken that is fried on a regular basis, and the crumbs or batter that encase the meat are as much a part of the attraction as the chicken itself. The popularity is undeniable. Indeed, properly fried chicken coated in homemade bread crumbs makes a great summer meal, especially when served with a crisp salad and well-flavored relish or dressing.

One way to prepare fried chicken is to pound out the leg or breast into a flat cutlet, coat it in bread crumbs, and fry it like Wiener schnitzel (see opposite). Another method is the traditional Southern-fried chicken. For this, I sometimes poach the chicken pieces and cool them before coating them with crumbs and frying. This enhances the flavor in much the same way as a roasted potato that has been parboiled first. Also, it means the chicken needs less time in the oil, and turns out less greasy and less prone to being undercooked at the center. But it still has the crisp coating that makes the dish so appetizing.

When frying chicken in batches, clean the pan and renew the oil between each batch to prevent any loose crumbs from burning.

FRIED CHICKEN WITH BACON

The temperature of the cooking oil is crucial for the success of this recipe. If the oil is too hot, the coating of bacon and crumbs will crisp before the chicken is cooked all the way through. If the oil starts to smoke—a sure sign that it is too hot—add a little more cold oil to quickly reduce the overall temperature.

2 skinless, boneless chicken breast halves
2 skinless, boneless chicken thighs
1 tbsp Dijon mustard
1 tsp salt
1 tsp freshly ground black pepper
pinch of cayenne pepper
⅔ cup buttermilk
4 thick-cut slices of lean bacon
3 cups fresh white bread crumbs
sunflower oil for frying

1 Using a sharp knife, slice each breast half and thigh diagonally into four pieces.

2 Mix the mustard with the salt, pepper, and cayenne, then brush this mixture over the chicken pieces. Place the pieces in a bowl and pour the buttermilk over them. Turn the pieces gently so that they are all coated.

3 Pour oil into a heavy frying pan to a depth of ½in (1cm) and heat it, then fry the bacon until crisp. Lift out the slices and, when cool enough to handle, crumble or chop them into very small pieces. Mix the bacon with the bread crumbs. Coat each piece of chicken with the mixture, patting it on gently.

4 If necessary, add more oil to the pan so that it returns to a depth of ½in (1cm) and heat gently. When it is hot, fry the chicken pieces, turning them once, until they are golden brown and cooked—about 10 minutes, depending on the thickness of the pieces.

5 Your pan is unlikely to be large enough to cook all the chicken at once. Either cook the pieces in batches and keep them warm in the oven, or use two pans. Sprinkle the chicken with salt before serving.

FRIED CHICKEN CUTLETS

Boneless pieces of chicken that are to be rolled in crumbs and fried, or brushed with oil and herbs and then broiled, should be flattened first. Partly this is a tenderizing technique, and partly it helps the meat to cook evenly by obtaining a uniform thickness.

Chicken legs have more flavor than breasts, but you can substitute more breasts for the legs if you are not confident about boning the chicken parts yourself.

When frying, the oil should reach halfway up the cutlet as it cooks. Cook the cutlets individually, keeping the cooked ones warm in the oven while you finish the job.

1 chicken, about 3lb 3oz (1.5kg), cut up into 8 pieces, boned and skinned

1 small loaf of white bread, preferably 2 days old, crusts removed

1 tbsp Dijon mustard

1 tbsp chopped herbs, such as tarragon and parsley

2 eggs, beaten

sunflower oil for frying

1 Remove any sinews from the chicken, then place each piece between two sheets of plastic wrap. Flatten the pieces with a rolling pin until they have increased in size by half and are an even thickness.

2 Dice the bread and process to fine crumbs, then put in a wide bowl. Season the cutlets with salt and pepper. Brush them with the mustard and sprinkle each with some of the chopped herbs.

3 Heat ½in (1cm) of oil in a heavy frying pan. Dip the cutlets, one at a time, into the beaten egg to coat on all sides.

4 Turn the cutlets in the bread crumbs to coat well. Add to the hot oil and fry until golden brown on both sides, 4–5 minutes. Drain on paper towels and serve.

DEEP-FRYING

Deep-frying has more in common with boiling than it has with pan-frying. The meat is completely immersed in liquid—in this case oil or fat—and is cooked simultaneously from all sides. The temperatures reached by oils compared to water are much higher, of course, so Maillard reactions—the caramelization of surface proteins that occurs in anything roasted or grilled—will take place, allowing the meat to be browned and crisped. The thicker the

piece of meat, the lower the temperature must be, so that there is time for the heat to cook through to the center at the same time as the outside turns golden. The oil is important. An unobtrusively flavored oil is best, and one with a reasonably high smoke point (the temperature at which the oil starts to burn). Oils such as olive oil, which has a low smoke point, are unsuited to deep-frying, whereas sunflower, peanut, and vegetable oils are ideal.

DEEP-FRIED BREADED CHICKEN

Chicken has to be cooked thoroughly. If you are frying chicken for a number of people, then do so in small, controllable batches, keeping the cooked chicken in a moderate oven while the remainder is frying.

| ½ cup unsalted butter, softened |
| grated zest and juice of 1 lemon |
| 2 tbsp chopped tarragon |
| 4 large skinless, boneless chicken breast halves |
| 1 extra large egg |
| 2½ cups fresh white bread crumbs |
| sunflower oil for deep-frying |

1 Cream the butter, lemon zest, and tarragon in a bowl. Add the lemon juice and season to taste with salt and pepper. Shape the butter into a rectangular block on a piece of foil, then wrap up and leave in the freezer to set solid.

2 Meanwhile, place each chicken breast half between two pieces of plastic wrap and flatten out gently to a cutlet (p169).

3 Cut the flavored butter into four pieces. Place a piece in the center of each cutlet and roll up tightly, making sure the butter is completely enclosed.

4 Stick a wooden toothpick into both ends of each filled cutlet to secure it.

5 Lightly beat the egg in a shallow dish. Dip in the filled cutlets to coat on all sides, then roll them in the bread crumbs, pressing on the crumbs to coat evenly. Refrigerate the breaded chicken until the coating has set.

GRILLING & BROILING

In a professional kitchen, the chef's grill comprises bars that are heated from below and onto which food is placed for cooking, like an outdoor grill. A salamander blasts heat from above, toasting and crisping food, like a broiler but more fierce. In essence, they achieve the same thing—a caramelized seal on the food and fast cooking. They are both poor for slow cooking. The advantage of the grill is that the wood used will affect the flavor—a sort of small-scale smoking at the same time as the cooking—and there is an instant searing of whatever is cooking. The advantage of the salamander is that it can crisp delicate surfaces, brown gratin toppings, and deal effectively with poultry that is in a wet marinade.

For both grilling and broiling, the poultry must be brushed with butter or oil before cooking, so that its surface can color without drying. Use tender, fast-cooking cuts like boneless breast halves. Marinades will tenderize and leave on a protective oil coating.

Pan-grilling is a method halfway between frying and grilling. The difference between it and frying is that the meat, rather than the pan, is coated with oil. The difference between pan-grilling and charcoal grilling is that there is no flavor from wood smoke. I think the best use for a grill pan is for the initital searing at high temperature, after which the meat is placed in a roasting pan and cooked in the oven at a less ferocious pace.

BUTTERFLYING A BIRD

A butterflied bird is flattened and transformed into something more two-dimensional that can be grilled or broiled evenly. There is little point in the process otherwise. Once butterflied, the bird can be marinated in olive or some other oil mixed with, say, tarragon or oregano, then brushed with mustard and cooked. If you intend to cook it in the oven, it can be brushed with mustard after roasting, topped with a mixture of fresh bread crumbs and herbs, and then crisped under the broiler.

Squab chickens are ideal candidates for butterflying and then grilling or broiling. Other small birds—such as Rock Cornish game hens, young guinea fowl, quail, and squabs (pigeon)— can also be prepared in this way.

1 Turn the chicken upside-down. Using poultry shears, cut along one side of the backbone, then cut along the other side and remove the backbone completely. Open out the bird and turn it over.

2 Using the heel of your hand or the flat side of a heavy knife, lightly crush the bird all over. This will flatten the bird to an even thickness and ensure that it cooks more evenly.

3 Using a sharp knife, cut a few slashes in the meat of the legs and thighs, so they will cook more quickly.

4 Push a skewer through the left leg to the right wing, and another skewer through the right leg to the left wing.

5 If wished, the butterflied bird can now be marinated before being grilled or broiled, or it can be roasted in the oven.

GRILLED PHEASANT BREAST WITH BRAISED CHESTNUTS

Pheasant needs help if it is to be moist when grilled or roasted. The legs are a lost cause and are best braised, whatever the dish. However, this can be an advantage, for any fast-cooking method like grilling or frying will produce good texture in tender breasts but without any pronounced pheasant flavor. The legs can provide this. After all, there is little point in using pheasant—rather than guinea fowl or chicken—if its distinctive flavor is lost.

4 young pheasants, wishbones removed (p152), cut up into breasts, thighs, and drumsticks (p167), breasts skinned, and skin reserved

1½ tbsp butter

5 thick-cut slices of bacon, cut into 1in (2.5cm) strips

6 small carrots, cut into 1in (2.5cm) strips

12 shallots

1 tsp grated nutmeg

1 tsp ground cinnamon

½ cup white wine

1 tbsp tomato purée

1 cup chicken stock

1 tbsp brown lentils, soaked for 1 hour, then boiled until tender

8 peeled fresh chestnuts (p481) or unsweetened vacuum-packed chestnuts

¼ cup olive oil

1 Preheat the oven to 350°F (180°C). Heat the butter in a heavy-based stovetop-to-oven casserole and fry the thighs and drumsticks until browned. Add the bacon, vegetables, spices, and skin from the breasts.

CHEF'S TIPS

■ Pheasant legs—especially the drumsticks—have lots of little bones and gristle. These need careful removal before the meat is blended in the sauce.

■ Pheasant skin has little to recommend it, so it is removed from the breasts and added to the stock.

■ As an alternative, you could cook the legs over a low heat on the stovetop.

2 Season with salt and pepper, then stir in the wine, tomato purée, and stock. Add the lentils and chestnuts. Bring to a boil, then cover the pot and transfer it to the oven. Cook for about 1 hour.

4 Remove the vegetables, meat, and chestnuts from the casserole and reserve. Discard all the bones, skin, and gristle from the meat.

3 Meanwhile, place the pheasant breasts between two sheets of plastic wrap and flatten to an even thickness. Season with salt and pepper, and brush generously with olive oil ready for pan-grilling.

5 Pour the remaining liquid, including the bacon and lentils, into a blender and add the meat from the legs. Blend, in batches if necessary, into a smooth sauce. Pour back over the vegetables and chestnuts, and reheat.

6 Pan-grill (or grill) the breasts for a few minutes on each side, then serve on top of the braised chestnuts and vegetables.

Grilling & broiling times

BIRD	TIME*
Chicken cutlets	7–10 minutes each side
Chicken pieces	15 minutes each side
Kabob strips	5–6 minutes
Pheasant breasts	3–4 minutes each side
Squab chickens, butterflied	15 minutes each side
Quail, butterflied	12 minutes each side

*Turn regularly and baste if directed in the recipe

MARINATING POULTRY

Marinades

Each of the following marinades makes enough to coat a small chicken, cut up, or 4 breast halves. Brush the marinade over the chicken pieces. Let marinate for 1 hour, then grill the pieces over charcoal, or broil, brushing from time to time with the reserved marinade.

Sesame & chili marinade

Whisk together ½ cup light toasted sesame oil, 1 seeded and minced, small, hot chili, 1 tbsp soy sauce, and 1 tbsp yuzu juice (p88), to form an emulsion.

Orange & olive oil marinade

Whisk together ½ cup olive oil, the grated zest of 1 orange, 3 large crushed garlic cloves, 1 tbsp chopped oregano, and freshly ground black pepper, to form an emulsion.

Cumin & cinnamon marinade

Whisk together ½ cup olive oil, 1 tbsp ground cumin, 1 tsp paprika, 1 tsp ground cinnamon, the grated zest of 1 lime, 1 crushed garlic clove, ½ seeded and minced, small, hot chili, and plenty of freshly ground black pepper, to form an emulsion.

Marinating poultry serves one of two purposes. If the marinade has an acid component—such as red wine or vinegar—it will break down any tough proteins or connective tissue in the meat and, in theory at least, make it that much more tender to eat. This process has to be used with care when dealing with the delicate white meat of chicken or pheasant, since it can dominate their fragile quality, leaving you little but the taste of wine and peppercorns. Also, there is the danger of drying out the meat that contact with any non-oil or fat liquid brings. One hour is long enough for poultry to be left in this type of acid marinade.

The object of marinating for most types of poultry, and its second purpose, is to avoid any dryness in the meat and maybe to add some nuances of spicing to the finished dish. For this, you need a marinade that is oil-based. Added interest will be given to the meat by using aromatic ingredients such as grated orange zest, garlic, or chili, as well as whatever herbs and spices are appropriate to the dish.

Poultry can be left in this kind of oil-based marinade for a longer period of time—the cilantro-marinated chicken kabobs opposite can be left in the seasoning for at least 4 hours, for example.

DRY-MARINATING

A third type of marinade just about qualifies for inclusion. Dry-marinating, also called dry rub, which involves no liquid, is an extension of the process of seasoning the poultry ahead of its cooking. The recipe for squabs with spices (p162) is an example of this. The spice mixture is left on the bird for an hour or so to penetrate the meat more than just skin-deep.

Cilantro-marinated chicken kabobs

Versions of this dish are served as a main course across a large part of the Middle East and eastern Mediterranean. The method leaves the meat completely tender and the flavors nicely balanced between the acidity of the yogurt and the light sweetness of the chicken. The difference between the dish when made with high-quality ingredients and one made with standard-issue ingredients is dramatic.

Small fingers of the marinated chicken also make a first-rate hot canapé—the lime and cilantro tang will stimulate appetite without the bulk necessary to satisfy it.

Pairs of skewers keep the strips of chicken flat during cooking

4 skinless, boneless chicken breast halves

½ cup thick plain yogurt

1 scant tsp salt

juice of 1 lime

1 tbsp chopped cilantro plus extra for garnish

1 tsp freshly ground black pepper

1 tsp crushed coriander seeds

few drops of olive oil

Cut the chicken breasts into strips that are ¾in (2cm) wide. Mix the yogurt with the salt, lime, cilantro, and spices. Coat the chicken in this mixture and let marinate for 4 hours. (The longer the chicken is left in the marinade, the more effect it will have. Four hours is ideal if you still want some vestige of chicken taste coming through the spices.)

Preheat the broiler or prepare a charcoal grill. Thread the chicken strips onto pairs of skewers, spacing them out evenly, and putting about four strips of chicken on each pair.

Sprinkle a few drops of olive oil on the kabobs, then broil or grill them until they are done, about 7 minutes on each side.

INDIAN COOKING

ATUL KOCHHAR

Indian cuisine can be divided broadly into four main regions—north, south, east, and west—which are themselves subdivided into individual Indian states. All the states vary in the spices they grow and use, and the cooking techniques they employ. Tandoori chicken is a northern Indian recipe. It is cooked in a tandoor, a charcoal-fired clay oven that gives food a characteristic finish and flavor. In this oven meats and vegetables are cooked skewered on iron spikes, and breads are baked by slapping them onto the oven's clay walls. It is common to serve the dish with bhajis, a type of savory fritter also used as a snack or appetizer. The onion bhaji, from western India, is one of the most delicious examples, often served as an appetizer with mint chutney.

Cooking techniques India has more than 4,350 miles (7,000km) of warm water coasts, so seafood is an essential part of Indian gastronomy. The two seafood recipes in this chapter involve very different types of cooking—kadhai (Indian wok) and curry (poaching in a sauce). Kadhai cooking combines stir-frying and sautéing; curry cooking combines sautéing and poaching. Both methods employ their own set of spices. Kadhai spices are usually specific and are listed in recipes, whereas curry's spice combinations vary according to regional differences and the main ingredients used.

Bhuna is a sautéing technique that gives numerous Indian recipes a distinct flavor due to its heat treatment of spices. Fresh or dried spices are lightly toasted to release their essential oils, which then flavor lamb, chicken, shrimp, and vegetables. The bhuna technique also varies from region to region in the spices and ingredients used. For example, yogurt is not always the cooking liquid used.

Dum cooking, or slow cooking of food in its own steam, is an ancient Indian method first used in the city of Awadh (now Lucknow), in India. In biriyani dishes made by this method, meat or vegetables are partly cooked and mixed with partly cooked rice, spices, and other flavorings. The food is baked slowly at a low temperature in a sealed pot. Spices such as mace (the aril that surrounds the nutmeg) and green cardamom play a major role, and saffron, rose water, cream, and yogurt are used liberally to enhance the dish. Tadka is a technique in which foods such as lentils, prepared with little or no spicing, are spiced just before they are served. This technique is also used to further enhance preparations that are already spiced.

The spicing process In Indian cooking, spices are sizzled and made to release their flavors in hot oil. The oil becomes the carrier of the flavors and distributes them evenly throughout the dish. The temperature of the oil is critical. If too hot, the oil burns the spices, destroying the flavors and giving the preparation a burned taste. If too cold, the oil fails to release the flavors from the spices, and the preparation becomes a poor or unworthy dish.

Spices are used in various forms—fresh and dried, whole and ground, and in coarse and fine pastes. Most notable are the whole and ground dried spices. Generally, whole spices are added to hot oil at the start of the preparation, and ground or powdered spices are used during or at the end of the preparation to complete the flavorings. Ground spices are rarely added directly to hot oil, since they burn readily and their flavors are spoiled.

Planning an Indian meal A traditional Indian meal may or may not have appetizers—fried snacks such as bhajis; a salad of cucumber, tomatoes, and onions; a lentil soup (rasam); or a tangy drink made with toasted cumin and mango powder. For the main course, a meat curry might be the central dish, with two vegetable accompaniments and a lentil preparation. Different spicing, cooking methods, ingredients, and textures are used to vary vegetable dishes; this is especially important for vegetarian meals. The main dish is served with an Indian bread such as a chapatti and either plain steamed rice or pilau rice. Pickles, chutneys, and poppadums are also served. Desserts vary from region to region, but fresh fruits, kulfi, or rice pudding satisfy most palates.

MENU

- Tandoori murg

- Onion bhajis

- Raita

- Kadhai jhinga

- Paneer & baby corn with ginger

- Tadka dal

- Bhuna gosht

- Meen molee

TANDOORI MURG

The Indian culinary scene has been dominated for a long time by tandoori chicken dishes. This is a simple recipe that can be produced easily in household ovens or on a grill. Marinating (see opposite) helps to retain flavor in the meat during and after cooking. Birds are generally cooked without the skin because it is considered unhealthy.

1 chicken, about 2¼lb (1kg)

For the first marinade

1 tsp salt

1 tbsp ginger-garlic paste (see opposite)

1 tsp hot chili powder

2 tbsp lemon juice

For the second marinade

1 cup thick plain yogurt

1 tsp garam masala

7 tbsp vegetable oil

½ tsp ground cinnamon

½ tsp hot chili powder or paprika

1 tsp salt

few drops of red food coloring (optional)

For serving

2 tbsp butter

2 tbsp vegetable oil

1 tbsp lime juice

1 tsp chat masala (mixed spices)

1 Skin the chicken and, with a sharp knife, cut into four pieces (two breasts and two legs). Pull the legs through the ball and socket joint, leaving some meat attached to the end of the bone for less shrinkage. Marinate the chicken pieces (see opposite).

2 Preheat the oven to 400°F (200°C) or prepare a charcoal fire. Bake the chicken (on a baking sheet) or grill for 10 minutes. Baste with half of the butter and oil, and cook for 15 minutes longer.

3 Remove the chicken from the oven or grill and baste with the remaining butter and oil. Sprinkle with the lime juice and chat masala. Serve hot, with a leafy salad and mint chutney.

RAITA

Lightly whisk 1 cup thick plain yogurt with ½ tsp dry-roasted and crushed cumin seeds (p79), 1 tbsp diced red onions, 1 tbsp chopped mint, 1 tbsp peeled and grated cucumber, and salt to taste.

ONION BHAJIS

Bhajis—or bhajias or pakoras—are deep-fried vegetable snacks. The vegetables are coated in a batter made from besan or gram flour, which is ground dried chickpeas. Alternatively, you can use cornmeal or rice flour. Other vegetables, such as cauliflower florets, cabbage, and carrots, are also suitable for making crisp bhajis. The bhajis are best made just before serving.

Makes 12–15

3 onions, finely sliced

vegetable oil for deep-frying

For the batter

scant 1 cup besan or gram flour

¼ tsp baking soda

½ tsp ground turmeric

1 hot green chili, minced

1 tbsp chopped cilantro

½ tsp salt

5 tbsp water

Prepare the batter, then fry the bhajis (see opposite). Serve hot with raita (see left).

MARINATING

In Indian cooking, meats may be marinated twice: The first removes excess moisture and the second introduces flavors and spices.

1 With a sharp knife, make three or four deep incisions, to the bone, in each piece of chicken. This helps the marinade penetrate the meat and stops it from shrinking during the dry-heat cooking.

2 Mix all the ingredients for the first marinade in a bowl. Coat the chicken with the marinade (wear plastic or rubber gloves). Place the chicken in a strainer set over the bowl and let drain at room temperature for 20 minutes.

3 In another bowl, mix together all the ingredients for the second marinade. Coat the chicken thoroughly, then cover the bowl and refrigerate for 2–3 hours.

GINGER-GARLIC PASTE

You will need kitchen scales to prepare this. Put equal weights of peeled fresh ginger and garlic in a blender with 10 percent of their total weight in water. Blend to a smooth, fine paste. Store in a sealed container in the refrigerator for up to a week.

If you want to keep the paste longer than this, add 5 percent vegetable oil and 2 percent lemon juice when you blend the paste. This makes it last longer and also lightens the color. Alternatively, freeze the paste in ice-cube trays for future use.

MAKING ONION BHAJIS

In India, frying in a wok or deep-fryer is called "talna." If you are making fried foods such as bhajis in advance, reheat them in the oven or flash-fry in hot oil to regain their crispness.

1 Combine all the ingredients for the batter in a bowl and whisk well together. The quantity of water given is only a guide—the batter should be thick, but still drop off a spoon, so add more water if needed.

2 Mix the onions into the batter with a spoon. Fill a wok with oil to a depth of 2–3in (5–7.5cm), or use a deep-fryer. Heat the oil to 325–350°F (160–180°C).

3 With two spoons, shape small portions of the onion batter into patties and drop into the hot oil. Fry until golden brown. It will take 3–4 minutes to fry the 12–15 bhajis. Drain on paper towels.

COOKING BHAJIS

■ If the batter gets too thin, add extra besan flour to thicken it. You may also have to increase the spicing by a fraction to maintain the flavors.
■ Sometimes onion bhajis need to be fried twice if the onions are very watery. If this is the case, part-fry the onion bhajis, remove, and drain on paper towels. Press more towels on top to dry, then fry again in hot oil until crisp. The patties will be flat.

KADHAI JHINGA

Kadhai is the Hindi name for a wok. This is a recipe for shrimp cooked with tomatoes. Kadhai cooking is a style that has its own set of essential spices. Extremely fresh ingredients and quick cooking are the key to good kadhai dishes.

4 tbsp vegetable oil

1 tsp crushed garlic

4 tsp coriander seeds, pounded in a mortar

3 dried, hot, red chilies, roughly crushed

6 large tomatoes, roughly chopped

1 tsp hot chili powder

1 tsp fenugreek leaf powder

1 tsp finely chopped fresh ginger

1 green bell pepper, cut into julienne

20 large raw shrimp, peeled and deveined (p126)

1½ tsp garam masala

2 tbsp finely chopped cilantro

1 Heat 3 tbsp of the oil in a wok or heavy-based pan. Add the garlic, 3 tsp of the pounded coriander seeds, and the crushed chilies. Stir, then cook until the spices crackle and the garlic turns golden brown, 1–2 minutes.

2 Add the tomatoes and a pinch of salt, cover with a lid, and cook until the tomatoes are soft, 8–10 minutes. Remove the lid, add the chili powder, fenugreek, and remaining coriander, and cook until the fat separates from the sauce, 3–5 minutes longer.

3 Heat the remaining oil in another pan. Add the ginger and bell pepper, and sauté for 1 minute. Add the shrimp and stir until almost cooked, 3–4 minutes.

4 Add the sauce to the shrimp and cook until they turn pink, 2–3 minutes longer. Sprinkle with the garam masala and cilantro. Serve the dish in the wok or pan, with an Indian bread like chapatti, roti, or naan (p362).

Variations
Similar weights of boiled chickpeas, soft spring vegetables, fish, and chicken, cut into small pieces, can be cooked following this recipe. If your tomatoes are a bit sour, add 1 tsp sugar. A little tomato paste can be added to enhance the color of the dish.

PANEER & BABY CORN WITH GINGER

Foods cooked on a tawa, or griddle, are common in India, and many of the preparations that adorn roadside cafés are cooked in this way.

1⅓lb (600g) paneer, cut into 1in (2.5cm) cubes

6 cups vegetable oil

1 tsp ajwain seeds or thyme leaves

1 tsp coriander seeds

2 tbsp minced fresh ginger

1 tsp minced hot green chili

2 onions, finely chopped

1 tsp salt

1 tbsp finely diced red bell pepper

1 tbsp finely diced green bell pepper

2 tomatoes, finely chopped

1 tsp hot chili powder

1 tsp fenugreek leaf powder

1 tsp garam masala

4oz (115g) baby corn, sliced in half

For serving

2 tbsp minced cilantro

1 tbsp fresh ginger julienne

1 scallion, cut into thin strips

First, deep-fry the paneer for 2–3 minutes in the vegetable oil (see opposite), then set aside for later combination with the freshly cooked tawa masala (see opposite).

TADKA DAL

This is an easy dish of dried legumes highly seasoned with chili and garlic. The technique used to season the dish is called variously tadka, bhagar, or chowkna.

1½ cups yellow split peas or lentils
1 tsp ground turmeric
4 cups water
1 tbsp vegetable oil
1 tsp butter or ghee
1 tsp minced garlic
1 tsp hot chili powder
2 tomatoes, chopped
1 tsp salt
1 tsp chopped cilantro
½ tomato, julienned, for garnish

1 In a heavy-based pan, bring the split peas or lentils to a boil with the turmeric and water. Simmer until the split peas or lentils are cooked, approximately 15–20 minutes.

2 In a sauté pan, heat the oil and butter, and fry the garlic until it is lightly browned, about 2 minutes. Add the chili powder and sauté for 1 minute. Add the tomatoes and cook for 3–4 minutes longer.

3 Add the spiced tomato mixture and the salt to the cooked lentils and simmer for 5–7 minutes. Sprinkle with chopped cilantro and the julienned tomato, and serve hot.

DEEP-FRYING PANEER

Paneer—Indian cottage cheese—is very different from cottage cheese in Western countries. It is cooked as a vegetable and used on its own or in combination with true vegetables, either as the main dish or as an accompaniment. Paneer has no taste of its own, so mixes easily with other flavored ingredients, while providing texture to the dish. To use in the dish opposite, deep-fry the cheese in hot oil until lightly browned, then keep in lukewarm water until required.

MAKING THE TAWA MASALA

When making this accompaniment for the paneer, take care not to char the spices or onions over too high a heat, or you will have to start again.

1 Heat a little oil in a frying pan. Add the ajwain and coriander seeds, minced ginger, and green chili. Sauté until the spices crackle, about 1 minute, then add the onions and salt.

2 Cook until the onions are translucent, 3–5 minutes. Add the bell peppers and tomatoes, and cook until soft, about 2 minutes.

3 Add the powdered spices and cook until the fat separates out. Add the paneer and baby corn to the sauce and simmer for 3–5 minutes. Taste and adjust the seasoning, if necessary. Garnish with the chopped cilantro, ginger julienne, and scallion.

Variations

Most vegetables, such as diced blanched carrots and potatoes, zucchini, and bell peppers, are suitable for tawa cooking. Even meat, poultry, and seafood, if cut small, can be cooked by this method, using equivalent weights to the paneer.

MAKING BHUNA GOSHT

Bhuna literally means roasted, but for this type of preparation the term can also mean sautéed. The lamb is marinated in yogurt before being cooked in a spicy paste. Chili and turmeric are used in the marinade, but the dish's other spices are all cooked in oil to extract their flavors.

1 Mix together the salt and yogurt in a stainless steel bowl, then stir in the chili, turmeric, and lamb. Let marinate for 15 minutes. Mix the poppy seeds with the ginger, and grind to a fine paste in a mortar with a pestle.

2 In the mortar, grind the cloves, coriander powder, cinnamon sticks, cardamom, and garlic to a fine paste. Heat the oil in a deep saucepan and sauté the onions until lightly browned, 5–7 minutes. Add the spices and sauté for 2–3 minutes.

3 Add the lamb and its marinade and stir well to mix with the spice mixture. Cook on a low heat until the lamb is tender, about 30 minutes. Stir in the butter.

MAKING COCONUT CURRY SAUCE

This coconut curry sauce is used opposite as the basis for a fish curry, but it serves equally well as a basis for chicken and vegetable curries. It has the strong flavorings of southern India.

1 Heat the coconut oil in a wide saucepan and fry 10 of the curry leaves until crisp. Remove with a perforated spoon and drain on paper towels. Set aside for the garnish. Reheat the oil and add the onions, chilies, and garlic.

2 Add the remaining 10 curry leaves and cook until the onion is translucent, 3–5 minutes. Add the remaining salt and turmeric, and pour in the coconut milk. Bring the sauce to a simmer, then let simmer for 5 minutes.

REHEATING

■ Meen molee should be prepared close to serving, but if you have to hold the dish for a while, you can keep it warm, preferably with the fish separate from the sauce.

■ The sauce may thicken while being kept warm, but can be thinned down with 3–4 tbsp of warm water during reheating. Add the fish after the sauce has been reheated.

BHUNA GOSHT

This lamb dish is often seen on the menus of Indian restaurants. It is easy to prepare and delicious with rice or Indian breads.

1 tsp salt, or to taste
1 cup plain yogurt
½ tsp hot chili powder
½ tsp ground turmeric
1lb 2oz (500g) boneless lamb, cut into ½in (1cm) cubes
1½ tsp poppy seeds
1in (2.5cm) piece of fresh ginger
3 whole cloves
1 tsp ground coriander
2 cinnamon sticks, each about 1in (2.5cm) long
3 green cardamom pods
1 black cardamom pod
8 garlic cloves
3 tbsp vegetable oil
2 onions, thinly sliced
1 tbsp butter
For serving
1 tsp garam masala
pinch of ginger julienne
1 tbsp chopped cilantro
10 cashew nuts, deep-fried

Prepare the bhuna gosht (see left). To serve, sprinkle the garam masala, ginger julienne, cilantro, and cashew nuts over the dish.

MEEN MOLEE

Curry in India means a sauce preparation, so to use the word to describe a whole range of Indian foods is misleading. This fish curry is one of the simplest dishes and needs little advance planning. The sauce is made by simmering coconut milk with flavorings, and the fish is then poached in it. In Indian cooking, fish, poultry, or meats are marinated with salt to draw out excess moisture, so that during cooking the flavors will be better absorbed.

4 small fillets of sea bass or porgy, about 5oz (150g) each, skin on
1 tsp salt
1 tsp ground turmeric
2 tbsp coconut oil
20 curry leaves
2 onions, finely sliced
6 hot green chilies, slit lengthwise
3 garlic cloves, sliced into fine strips
1¾ cups coconut milk (p305)
small bunch of cilantro, chopped

Variations

Some chefs add black mustard seeds to this recipe. If desired, stir in 1 tsp black mustard seeds before the onions. Let them splutter in the oil, then continue with the recipe.

Other seafood can be cooked in the sauce. Use the equivalent weight of shrimp, lobster, scallops, or whatever you prefer, and adjust the cooking time accordingly.

1 Score the fish fillets. Mix ½ tsp of the salt with ½ tsp turmeric and gently rub into the fish. Let marinate for at least 30 minutes, or until required.

2 Make the coconut curry sauce (see opposite). Add the fish fillets, skin-side up, and simmer very gently until the fish is just cooked, 3–5 minutes. Garnish with the fried curry leaves and cilantro, and serve.

MARCUS WAREING

The first step in ensuring success in meat cooking is to purchase meat of good quality, if possible from a knowledgeable butcher. When searching for a supplier in your area, try to find a butcher who prepares the cuts on site. Ask the staff where they obtain their meat: A really good butcher will know the farmer, the breed, and when the animal was slaughtered. Some supermarkets now encourage the sale of local meats by providing specialist meat counters in their stores. This is a good service as long as trained staff are available to advise and assist you with your purchase.

When purchasing ground meat, always buy meat that was ground on site.

Farmers' markets can be a source of good meat, and you also have the opportunity to talk to the farmers about their animals and produce. In the United States alone there are 3,000 farmers' markets supporting 20,000 farmers. If you go further still and visit the farms themselves, you are able to assess the cleanliness and general appearance of the farm before buying. Some producers market their meat via mail order and the internet, although for the consumer these have the disadvantage of not allowing the meat to be viewed before it is purchased.

Selecting meat Good meat has little odor. Lamb and beef fat should be slightly creamy, whereas pork fat should be white. Meat should not be unduly moist, and never slimy. The most tender cuts are from the loin and round (where the muscles are less active), and these cuts are also the most expensive. However, lesser cuts of meat make equally stunning meals if cooked correctly.

With the exception of organ or variety meats, which should be eaten as soon as possible, meat has to be hung for some time after slaughter. If cooked immediately after slaughter meat is quite acidic, due to the lactic acid present at the time of death (lactic acid is present in all exercising muscle). Rigor mortis also affects meat and can remain in a carcass for up to 30 hours.

The optimum period of time for which meat should be hung varies according to the animal and the breed. Veal and pork can be hung for as little as a week, lamb for 1–3 weeks, and some beef for up to 5 weeks. Venison is normally hung for 1–3 weeks, while rabbit requires just 4–5 days. The main reason for hanging meat is to maximize its tenderness, but remember that the longer the meat is hung, the "gamier" and stronger the taste will be.

Meat is hung for a shorter period than in centuries past for a number of reasons. Modern breeding techniques produce animals with relatively tender flesh, so the meat requires less hanging time. Further, most westerners have lost their taste for the stronger flavors of well-hung meat. Hanging meat takes time and uses storage space, leading to expenses that make the meat business less financially attractive to producers and supermarkets. A further expense is incurred by the weight of the carcass actually falling slightly during hanging—in a market driven by price per pound, lost weight equals lost earnings. Large producers therefore minimize meat hanging so that the produce can go into the food chain quickly, tying up their capital for as little time as possible.

Storing meat Raw meat carries bacteria and should be stored carefully to keep all your food safe from contamination. In warmer countries, newly purchased meat should be carried home in an insulated bag to ensure that it does not become too warm. Before refrigeration, the meat should be removed from any plastic packaging to prevent it from sweating. Place the meat at the bottom of the refrigerator, and never above cooked foods that could be contaminated by liquids dripping from the uncooked meat. Ideally, the refrigerator in which you store your meat should be maintained at a temperature of 39°F (4°C) and should not exceed 46°F (8°C).

ROASTING

One of the simplest of culinary techniques, roasting requires little more than basic skills in managing temperature and timing. It is also one of the least labor-intensive—meat needs little or no attention during cooking, apart from occasional basting with fat.

Roasting time is calculated by the weight of the meat and the degree of doneness you desire. For timing to be accurate, meat should be at room temperature before cooking or it will take longer to cook, and it will steam rather than roast. Take the meat out of the refrigerator at least 30–60 minutes before roasting, and wait to season until just before you put it in the oven. Salt will draw the juices from raw meat if it is left to stand for any length of time, resulting in dry meat.

A meat thermometer is useful to check the internal temperature of meat accurately, but is not essential.

ROAST RIB OF BEEF

To begin with, the meat is seared in a hot oven for 15 minutes, then the temperature is reduced. This technique ensures a good, appetizing color on the outside, and also helps prevent the juices from "bleeding" and the meat from becoming dry.

I like to serve this roast in traditional British style—with Yorkshire puddings (see opposite), gravy (p38), and English mustard and horseradish sauce alongside.

Serves 8–10

4-rib beef rib roast (standing rib roast), about 10lb (4.5kg), chine bone removed

¼ cup olive or vegetable oil

2 large sprigs of thyme

1 Preheat the oven to 425°F (220°C). Calculate the roasting time according to the precise weight of the roast. Stand the beef, fat-side up, in a roasting pan and brush with the oil. Scatter with leaves from the thyme sprigs, season, and place in the oven.

2 After 15 minutes, reduce the oven temperature to 350°F (180°C). Continue roasting the beef for the remainder of the calculated cooking time, basting occasionally with the rendered fat in the pan. For the most accurate result, test the roast for doneness by using a meat thermometer.

RESTING MEAT

Letting the meat rest for 15–30 minutes after roasting allows the muscles to relax, so the juices are retained within the meat and carving is easier. The meat will not go cold during this time—as long as it is not cut into, it will stay hot inside. This leaves plenty of time for you to make the gravy, and attend to any last-minute cooking of vegetables to serve with the meat.

3 Transfer the roast to a carving board, cover loosely with foil, and let rest in a warm place for 15–30 minutes before carving.

4 To carve, stand the roast with the ends of the bones up. Steadying the meat with a carving fork inserted into the fatty side, and using a sawing action with the carving knife, cut downward between the bones and the meat to separate them. Discard the bones.

YORKSHIRE PUDDINGS

Combine 1⅔ cups all-purpose flour, 2 eggs, 1 cup whole milk, 1 cup water, ⅔ cup olive oil, and a pinch of salt in a food processor and process to make a smooth, creamy batter, 2–3 minutes. Cover the processor bowl and let rest at room temperature for at least 3 hours.

Preheat the oven to 400°F (200°C). Put 1 tbsp olive oil each in 10 cups of a standard muffin pan and put into the oven to heat for 5 minutes.

Pulse the batter briefly in the food processor, then pour into the muffin cups. Return the pan to the oven and bake until risen and golden, about 25 minutes. Tap the pan on the work surface: The puddings should then lift out easily. Serve immediately.

5 Turn the boneless piece of meat fat-side up on the carving board. Holding it steady with the fork, cut downward across the grain into thin slices, again using a sawing action with the knife.

Tender beef with gravy and Yorkshire puddings is a British favorite

ROAST LEG OF LAMB WITH ROSEMARY & GARLIC

Studding a roast with rosemary and garlic has
a twofold effect: It imparts flavor to the meat,
and makes the roast look attractive when served.
This technique can be applied to any roast.

Serves 4–6

1 bone-in leg of lamb, about 5½lb (2.5kg)
12 sprigs of rosemary
6 garlic cloves
olive oil for brushing

1 Preheat the oven to 425°F (220°C). Calculate
the roasting time according to the precise
weight of the roast. Make 12 incisions in the fat
side of the lamb using the tip of a small, sharp
knife. Tear the tops off the rosemary and halve
each garlic clove lengthwise. Insert the rosemary
and garlic into the slits in the meat.

2 Brush the fat with oil and season liberally.
Put the lamb in a roasting pan and roast
until lightly browned, about 15 minutes.

3 Reduce the temperature to 350°F (180°C) and continue roasting for the remainder of the
cooking time, basting occasionally with the rendered fat in the pan. When the lamb is done,
transfer to a carving board. Cover loosely with foil and let rest in a warm place for 15–30 minutes.

4 To carve, hold the roast upright by the bone, and slice off the plump "lobe" of meat (the front of the thigh) by following along the bone with your knife. Now stand the roast on its cut surface and slice off the larger lobe of meat on the other side (the back of the thigh) by working your knife along the bone with an even sawing action.

5 Remove the remaining meat from the bone so you have three chunks of boneless meat. Lay the chunks on their flat, cut sides, and carve thick slices downward and against the grain. The slices should be thick, almost like steaks. If they are too thin, they will be bloodless and the meat will be dry. Serve one slice per person.

SLOW-ROAST SHOULDER OF PORK

For me, the cracklings (crisp skin) on a pork roast enhance the appeal of the meat. To get the crispest cracklings, score the skin, rub it with salt and oil, roast at a high temperature for the first 15 minutes, and then do not baste at all during the remainder of the roasting.

Serves 6–8

7¾lb (3.5kg) skin-on boneless pork shoulder roast

coarse sea or kosher salt

¼ cup vegetable oil

2 red onions, quartered lengthwise

2 white onions, quartered lengthwise

2 large lemons, quartered lengthwise

2 tbsp clear honey

2–3 tbsp chopped sage

1 wine glass of dry white wine or hard cider

sage leaves for garnish

1 Preheat the oven to 425°F (220°C). Score the skin widthwise using a very sharp knife or a scalpel, keeping the lines parallel and close together. First work from the middle toward one edge, then turn the meat around and work from the middle toward the other edge. This is easier than scoring in a long line.

2 Massage the skin liberally with sea salt, then rub all over with a little oil. Stand the pork, skin-side up, on a rack in a roasting pan and splash a little oil in the bottom of the pan. Roast for 15 minutes, then reduce the oven temperature to 300°F (150°C) and continue roasting for 2 hours longer, without basting.

3 Remove the pork and rack from the pan and set aside. Put the pan on the stovetop and sauté the onions and lemons until just caramelized, about 10 minutes. Add the honey and sage, then push this mixture to the outside of the pan and set the pork in the middle.

4 Return to the oven and roast for 1¼ hours, basting the onions and lemons occasionally, but not the pork. The cracklings will be crisp, and the meat will be tender when pierced through the middle with a thin, metal skewer.

5 Transfer the pork to a carving board, cover loosely with foil, and let rest in a warm place for 15–30 minutes. Transfer the onions and lemons to a dish using a slotted spoon; cover and keep warm.

6 Pour or skim off as much oily fat from the pan juices as possible. Place the pan on the stovetop and deglaze with the wine, scraping the pan bottom to release the sediments. Simmer until reduced by one-third, then season and strain. Keep this pan gravy warm.

7 Steadying the meat with a carving fork, slice between the cracklings and the meat so the cracklings lift off in one piece.

8 With kitchen scissors or a sharp knife, cut the cracklings in half crosswise to give short pieces that are easy to eat.

9 Carve the meat downward and across the grain into thick slices, using a sawing action with the carving knife.

Arrange the pork and cracklings on a platter with the onions and lemons, and garnish with sage; serve the gravy alongside

BAKING

When meat is baked in the oven, it is covered, and so protected from direct heat. Coverings can be pastry, mashed or sliced potatoes, or thick layers of vegetables. This method suits lean, tender cuts and cheaper tough cuts, both of which need protection to prevent them from drying out. For the meat to be a good, appetizing color, it should always be seared or browned before covering and baking, but once this is done and the dish is in the oven, it will need little or no further attention.

SHEPHERD'S PIE

Baking ground lamb under a plump pillow of rich and creamy potato purée transforms this humble cut of meat into a very special dish. This is no ordinary shepherd's pie.

6 small shallots

1 large carrot

2 tbsp vegetable oil

3½ tbsp unsalted butter

1 bay leaf

1 sprig of fresh thyme

1lb 2oz (500g) ground lamb

1 tbsp tomato paste

dash of Worcestershire sauce

4 cups lamb or chicken stock

1⅔ cups frozen peas

piccalilli for serving (see opposite—optional)

For the topping

1lb 2oz (500g) floury baking potatoes, peeled and cut into large chunks

½ cup milk

½ cup butter

2 egg yolks

PIPING

I like to pipe the mashed potato because it gives a smoother, neater finish, but you can just spread it on with a metal spatula, if you prefer.

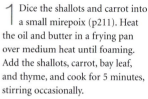

1 Dice the shallots and carrot into a small mirepoix (p211). Heat the oil and butter in a frying pan over medium heat until foaming. Add the shallots, carrot, bay leaf, and thyme, and cook for 5 minutes, stirring occasionally.

2 Add the ground lamb and cook until it is all colored, stirring and pressing with a fork to break up any lumps. Season, then stir in the tomato paste, Worcestershire sauce, and stock. Cook until reduced to a saucelike consistency, about 20 minutes, adding the peas for the last 5 minutes of cooking.

3 Put the potatoes in a pan of cold water, bring to a boil, and simmer until soft but not mushy, about 20 minutes. Drain and press through a potato ricer while still hot. Warm the milk and butter until the butter has melted, then mix into the potato along with the egg yolks and seasoning.

4 Preheat the oven to 375°F (190°C). Pour the lamb mixture into a baking dish and spread out evenly. Spoon the potato purée into a pastry bag fitted with a large, round tip and pipe the purée in straight lines on top.

5 Smooth the piped potato with a metal spatula, then mark a pattern on top by drawing up the end of the spatula at regular intervals. Bake until the top of the shepherd's pie is golden brown, about 30 minutes.

PICCALILLI

Whenever my mother made shepherd's pie, she always put a jar of piccalilli on the table. Now I do the same, to continue the tradition.

Makes 2 large jars

12 pearl onions
1 head of cauliflower, cut into small florets
2 large gherkins, sliced
2½ cups white wine vinegar
1¼ cups malt vinegar
½ tsp chopped fresh, hot red chili
1¾ cups sugar
⅓ cup English mustard powder
¼ cup ground turmeric
¼ cup cornstarch

Let the pie stand for 10 minutes, then serve straight from the dish

1 Blanch the onions in boiling salted water for 2 minutes; drain and refresh in cold water, then peel. Mix the onions in a bowl with the cauliflower and gherkins. Bring the vinegars to a boil with the chili. Cool, then strain. You can get to this stage the day before, then leave the vegetables in salted water overnight.

2 Mix the sugar, mustard, turmeric, and cornstarch to a paste with a little of the cold vinegar. Boil the remaining vinegar, whisk into the paste, and return to the pan. Boil until thickened, about 3 minutes.

3 Drain the vegetables, return them to the bowl, and mix in the vinegar and seasoning. The piccalilli can be served when cold, or kept in a sealed jar in the refrigerator for up to 1 month.

PORK CHOPS WITH CARAMELIZED ONIONS

This is a dish for all sage and onion lovers. The pork chops are smothered in sweetly caramelized onions, which ooze into the meat during baking to give an exquisite flavor.

5 tbsp olive oil
6 tbsp butter
4 pork loin chops
8 small onions, thinly sliced
2 garlic cloves, sliced
leaves from 6 sprigs of thyme
leaves from 1 bunch of sage, roughly chopped
1 tsp dried sage
4 bay leaves

1 Preheat the oven to 350°F (180°C). In a large, heavy frying pan, heat 2 tbsp of the oil with 2 tbsp of the butter until they are just beginning to turn brown.

2 Place the chops in the pan and cook quickly over medium-high heat, turning, until well colored. Transfer the chops to a roasting pan and season. Heat the remaining oil and another 2 tbsp of the butter in the frying pan and sauté the onions until well colored and almost caramelized, 10–15 minutes.

3 Spread the onions over the chops and sprinkle with the garlic, thyme, and both chopped and dried sage. Dot with small pieces of the remaining butter and put a bay leaf on each chop. Season well. Cover with foil and bake for 45–60 minutes. Transfer the chops and onions to plates and keep warm.

Boil the cooking juices until reduced, then spoon them over the chops and serve

CHEF'S TIPS

■ This is my mother's recipe, which I have adapted. My parents liked their chops well done, so my mother used to put the onions over the chops raw and bake the chops for 2–2½ hours in a low oven. I prefer my meat less well cooked, so I caramelize the onions first to cut down on the baking time.

■ Use as many onions as you like—they break down during baking and mingle their juices with the butter and herbs to become so deliciously sweet and sticky that you can never have too much.

VENISON RAGOUT

I think of this as the French equivalent of Lancashire hotchpotch—a homey, comforting stew in which potatoes make the meat go further.

2 tbsp olive oil

2 onions, finely chopped

2¼lb (1kg) boneless leg of venison, diced

2 cups veal stock

1 cup brown ale

1 garlic clove, chopped

2 tbsp paprika

1 tsp caraway seeds

1lb 2oz (500g) boiling potatoes, peeled and cut into ¼in (5mm) cubes

3 tomatoes, peeled, seeded, and chopped

¼ cup chopped parsley

1 Heat the oil in a large stovetop-to-oven casserole. Add the onions and sauté over low heat until softened but not colored, 2–3 minutes. Remove with a slotted spoon and set aside.

2 Add half the meat and fry over high heat until well browned. Remove and repeat with the remaining meat. Lower the heat to medium and return all the meat and the onions to the pot. Toss to mix. Add the stock, ale, garlic, and spices, season well, and bring to a boil. Cover, reduce the heat, and simmer for 2 hours.

3 Add the potatoes and tomatoes, and continue simmering until the venison is really tender, about 1 hour longer. Check the seasoning, then sprinkle with the chopped parsley and serve.

WILD BOAR

This stew can also be made using wild boar instead of venison. The flavor of boar can be mild and delicate or very gamy—ask your butcher for advice. Boneless shoulder, either sliced or diced, is a good cut for stewing.

BRAISING & STEWING

The connective tissue, fat, and sinew that hold the muscles of meat together are broken down by braising and stewing, rendering the meat tender and releasing gelatinous juices to create a rich, full-bodied gravy. Tougher, cheaper cuts respond well, and marinating before cooking adds flavor, with melt-in-the-mouth results.

The differences between braising and stewing are subtle. In a braise, the meat is usually in large pieces (if the cut is whole, it is called a pot roast) and is cooked in enough liquid barely to cover, whereas in a stew the pieces of meat are smaller and there is generally more liquid. There are two methods of starting the cooking. The meat can be seared in hot fat until colored before the addition of vegetables and liquid, or the meat, vegetables, and liquid can be put into the pan raw at the beginning. In either case, the subsequent cooking is always long and slow, either on the stovetop or in the oven. Cooking times are intended as a guide: The meat is ready when it is tender and moist, by which time the gravy will be rich.

IRISH STEW

A humble cut of meat combined with wholesome ingredients and the clever use of two types of potatoes creates a perfect dish to my mind. Floury-textured potatoes break down to thicken the sauce, while waxy potatoes keep their shape and looks.

2lb (900g) boneless lamb stew meat from the neck or shoulder
1½lb (675g) carrots
1 onion
1lb (450g) floury baking potatoes
1lb (450g) waxy new potatoes
5 cups hot lamb stock
leaves from 6 sprigs of thyme
chopped parsley for garnish

1 Cut the lamb across the grain into large chunks about 2in (5cm) thick. Cut the carrots into bite-sized pieces, and thickly slice the onion. Peel both kinds of potatoes and cut them into 1in (2.5cm) chunks.

2 Put the meat into a pot and pour in the stock. Bring to a boil over high heat, then reduce to a simmer. Cook, uncovered, for 30 minutes.

3 During simmering, use a large spoon to skim off the froth and impurities as they rise to the surface.

4 Remove the lamb and set aside; strain the stock. Return the lamb and stock to the cleaned pot and bring to a boil. Reduce the heat, cover, and simmer gently for 10 minutes. Add the onion, floury potatoes, and carrots, then continue simmering, covered, for 10 minutes.

5 Add the thyme and waxy potatoes. Cover again and simmer until the lamb is very tender, 15–20 minutes longer. The floury potatoes will break down to thicken the sauce; the waxy potatoes will retain their shape. Remove from the heat and let stand, covered, for about 15 minutes.

Check the seasoning before serving, sprinkled generously with chopped parsley

RABBIT WITH GARLIC & THYME

Rabbit is a tender meat that cooks quickly, so I have used a cartouche of parchment paper to prevent the cooking liquid from evaporating during the short stewing time. If you are cooking a stew for a long time, you should use a tight lid rather than a cartouche. With a lid, moisture drips down inside the pan and creates extra liquid, which develops into a rich sauce over time.

4 tbsp olive oil

6 rabbit legs

1 onion, thinly sliced

24 garlic cloves, peeled

15 sprigs of thyme

1 bay leaf

1 tsp tomato paste

½ cup dry white wine

6 ripe tomatoes, peeled, seeded, and chopped

2½ cups chicken stock

6 scallions, with 2in (5cm) of the green part attached

12 baby onions, peeled

4 tbsp unsalted butter

6 thin slices of prosciutto or Bayonne ham

1 Heat 2 tbsp of the oil in a wide, heavy pot, add the rabbit, and brown on all sides over medium-high heat. Season the rabbit and lift out; set aside. Drain off the excess fat from the pot.

2 Add the remaining oil to the pot and cook the onion over medium heat, stirring occasionally, until softened, 5–6 minutes. Add 23 of the garlic cloves and cook for 2 more minutes before adding 5 of the thyme sprigs, the bay leaf, the tomato paste, and wine.

3 Bring to a boil and simmer for 1 minute, then return the rabbit to the pot. Add the tomatoes and stock. Stir well, then cover with a cartouche (see opposite). Simmer until the rabbit pieces are tender, 35–45 minutes.

4 Blanch both kinds of onions in a pan of boiling salted water for 3–4 minutes, then drain. Melt half the butter in the pan and add the onions with 5 sprigs of thyme and the remaining garlic clove (crushed). Cover with buttered parchment paper and soften over low heat for 4–5 minutes.

5 Meanwhile, broil the slices of prosciutto until crisp; set aside. Remove the rabbit and garlic from their pot and keep warm. Pass the liquid through a coarse strainer into a clean pan. Add the onions, the remaining thyme leaves, and butter, and bring to a boil.

6 Check the sauce for seasoning then pour over the rabbit and garlic in a warmed serving bowl. Surround with the crisp prosciutto.

Making a cartouche

It is as easy as child's play to make a cartouche, which is a disk of parchment paper cut to be the perfect fit for your pan. Use it instead of, or in addition to, the pan lid. When placed in direct contact with the surface of the stew in the pan, it will prevent evaporation. If the meat is not covered by liquid, a cartouche will also help to prevent it from drying out.

1 Cut a large rectangle of parchment paper. Fold it lengthwise in half, then fold it crosswise in half.

2 With the closed corner as the point, fold the paper diagonally in half, then in half again to make a fan shape.

3 Holding the point over the center of the pan, cut the paper about 1in (2.5cm) larger than the circumference, using the edge of the pan as a guide. Snip off the point and unfold the paper to reveal a disk with a hole in the middle.

4 Fit the cartouche in the pan so that it rests right on top of the stew and about 1in (2.5cm) up the sides of the pan.

HARE IN RED WINE

This is how I learned to cook hare at Guy Savoy in Paris, where it was served with pommes purée. Now I make this to serve at home to friends—it is a lovely, rustic winter dish. If you are going to make it, allow plenty of time. The hare needs to marinate for 24 hours and then gently braise for a further 8 hours.

Serves 4–6

1 hare, cut up
4 cups chicken stock
4 cups veal stock
2 shallots, thinly sliced
For the marinade
3 quarts (3 liters) red wine
2 tbsp olive oil
1 large carrot, finely diced
1 large leek, finely diced
1 onion, finely diced
10 garlic cloves, crushed
1 bouquet garni (p75)

1 To make the marinade, boil the wine in a pot until reduced by half. Heat the oil in a frying pan, add the vegetables and garlic, and cook over medium-high heat until golden brown, 5–6 minutes. Pour in the wine reduction and boil until reduced by half again, then pour into a shallow, nonreactive container. Add the bouquet garni and let the marinade cool.

2 Add the pieces of hare to the cold marinade and turn to coat. Cover tightly and marinate in the refrigerator for 24 hours, turning the pieces of hare occasionally during this time.

3 Transfer the hare and marinade to a large, heavy pot and pour in the stocks, ensuring that the meat is completely submerged (add some water, if necessary). Season and add the shallots. Bring slowly to a boil, then reduce the heat to very low. Cover and braise for 8 hours.

BRAISED LAMB SHANKS

This really is a superb dish for a family meal, particularly if you like succulent well-done meat that literally falls off the bone. It is simple to prepare, because the vegetables are cooked with the meat and the gravy evolves naturally, cutting down on the number of pans that need to be washed. When lamb shanks are braised, meat shrinkage is minimal, so a little goes a long way. I wish my mother had known this when feeding the six of us.

4 lamb shanks

2 tbsp olive oil

1 carrot, cut into ⅜in (1cm) dice

1 onion, cut into ⅜in (1cm) dice

2 celery stalks, cut into ⅜in (1cm) dice

2–3 sprigs of thyme

2 bay leaves

2 garlic cloves, finely chopped

¼ cup tomato paste

3 cups dry white wine

about 4 cups lamb or chicken stock

2 tbsp minced rosemary

For the marinade

⅔ cup olive oil

1 whole head of garlic, smashed with skin on

4 large sprigs of rosemary

2 bay leaves

1 Put the lamb shanks and all the marinade ingredients in a bowl and turn the shanks to coat. Cover the bowl with plastic wrap and let marinate in the refrigerator for 24 hours, turning the shanks occasionally.

2 Heat the oil in a large stovetop-to-oven casserole and sweat the carrot, onion, and celery over a gentle heat for 5 minutes without browning. Add the thyme, bay leaves, garlic, tomato paste, and wine. Bring to a boil and simmer until reduced by about half.

3 Meanwhile, heat a heavy frying pan over medium-high heat and add the lamb shanks with their marinade. Season the meat, then brown well on all sides, 10–15 minutes. Preheat the oven to 350°F (180°C).

4 Transfer the lamb to the casserole and pour in the stock. Bring to a boil, then cover and place in the oven. Braise until the meat is tender, about 2 hours. Remove the shanks and keep them warm. Skim off all the excess fat from the cooking liquid, then boil it until reduced to a saucelike consistency. Check the seasoning.

Serve the lamb shanks with a generous amount of sauce and a sprinkling of minced rosemary

DAUBE OF PORK WITH APRICOTS

Braised dishes like this are good made ahead and reheated before serving—not only is this convenient if you are working, but the flavor improves with keeping. Start marinating the pork 2 days before you intend to serve it, then cook it the day before.

Serves 6

sunflower oil for frying

2¼lb (1kg) boneless lean pork shoulder, cut into 3in (7.5cm) slices

12 dried apricots

1¼ cups dry white wine

1 cup orange juice

sugar to taste

about 1 cup veal stock

about 1 cup brown chicken stock

For the marinade

1½ cups full-bodied red wine

1 cup olive oil

3–4 plum tomatoes, halved lengthwise

6 garlic cloves, crushed

1 carrot, sliced

2 celery stalks, chopped

1 leek, trimmed and sliced

1 onion, sliced

tiny pinch of cumin seeds

tiny pinch of fennel seeds

½ bunch of mint, chopped

few sprigs of thyme

1 bay leaf

1 Heat a small amount of sunflower oil in a heavy roasting pan over medium-high heat and fry the pork slices, in a single layer, until rich dark brown on both sides. This should take approximately 10–15 minutes.

2 Mix the marinade ingredients in a bowl with some seasoning. Remove the roasting pan from the heat and drain off excess fat, then spoon the marinade over the pork. Let cool, then cover and let marinate in the refrigerator for 24 hours.

3 Combine the apricots with the wine, orange juice, and a little sugar in a saucepan and bring to a boil. Remove from the heat and let soak overnight to rehydrate.

4 Preheat the oven to 350°F (180°C). Transfer the pork slices from the marinade to a stovetop-to-oven casserole. Boil the marinade in a saucepan for 15 minutes, skimming off any foam. Add the stocks and bring to a boil, then pour into the casserole, making sure the meat is covered. Cover and braise in the oven for 2 hours.

5 Transfer the pork to a serving dish and keep warm. Pass the liquid through a fine strainer into a saucepan and reheat, boiling to reduce the sauce if it seems a bit thin. Add the drained apricots and heat through, then taste to check the seasoning.

Spoon the apricots and sauce over the pork and serve

BRAISED OXTAIL

This braise is in the oven for a fairly long time, so the vegetables are not cut small—they would disintegrate into the sauce and make it cloudy. The opposite is true for the finely diced vegetable garnish at the end—it is only briefly blanched so the tiny pieces retain their shape.

2 oxtails, each cut into 4 sections (ask your butcher to do this or see step 1)

4oz (125g) carrots

4oz (125g) onions

4oz (125g) celery stalks

4oz (125g) leeks

3–4 tbsp olive oil or beef drippings

1lb 2oz (500g) tomatoes

8 sprigs of fresh thyme

2 bay leaves

4 garlic cloves, crushed

1¼ cups red wine

about 4 cups veal stock or chicken stock

For the vegetable garnish

1 carrot, finely diced

1 onion, finely diced

2 celery stalks, finely diced

½ small leek, finely diced

4 tomatoes, peeled, seeded, and finely diced

1 heaped tbsp chopped parsley

CHEF'S TIPS

■ To deepen the flavor, the oxtail can be marinated in the wine and herbs for 48 hours before cooking.

■ If you have cut up the oxtail yourself, there will be tail ends. Cook these with the oxtail sections to enrich the sauce with their marrow, then discard them before straining the sauce.

1 With a cleaver, trim off the tail ends, then chop each oxtail into four sections. If you locate the space between each joint, you will find it easier to get a clean cut. Season well. Cut the carrots, onions, celery, and leeks into a medium mirepoix (see opposite).

2 Preheat the oven to 350°F (180°C). Heat the oil in a large frying pan over medium-high heat and brown the oxtail well—let the pieces sit undisturbed until they are brown underneath before turning them. Remove with a slotted spoon and drain in a colander. In the same pan, brown the tail ends, then remove and drain.

3 Add the mirepoix and stir well with a wooden spatula to collect the meat residue from the bottom of the pan, then cook until the vegetables are browned. Stir in the tomatoes, thyme, bay leaves, and garlic, and continue to cook for a few minutes.

4 Put the oxtail pieces in a stovetop-to-oven casserole and top with the vegetables. Pour in the wine and boil over a high heat until nearly all evaporated, then add enough stock to cover the meat. Bring to a simmer, then cover with the lid and transfer to the oven. Braise until the meat is tender, 1½–2 hours.

Serve the oxtail in warmed shallow bowls, spooning the rich sauce over

MIREPOIX

This is a mixture of chopped celery, carrot, leek, and onion. The size of the vegetables varies from very large chunks to bite-sized, according to the length of time the mirepoix is to be cooked—the longer the cooking, the larger the pieces of vegetable.

Large

Used in long-cooking stocks and some braised dishes. Cut the celery, carrot, and leek into 2in (5cm) chunks. Cut the onion lengthwise into quarters and retain whole.

Medium

Used in braised dishes and stews. Cut the celery in half crosswise, then lengthwise. Gather the pieces together and cut across into ¾in (2cm) dice. Cut the carrot and leek into 2in (5cm) lengths, quarter lengthwise, and cut across into thirds. Halve the onion lengthwise, then slice across into ¾in (2cm) pieces.

Small

Used for garnishing, with a short cooking time. Cut the celery, carrot, and leek into sticks. Stack the sticks and cut across into ¼in (5mm) dice. Finely dice the onion (p242).

5 Lift out the oxtail and keep warm. Pass the sauce through a strainer into a clean pan and skim off any fat and scum. Boil until glossy, about 10 minutes, skimming often. Blanch the garnish vegetables (except the tomatoes) for 5 minutes, then drain and add to the sauce with the tomatoes and parsley. Simmer for 2 minutes.

BRAISED SHOULDER OF LAMB

In this classic example of French home cooking, the meat is braised under a loose covering of parchment paper. This allows for evaporation of the liquid, which concentrates the sauce at the same time as richly coloring the meat.

Serves 4–6

2 bone-in shoulders of baby or spring lamb

olive oil for frying

24 baby onions, peeled

6 plum tomatoes, peeled, seeded, and chopped

3 garlic cloves, roughly chopped

1 tsp cumin seeds

1 fresh, hot chili, cut in half lengthwise and seeded

3 sprigs of rosemary

½ cup Madeira

½ cup port wine

1 cup fresh orange juice

2 cups chicken stock

To finish

olive oil for frying

1 head of garlic, halved crosswise

few sprigs of thyme

few bay leaves

1 Preheat the oven to 375°F (190°C). Season the lamb well. Take a heavy frying pan large enough to accommodate one shoulder and place over a high heat. Add some olive oil and brown one of the shoulders well on all sides, basting often. Remove, and brown the second shoulder. Lay them side by side in a large roasting pan.

2 Put the onions in the frying pan, with a little more oil if needed, and sprinkle with salt. Let the onions color for 5 minutes. Then add the tomatoes, garlic, cumin, chili, and rosemary, and stir well. Add the Madeira and port, turn up the heat to high, and bring to a boil. Pour this mixture over the lamb.

3 Set the roasting pan on the stovetop over medium-high heat. Pour in the orange juice and stock, and bring to a boil. Cover the pan loosely with parchment paper and transfer to the oven. Braise for 1–1¼ hours, turning the meat occasionally and stirring the vegetables at the same time. The lamb is done when the meat on the knuckle bone shrinks away.

4 Remove from the oven and let the lamb cool completely in the pan. Lift out the lamb and chill in the refrigerator for 1 hour.

5 Lay the lamb skin-side down on a board. Using a heavy knife or a cleaver, cut each shoulder into three at the joints.

CHEF'S TIP

This is a beautiful way to cook a shoulder of baby or spring lamb, but older lamb can be cooked like this too. An extra-large roasting pan will be essential, unless you cook the shoulders in separate pans.

6 Heat a few spoonfuls of olive oil in a frying pan until very hot. Add the pieces of lamb, along with the garlic, thyme, and bay leaf, and brown over medium-high heat until the lamb is almost caramelized.

7 Meanwhile, strain the cooking liquid into a pan; reserve the vegetables but not the chili. Boil the liquid until reduced to a saucelike consistency, skimming off excess fat. Return the vegetables to the sauce and heat through.

8 Serve a chunk of meat in the middle of each shallow dish, with the sauce and vegetables spooned over and around. To get the most out of the meat, pick up the bone as you would chicken—remember, this is a homey meal.

Lamb braised like this is wonderfully tender and succulent

BOILING & STEAMING

Boiling, simmering, and poaching are very similar techniques. The main difference is the slight variation in their temperatures: When water is boiling, it is at 212°F (100°C), whereas simmering water is at 185–200°F (85–95°C), and water for poaching is slightly lower at 170–180°F (77–82°C). In a professional kitchen we use a thermometer for absolutely accurate results, but at home you can judge the difference by eye—boiling liquid moves vigorously, while simmering liquid shows a little agitation; liquid for poaching resembles more of a gentle murmuring.

With any of these three cooking methods, it is important to use the right one for each stage in a recipe. For example, meat may be boiled in the first stage, then the temperature is lowered to a simmer or a poach for the remainder of the cooking time—this is especially useful for tough cuts of meat that need long and slow cooking to make them tender. If meat is boiled continuously and vigorously throughout cooking, it becomes stringy and tough.

Meat can also be steamed (i.e. cooked in the vapor produced by boiling water), but only indirectly. In direct steaming, food is placed in a steamer or steaming basket above the water, which would make meat insipid, gray, and unappetizing, but with indirect steaming the food is sealed to protect it. A classic example of this is traditional steak and kidney pudding (p216), in which the meat is encased in suet pastry so that it cooks in its own juices to become rich and more tender.

BOILING A HAM HOCK

Ham hocks are usually cooked in a lot less time than in my recipe here, but I have found that the gentler the heat and the longer they cook, the more juicy and tender the meat becomes.

I use boiled ham for a variety of different things—sliced hot off the bone, it makes an inexpensive and comforting meal served with parsley sauce and boiled potatoes, while shredded ham is good in sandwiches and soups such as traditional pea and ham (for which I also use the strained ham stock).

2 cured, unsmoked ham hocks, 2¼lb (1kg) each
1 large onion
1 large carrot
1 large leek
2 celery stalks
10 sprigs of thyme
3 bay leaves
12 white peppercorns
handful of parsley stems
about 8 cups chicken stock

1 Put the ham hocks in a large pot. Cover with cold water and bring to a boil, then simmer for 5 minutes. Drain the hocks in a colander and rinse under cold running water, then return them to the cleaned pot. Add all the vegetables and flavorings, and pour in enough stock to cover the hocks well.

2 Bring to a boil, then cover and simmer over very low heat for 2½ hours. To check if the hocks are done, lift out one of them and pull out the small bone that lies next to the knuckle bone—it should come away easily. To serve hot, slice the meat thickly off the bone, stripping off and discarding all the skin and fat.

3 To shred the ham for use in sandwiches, soups, and terrines, let the hocks cool in the stock until you can handle them, then lift them out onto a board. Pull all the meat away from the bones and shred it into chunky pieces, discarding all the skin and fat. Strain the stock and reserve for making soup.

Caramelized boiled bacon

Here, I have taken a salty piece of bacon, boiled it and pressed it overnight, then coated it in perfumed spices and a sweet and sour caramel—flavors that everyone loves. The presentation is pure Pétrus.

Serves 6

3 carrots

2 large onions

2 celery stalks

1 large leek

12 black peppercorns, lightly crushed

2 bay leaves

small bunch of fresh thyme

6½lb (3kg) piece of slab bacon

For the spice mixture

5 tsp ground cinnamon

5 tsp ground star anise

5 tsp ground coriander seed

For the sweet and sour caramel

½ cup port wine

½ cup clear honey

½ cup rice vinegar

Cut the carrots, onions, celery, and leek into a large mirepoix (p211). Put into a very large pot with the peppercorns, bay leaves, and thyme. Add the bacon and fill the pot almost to the top with cold water. Bring to a boil, then reduce the heat and simmer, uncovered, until the bacon is tender when pierced with a skewer, about 2 hours. During simmering, skim off all the scum and replenish the water to keep the bacon submerged.

Remove the bacon, place on a tray, and place another tray on top. Put weights (such as cans of food) on the top tray to press the bacon down. Leave until cold, then refrigerate overnight.

The next day, let the bacon come to room temperature. Strip off the skin, plus any dry meat underneath and around the sides, to reveal the pink meat. Cut this into five strips that are 1½in (4cm) wide, following the grain of the meat. Square off the edges to make neat rectangles. Mix the spices together and use to season the strips of bacon (you will not need all of the spice mixture at this stage).

Heat the caramel ingredients in a saucepan. Pour half into a frying pan and bubble over high heat until reduced by half. Put a bacon strip in the frying pan and let it sit undisturbed until it turns golden brown underneath, adding a little more caramel from the saucepan if it gets brown too quickly. Turn the bacon over and repeat, sprinkling with more spice mix as the sauce caramelizes. Repeat with the remaining strips. Let the strips cool a little before slicing across, against the grain.

At Pétrus, we serve the bacon on red onion tartes Tatin and garnish with parsnips and baby carrots. We decorate the plate with Banyuls sauce, a classic Bordelaise sauce made with Banyuls wine instead of Bordeaux.

STEAK & KIDNEY PUDDING

This was on the menu at The Savoy when I first worked there. It was made in large pots of 8–10 portions, which were wheeled around the restaurant on trolleys.

1 quantity of suet pastry dough (see below)

14oz (400g) beef chuck or round steak

4oz (125g) trimmed veal or beef kidney

1 onion, thinly sliced

leaves from 6 sprigs of fresh thyme

1 garlic clove, finely chopped

3–4 tbsp all-purpose flour seasoned with salt and pepper

Worcestershire sauce to taste

1 egg yolk, beaten

Guinness gravy (see opposite) for serving

1 Divide the suet pastry dough in half and roll out each piece to a rectangle about ⅛in (3mm) thick. Let rest for 10 minutes, then cut out four 7in (18cm) disks and four 3in (7.5cm) disks. Let the disks rest for 10 minutes on a floured tray, then cover with plastic wrap and refrigerate while you make the filling.

2 Chop the steak and kidney into small cubes (save the trimmings for the Guinness gravy, opposite). Mix the steak and kidney with the onion, thyme, and garlic in a bowl, then toss in enough seasoned flour to coat everything evenly.

3 Dampen four dariole molds and line each with three layers of plastic wrap, letting it overhang generously. Then line each mold with a large suet pastry disk, pushing it in around the bottom edge and pressing it smoothly against the sides so that it protrudes ½in (1cm) above the rim. Discard the dough trimmings.

SUET PASTRY

Sift 2 cups self-rising flour and a pinch of salt into a large bowl. Add 5oz (150g) finely chopped beef suet and some black pepper, and mix until evenly blended. Sprinkle a few drops of cold water over the flour and suet, and mix in with your hands. Continue adding water, a few drops at a time, until the mixture comes together as a dough—it should not be too sticky. Knead until you have a smooth, elastic dough that leaves the sides of the bowl clean.

5 Brush inside each pastry edge with egg yolk, then put a small disk on top, and press and pinch to seal to the pastry lining. Trim the edges with scissors and brush with more egg yolk. Roll the pastry edge over toward the middle to make a border, and press down to seal.

6 Wrap each mold in a double thickness of plastic wrap, pulling it very tight to exclude all air. This will prevent water from getting into the molds and making the pastry soggy, and it will also keep the flavors of the filling ingredients from leaching out into the water.

Guinness gravy

steak and kidney trimmings (see opposite)

3–4 shallots, finely chopped

3 garlic cloves, crushed

1 sprig of thyme

1 bay leaf

10 white peppercorns, crushed

2½ cups Guinness

2 cups red wine

4 cups chicken stock

4 cups veal stock

large pinch of sugar

Put the steak and kidney trimmings in a saucepan with the shallots, garlic, herbs, peppercorns, and some sea salt. Sweat over low heat for about 10 minutes, then increase the heat and cook, uncovered, until caramelized. Add the Guinness and boil to reduce by three-fourths, then add the wine and reduce in the same way. Repeat with the two stocks, adding them one after the other, reducing until the gravy has the consistency you like. Strain the gravy, then taste and add the sugar and a seasoning of salt and pepper.

4 Divide the steak and kidney filling among the molds, then pour in enough cold water to fill them by three-fourths. Sprinkle a few drops of Worcestershire sauce into each mold.

Serve the puddings with Guinness gravy, garnished as shown here if desired—on a bed of wilted spinach, surrounded with blanched diced carrot, rutabaga, and celery, and topped with an oyster

7 Set the puddings in the top of a steamer over boiling water, cover with the lid, and steam for 2½ hours, replenishing the water as necessary. To unmold, unwrap the plastic wrap and open it out at the top, then turn the molds upside-down on plates. Lift off the molds and gently ease the film off the sides of the puddings.

BEEF STROGANOFF

Stroganoff was one of the first things I learned to cook at catering schools. The raw ingredients were cooked in front of guests in the dining room, and the meat was flambéed with brandy.

1 tbsp olive oil
3½ tbsp unsalted butter
2 large onions, thinly sliced
3½ cups thinly sliced small button mushrooms
2¼lb (1kg) beef tenderloin (see below)
2 tbsp chopped parsley
½ cup heavy cream

CUTTING BEEF TENDERLOIN

To get perfectly even-sized pieces of meat, it is best to cut it yourself. Cut the beef tenderloin across into 3in (7.5cm) pieces, then cut each piece against the grain into slices about 3in (7.5cm) square and 1in (2.5cm) thick. Lay the slices flat and cut the squares into 3 by 1in (7.5 by 2.5cm) strips.

1 Heat the oil and half of the butter in a large frying pan over medium-high heat and fry the onions until translucent. Add the mushrooms and fry until they begin to soften, 2–3 minutes. Remove the onions and mushrooms from the pan with a slotted spoon.

2 Add the rest of the butter to the pan and heat until beginning to foam. Add the steak and sauté quickly over a high heat until browned on all sides, 3–4 minutes.

3 Return the onions and mushrooms to the pan, and stir and shake to mix with the meat. Sprinkle with the parsley, then pour in the cream and cook for 1 minute longer. Season well before serving.

Stroganoff is quickly made using
the tenderest beef steak

GRILLING & BROILING

Tender cuts of meat are suitable for grilling—either over charcoal or on a ridged cast-iron grill pan on top of the stove (a method described as pan-grilling or pan-broiling)—as well as for broiling in the oven. All three of these methods are fast ways of cooking and the heat is intense, so you need to take care that the meat does not dry out, particularly because tender cuts are mostly lean. Marinating before cooking is a sure way to safeguard against dryness, coupled with basting during cooking.

PAN-GRILLING STEAKS

A ridged cast-iron grill pan mimics a charcoal grill by imprinting charred lines on the meat. The technique shown here with sirloin steaks can be applied to the grill pan or grill, as you prefer. The cooking time is for rare steaks – if you like yours cooked more, add at least 2 minutes.

1 Heat the grill pan over high heat until very hot. Brush the steaks on both sides with a little peanut oil and season them with salt and freshly ground black pepper.

2 Put the steaks on the pan, arranging them diagonally across the ridges. Cook for 1 minute, then turn them at a 45° angle and cook for 1–2 minutes longer. Now turn the steaks over and repeat on the other side. Remove the steaks from the pan and let rest in a warm place for a few minutes before serving.

GUIDELINES FOR GOOD GRILLING & BROILING

■ Make sure that the grill, grill pan, or broiler are hot before starting to cook. Coals should be ash gray.

■ Always oil the meat before cooking, not the pan, grid, or rack. This will help prevent smoking.

■ Season meat just before cooking, or immediately after. If meat is salted and left for any length of time before cooking, the juices will be drawn out and when cooked the meat will be dry.

■ When cooking over charcoal or on a grill pan, allow time for the meat to brown underneath before turning it over. If moved too soon, it will stick.

■ Use tongs to turn the meat. A fork will pierce the meat and cause the juices to flow.

■ When cooking meat for an extended time under the broiler, after an initial browning, move the rack or pan farther away from the heat source.

ENTRECÔTE STEAKS BORDELAISE

With its intense beefy flavor, melt-in-the-mouth marrow provides an extra element of indulgence in this very special dish, and it goes really well with the red wine sauce.

| 4 entrecôte (rib) steaks, 12oz (340g) each, trimmed of fat |
| 8oz (225g) marrow bone (see opposite) |
| 1 tbsp peanut oil |
| 3½ tbsp butter |
| 12oz (340g) fresh porcini, cleaned (p249) and sliced lengthwise |
| 2 tbsp chopped flat-leaf parsley |
| **For the Bordelaise sauce** |
| ½ cup butter |
| 8 shallots, finely chopped |
| 6 garlic cloves, lightly crushed |
| 1¼ cups red Bordeaux wine |
| 1 bouquet garni (p75) |
| 24 white peppercorns, crushed |
| 6 sprigs of fresh thyme |
| sprig of fresh rosemary |
| ¾ cup veal stock |
| ¾ cup chicken stock |

1 To make the sauce, melt half the butter in a large pan, add the shallots and garlic, and cook over low heat, stirring often, until soft, about 5 minutes. Add the wine, bouquet garni, peppercorns, thyme, and rosemary. Bring to a boil and reduce to a syrupy consistency.

2 Pour in the stocks and simmer gently over a low heat for 40 minutes, skimming frequently. Meanwhile, prepare the marrow (see opposite) and let cool.

3 Remove the bouquet garni and herb stems from the sauce, leaving in the shallots, garlic, thyme, and rosemary leaves. Finish the sauce by whisking in the remaining butter.

4 Pan-grill the steaks (see left). While they are resting, heat the oil and butter in a frying pan and sauté the porcini until golden brown. Sprinkle with sea salt and drain on paper towels.

5 Slice each steak diagonally, against the grain, into four or five thick slices, using a gentle sawing action with the knife.

6 Arrange the slices of steak on warmed plates and top with the marrow. Spoon the sauce over the top. Garnish with the porcini and a sprinkling of parsley. Serve immediately.

PREPARING MARROW

Dig pieces of the marrow out of the bone with a spoon into a small saucepan of cold water. Bring to a boil, then remove the marrow and set aside to cool.

Entrecote bordelaise is a very rich dish for true meat lovers

SPIT-ROASTING

A cross between grilling and conventional roasting, spit-roasting uses either a rotisserie attachment in the oven, in which case the heat source is the broiler above the meat, or an electrically operated spit in a barbecue unit, where the heat comes from the coals. Both of these modern techniques mimic the original method of roasting meat on a spit over an open fire. Suitable cuts are pork loin, tunnel-boned leg of lamb, and boneless beef rib-eye roast. With these cuts, there is little shrinkage and the fat responds well to the direct heat.

BRINING PORK FOR SPIT-ROASTING

Soaking a fresh pork roast in a brine of salt, sugar, spices, and herbs gives the meat a "cured" flavor and a brighter pink color, as well as having a tenderizing effect. This brining is not an essential technique before spit-roasting, but I think of it like soaking in a warm bath—it enables the muscles to relax. The more the meat relaxes, the more tender it will be. It will also be easier to carve.

5½lb (2.5kg) skin-on pork loin roast, boned, with skin scored (p198)

For the brine

½ cup sugar

⅔ cup coarse sea salt

20 black peppercorns

10 juniper berries

4 star anise

2 tbsp fennel seeds

20 coriander seeds

10 sprigs of rosemary

10 sprigs of thyme

5 bay leaves

4 cups boiling water

about 4 quarts (3.8 liters) cold water

3 Pour in the boiling water and stir until the sugar and salt have dissolved, then pour in the 4 quarts of cold water.

4 Put the pork in the brine. If it is not submerged, add more cold water. Cover and keep in the refrigerator for 48 hours.

5 Remove the pork from the brine and dry it well. Let the meat come to room temperature before cooking. Retain brine for basting.

1 Form the pork into a sausage shape by rolling and pressing it together with your hands, then tie at regular intervals with kitchen string. Do not tie too tightly.

2 Put all the dry ingredients for the brine in a nonreactive pot that is large enough to hold the pork comfortably.

6 To get the meat ready for spit-roasting, push sprigs of rosemary and thyme under the string on the meaty side of the pork, and insert the spit prongs through each end.

SPIT-ROASTED BRINED PORK

Once spit-roasting is under way, the fat on the pork begins to melt and self-baste the meat as it turns around. Do not worry if the herbs start to singe—this all adds to the flavor.

Serves 6–8

1 brined pork loin (see opposite)

5 sprigs of rosemary

5 sprigs of thyme

fresh bay leaves for garnish

1 Prepare the pork for spit-roasting with sprigs of rosemary and thyme (see step 6, opposite).

2 Preheat the broiler or get the barbecue ready for cooking. Spit-roast the pork, with a drip tray underneath, for 2 hours. Baste often with the reserved brine, to keep the meat moist and prevent burning.

3 When the roast is cooked, let it rest in a warm place for 15–30 minutes before removing the string and carving into thick slices.

CHEF'S TIP

I like to serve roast vegetables with spit-roasted pork. Chop 8 carrots and 1 large leek, and mix in a roasting pan with 4 red onions, quartered, 3 heads of garlic, and a few sprigs of rosemary and thyme. Toss with some of the juices from the pork (or olive oil) and roast in a preheated 400°F (200°C) oven for 1 hour. Before serving, press the garlic cloves out of the skin and mix with the vegetables.

Garnish succulent spit-roasted pork with fresh bay leaves

CHINESE COOKING

KEN HOM

Chinese cooking is a sophisticated cuisine involving a number of cooking methods that are relatively uncommon in the West. Several different techniques may be used in the preparation of a single dish, but most of them can be easily mastered with a little practice. When planning a meal, it is more challenging to select dishes that use a range of techniques. Limit yourself to one stir-fried dish per meal until you have become accustomed to this method of cooking.

Meticulous preparation The initial preparation of foods is probably more important and more time-consuming in Chinese cookery than in any other cuisine. Although many dishes are cooked rapidly, this presupposes that every ingredient has been properly prepared beforehand—usually chopped into smallish, well-shaped pieces to ensure even and quick cooking. Food can then be cooked in the minimum time to preserve its natural texture and taste.

Careful cutting also enhances the visual appeal of a dish. This is why most Chinese cooks are so specific about cutting techniques, particularly where vegetables are concerned. The Chinese use a cleaver for cutting, wielding it with skill and dexterity. Of course, a sharp knife can be used instead.

Chinese meals traditionally consist of a soup; a rice, noodle, or bread dish; a vegetable dish; and at least two other dishes, which may be mainly meat, fish, or chicken. The meal may be preceded by and concluded with tea, but soup—really a broth—will be the only beverage during the meal itself. Soup is drunk not as a first course, but throughout the meal. The exception to this is a banquet, when soup, if it is served at all, comes at the end of the meal or as a palate-cleanser at several points during the dinner. On such occasions, wine, spirits, beer, or fruit juice will be drunk with the food. At banquets (which are really elaborate dinner parties), there may be as many as eight to twelve courses. Dishes are served one at a time so that the individual qualities of each can be properly savored. Rice is not served except at the end of the meal, when fried rice might be offered.

At ordinary meals, all the dishes are served together, including the soup, and the food is placed in the center of the table. Everyone has their own rice bowl, into which they put a generous amount of steamed rice. Then, using chopsticks, they each help themselves to a little of one dish, transferring this to their rice bowls. Once this has been eaten together with some of the rice, they will have a chopstick-full of another dish. Eating is a communal affair, and each diner takes care to see that everyone at the table receives a fair share of each dish.

Creating Chinese meals When devising a Chinese meal, aim for a good mix of textures, flavors, colors, and shapes. Apart from a staple, such as steamed rice, choose a variety of meat, poultry, and fish. It is better to serve one meat and one fish dish rather than two meat dishes, even if the meats are different. It also will be a better-balanced meal (and easier to prepare) if you use a variety of cooking methods. Serve a stir-fried dish with a braised, steamed, or cold dish. It is a good idea to select one or two things that can be prepared in advance.

You do not need any special dishes or implements to enjoy Chinese food, although I think it tastes decidedly better when it is eaten with chopsticks, rather than a fork. Knives are unnecessary, since Chinese food is always cut into bite-sized pieces before it is served. Each person will need a rice bowl, a soup bowl, a teacup if you are serving tea, and a small plate for any bones and such. A small dish or saucer each will be needed if you serve dipping sauces. Soup or cereal bowls will do for the rice and soup. Chopsticks are usually set to the right of the rice bowl. A spoon—metal or china—will be needed for soup and as an adjunct to chopsticks for noodles. The Chinese help themselves (and others) to food using their own chopsticks. Some people provide separate serving chopsticks, but these are often abandoned in the enthusiasm of communal eating.

MENU

- Steamed fish with scallions & ginger

- Stir-fried broccoli

- Red-braised chiu chow duck

- Sichuan green beans

- Steeped chicken with Cantonese-style sauce

SLICING

Food is cut into fine slices on a chopping board. Slicing meat across the grain cuts its fibers and makes it more tender.

When using a cleaver, keep your index finger over the top of the blade for greater control. Hold the food with your other hand, using your knuckles to guide the cutting edge and turning your fingers under for safety.

STIR-FRYING

Stir-frying depends upon having all the ingredients prepared, measured, and immediately to hand, and upon having a good source of fierce heat. Properly executed, stir-fried foods can be cooked in minutes in very little oil so they retain their natural flavors and textures. Use a steep-sided wok or pan for stir-frying. Peanut oil is best; corn and sunflower oil will do, but not olive oil.

1 Heat the wok or pan and add the peanut oil, spreading it evenly with a spatula. When the oil is very hot, add any flavorings, such as garlic, ginger, chili, or scallions, and quickly toss.

2 Add the recipe's ingredients and toss them across the wok or pan, moving the food from the center to the sides. When stir-frying meat, let each side rest for a few seconds before continuing to stir.

3 Some stir-fried foods, such as this broccoli dish, benefit from the addition of a little water before the wok or pan is covered. This late steaming, combined with the earlier frying, perfects the dish.

SHREDDING

The shredding process is like the French julienne technique, in which food is cut into thin, fine, matchsticklike shreds.

Pile slices of food on top of each other and cut into fine strips. Some foods shred better if stiffened in the freezer for about 20 minutes.

STEAMING

Along with stir-frying and deep-frying, steaming is the most widely used Chinese cooking technique. Steaming works with a gentle, moist heat. It is an excellent method for bringing out subtle flavors and so is particularly appropriate for fish. The Chinese use bamboo steamers in woks, but a large roasting pan or pot is just as good. It is important that the simmering water never makes contact with the food.

1 Place a bamboo steamer or a metal or wooden rack into a wok holding 2in (5cm) water. Bring the water to a simmer.

2 Put the food to be steamed onto a heatproof plate and place it on the rack. Cover the steamer or wok tightly with a lid.

3 Occasionally check the water level and replenish if needed. Remove any water from the plate when the food is cooked.

STEAMED FISH WITH SCALLIONS & GINGER

Steaming fish is a favorite Chinese cooking tradition. It is a simple, gentle technique that preserves the pure flavors of the fish, while keeping it both moist and tender.

1lb (450g) firm white fish fillets, such as cod or sole, or a 2lb (900g) whole fish, such as sole or turbot

1 tsp coarse sea salt or kosher salt

1–1½ tbsp finely shredded fresh ginger

3 tbsp finely shredded scallions

1 tbsp light soy sauce

1 tbsp dark soy sauce

1 tbsp peanut oil

2 tsp toasted sesame oil

handful of cilantro sprigs

1 Pat the fish fillets or whole fish dry with paper towels. Rub both sides evenly with the salt, and the inside as well if you are steaming a whole fish.

2 Put the fish onto a heatproof plate and scatter the ginger evenly over the top.

3 Put the plate of fish into the steamer. Cover tightly and gently steam the fish until it is just cooked. Fillets take 5–8 minutes to cook, depending on thickness. Whole fish take 10–14 minutes.

4 Remove the plate of cooked fish, pour off any excess liquid that may have accumulated on it, and scatter the scallions on the fish along with the light and dark soy sauces. Set aside.

5 Heat the peanut and sesame oils together in a small pan. When the oils are hot—almost smoking—pour them quickly over the fish.

6 Scatter the cilantro sprigs on top and serve at once.

STIR-FRIED BROCCOLI

Stir-frying is one of the most appealing ways to prepare broccoli. The secret to success with this simple dish is the late addition of water to round off the cooking process with 4–5 minutes of steaming.

1lb (450g) broccoli

1–1½ tbsp peanut oil

4 garlic cloves, lightly crushed

1 tsp salt

½ tsp freshly ground black pepper

6 tbsp water

2 tsp toasted sesame oil

1 Separate the broccoli into small florets; peel and slice the stems. Heat a wok or frying pan over high heat until it is hot. Add the peanut oil and, when it is almost smoking, add the garlic, salt, and pepper.

2 Stir-fry until the garlic is lightly browned, 30 seconds. Add the broccoli and stir-fry for 2 minutes. Add the water, cover the wok tightly with a lid, and cook over high heat for 4–5 minutes.

3 Stir in the sesame oil and stir-fry for 30 seconds, then serve immediately.

RED-BRAISED CHIU CHOW DUCK

Throughout China and Southeast Asia—and in Chinatowns all over the world—you will see this red-braised duck hanging from hooks in the windows of food shops and restaurants. It is easy to make at home and can be served warm or at room temperature. Rock sugar, which has a richer, more subtle flavor than granulated sugar, gives a lustrous glaze to red-cooked dishes such as this. You can find rock sugar in Chinese markets.

1 duck, 3½–4lb (1.6–1.8kg), preferably organic, fresh or frozen and thawed

5 cups peanut oil

For the sauce

5 cups chicken stock

5 cups dark soy sauce

1¼ cups light soy sauce

2 cups Shaoxing rice wine or dry sherry, or 1 cup dry sherry mixed with 1 cup chicken stock

½ cup rock sugar (or granulated sugar)

5 star anise

3 pieces of cassia or cinnamon sticks

2 tbsp fennel seeds

1 tbsp cumin seeds

cilantro sprigs for garnish

1 Using a cleaver, chop the duck in half lengthwise. Dry the halves well with paper towels.

2 Heat the oil in a wok or large frying pan until it is almost smoking. Add the duck halves, skin-side down. Turn the heat down to medium and deep-fry slowly until the skin is lightly browned, 15–20 minutes. Do not turn the pieces over, but baste the duck with the hot oil as it fries. Drain the duck on paper towels.

3 Mix together all the sauce ingredients in a large pot or wok and bring to a boil. Add the duck halves. Turn the heat down so that the sauce is gently simmering and then cover the pot or wok. Braise the duck until it is tender and cooked through, about 1 hour, occasionally skimming off fat from the surface of the sauce.

4 When the duck is cooked, skim off any remaining surface fat, then remove the duck pieces with a slotted spoon. Let them cool slightly before chopping them into smaller serving-size pieces.

5 Arrange the pieces of duck on a warm platter, garnish with cilantro, and serve. Alternatively, let the duck cool to room temperature before serving.

SICHUAN GREEN BEANS

Chinese asparagus or long beans are traditionally used in this tasty dish from western China, but green beans are equally good.

2½ cups peanut oil

1lb (450g) green beans

2 tbsp chopped garlic

1 tbsp finely chopped fresh ginger

3 tbsp finely chopped scallions (white part only)

1½ tbsp chili bean sauce

1 tbsp whole yellow bean sauce

2 tbsp Shaoxing rice wine or dry sherry

1 tbsp dark soy sauce

2 tsp sugar

1 tbsp water

2 tsp chili oil

1 Heat a wok or large frying pan over high heat and add the oil. When it is very hot and slightly smoking, add half of the green beans and deep-fry until they are slightly wrinkled, 3–4 minutes. Remove with a slotted spoon to drain. Deep-fry the remaining beans and drain. Set aside.

2 Pour off the oil from the wok and reserve. Clean the wok, then return about 1 tbsp of the oil and heat it. Add the garlic, ginger, and scallions, and stir-fry for about 30 seconds.

3 Add the rest of the flavoring ingredients and stir-fry for another 30 seconds.

4 Return the green beans to the wok and stir until they are thoroughly coated with the spicy mixture. Serve as soon as the beans are heated through.

CHOPPING

This term denotes completely cutting through food, and is usually applied to whole birds or cooked food with bones.

1 Using a heavy-duty cleaver or knife, chop with a straight, sharp, downward motion.

2 To chop through bones, hit with the blade, then strike with your hand or a mallet on the back edge of the cleaver or knife.

DEEP-FRYING

In China, a wok is used for deep-frying, one of the most important techniques in Chinese cooking. The trick is to regulate the heat of the oil so that the surface of the food does not brown so fast that the food is uncooked inside. Fresh, clean oil gives the best results.

1 To prevent splattering, dry food thoroughly with paper towels before adding it to hot oil. If the food is in a marinade, drain it well. When using a batter, dip in the food, then hold it up so excess batter can drip off.

2 Wait for the oil to get hot enough before adding the food. At the right temperature, the oil should give off a haze and almost produce little wisps of smoke. You can test by dropping in a small piece of food. If it bubbles all over, the oil is sufficiently hot. During frying, adjust the heat as necessary to prevent the oil from smoking or overheating.

3 Do not turn large pieces, but instead baste them with the hot oil as they fry.

4 Using tongs or a slotted spoon, remove the fried food from the hot oil and drain it on paper towels. Serve as soon as possible.

RED-BRAISING

Used for tougher cuts of meat, poultry, and certain vegetables, this cooking method gives food a reddish-brown color. The food is usually browned first, then simmered in a dark liquid based on soy sauce, and flavored with strong seasonings and spices. The braising sauce can be saved and frozen, then reused many times, becoming richer in flavor.

1 Combine the sauce ingredients in a wok or large pot and bring to a boil. Add the browned food, reduce the heat, and cover the wok.

2 Simmer gently until cooked. If necessary, skim off any fat from the surface of the sauce.

3 Remove the red-braised food. Once the sauce is cool, skim off all the fat, then save the sauce for future use.

STEEPING

In steeping, foods are immersed in liquid (usually stock, but sometimes Shaoxing rice wine) and simmered for a short time, then removed from the heat. The heat remaining in the liquid finishes off the cooking process. Delicate foods with a subtle taste lend themselves best to steeping. Chicken is the most used, but fish, seafood, and even very thin slices of meat can also be steeped.

1 Place the food (in this case a whole chicken) in a large pot and immerse in stock or water.

2 Bring to a boil, then cover tightly and simmer for a short time, about 20 minutes. Remove from the heat, then leave, still tightly covered, for 1 hour to complete the cooking.

3 Remove the food from the pot and plunge into a bowl of ice water to cool thoroughly.

4 Lift the food from the ice water and drain well, then pat dry with paper towels.

5 Prepare the food according to the recipe and serve.

CANTONESE-STYLE SAUCE

The pure, simple flavors of steeped chicken (see right) call for a pungent counterpoint in the dipping sauce. Scallions and fresh ginger, jolted to a full fragrance by a quick dousing of hot peanut oil, offer the perfect flavor combination.

¼ cup finely chopped scallions (white part only)

2 tsp finely chopped fresh ginger

2 tsp salt

2 tbsp peanut oil

1 Place the scallions, ginger, and salt in a bowl and mix well.

2 Heat a wok until it is hot, then add the peanut oil and spread it over the bottom.

3 When the oil is very hot and slightly smoking, pour it onto the ingredients in the bowl and mix well. Pour the sauce into a bowl and serve.

STEEPED CHICKEN

This is a classic Cantonese chicken dish that my mother often made. The gentlest possible heat is used so that the chicken remains extremely moist and flavorful with a satiny, almost velvetlike texture. The dish is not difficult to make. Save the cooking liquid for cooking rice or use as the base for chicken stock.

1 chicken, 3½–4lb (1.6–1.8kg), preferably organic

1 tbsp salt

chicken stock or water to cover

6 scallions

6 slices of fresh ginger

1 Rub the chicken all over with the salt, aiming to achieve an even covering.

2 Place the chicken in a large pot, cover with chicken stock or water, and bring to a boil. Add the scallions, ginger slices, and a few grinds of black pepper. Cover the pot tightly and reduce the heat. Simmer for 20 minutes.

3 Remove from the heat. Leave the chicken in the pot, still tightly covered, for 1 hour.

4 Lift the chicken from the stock and immediately plunge it into a large bowl of ice water to cool quickly and thoroughly.

5 Remove the chicken and drain well. Pat dry with paper towels. Discard the water used for cooling.

6 Place the chicken on a chopping board and cut into bite-sized pieces. Arrange on a platter. Serve the chicken pieces with Cantonese-style dipping sauce (see opposite) alongside.

VEGETABLES

CHARLIE TROTTER

I have long been an advocate of small farms and organic farming, as much from the standpoint of flavor as that of politics. Just as foods are absolutely at their best at the height of their season, they also taste better when they are naturally raised. You can't fudge it with the seasons—tomatoes are available for only six weeks, not 12 months of the year. Farmers who embrace sustainable agriculture and grow natural, organic produce are forced to go by the rules of nature.

Heritage varieties Many of these farmers produce heritage varieties that have never been hybridized to extend their growing season, withstand frost, or "improve" their qualities in other ways. Many heritage varieties are astonishing in their appearance and flavor. In America, most people think that tomatoes are available year round and come in only one color: red. Little do they know that there are 80–90 heritage varieties of tomato native to the U.S., such as Purple Cherokee, Yellow Taxi, Tiger Stripe, and Sunburst, and many European varieties such as the Russian Black Prince and the Italian Principe Borghese. Some are meaty, some have very thin skin; others are high in acid, or so sweet you can eat them as a dessert. There are also various strands of heritage corn, squash, and lettuce. Farmers can now go to seed-saving groups to obtain seeds for heritage products.

Heritage varieties tend not to be available in large supermarkets, but increasingly small farmers are bringing their wares to farmers' markets. Food doesn't get any fresher, coming straight from the ground or right off the tree. Serve meat or fish with farmers' market vegetables, perhaps braised cabbage or caramelized onions, and you will find that the flavors just explode. It won't be long before you will be experimenting and having fun with all the delicious vegetables now to be found.

Always buy vegetables in season, when they are of the highest quality, have the best flavor, and typically cost less than when purchased out of season. Look for bright, vibrant colors, and avoid yellowing, especially in cauliflower and leafy greens—these should be young and tender. Make sure members of the cabbage and root families are firm and unblemished, and that beans are firm and bright with no blemishes or soft spots. Corn should be freshly picked, with small firm kernels; there should be no sign of mold, or brown silks overlaying the kernels.

Storing vegetables Most fresh vegetables, including winter squash and members of the onion family, should be kept in a vegetable cooler at 50–65°F (10–18°C). If you don't have a vegetable cooler, keep the vegetables in a cool, dry place with ample ventilation. Other vegetables should be stored in the refrigerator, which is colder and has a higher humidity than a vegetable cooler. Cover or wrap different vegetable types and store them separately. Keep greens and other delicate vegetables away from tomatoes, which release ethylene gas that causes green vegetables to wilt. Keep potatoes in the vegetable cooler because fridge temperatures break down their texture and flavor.

Vegetables are ideally purchased in season when they are fully ripe, but tomatoes, and some fruits, are ripened in the home. Store unripe tomatoes at room temperature. The ethylene gas produced by tomatoes is a ripening agent, and placing a ripe tomato with unripe ones in a box or brown paper bag helps to speed up the ripening of all the unripe ones.

Preparing vegetables Some vegetables are peeled to remove their tough skin. Peeling also serves to remove skin that might contain traces of pesticides and other chemicals that cannot be removed by washing. Otherwise, before washing, you can spray them using a spray bottle containing one part lemon juice to five parts water. This mixture will aid the removal of wax, surface contaminants, and moisture-resistant chemicals, some of which are otherwise stored in the body.

Delay the washing, peeling, and cutting of vegetables until just before cooking, as exposure to air and moisture causes vegetables to deteriorate and lose their vitamins. Discoloration can be minimized by immersing the vegetables in water to which lemon juice or vinegar has been added.

LEAFY VEGETABLES

Vegetables in this family are often used in salads. The most common of these is lettuce, but there is also a wonderful variety of other salad leaves, in all shapes, sizes, and colors.

Heartier leafy greens—such as collards, spinach, dandelion, Swiss chard leaves, kale, and sorrel—are usually richly colored. They range in flavor from piquant to peppery, and even bitter.

TRIMMING, WASHING & DRYING SALAD LEAVES

Greens intended for a salad need to be trimmed and broken or cut into manageable pieces. Leaves that typically have the rib cut out include romaine, endive, and radicchio. After thorough washing, the leaves must be dried well to prevent the salad dressing from being diluted. This method of washing and drying is also suitable for leafy greens such as spinach and sorrel.

1 Trim off the ends of the leaves, discarding any that are discolored. If leaves are tough, separate them and cut out the rib from each one. Break or cut the leaves to the desired size.

2 Gather the salad greens loosely and hold under running water or immerse in cool water. Shake or swirl gently to loosen dirt.

3 Drain the leaves in a colander, then pat dry in a clean kitchen towel or with paper towels. Alternatively, use a salad spinner to dry the leaves.

Dressing a salad

The most basic form of a salad is lettuce tossed in vinaigrette (p51). But there is an incredible variety of greens available for salads today. You don't have to limit yourself just to greens—many root vegetables, bell peppers, and other vegetables also make wonderful bases for salads. For complexity, add cooked meat, fish, cheese, nuts, and fruit. Have fun mixing vegetables such as roasted beets with goat cheese and balsamic vinegar, or fennel with oranges.

Another interesting way to prepare salads is to heat the greens slightly before tossing with the other elements. Composed salads are lovely too, with elements placed separately on the plate.

When making a green salad:
- Add just enough dressing to give the leaves a light coating—that is all they need.
- Gently toss and turn over the leaves—use salad servers or your clean hands.
- Serve without delay: If a dressed salad waits to be served, the leaves will wilt.

TRIMMING & SLICING HEARTY GREENS

Leafy green vegetables such as spinach may be young and tender enough to eat raw in a salad, but most hearty greens—such as Swiss chard, kale, collard greens, and the leaves of vegetables such as turnips and beets—are cooked, most commonly by boiling, steaming, or sautéing.

Hearty greens are most often trimmed to remove the central rib and then sliced into strips (called a chiffonade). With mature leaves, the rib is cut out; with more tender leaves, such as spinach and sorrel, you can just pull off the stem and rib (see below). This method of slicing into a chiffonade is suitable for hearty greens such as collards (which are shown in the photographs), as well as for salad leaves.

1 Discard all limp or discolored leaves. Using a chef's knife, quickly slash each leaf on each side of the rib. Remove and discard the rib.

2 Rinse in water as described for salad leaves (see opposite), and pat dry in a dish towel or with paper towels.

3 Grab a handful of leaves and roll loosely into a bunch. Cut across the roll into strips of the desired width.

PREPARING SPINACH

Spinach tends to trap a lot of soil as it grows, so the leaves need to be washed thoroughly.
- Immerse the spinach in several changes of cold water, agitating the water to clean the spinach.
- After draining in a colander, pat dry in a dish towel or with paper towels.
- Fold each leaf in half and pull off the midrib and stem. The spinach is now ready to eat raw or cook.

CABBAGE FAMILY

The most common way to prepare tight, round heads of cabbage is to quarter them and cut out the hard central core, then to shred coarsely or finely. The cabbage can then be used raw in a salad or coleslaw, or cooked by boiling or steaming, sautéing, or braising. Whole heads of cabbage and rolled leaves may also be stuffed and baked. Loose-leaf heads, such as Napa cabbage and Chinese cabbages, are prepared more like hearty greens (p239).

Both broccoli and cauliflower have tightly packed heads of buds or florets. The usual method of preparing broccoli and cauliflower is to trim the stem and separate the florets, although heads are also sometimes cooked whole. Cooking methods include boiling and steaming, sautéing, stir-frying (blanch first), microwaving, and baking or simmering in a sauce. Florets can also be served raw as part of a selection of vegetable crudités.

CORING & SHREDDING CABBAGE

1 Holding the head of cabbage firmly on the board, use a chef's knife to cut it lengthwise in half, cutting straight through the stem end.

2 Cut each cabbage half lengthwise in half again, cutting through the stem end, then cut out the hard central core from each quarter.

SPEEDY SHREDDING

Cabbage can be quickly shredded by hand with a chef's knife (see right). For the most efficient action and control, keep the point of the knife on the board as you raise and lower the handle; guide the knife blade with the knuckles of your other hand. Alternatively, you can use the shredding disk on a food processor, which will cut cabbage very quickly into the finest slices.

3 Take one cabbage quarter and place it cut-side down on the board. Cut across the cabbage, creating shreds of the desired thickness.

OUR FAVORITE COLESLAW

Coleslaw is a true American classic. While this recipe is traditional, you can easily change it. For an exotic twist, add 1 tbsp chopped Thai chili and substitute ½ cup of your favorite Asian vinaigrette for the sour cream and mayonnaise.

Serves 4–6

½ cup sour cream
2 tbsp mayonnaise
¼ cup cider vinegar
2 tbsp sugar
3 cups shredded green cabbage
1 cup grated carrots

1 Combine the sour cream, mayonnaise, vinegar, sugar, and salt and pepper to taste in a bowl. Stir until evenly mixed.

2 Add the cabbage and carrots, and toss to coat evenly. Cover and keep refrigerated until ready to serve.

TRIMMING BROCCOLI & CUTTING FLORETS

1 Lay the head of broccoli flat on the board. With a chef's knife, cut off the thick portion of the stem, cutting just below the floret stems.

2 Remove the florets by sliding the knife between their stems to separate them. Rinse the florets in cold water and drain in a colander.

TRIMMING CAULIFLOWER & CUTTING FLORETS

1 Lay the head of cauliflower on its side on the board. With a chef's knife, cut off the end of the stem. Pull or cut off any leaves.

2 Turn the head core-side up and use a paring knife to carefully cut the florets from the central stem. Rinse the florets in cold water and drain in a colander.

ONION FAMILY

Sometimes cooked as a vegetable—by roasting, braising, or baking—or added raw to a salad, onions and shallots are most often used as a seasoning in a cooked dish. They are peeled and diced or sliced in the same way, then usually sweated so they soften without coloring. If cooked too rapidly or at too high a temperature they can become dark brown and bitter.

Used primarily as a flavoring, the pungency of garlic depends on how it is prepared. When it is left whole—in a head or individual cloves—and roasted or boiled, it is mild and sweet; when it is chopped the flavor is stronger. The more finely garlic is chopped, the more pungent it becomes.

Although occasionally used raw in salads, leeks are most often cooked, whole or cut up, by boiling, braising, or baking in a sauce, or in a vegetable mixture.

PEELING & DICING ONIONS

1 Using a chef's knife, cut the onion lengthwise in half. Peel off the skin, leaving the root in place to keep the onion halves together.

2 Lay one half flat-side down. Make two or three slices into it horizontally, cutting up to but not through the root end.

3 Cut the onion half vertically now, slicing down through the layers, again cutting up to but not through the root end.

SLICING ONIONS

Onions may be sliced into half moons or rings of varying thicknesses.

■ To slice half moons, cut the onion in half and peel it (see step 1 above). Lay each half cut-side down on the board and slice across (not lengthwise).

■ For rings, peel the onion, keeping it whole. Hold it firmly on the board, and slice across into rings. Discard the root and stem ends.

4 Cut across the vertical slices to get even dice. Discard the root end.

PEELING & CHOPPING GARLIC

WASHING LEEKS & CUTTING INTO JULIENNE

This mildest member of the onion family often collects soil between its many layers, so it needs to be thoroughly washed before use.

1 Lay a garlic clove flat on the cutting board and place the side of the blade of a chef's knife on it. Lightly strike the blade to break the garlic skin. Peel off the skin.

1 With a chef's knife, trim off the root end and some of the dark green leaf top. Cut the leek in half lengthwise and fan it open, holding the white end.

2 Chop the garlic roughly, then sprinkle it with a little salt (this prevents the garlic from sticking to the knife). Continue chopping it until it is very fine. When it is very finely chopped it is described as being minced. To make a paste, continue chopping as you press and smash the garlic on the board.

2 Rinse under cold running water to remove the soil from between the layers. Gently shake the leek to remove excess water, then pat dry with paper towels.

3 For julienne, cut off all the green part. Cut the white part across into sections of the required length. Lay a section flat-side down and slice into fine strips about ⅛in (3mm) thick.

GOURD FAMILY

Gourds—or squashes—come in all shapes, colors, and sizes. The winter squashes, such as pumpkin, butternut, acorn, hubbard, and turban, are always cooked, most often by boiling or steaming (and often then puréed) or by baking or roasting. Halves may also be stuffed and baked. In addition to the popular zucchini, summer squashes include pattypan, crookneck, and chayote. Cucumber is also in this family. Summer squashes can be cooked whole or cut up, by steaming, baking, sautéing or frying, and grilling.

HALVING, SEEDING & PEELING WINTER SQUASH

The skin of winter squashes is thick and hard, and the seeds are fully developed. Because of this, winter squashes are always peeled (either before or after cooking) and the seeds and central fibers are removed. Use a sharp, heavy knife for cutting. Butternut squash is shown in these photographs.

1 Hold the squash firmly on the board, then cut in half, cutting from the stem end directly through the core end.

2 Use a spoon or a small ice cream scoop to remove the seeds and fibers from each squash half. Discard the seeds and fibers.

3 Cut the squash into sections. If removing the skin before cooking, peel the sections using a vegetable peeler or knife.

GRATING SUMMER SQUASH

Soft-skinned summer squashes can be eaten peel and all. However, because their flesh is tender and moist, they can become mushy if overcooked. Draining or squeezing out excess moisture before cooking can help to prevent this.

This preparation technique is suitable for summer squashes such as zucchini (shown here), as well as for cucumber.

1 If desired, peel the squash. Grasp the squash firmly and grate the flesh on the side of the grater with large holes.

2 Wrap the grated squash in a piece of cheesecloth and squeeze to remove excess moisture. Discard all the liquid.

CUTTING BATONNETS

This method of cutting batonnets is also suitable for other slim vegetables, such as carrots, parsnips, and salsify. Zucchini is shown here.

1 Cut off both ends of the squash, then cut it in half lengthwise. Cut each half again to make slices ¼in (5mm) thick.

2 Lay each slice of zucchini flat on the board, hold firmly, and cut across to make sticks or batonnets ¼in (5mm) wide.

ROOT & TUBER FAMILY

Vegetables that grow underground include carrots, turnips, potatoes, parsnips, rutabaga, beets, salsify, celeriac, radishes, and Jerusalem artichokes. Some, such as radishes, are usually eaten raw; others, such as carrots, may be eaten raw or cooked. But it is more common to cook roots and tubers by boiling or steaming—often to make a purée—sous vide, or by baking or roasting, en papillote, sautéing, or frying. Many are also delicious thinly sliced and deep-fried. Most roots and tubers are peeled, before or after cooking.

TOURNER

Also called turning, this is a common preparation technique for vegetables in the root and tuber family, such as carrots (shown here), turnips, and potatoes, as well as for summer squashes. The vegetable is shaved into classic seven-sided oval shapes.

1 Peel the vegetables, if necessary, then cut into pieces that are 2in (5cm) long.

2 Holding one vegetable piece between thumb and index finger, start shaving off the sides of the piece to curve them.

3 Continue cutting while turning the vegetable piece in your hand, to create an oval shape with seven curved sides.

SHOOTS & STALKS FAMILY

Vegetables in this family include young shoots (asparagus), leaf stalks (celery and fennel), and flowerheads atop stalks (globe artichokes). Asparagus are rarely eaten raw, unless very young and slim, whereas celery and fennel may be used raw or cooked. Even when young, globe artichokes are always cooked before eating, either whole or trimmed down to the fleshy bottom or heart.

TRIMMING GLOBE ARTICHOKES TO SERVE WHOLE

Whole globe artichokes are cooked by boiling or steaming. The hairy "choke" in the center can be scooped out after cooking or before eating. When cut and exposed to the air, globe artichokes will quickly discolor. To prevent them from browning prior to cooking, drop them into a bowl of water acidulated with lemon juice or rub all the cut surfaces with lemon.

2 Use a chef's knife to cut off the stem flush with the base, so that the artichoke will sit upright on a flat bottom.

1 Holding the stem, cut the tough tips from the artichoke leaves with sturdy kitchen scissors.

3 Cut off the pointed top. The artichoke is now ready to be cooked.

PREPARING ARTICHOKE BOTTOMS

When all the leaves are removed from a globe artichoke, what is left is the fleshy, cup-shaped bottom or heart, which is completely edible apart from the central hairy "choke." The bottom can be cut up for cooking or left whole. If it is to be served whole, it will be easier to remove the choke after cooking. As you work, keep rubbing the exposed flesh of the artichoke with lemon juice to prevent browning.

1 Pull away or cut off all of the large leaves from the artichoke. Then cut off the stem flush with the base.

2 Cut off the remaining soft "cone" of leaves in the middle, cutting across just above the choke (you will see the hairy fibers).

3 Neaten the bottom with a paring knife, trimming off all the remaining leaves and trimming the base so it is slightly flattened.

4 If cutting up the artichoke for cooking, scoop out the choke with a small spoon. Take care to remove all of the hairy fibers.

5 Rub the exposed surface of the hollow generously with lemon juice. The artichoke bottom is now ready to be cut up.

PREPARING ASPARAGUS

Asparagus need little preparation, apart from trimming off the ends of the stalks. However, if the spears are larger you may want to peel them. Cook asparagus by boiling or steaming, or try roasting or pan-grilling them.

1 With a chef's knife, cut the hard ends from the asparagus spears.

2 Holding the tip of a spear gently, use a vegetable peeler to peel off a thin layer of skin from the stalk, rotating to peel all sides.

STRINGING CELERY

The thick, outer stalks of celery have long, stringy fibers that are best removed. Separate the stalks from the bunch and wash. Then, using a vegetable peeler, peel off a thin layer from each stalk to remove the strings. Florence or bulb fennel and cardoons also have strings that are usually removed in the same way.

PODS & SEEDS

There are three types of peas and beans: Those where the unripe seeds are eaten in the pod (e.g. green beans, yellow wax beans, snow peas, and sugarsnap peas); those where the seeds are mature and removed from the pod to be eaten fresh (e.g. garden peas, fava beans, and lima beans); and those where the shucked mature seeds are dried before eating (e.g. navy beans, pinto beans, and black-eyed peas). The fresh types are usually cooked by boiling or steaming, although they may also be braised, sautéed, or stir-fried. Although not in the same botanical family as peas and beans, corn is treated in the same way in the kitchen.

REMOVING STRINGS

Snow peas (shown below) and some green beans—in particular heritage varieties—have tough strings along one or both sides of the pod that need to be stripped off before cooking.

Carefully tear off the tip, which will be attached to the string, then pull it along the side to remove the string. With snow peas, the flat side has the string. If you are preparing beans that have a tough string on the other side too, carefully tear off the tail of the bean and pull off the attached string.

SHUCKING CORN & CUTTING OFF KERNELS

After shucking (removing the husks and silk), the whole ear of corn may be boiled and the kernels served on the cob. Or, the kernels can be cut off to be boiled or steamed, sautéed, or simmered or baked in a sauce or soup.

1 Pull off the husks and all of the silk from the ear of corn.

2 Hold the ear upright on a cutting board and, using a chef's knife, slice straight down the sides to cut the kernels off the cob.

3 Hold the cob upright in a bowl, at a slight angle, and scrape down the length of the cob with the knife to extract the rest of the corn "milk."

MUSHROOMS

Mushrooms, both cultivated and wild, and truffles make up this vegetable family. Before cooking, most fresh fungi need only to be cleaned to remove earth or sand—only a few varieties of wild mushrooms need to be peeled. If the stems are woody, trim the ends or cut them off completely. When they are cooked—sautéing and stewing are the most popular methods—fresh mushrooms produce a lot of liquid, which may need to be drained off or boiled to evaporate. Mushrooms preserved by drying, which intensifies their flavor, need to be soaked before use. Once reconstituted, they can be treated like fresh mushrooms.

REHYDRATING DRIED MUSHROOMS

1 Place the dried mushrooms (either cultivated or wild) in a bowl of hot water. Let soak for at least 15 minutes to rehydrate them.

2 Use a slotted spoon to remove the mushrooms from the soaking liquid. If you are going to use the soaking liquid in the dish with the mushrooms, strain the liquid through fine cheesecloth or a coffee filter paper to remove all sand and grit.

CLEANING FRESH MUSHROOMS

Use a wet paper towel to clean all soil from fresh mushrooms, wiping it off gently. If the mushrooms are sandy, you may need to plunge them into cold water and shake them around to loosen the sand (this is most likely to be needed with species that have deep gills). However, do not leave cultivated fresh mushrooms to soak, because they quickly absorb moisture and become bloated.

PREPARING WILD MUSHROOMS & TRUFFLES

Fresh wild mushrooms need thorough cleaning, and may need to be soaked for up to 5 minutes to loosen grit in their gills or indentations. Some species have a thick skin, which should be peeled off.

Fresh truffles usually only need to be brushed gently to remove any loose dirt, but if they contain a lot of grit and dirt, they may need to be rinsed. Once the truffle is clean, peel off the rough skin (reserve the skin and use for flavoring).

FRUIT VEGETABLES

Tomatoes, eggplants, sweet bell and chili peppers, tomatillos, and avocados, which are fruits according to botanists, are treated as vegetables in the kitchen. With the exception of tomatillos, all are ideal for stuffing with a savory mixture (p263).

Eggplant is never used raw, while avocados are rarely cooked; tomatoes and bell peppers are extremely versatile and can be used either raw or cooked. Popular cooking methods include baking, grilling, and sautéing.

HALVING & PITTING AN AVOCADO

Once avocado flesh has been removed from the skin, it can be added to salads, or mashed or puréed to use in uncooked soups and dips such as guacamole (see opposite). It may also be cooked lightly and briefly. Take care, though, because if it is heated for too long, avocado will quickly lose its flavor.

PREVENTING BROWNING

The flesh of avocado will discolor quickly when exposed to the air, so serve it promptly or rub or toss it with lemon or lime juice.

1 Using a chef's knife, slice into the avocado, cutting all the way around the pit.

2 Twist the cut halves gently in opposite directions to separate them.

3 Strike the pit with the knife blade to pierce it firmly. Lift up the knife to remove the pit from the avocado half.

4 Use a wooden spoon to pry the pit off the knife (do this carefully). Discard the pit.

5 Holding an avocado half in your hand, gently scoop out the flesh with the help of a rubber spatula. Repeat with the other half.

PEELING & DICING AVOCADO

1 After cutting the avocado in half and removing the pit (see opposite), cut the half into fourths and remove the peel.

2 Cut the avocado flesh into neat slices. To dice the flesh, slice thinly and then cut across the slices to make dice.

EASY GUACAMOLE

Makes about 2 cups

3 small avocados

1 ripe but firm tomato, peeled, seeded, and chopped

1 small jalapeño chili, seeded and finely chopped

½ small white onion, chopped

½ cup loosely packed cilantro, chopped

2 tbsp fresh lemon or lime juice

pinch of salt

1 Scoop the flesh from the avocados. Mash the flesh until smooth with a few slight lumps. Lightly stir in the rest of the ingredients without overmixing.

2 Use immediately, or cover by pressing plastic wrap directly onto the guacamole (not on top of the bowl) to prevent browning, and store in the refrigerator. Serve as a dip for tortilla chips or raw vegetables, or with tacos.

ROASTING, PEELING & SLICING BELL PEPPERS

Red and yellow bell peppers can have thick skins, which some people find indigestible. Roasting the peppers, which makes the skin easier to remove, also imparts a slightly smoky taste and enhances the sweetness of the pepper flesh. The same roasting and peeling method can be used for chili peppers as well as for tomatoes and even garlic.

BROIL-ROASTING

You can also char bell peppers under the broiler. Place them on a baking sheet, about 4in (10cm) from the heat source, and broil until the skin blisters and blackens, about 5 minutes. Turn the peppers over and char the other side in the same way.

1 Using long-handled tongs, hold each pepper over an open flame to char it on all sides. (Alternatively, char under the broiler; see box right.)

2 Put into a plastic bag and seal tightly. Set aside to allow steam to loosen the skin.

3 Using your fingers, peel away the charred skin from the pepper.

4 Pull off the stem, taking the core with it, and remove all the seeds from inside.

5 Tear the peeled pepper into sections. Lay them flat and cut lengthwise into strips.

PEELING, SEEDING & CHOPPING TOMATOES

When tomatoes are used in a soup or sauce that is not going to be passed through a strainer or food mill, they are often peeled and seeded before use. This peeling method is also suitable for fruit such as peaches and plums and for chestnuts.

1 With the tip of a paring knife, cut around the core of the tomato to remove it.

2 Score an "X" in the skin on the base of the tomato. Immerse it in a pot of boiling water.

3 Leave the tomato in the boiling water until the skin splits, about 20 seconds.

4 Lift the tomato out of the pot and immediately submerge it in a bowl of ice water to cool.

5 Pull off the skin with the help of the paring knife.

6 Cut the tomato in half and gently squeeze out the seeds.

7 Place each half cut-side down and cut into strips. Cut across the strips to make dice.

RAW

There is no better way to celebrate the pure, clean flavors and textures of vegetables than with the RAW approach. RAW is an intriguing style of vegetable preparation that includes such techniques as soaking and sprouting nuts and legumes, and marinating vegetables in order to break down their undesirable starchy complexity and make them more easy to digest.

The overall concept of RAW is that nothing is ever heated over 118°F (48°C), because above that temperature enzymes in food are destroyed and food begins to lose its nutritional value. Leaving food in its natural—or RAW—state helps to retain most of the nutrients, as well as offering incredible flavor and texture.

Many people are adopting a 100-percent RAW food regime as their way of life. While this is not what I'm proposing, I encourage you to try some of the RAW approach to explore flavors and textures.

DEHYDRATING TOMATOES

Tomatoes are one of the best vegetables to dry for using in RAW preparations. You can also use this technique to dry mushrooms, fruit such as pears and apples, and even squash.

1 Using a serrated knife, cut the tomatoes into very thin slices—about ⅛in (3mm) thick.

2 Lay the slices in one layer on the dehydrator shelf. Lightly brush them with olive oil.

3 Dehydrate the tomatoes at 105°F (40°C) until dry, 6–8 hours. Remove the tomatoes from the dehydrator and let cool. Store in an airtight container until ready to use.

Chilled clear cucumber soup with watermelon, apple & jicama

This cucumber soup is so light and refreshing it could almost work as a summer beverage. Tart apple and sweet watermelon contrast deliciously. Togarashi powder is ground small, hot, red, Japanese chili peppers.

2 English cucumbers

2 tbsp plain yogurt

1 tsp freshly squeezed lemon juice

½ tsp togarashi powder

¼ cup cucumber julienne 1in (2.5cm) long

¼ cup green apple julienne 1in (2.5cm) long

8 tsp watermelon batonnets, seeds removed

¼ cup diced avocado

8 tsp diced jicama

8 tsp diced tomatillo

8 slices of dehydrated tomato (see opposite), julienned

4 tsp snipped dill

4 tsp green herb oil (p77)

Cut one of the cucumbers into eight 1in (2.5cm) pieces. Using a round cutter or a paring knife, remove the skin. Hollow out the inside of each cucumber piece using a spoon or small melon baller, to make a cup. Put the scooped-out pulp in a blender.

Peel and chop the second cucumber and add to the blender along with 1 tsp salt. Purée until smooth. Pour the cucumber purée into a strainer lined with three layers of cheesecloth and set in a bowl. Let it sit in the refrigerator until all of the liquid has strained through. Season this cucumber broth with salt if necessary and keep refrigerated until needed.

Combine the yogurt, lemon juice, and togarashi in a small bowl. Add the julienned cucumber and apple, and toss to mix.

To assemble, set two cucumber cups in the center of each wide serving bowl. Fill the cups with the cucumber and apple mixture. Place the watermelon, avocado, jicama, tomatillo, and tomato around the cups. Ladle the cucumber broth into each bowl and sprinkle with the dill. Drizzle 1 tsp herb oil onto each serving and finish with freshly ground pepper.

Scoop out the pulp to make cucumber cups

BOILING

Almost all vegetables can be boiled. It is important, however, to note some differences when boiling vegetables of different color or texture. As a general rule, all tough-textured, starchy root vegetables, such as potatoes, turnips, and celeriac, should be started in cold water in order to ensure even cooking, whereas green vegetables should be added to boiling water. To ensure even cooking, cut or trim all vegetables to a uniform size.

When boiling vegetables with bright colors—red (e.g. beets), white (e.g. turnips), yellow (e.g. squash), and orange (e.g. carrots)—cover the pot during boiling in order to retain acids that help hold the color fast. However, never cover green vegetables when they are boiling, as they will lose their color.

Root vegetables should be fast-boiled (at 212°F/100°C), whereas all other vegetables should be simmered more slowly.

BOILING GREEN VEGETABLES

This simple and healthy cooking method is suitable for green vegetables such as broccoli florets, Brussels sprouts, shredded green cabbage, green beans, garden peas, sugar snap peas, snow peas (as shown in the photographs), and asparagus spears.

1 Salt the water or other cooking liquid and bring it to a boil. Add the vegetables to the boiling water in small batches to minimize temperature reduction.

2 Bring the water back to a boil, then reduce the heat and gently simmer the vegetables to the desired degree of doneness (see right and the chart opposite for approximate timings).

3 Drain in a colander. If needed, refresh the vegetables by rinsing under cold running water (for delicate vegetables, immerse them in ice water). This stops the cooking and sets the color. Drain again well, then serve.

 ### DEGREES OF DONENESS

Vegetables can be boiled for varying lengths of time, according to how they are to be used or served, as well as how well done you prefer them to be. These terms are commonly used when boiling vegetables.

■ Blanch: To immerse in boiling water for a very short time, usually no more than a minute. This is followed by a quick cool down in ice water (called refreshing or shocking). A vegetable is blanched to set color, to loosen skin so that it can be removed more easily, or to eliminate strong flavor.

■ Parboil: To partially cook. A vegetable is parboiled to prepare it for other finishing (by braising or stewing, grilling or pan-grilling, sautéing, baking en papillote, roasting, etc.).

■ Al dente: Literally "to the tooth," to cook until just firm or crisp-tender. This degree of doneness suits green vegetables, such as green beans and snow peas, as well as summer squash.

■ Fully done: To cook until tender. Root vegetables and potatoes are always cooked until fully done.

STEAMING

Steaming vegetables results in a pure, clean flavor like no other. In addition, the end result is a vegetable that is firmer and more crisp than one that was boiled. This is primarily because the vegetable has had no contact with the liquid in the pan, just with steam. Any vegetable that can be boiled can be steamed.

It's a good idea to cut larger root vegetables into small pieces for steaming. Smaller vegetables can be left whole.

In general, the amount of liquid you use for steaming should be about the same as the amount of vegetables. You can add seasonings to the liquid (for example, herbs and citrus zest), which will impart flavor to the vegetables. Be sure that there is adequate room for steam circulation around them so that they cook evenly.

STEAMING BROCCOLI

Follow this method of steaming for all kinds of vegetables. You can use a steamer (as shown here) or stacking Chinese bamboo steamers.

1 Put water into the bottom of a steamer and bring to a boil. Place the broccoli on the steamer rack, spreading the florets out in a single layer. Cover the steamer.

2 Cook the broccoli to the desired doneness (test by pricking the thickest part—here the stem of a floret—with the tip of a paring knife). Remove from the steamer and serve.

Boiling & steaming vegetables

This chart suggests times for boiling and steaming vegetables. Some people like vegetables to be fully done, while others prefer some to be cooked al dente or until crisp-tender, so a range of timings is given. The range also covers differences that may result from the vegetable's age, size, or variety. Whether you start in cold or boiling water (see opposite), time the cooking from the moment the water reaches or returns to a boil. Then cover the pan if this is indicated. For perfect results, test for doneness with the point of a sharp knife or a fork.

VEGETABLE	BOILING			STEAMING
	Times (in minutes)	Cold/boiling start	Cook covered?	Times (in minutes)
artichoke bottoms	20–30	cold start	no	15–20
artichokes, whole	20–40	cold start	no	25–35
artichokes, baby	15–18	cold start	no	15–20
asparagus	3–4	boiling start	no	4–10
beans, green	2–8	boiling start	no	5–12
beets, whole	30–60	cold start	yes	30–60
broccoli florets	2–3	boiling start	no	5–10
Brussels sprouts	5–12	boiling start	no	10–15
cabbage, quartered	5–15	boiling start	no	6–15
cabbage, shredded	3–5	boiling start	no	5–10
carrots, baby	3–4	boiling start	yes	10
carrots, sliced/diced	5–10	boiling start	yes	8–10
cauliflower florets	2–3	boiling start	no	5–8
cauliflower, whole	10–15	boiling start	no	15–20
celeriac, cubed/wedges	8–10	cold start	no	8–10
corn-on-the-cob	3–4	boiling start	no	6–10
greens, hearty, sliced	5–7	boiling start	no	10–12
leeks, whole/halved	10–15	boiling start	no	12–15
peas, fresh garden	3–5	boiling start	no	5–10
potatoes, boiling/new	10–25	cold start	no	15–35
potatoes, Idaho, cubed	15–20	cold start	no	15–35
rutabaga, thickly sliced	8–12	cold start	yes	10–15
snow peas	2–3	boiling start	no	5–10
spinach	1–2	boiling start	no	3–4
squash, summer, sliced	5–8	boiling start	no	5–10
squash, winter, pieces	12–15	boiling start	yes	15–30
sweet potatoes, cubed	15–35	cold start	yes	30–45
turnip, thickly sliced/cubes	8–12	cold start	yes	10–15

COOKING EN PAPILLOTE

This is a delicate way to cook vegetables quickly while retaining much of their texture, flavor, and aromas. The vegetables are wrapped in a package ("papillote" is French for package) and cooked in the oven. However, they are really steamed, not baked.

Tender vegetables are the best suited for cooking en papillote, because they do not need long baking. Always consider sweating or parboiling potatoes and other roots and tubers first, to ensure even cooking and to speed up the process.

BABY CARROTS & TURNIPS EN PAPILLOTE

Cooking in individual paper packages turns otherwise humble vegetables, such as carrots and turnips, into something special.

8oz (225g) baby carrots, peeled and green ends trimmed

8oz (225g) baby turnips, halved or cut into wedges, according to size

extra virgin olive oil for brushing

sprigs of thyme

sprigs of rosemary

1 Preheat the oven to 450°F (230°C). Drop the baby carrots and turnips into a pan of boiling salted water and parboil for 3 minutes. Drain and refresh in ice water.

2 Cut out four large, heart-shaped pieces of parchment paper and brush them with extra virgin olive oil. Divide the vegetables into four individual portions.

3 For each package, place the vegetables on one side of a heart and season with salt and pepper. Add thyme and rosemary sprigs. Fold the other half of the heart over the vegetables.

4 Starting at the top of the heart, crimp all around the edge to seal the two open sides of the halves together, ensuring the crimps overlap each other.

COOKING EN PAPILLOTE

This is done primarily in parchment paper or foil, which is cut into a heart shape and then folded around the food to be cooked and its flavorings, to seal them in tightly. During cooking the ingredients produce steam, which causes the package to puff up. The result is very juicy and full of flavor. The same effect can be achieved by wrapping food in banana leaves, grape leaves, and corn husks.

5 When you reach the bottom, fold the point under to hold all the crimping in place.

6 Place the packages on a baking sheet and bake until the paper puffs, 5–8 minutes.

MICROWAVING

Microwave cooking is a form of steaming—
the microwaves agitate water molecules,
which in turn create steam. The water is
either found naturally in the food or is
added to the dish. Any vegetable that can
be steamed can be successfully microwaved.

MICROWAVED BABY ARTICHOKES

1 Place the artichokes in a microwave-safe
dish. Add enough water to cover the bottom
of the dish plus some sprigs of rosemary.

2 Cover the dish with plastic wrap that has
been punctured for ventilation of steam, or
cover with a lid. Cook to the desired doneness.
Remove from the microwave and let stand for a
few minutes. Then remove the cover and serve.

MICROWAVE TIPS

■ Cooking times will vary according to the wattage
of your microwave, as well as the freshness of the
vegetable you are cooking, the type of vegetable,
the quantity, and how it is prepared. Consult your
owner's manual for guidelines.
■ Be sure to allow vegetables to stand for a few
minutes after they are removed from the microwave.
This will complete the cooking.
■ Take care when uncovering the dish since steam
trapped inside will be very hot. If you have used
plastic wrap, make a large cut in it before removing.

Open the packages for serving, or
let each person open his or her own

BAKING & ROASTING

These are both dry-heat methods of cooking wherein the food is surrounded by hot air, usually in an oven although sometimes on a spit over an open fire. The term roasting is usually applied to meats and poultry, while baking typically is used for breads, pastries, and fish. In reality, though, there is little difference in the techniques.

Both baking and roasting concentrate the flavors of vegetables and also often produce a delicious browned, caramelized exterior.

Thick-skinned vegetables, such as potatoes, turnips, winter and summer squashes, beets, eggplant, and bell peppers, are well suited for baking or roasting. Also try roasting mushrooms. The vegetables may be baked or roasted in their skins or peeled.

Potatoes and other roots and tubers cut in pieces are often parboiled before roasting. Many vegetables are baked or roasted as a first step when making a purée (p262).

BAKED BEETS

Potatoes are often baked in their skins, with or without wrapping in foil, but this cooking method is also excellent for many other roots and tubers. Here, beets are baked in foil. Turnips, rutabaga, and salsify are also excellent baked like this. For even cooking, choose vegetables of equal size. Once baked, peel the vegetables or serve in their skins.

4 beets, preferably the size of a baseball

olive oil for drizzling

1 Preheat the oven to 400°F (200°C). Trim all but 1in (2.5cm) from the stem of each beet, then wash thoroughly and dry well. Drizzle some olive oil over the beets and rub it on evenly, then sprinkle them with coarse kosher or sea salt. Wrap individually in foil.

2 Place in a shallow roasting pan and bake in the middle of the oven until tender, about 45 minutes. Test for doneness with a fork: It should come out easily. Remove from the oven and set aside until cool enough to handle.

3 When the beets have cooled, peel away the skins using a paring knife (wear disposable gloves to prevent your hands from being stained with the beet juice).

4 Slice the beets, and season with salt and pepper to taste. Serve warm or cool.

ROASTED BUTTERNUT SQUASH

Butternut squash is particularly good cooked this way, as are pumpkin and acorn, hubbard, turban, and kabocha squashes. Other vegetables to roast like this include potatoes, turnips, parsnips, and rutabaga.

You can add extra flavor by tossing the buttered squash with chopped fresh herbs, such as rosemary, oregano, or thyme, before roasting. Or, for a sweet touch, try mixing a bit of brown sugar into the melted butter or oil.

1½lb (675g) butternut squash, halved, seeded, and peeled (p244)

3 tbsp melted butter or olive oil

1 Preheat the oven to 400°F (200°C). Cut the butternut squash into uniform-sized cubes, about 1in (2.5cm). Put onto a foil-lined baking sheet. Drizzle with the melted butter or oil and toss until the cubes are evenly coated.

Timings for baking & roasting vegetables

Bake or roast at 350–375°F (180–190°C), unless a hot oven (400–425°F/200–225°C) is noted. The size of the vegetables will affect the cooking times suggested.

SOME SUITABLE VEGETABLES	APPROXIMATE COOKING TIMES
asparagus	8–10 mins (hot oven)
beets (in skin)	45 mins (hot oven)
Belgian endive (in sauce)	20–30 min
cabbage, quartered and sliced (in sauce)	45–60 mins
carrots, baby	45–60 mins
corn-on-the-cob (in husk)	20–30 mins
eggplant, halved	25–35 mins
mushrooms, whole	15–20 mins
parsnip pieces	30 mins (blanch first)
potatoes, baking (in skin)	50–60 mins
potato pieces	30 mins (blanch first)
sweet potatoes (in skin)	45–60 mins
winter squash, cubed	45 mins (hot oven)
winter squash, halved	45–60 mins

2 Season the cubes of squash with salt to taste, then spread them out in a single layer. Put into the oven and roast until tender, about 45 minutes (test for doneness with a fork or tip of a knife). Serve the squash hot.

ROASTED GARLIC

Preheat the oven to 350°F (180°C). Cut the tops off 4 whole garlic bulbs. Put them in a small saucepan and cover with 3 cups of milk. Bring to a simmer, then cook on low heat for 10 minutes (cooking in milk helps to sweeten the garlic and preserve the color). Drain. Set the bulbs upright in an ovenproof dish. Add ½ cup olive oil and cover. Roast until the bulbs are soft, 1–1½ hours. Let the garlic cool in the oil, then squeeze the soft cloves out of the skins. Use immediately or refrigerate (in the oil) for up to 3 days. This makes ¾ cup.

POTATO GRATIN

One of the most popular ways to bake vegetables is in a gratin. Baking is done uncovered, so that an appetizing and flavorful crust can form.

Serves 6

butter for the pan

8 medium Yukon Gold potatoes, about 2lb (900g) in total, peeled and thinly sliced

2 cups freshly grated Parmesan or other well-flavored cheese

2 cups heavy cream

1 Preheat the oven to 350°F (180°C). Butter an 8in (20cm) square baking pan. Arrange a layer of potato slices on the bottom of the pan. Season with salt and pepper, and sprinkle with some of the cheese. Continue the layering until all the potatoes are in the pan, finishing with the last of the cheese on top.

2 Pour the heavy cream evenly over the surface. Bake the gratin until the potatoes are tender (test with a skewer) and the top is golden brown and crisp, about 1½ hours. Serve the gratin immediately.

PURÉEING

Cooked vegetable purées can be served as they are or used as a component of another recipe. They can also be mixed with other ingredients to make soufflés and terrines. Try experimenting with different combinations for purées, such as fennel with apple.

The most common way to cook vegetables for a purée is to boil, bake, or steam them. In some cases, a microwave can be used. The vegetables can be peeled before or after cooking. Most tubers and root vegetables can be boiled in water. In the case of vegetables, such as celeriac, turnips, and parsnips, however, they are better cooked in milk, to retain their color as well as to add a hint of sweetness. Green vegetables should only be cooked until just tender, as overcooking will cause them to discolor. All other vegetables should be cooked until very tender, almost falling apart.

Puréeing with a ricer or food mill will remove any fibers and skin at the same time. If you use a blender or food processor to purée vegetables that are fibrous, you will then have to pass the purée through a strainer to remove the fibers and skin.

USING A FOOD MILL

1 Cook the vegetables (celeriac is shown here), then drain well. Transfer to a food mill set over a bowl and turn the handle to work the vegetables through the screen to make a purée.

2 Season the purée with salt and pepper to taste. It is now ready to serve (reheat if necessary) or to use in another recipe.

USING A STRAINER

If a cooked vegetable is fibrous (such as celeriac, shown here), first purée it in a blender or food processor, then transfer to a fine-mesh strainer set over a bowl. Use a rubber spatula to press the purée through the strainer to remove the fibers. The resulting purée will be very smooth.

STUFFING

This is a great way to present vegetables as a main course or as a side dish. Most vegetables are appropriate for stuffing, although the method will vary based on the vegetable's texture. Common stuffing ingredients are seafood, meat, cheese, rice, and crumbs.

Bell peppers, onions, winter and summer squashes, and tomatoes are all ideal for stuffing, and are usually baked. Other stuffed vegetables, such as squash blossoms, are cooked on the stovetop. In most cases the stuffing should include part of the vegetable being stuffed (i.e. a stuffed onion should include some onion in the stuffing), to bind the flavors together.

Stuffing a raw vegetable produces more integrated flavors in the finished dish; however, stuffing a partially cooked vegetable, such as a tomato, allows for easier control of flavor and texture. You can also stuff vegetables that are completely cooked. For example, roasted squash can be stuffed with a cooked filling and then simply warmed through in the oven before serving.

BELL PEPPERS WITH WILD RICE STUFFING

Ingredients
4 bell peppers
2 cups cooked wild rice
½ cup julienned sun-dried tomatoes
½ cup roasted, peeled, and diced green bell peppers (p252)
½ cup cooked, diced eggplant
2 tbsp snipped chives
2 tsp extra virgin olive oil
1 tsp fresh lemon juice

A HANDY TOOL

A melon baller is a great tool for removing cores and flesh when preparing vegetables for stuffing, especially tomatoes, onions, and squashes.

1 Preheat the oven to 375°F (190°C). Cut around the stem of each pepper and pull it off, taking the core with it. Rinse inside to remove all the seeds, then blot the peppers dry with paper towels.

2 Mix together all the remaining ingredients with seasoning to taste. Spoon this stuffing into the peppers. Stand them upright in an oiled baking pan and cover with foil. Bake until piping hot and very tender, about 1 hour.

SAUTÉING

For this quick method, vegetables are cooked in a small amount of fat in a shallow pan on the stovetop. The heat is very high and the vegetables are constantly kept moving in the pan. Sautéing is similar to pan-frying (p268), the differences being the amount of fat used and the fact that you don't "toss" the items when pan-frying.

Vegetables suitable for sautéing include tender leafy greens, onions, summer squashes, and mushrooms. Take care not to crowd the pan, so that all the vegetables cook quickly and evenly.

Sometimes sautéing is used as a finishing step for vegetables that have been parboiled, for example potatoes and other roots and tubers. Sautéed and parboiled vegetables may also be finished by glazing (see opposite). For this, a small amount of sugar and butter are added at the end of cooking. The sugar caramelizes, coating the vegetable with a sweet glaze.

If desired, once the vegetables have been removed, a sauce can be made in the pan, to capture all of the flavor.

SAUTÉING FIRM VEGETABLES

1 Set a sauté pan on high heat. When the pan is hot, add a small amount of clarified butter or oil (just enough to cover the bottom).

2 As soon as the fat is heated, add the vegetables to the pan (zucchini batonnets are shown here). Constantly turn and toss the vegetables in the pan so that they cook evenly.

3 When the vegetables are browned and tender, remove from the heat and serve.

SAUTÉING LEAFY GREEN VEGETABLES

Leafy vegetables, such as spinach (shown here), must be completely dry before cooking. Otherwise the hot fat in the pan will spit. Melt a small amount of butter in a sauté pan, then add the vegetables. If desired, add a smashed garlic clove, too, to enhance the flavor. Turn and toss until the leaves are wilted and tender, then season and serve immediately.

GLAZED SAUTÉED CARROTS

Here, baby carrots are finished with a delicious butter-sugar glaze. You can glaze other sautéed vegetables, such as baby turnips and cubes of winter squash, in the same way.

20 small baby carrots or 1½ cups sliced carrots, parboiled for 3 minutes and drained

3–4 tbsp butter

1½–2 tsp sugar

1 Put the carrots in a hot sauté pan with the butter and sugar (use the smaller amounts of butter and sugar for baby carrots).

2 Turn and toss the carrots until they are tender and coated in a delicious butter-sugar glaze. Serve immediately.

Timings for sautéing vegetables

The size of the vegetables will affect the cooking times indicated in the chart.

SOME SUITABLE VEGETABLES	APPROXIMATE COOKING TIMES
asparagus	3–4 mins
bell peppers, sliced	3–6 mins
cabbage, shredded	5–7 mins
corn kernels, fresh	3–5 mins
mushrooms	3–5 mins
onions, sliced	3–5 mins
porcini mushrooms, fresh	5–7 mins
radicchio	3–5 mins
shallots, whole (glaze)	10–15 mins
snow peas	3–6 mins
spinach	3–5 mins
winter squash pieces	3–5 mins

 ### FATS FOR SAUTÉING & FRYING

It is important to know which fats are good for sautéing. The oils I like to use are canola, safflower, grapeseed, peanut, corn, and olive. All of these are also suitable for pan-frying and deep-frying. Butter —whole or clarified (p24)—and rendered animal fat, such as bacon grease and duck fat, are also great for sautéing and pan-frying, but not for deep-frying.

When using olive oil for sautéing, take care that it doesn't overheat. Olive oil has a lower smoke point than other oils, so you can't get it as hot.

BRAISING & STEWING

The results of braising and stewing are amazing. For both of these methods, vegetables are gently simmered in a small amount of stock or other liquid (often flavored with a mirepoix or with other vegetables) for an extended period of time. Cooking can be done on the stovetop or in the oven.

A key difference between braising and stewing is that braising uses much less liquid. Also, in some braising recipes the flavoring agents are not sweated or browned before the vegetables are added. Fat is always used to start braising or stewing vegetables, because it imparts flavor and texture to the finished dish.

BRAISED RED CABBAGE

2 tbsp rendered bacon fat

1 cup roughly chopped mirepoix of carrot, onion, and celery (see below)

2 cups finely shredded red cabbage

1 tbsp sherry vinegar, or to taste

2 tbsp sugar, or to taste

1 Heat the bacon fat in a heavy-based pan, add the mirepoix, and cook over low heat to soften and release flavor, without letting the vegetables brown. Add the red cabbage and stir to mix with the fat and mirepoix.

2 Pour in enough water partially to cover the vegetables. Add the sherry vinegar and sugar. Bring to a boil, then cover and simmer until the cabbage is tender, about 1 hour.

3 Remove from the heat. Lift out and discard the mirepoix, then season the cabbage with salt and pepper to taste. Serve hot.

Timings for braising & stewing vegetables

Oven cooking is typically at 350°F (180°C). On the stovetop the pot is always covered and heat is very low.

SOME SUITABLE VEGETABLES	APPROXIMATE COOKING TIMES
artichokes, baby	30–45 mins
Belgian endive	15–20 mins
Brussels sprouts	30–40 mins
cabbage, shredded	20–60 mins
fennel	20–30 mins
greens, hearty	30–45 mins
leeks	20–30 mins
okra	30–60 mins
potatoes, new	20–30 mins
radicchio	40–45 mins
summer squash, sliced	8–15 mins

MIREPOIX

A mirepoix is a mixture of aromatic vegetables—usually carrots, onions, and celery—used as a flavoring agent. I prefer to have a mirepoix in larger chunks so that more flavor is released during the sweating process, and I always remove it at the end of cooking. However, the mirepoix can be cut into small dice and left in the finished dish. It is really a matter of personal preference.

PICKLING

These days, pickling is much more about flavor than it is about preserving in a spiced vinegar. The simplest way to pickle is to prepare a brine and add either cooked or raw vegetables. A typical brine is made with one part salt to eight parts water, but many other ingredients are added to help flavor the pickled vegetables.

The most popular vegetable for pickling is cucumber, but okra, mushrooms, garlic, chilies, beets, carrots, and globe artichokes can also be successfully pickled. Vegetables with a firmer texture tend to hold up best when pickled.

If you plan to keep pickled vegetables for an extended period of time, it is important to follow an appropriate canning technique. This involves submerging the closed jar in a pan of boiling water until a vacuum seal is created. If you don't do this, keep the pickled vegetables in the refrigerator and consume within a week or so.

PICKLED CUCUMBERS

2 English cucumbers
1 cup water
½ cup rice vinegar
⅓ cup sugar
2 tbsp kosher salt
1 whole clove
1 tsp mustard seed
1 tsp black peppercorns
2 fresh Thai chilies
2 bay leaves
2 sprigs of thyme

1 Prepare the cucumbers for pickling by quartering them lengthwise. If necessary, trim them so they'll fit in the jar. Combine all the remaining ingredients in a saucepan and bring to a boil. Stir to dissolve the sugar and salt.

2 Put the cucumbers in a nonreactive jar or container and cover with the hot brine. Cover the jar and let cool to room temperature. Keep in the refrigerator for at least 12 hours before serving. The pickled cucumbers can be kept, refrigerated, for up to 1 week.

PASTA & DUMPLINGS

MICHAEL ROMANO

"Pasta" is Italian for paste, or dough, and consists of a starch in the form of flour mixed with a liquid, frequently water. Pasta is made from starches. Perhaps most common is durum wheat (*Triticum turgidum* var. *durum*), a hard wheat with a high proportion of gluten content among the proteins; this is mostly used coarsely ground in the form of semolina. Hard wheat (*Triticum aestivum*) is used to make all-purpose flour for fresh pasta and is sometimes blended with durum wheat. Emmer (*Triticum dicoccum*), or farro in Italian, is an ancient form of wheat made into flour for dried pasta. Whole-wheat flour, milled with the bran and germ intact, is used in Venetian cooking to form bigoli, a type of fresh, thick spaghetti. Flour from buckwheat is used in Lombardy to make pizzoccheri, a rectangular-shaped pasta. Buckwheat flour is also made into dumplings and Japanese soba noodles.

Throughout Asia, barley, rice, millet, mung beans, seaweed, tapioca, soybeans, and oats are used to fashion different types of pasta. Also utilized are potato flour, cornstarch, cornmeal, dried legumes, and dried vegetables, such as artichokes and Jerusalem artichokes. The processed seeds of amaranth and quinoa, two highly nutritious plants known and widely used by pre-Columbian peoples, are also still used to make pasta today.

Pasta varieties To make commercial dried pasta, water is used almost exclusively. In parts of Italy, whole eggs, egg yolks, or a combination of the two, are used for fresh pasta. Some dried pastas use dried eggs or egg yolks instead of fresh. Cheese is used for pasta in Sicily, and flour and ricotta cheese are used to make the dough for gnocchi and cavatelli. Some recipes call for olive oil, white wine, or milk to be added to the flour for pasta dough. There is also a whole category of pastas that are flavored and colored by being made with puréed spinach, green chard, beets, mushrooms, or tomatoes. Squid ink is also used to make a distinctive black-colored fresh pasta.

In fresh pastamaking, some or all of the water used in the basic recipe is replaced with eggs and/or egg yolks with the possible additions of white wine, oil, and other flavoring liquids. The starch used is bread wheat, which is less hard than durum wheat. Fresh pasta is typically associated with the Italian regions of Emilia-Romagna—and its capital, the great gastronomic city of Bologna—and Piedmont, famous also for its intense wines and fragrant white truffles.

Every day, millions of people eat dried pasta, molded into hundreds of different shapes, in every part of the world. However, many people associate "fresh" with wholesomeness and better health, and view fresh pasta as better, or more special, than dried. This is simply not true. Dried pasta can be a product of very high quality. Indeed, some argue that dried pasta is more desirable than fresh, because durum wheat semolina retains more of its nutritious elements than the white flour used in fresh pasta. Today, one can even find Italian dried pasta made from organically grown wheat.

Dumplings Always made of some sort of cereal or starchy vegetable, dumplings consist of a kind of bread dough to which seasonings or herbs are added. The cooking process involves simmering and/or steaming in a flavored liquid, such as a broth or stew, to allow the proteins in the starch (or eggs) to expand, lighten, and set. Often, something is enclosed inside the ball or oblong of dough, such as meat or fruit. In southern Germany and Austria, eggs, butter, cheese, liver, milk, and other embellishments are added. In that part of the world, dumplings go by such names as Knödel, Nockerl, and Spaetzle, according to their size and shape.

The "dumplings" of Italian and Asian cuisine lie somewhat apart from the English and central European models. Gnocchi, for example, can be considered a type of fresh pasta, with a fairly well-defined shape, while in China, throughout central Asia, and in Russia, many types of stuffed "dumplings," such as wonton, mantu, mantou, shao mai, and pel'meni, more closely resemble the "ravioli" pasta prototype than that of the dumpling.

MAKING FRESH PASTA

Preparing fresh pasta from scratch definitely ranks among the most pleasurable and satisfying tasks in the kitchen. Like any other worthwhile endeavor, it takes patience and practice, but to my mind, there are few things that repay a little effort with such generous and delicious rewards.

There are two methods of making fresh pasta—by hand or in a food processor. While the latter is quicker, the former has the benefit of giving the pasta-maker, over time, a truer sense of the texture and feel of the dough, a sense of how much flour the eggs can absorb, and—ultimately—a more tender pasta. Remember, however, that "tender" does not mean flaccid: Fresh pasta, if it is worked correctly during the stretching process, should have texture and "tooth" when it is cooked.

Once the pasta dough is made, there are again two methods you can use to stretch the dough. The hand method, using the long, dowel-like European rolling pin, which is usually not more than 1½in (4cm) in diameter, is by far the more demanding skill. This rolling pin, by the way, is much recommended over the thicker American style with its ball-bearing mechanism. Using the latter is like driving an automatic transmission car, as opposed to a sporty

stick shift. With the plain, cylindrical pin, you can feel the dough as it stretches. I urge everyone to attempt hand-stretching the pasta dough, simply because it is so satisfying.

The alternative is a good-quality pasta machine, either hand-cranked or electric, which also produces an excellent result. To my taste, the hand-stretched pasta is a bit more porous, lighter, and more capable of absorbing sauce, while machine-stretching results in a denser, somewhat slicker, smoother strand.

Preferences for work surfaces vary, with wood, stone (marble or other), and stainless steel being the most popular choices.

Making fresh pasta entails four distinct steps:

■ The first step is the actual formation of the dough from the basic ingredients, which for homemade pasta are usually flour and eggs with a little salt, plus sometimes olive oil, white wine, or milk. Other flavorings and colorings can also be added.

■ The second step is the kneading of the dough to develop its "body." This enables it to be stretched thin.

■ The third step is creating "la sfoglia," which is what Italians call the thinly stretched sheet of dough (pasta-makers are "sfogline").

■ The final step is to cut the sfoglia into the desired shapes.

MAKING PASTA DOUGH BY HAND

Do keep in mind that in Italy—and, in fact, wherever people are familiar with making fresh pasta—the amounts given in a recipe are approximate. One speaks of making "an egg" of pasta, per person, as opposed to a definite amount of flour. The eggs will absorb as much flour as they want. In certain parts of Italy, such as Emilia-Romagna, salt is omitted from the dough. I like to include it in the recipe.

It is better to have a dough that is a bit too wet than too dry, as it is much easier to work in a bit more flour than it is to add more moisture. If you do find yourself needing to add some moisture, do it by wetting your hands and then working the dough, rather than by adding water directly to the dough.

Makes enough pasta to serve 4 as an appetizer or 2 as a main dish, depending on shape and thickness of cut

1⅓ cups all-purpose flour

½ tsp salt

2 eggs

1 Prepare a clean, well-lit work surface, at least 2ft (60cm) deep by 3ft (92cm) wide, and have at hand your rolling pin, a pastry scraper, a fork, and a fine-mesh strainer. Pour the flour and salt onto the work surface and form a well large enough to hold the eggs. Crack the eggs into the well and beat lightly with the fork.

2 Keeping one hand at the ready on the outside of the well, in case some egg should escape, begin drawing in small amounts of flour from the inside bottom of the well and mixing to incorporate the flour into the eggs. Gently stir the eggs all the while, and continue pulling in small amounts of flour.

3 When the egg and flour mixture is thick enough not to run, push all the remaining flour into the middle and gently mix to form a dough. When the dough has stiffened somewhat and will no longer absorb flour, move it to a corner of the work surface. Scrape the work surface clean, and wash and dry your hands.

4 Place the scraped-away flour and bits of dough in the strainer and sift the clean flour onto a corner of the surface. Discard the pieces of dough in the strainer. Place the dough on the clean surface and knead until it holds together well. If it seems very sticky, sprinkle with a bit of the sifted flour, but do not let it get too dry.

5 Continue to knead with a steady, firm motion, giving a quarter-turn with one hand while you press downward and forward with the heel of the other hand. Do this without rushing or exerting too much force, which will tire you out, but with a very steady, rhythmic motion, perhaps timed to your breathing.

6 Knead until the dough feels very smooth and elastic, about 5–8 minutes. Wrap the dough in plastic wrap and set aside at room temperature for at least 30 minutes, or up to 2 hours, before stretching it. This will give it time to soften enough to be stretched.

USING A MACHINE

A food processor is quick, but be careful not to overheat the dough by too much processing.

1 Combine the flour and salt in the bowl of a food processor and pulse a few times to aerate. With the machine running, add the beaten eggs (or eggs mixed with flavoring ingredients—see below) through the feed tube and process until the dough begins to form a ball. If it is too dry to do this, add water 1 tsp at a time and continue to process.

2 Turn the dough onto a clean, unfloured surface and form it into a ball. Knead (see step 5, left) until the dough feels smooth and elastic, 5–8 minutes. Wrap the dough and set it aside for at least 30 minutes to let it soften before stretching it.

FLAVORING & COLORING PASTA DOUGH

Mix one of the following with the eggs, then continue making the dough by hand or in a machine.

■ For spinach pasta (see below), use ½ cup cooked, finely chopped or puréed, and well-drained spinach. Finely chopped spinach will give you a pasta that is speckled green and purée a more uniform green.

■ For pasta rossa, add 2 tbsp tomato paste—ideally Sicilian sun-dried tomato paste.

■ For lemon-pepper pasta, add the grated zest of 2 small lemons, 1 tsp coarsely ground black pepper, and 2 tbsp freshly grated Parmesan (try to use Parmigiano Reggiano).

■ For mushroom and herb pasta, rehydrate and purée 1oz (30g) dried porcini, then add with 1 tbsp finely minced rosemary.

STRETCHING PASTA DOUGH BY HAND

Stretching the dough by hand, using a rolling pin, is the part of the pasta-making process that requires the most skill—and patience. It is not all that difficult to master, however, and once you've gotten the knack, and the rhythm, you will find that it is definitely the most satisfying part. Remember that it is important to work quickly, because if the dough is allowed to dry out and become stiff, it will no longer stretch.

When beginning to roll out the dough, apply pressure only in the outward direction, not on the return of the pin, and remember to think of this motion as pushing the dough out and away from you, rather than pressing it into the table. If the dough feels sticky at any time during the stretching process, sprinkle it with a small amount of flour to ease movement.

If you are intending to use the dough for stuffed pasta, you can either stuff and cut each sheet as it is done, or cover each rolled out sheet with a slightly damp dish towel and then stuff them all at once.

1 Unwrap the dough and cut it in half or into thirds or even fourths, depending on how skilled you are at stretching. Re-wrap all but one piece of the dough. Form the dough into a ball and flatten it slightly with your hands to create a disk. Sprinkle the worktable lightly with flour and place the dough in front of you.

2 Begin gently rolling the dough outward from a point about one-third of the way into the disk. Do not use too much pressure, and give the dough a quarter turn each time you complete an outward motion. Continue this process until you have formed a round piece of dough of equal thickness—about ⅛in (3mm).

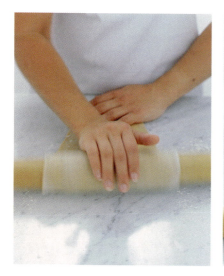

5 Continue, adding a bit more of the dough each time, until you have rolled up and unfurled the entire round. Roll all the dough onto the rolling pin and turn the pin around (not over) so that each hand is now grasping the other end, then unroll the dough on the table.

6 Begin the process again, starting on the opposite end to where you last began. Keep repeating the curling, stretching, and unfurling process until the dough reaches the desired thickness (for stuffed pasta, roll as thinly as possible; for cut pasta, roll to about 1mm).

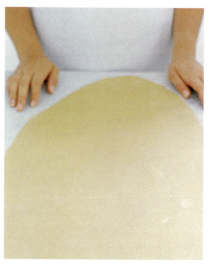

7 At the end of this process, you will have a very elongated oval shape of thinly rolled dough—the sfoglia—which I find easier to achieve, and to work with, than a perfect circle.

CUTTING PASTA DOUGH BY HAND

Before cutting, you can trim the dough that results from hand-stretching. I prefer not to, as it causes waste and lowers yield. Also, part of the hand-made process is the irregularity of lengths and shapes. It is generally just fine to use your eye to measure the widths of the various shapes and noodles. Flour the work surface and use a sharp chef's knife for cutting.

Square or rectangular shapes

Cut the dough to the required size: 5in (12cm) squares for fazzoletti, or 5 by 6in (12 by 15cm) rectangles for lasagna or cannelloni.

Noodles

Fold the dough into thirds, like a letter. Place it with the folds at top and bottom, then cut lengthwise into strips: ¼in (5mm) wide for fettuccine and ½in (1cm) wide for pappardelle.

3 Place the rolling pin on the top edge of the dough round. Curl the dough over the pin and roll up about one-fourth of the dough, using a light pressure. Anchor the dough on the table with your other hand. Using a somewhat staccato forward-and-back, rolling-and-pushing motion, quickly unfurl the dough from the pin.

4 Repeat the curling of the dough edge over the pin, but this time roll up a bit more of the dough than the last time, say one-third. Once again, anchor the dough with your other hand and give it the same forward-and-back unfurling motion. These movements should be quick, but smooth and even.

8 If you are going to cut the pasta into shapes, roll up the sheet of dough on your pin and unroll it onto a clean, dry dish towel. Let it dry for 15–25 minutes, depending on the humidity of the room, then cut. If using for stuffed pasta, proceed immediately (see opposite page).

STRETCHING & CUTTING PASTA DOUGH WITH A MACHINE

You can use either a hand-cranked or electric pasta machine. I have included a little trick to make the work easier—pressing the ends of the strip of dough together to make a continuous loop. This technique works well for a large amount of dough, which, when stretched, becomes tricky to keep removing from and feeding back into the rollers. To start, set up the machine on the work surface, and lightly flour the surface in front of the machine. During the initial folding and stretching process, drag the dough strip through the flour every now and then.

1 Cut the pasta dough into fourths; wrap three of the pieces in plastic and set aside. Flatten the remaining piece of dough into a rough circle and pass it through the widest setting on the machine. Decrease the setting a notch and pass the dough through once again. Decrease another notch, and pass the dough through once more.

2 Fold the strip of dough into thirds and flatten it with your fingers. Return the machine to its widest setting. Turn the dough so that an unfolded end is against the rollers, then pass it through the machine. Repeat this folding and stretching process five or six times, until the dough feels silky and elastic.

3 Now begin rolling the dough through the machine on decreasing settings until you reach the desired thickness. For cut pastas, this will usually be one notch before the finest setting; for stuffed pastas it will be all the way to the finest setting. To try my trick, pause three or four notches before the final setting.

5 Roll the loop through the machine several times to even it out, then continue rolling as you click down the settings to reach the desired thickness. Cut the dough with a paring knife and finish unrolling it from the machine.

6 If you are intending to use the dough for stuffed pasta, proceed immediately, without letting the sheet dry (see p279). If you are going to cut the pasta into shapes, lay it flat on a clean, dry dish towel on the work surface and let dry for 15–25 minutes, depending on the humidity of the room.

COOKING FRESH OR DRIED PASTA

In spite of its being a simple procedure, there seems to be a lot of erroneous information about the cooking of pasta. Here are my tips.

■ Do be sure to have an abundant amount of rapidly boiling water in the pot—on the order of 4 quarts (4 liters) for 12–16oz (350–450g) dried or fresh pasta. There is nothing worse than cooking pasta in insufficient water that is not at a rapid boil.

■ Season the 4 quarts (4 liters) boiling water with 2 tbsp salt—preferably kosher or sea salt. It is not possible to "season up" undersalted pasta once it is cooked; the salt will not penetrate.

■ Do not add oil to the water, because this will only make the pasta slippery and less able to absorb the sauce. The reason people add oil is to prevent the pasta shapes from sticking together. This is better accomplished by stirring the pasta once it has been added to the pot.

■ It is sometimes a good idea, especially if your burners are not too strong, to cover the pot after you have added the pasta. This will help the water return to a boil more quickly. Once it has started boiling again, remove the lid and continue cooking uncovered.

■ While the pasta is cooking, be sure you have everything at hand, ready to go, so that the pasta can be quickly drained and sauced, then served immediately.

■ After draining the pasta, do not run cold water over it to stop the cooking—you will wash away all the starch and seasoning.

■ To sauce pasta, I recommend tossing it in the skillet or pan with the sauce, to coat the pasta evenly and help it soak up the flavors. Make sure that the skillet or pan in which you are making the sauce is large enough to eventually hold all the cooked pasta, too.

1 Be sure the water is at a rapid boil, then add the salt and plunge the pasta into the pot. Stir immediately to prevent the pasta from clumping together. When the water comes back to a boil, cook until the pasta is done (see below), continuing to stir occasionally.

2 Drain the pasta by pouring it into a large colander. Always reserve a small amount of the cooking water—it comes in very handy in many recipes to thin out and season the sauce. Do this by immediately placing the colander over the pot you cooked the pasta in.

4 Pass about half of the pasta strip through the rollers and stop. Press the edge of the other half onto the top surface of the machine in front of the rollers, then bring up and connect the edge of the extended half to it, pressing with your fingers to form a continuous loop of dough. Be sure that the edges line up accurately.

7 Use the cutters provided with the pasta machine to cut the pasta shape you desire, such as fettuccine or tagliarini (as shown above). Feed the strip of dough carefully into the machine so it falls straight onto the cutters. For square or rectangular shapes, cut it by hand.

HOW DO YOU KNOW WHEN PASTA IS DONE?

When I was growing up, I remember hearing about the notion of testing the doneness of pasta by tossing a strand against the wall. If the pasta stuck, so the story went, it was done. I can assure you that I've never tried this system, and it is entirely unnecessary. Follow the timing suggestion on the package of pasta and—most importantly—taste a strand or piece of pasta at several points during the duration of the cooking.

Dried pasta is cooked until it is "al dente," which means it should offer a slight resistance to the tooth when you bite into it. Also, if you break open a strand or piece of the cooked pasta, you should see a small white dot at the center. Fresh pasta is cooked slightly beyond al dente—until it is tender. When cooked, the pasta will have lost its raw taste, and it will be tender to the bite while retaining some body.

SERVING FRESH PASTA

Following are two of my favorite pasta recipes. Fazzoletti, which are large, flat pasta squares whimsically named for their resemblance to a silk handkerchief, can be folded, casually draped, or laid flat on a plate. At Union Square Café, we sauce the fazzoletti with a delicious zucchini-marjoram purée.

Fettuccine with sweet corn has long been a late-summer pasta staple at USC. For the sauce, we've borrowed from classic corn chowder recipes, steeping corncobs with white wine and cream to lend a richly complex corn flavor. The addition of Gorgonzola, pancetta, and sun-dried tomatoes completes the dish.

FAZZOLETTI WITH ZUCCHINI-MARJORAM SAUCE

Serves 12 as an appetizer or 6 as a main course

1 quantity of fresh pasta dough made with 2 eggs (p276)

4 quarts (4 liters) boiling water with 2 tbsp kosher or sea salt for cooking

For the sauce

2 tbsp extra virgin olive oil

1 garlic clove, sliced

12oz (340g) zucchini, quartered lengthwise and thinly sliced

½ tsp chopped marjoram

½ cup peeled, seeded, and diced tomato

½ cup chicken stock, or more as needed

To finish

1 cup all-purpose flour for the cookie sheets

4 tbsp butter

⅓ cup water

fresh shavings of Parmesan (Parmigiano Reggiano)

1 To make the sauce, put the oil and garlic in a large, straight-sided skillet. Cook over low heat until the garlic is soft but not browned, 2–3 minutes. Raise the heat to high and add the zucchini, marjoram, tomato, and some salt and pepper. Cook, stirring occasionally, until the zucchini have softened somewhat. Add the chicken stock and cook for 4–5 minutes longer.

2 Transfer the zucchini mixture to a food processor and pulse until smooth, but not too finely puréed. Return the purée to the skillet and warm it through over medium heat, stirring constantly. Adjust the consistency to your taste (by adding more stock or water if it seems too thick) and check the seasoning. Set aside.

3 Dust two cookie sheets with the flour. Stretch the pasta dough to not quite paper-thin if you are doing it by hand, or to within one notch

of the finest if using a machine. Let dry, then cut into twelve 5in (12cm) squares (fazzoletti) and place in a single layer on the floured sheets.

4 Combine the butter, water, ½ tsp salt, and a pinch of pepper in a very large skillet. Bring to a boil to melt the butter, then swirl the ingredients to combine. Remove from the heat.

5 Cook the fazzoletti in the boiling salted water until tender, about 2 minutes. Return the zucchini-marjoram sauce to a simmer. Drain

the fazzoletti and immediately add them to the butter mixture in the skillet. Place it on medium heat and toss the fazzoletti gently to coat with the seasoned butter.

6 Spoon the zucchini sauce onto the serving plates and spread the sauce to cover the bottom. Using tongs, place a fazzoletto (or two, if serving as a main course) on top of each pool of sauce, draping the pasta so that it looks like a handkerchief. Sprinkle with Parmesan shavings and freshly ground black pepper, then serve.

FETTUCCINE WITH SWEET CORN & GORGONZOLA CREAM

Although this sauce has been designed to be served with freshly made fettuccine, you will also be satisfied if you use 1lb (450g) good-quality dried egg fettuccine.

Serves 6 as an appetizer or 3–4 as a main course

For the pasta

2 cups all-purpose flour

½ tsp salt

3 eggs

4 quarts (4 liters) boiling water with 2 tbsp kosher or sea salt for cooking

For the sauce

2 large ears sweet corn

1 tbsp olive oil

½ cup diced pancetta

½ cup sliced shallots

1 tbsp coarsely chopped garlic

½ cup white wine

2 cups heavy cream

2 heaping tbsp crumbled Gorgonzola

1 tsp kosher salt

⅛ tsp freshly ground black pepper

½ cup diagonally sliced scallions (white and green parts)

⅓ cup sliced basil leaves

12 oil-packed sun-dried tomatoes

1 Make the pasta dough following the master recipe (p276), but using the ingredients listed here. Stretch the dough to almost paper-thin if you are doing it by hand, or to within one to two notches of the finest if using a machine. Let dry, then cut into fettuccine, which are long strands about ¼in (5mm) wide.

2 Cut the kernels off the ears of corn. Set the kernels aside. Cut the cobs into 2in (5cm) sections.

3 Combine the oil and pancetta in a large, straight-sided skillet and cook over medium-high heat

to crisp the pancetta and render the fat, about 5 minutes. Remove the pancetta with a slotted spoon and set aside. Discard all but 1 tbsp fat from the pan.

4 Reduce the heat to medium. Add the shallots, garlic, and pieces of corncob to the pan, and

cook until the shallots are softened but not browned, about 3 minutes. Pour in the wine and reduce until almost dry. Add the cream and simmer very gently for 5 minutes. Remove from the heat, cover, and let steep for at least 15 minutes.

5 Strain the sauce through a fine-mesh strainer into another skillet or a saucepan that will be large enough to hold all the cooked pasta, too. Place over medium heat and gently whisk in the cheese in small pieces. Season with the salt and pepper. Add the pancetta, corn kernels, scallions, and basil. Cut the tomatoes in half lengthwise and stir in. Bring the sauce to a simmer, then remove from the heat, cover, and set aside.

6 Cook the fettuccine in the boiling salted water until it is tender, 30–60 seconds, then drain it in a colander. Add the pasta to the sauce in the skillet or saucepan.

7 Toss until all the strands of pasta are well coated with the sauce. Transfer to bowls and serve.

MAKING DUMPLINGS

In differentiating between pasta and dumplings, the distinguishing factor would appear to be shape, rather than ingredients. With pasta the dough is shaped or cut into a precise, well-defined form, whereas dumplings are generally left in a rather homey, irregular shape. For spaetzle, mainly seen in Alsace, Switzerland, Germany, and Austria, a batterlike dough is pressed into squiggly dumplings. Matzo balls and potato gnocchi are both shaped by hand, one into balls and the other into ridged ovals.

MAKING SPAETZLE

Spaetzle are quite simple to prepare: the dough is passed through a press directly into boiling salted water to create tiny, irregular dumplings. If you don't have a special spaetzle press, you can use a colander with ¼in (5mm) holes, and press the dough through it with a rubber spatula (as shown below). After boiling, spaetzle can be tossed with a sauce or sautéed.

1¾ cups all-purpose flour	5 tbsp hot water
2 eggs	**For sautéeing (optional)**
a scraping of freshly grated nutmeg	1 tbsp olive oil
5 tbsp milk	2 tbsp butter

1 Sift the flour into a large bowl. Form a well in the center and break in the eggs. Add a pinch of salt and the nutmeg. Stirring with your hand, begin mixing the eggs and flour together. Slowly pour in the milk, still stirring with your hand. Stir in the hot water.

2 Beat the mixture lightly with your hand for 30 seconds. The mixture should be the consistency of a very wet, soft dough. Let it relax for at least 30 minutes in a cool place. Meanwhile, bring a large pot of salted water to a boil and set a spaetzle press or colander on top.

3 Put the dough into the press or colander and begin pushing it through the holes. Cook in batches to avoid overcrowding the pot. As soon as the water resumes boiling, boil for 30 seconds. With a slotted spoon, transfer the cooked spaetzle to an ice-water bath, then drain well.

4 When all the spaetzle have been cooked and drained, reheat them in a sauce or sauté them: Heat the oil and butter in a large, heavy skillet. When sizzling, add the spaetzle and sauté until they are golden brown and slightly crisp. Serve hot as a side dish.

RED CHARD SPAETZLE

I really enjoy the earthy taste of red chard in combination with sautéed spaetzle. You could even include the chard stems as well as the leaves—thinly slice and sauté the stems separately, then add them with the leaves. Feel free to substitute green chard or spinach for the red chard.

1 quantity of spaetzle (see above)
1 tbsp olive oil
2 tbsp butter
12oz (340g) stemmed red Swiss chard leaves, cut into large pieces

Sauté the spaetzle in the oil and butter (see above) until they begin to turn golden brown. Add the chard leaves and continue cooking until the leaves are wilted. Season to taste with salt and pepper, then serve immediately, as an appetizer.

MATZO BALLS

Matzo balls—called kneidlach in Yiddish—are a type of dumpling made with a thick matzo meal batter. The dumplings are usually served in a rich chicken broth. Quantities to make 16 matzo balls are given in the recipe, right.

1 Put the eggs in a bowl and stir with a fork just to combine the white and yolks. Stir in the water or seltzer, the schmaltz, and some salt and pepper. Gradually add the matzo meal, stirring all the while to eliminate lumps. Refrigerate the batter for at least 1 hour.

2 With moistened hands, form the matzo balls, using about 2oz (55g) of batter for each one. As they are shaped, drop the balls, a couple at a time, into a large pot of boiling salted water. When the water returns to a boil, reduce the heat so it is simmering, then cover and cook for 30 minutes. Lift out with a slotted spoon, tasting one ball to be sure it is cooked through. Serve in rich chicken broth.

SUSAN FRIEDLAND'S MATZO BALL SOUP

This recipe for traditional matzo ball soup comes from my friend Susan Friedland, cookbook author and editor. The recipe for the broth makes twice the amount you need, but given the time and labor involved I think this is a good thing. Half of the broth can be frozen—it is useful to have on hand. If you want to serve the soup as a main course for 5–6, add the chicken meat to the broth.

Serves 8 as an appetizer

For the rich chicken broth

2 stewing hens, 6–8lb (2.7–3.6kg) each, including neck and giblets but not the liver

5–6 quarts (5–5.7 liters) water

4 large onions, halved

6 carrots, cut into large chunks

10 black peppercorns, crushed

15 parsley sprigs

dill and parsley for garnish

For the matzo balls

4 eggs

½ cup water or seltzer

6 tbsp melted schmaltz (chicken fat)

1 cup matzo meal

1 First make the broth: Remove the fat from the cavities of the hens. Place one hen in a stockpot with the water and half of the vegetables. The ingredients should barely be covered with water. Bring to a boil and skim the foam, then adjust the heat so that only a bubble or two appear on the surface. Add the peppercorns and parsley, partially cover, and simmer until the hen is tender but not falling apart, about 2 hours, skimming occasionally.

2 Remove the hen to a large platter. When it is cool enough to handle, take the meat from the bones (reserve for serving or for other use). Put the bones and skin back in the broth. Simmer, partially covered, for about 1 hour, then strain into a bowl. Let cool, and refrigerate overnight.

3 Remove the fat that has hardened on the surface of the broth. Pour into the cleaned pot and add the second hen, the remaining vegetables, and more water if necessary to cover. Repeat the cooking process, then strain and refrigerate. Reheat for serving.

4 Make the matzo balls (see left). Place two matzo balls in each soup bowl, add some of the reserved meat if desired, and ladle in hot chicken broth. Garnish and serve.

POTATO GNOCCHI

Potato gnocchi can be exquisitely delicate or quite leaden, depending on the handling and care they are given. The secret is to use a light touch and not over-handle or over-work the potatoes once they have been riced.

If not cooking the gnocchi the day you make them, freeze in a single layer, covered. They can be stored in the freezer for up to 1 week. Cook from frozen (they'll take a little longer to float to the surface).

Serves 6 as an appetizer or 4 as a main course

2 medium Idaho potatoes, about 1¼lb (600g) in total, unpeeled, cooked in boiling salted water until tender, then drained

⅓ cup finely grated Parmesan (Parmigiano Reggiano)

1 egg

½ tsp kosher salt

¼ tsp freshly ground black pepper

1 cup all-purpose flour, or more as needed

4 quarts (4 liters) boiling water and 2 tbsp kosher or sea salt for cooking

1 Peel the warm potatoes, then pass through a ricer or food mill onto a large cookie sheet, in an even layer. Refrigerate until cool, about 15 minutes. Mound the potatoes on a clean work surface and form a well in the center.

2 Add the Parmesan, egg, salt, and pepper to the well. With your fingertips, combine these ingredients with the potato, stirring to form a rough dough. Sprinkle the flour over the potato mixture and combine gently.

3 Knead the dough, using a downward press-and-quarter-turn motion, until smooth, elastic, and uniform in color, 8–10 minutes. Form into an 8 by 3in (20 by 7.5cm) loaf and cut crosswise into four pieces. Cover with plastic wrap.

4 Clean the work surface and your hands. Take one piece of dough and roll it back and forth on the surface while applying a gentle downward pressure, to form a cylinder 18–20in (46–50cm) long and as thick as your index finger. Lightly dust with flour. Repeat with the remaining pieces of dough.

5 Cut the cylinders into 1¼in (3cm) pieces. Form each into the traditional gnocchi crescent shape: Hold a fork backside up in one hand; with the thumb of your other hand, press the dough against the back of the fork, forming an indentation, while simultaneously rolling it down over the tines.

6 Lay the gnocchi on several cookie sheets, in a single layer so they don't stick together. Cover with plastic wrap and refrigerate until ready to cook.

7 Cook the gnocchi, in batches, in the boiling salted water. As soon as they float to the surface, remove them with a slotted spoon and drain in a colander. Spread out in one layer on cookie sheets or add directly to the sauce (in a large pan). When all the gnocchi are cooked, reheat them gently in the sauce for serving.

Porcini gnocchi with prosciutto & parmigiano cream

Each year, with the arrival of the first autumn chill, I bring our porcini gnocchi back to the menu. Our guests tell us how much they look forward to the return of this popular dish. As a variation on this theme, try using dried shiitake mushrooms in place of the porcini.

Serves 8 as an appetizer or 4–6 as a main course

For the gnocchi

2 cups boiling water

1oz (30g) dried porcini mushrooms

ingredients for potato gnocchi (see opposite)

For the parmigiano cream

3 tbsp butter

¾ cup sliced red onions

2 tbsp minced garlic

5oz (140g) shiitake mushrooms, stems removed and reserved, caps sliced

¼ cup parsley stems

1 cup dry white wine

2 cups heavy cream

2oz (55g) prosciutto, cut into thin strips 1in (2.5cm) long

1 cup stemmed and chopped red or green Swiss chard leaves or spinach

4 tbsp freshly grated Parmesan (Parmigiano Reggiano)

2 tbsp chopped parsley

Pour the boiling water over the porcini and let soak until fully rehydrated, about 15 minutes. Lift them out with a slotted spoon and set aside. Strain the liquid through a coffee filter to remove any grit. Reserve 1 cup of the liquid for the sauce. Squeeze the mushrooms with your hands until very dry, then purée to a smooth paste in a food processor.

Make the gnocchi dough following the master recipe (see opposite), adding the porcini purée with the Parmesan and egg. Shape the gnocchi, then lay them in a single layer on cookie sheets. Cover and refrigerate until ready to cook.

For the sauce, melt half the butter in a large nonreactive saucepan over medium heat. Add the onions, garlic, mushroom stems, and parsley stems. Cook until softened but not browned, about 4 minutes. Add the wine and reserved porcini liquid. Bring to a boil, then reduce to about one-third of the original volume. Add the cream and reduce again until the sauce coats the back of a spoon. Strain into a bowl and set aside.

In the cleaned saucepan, heat the remaining butter over medium-high heat until it is just beginning to brown. Add the shiitake mushroom caps and sauté for 2–3 minutes. Return the cream sauce to the pan, along with the prosciutto, Swiss chard, and half of the Parmesan. Cook over medium heat for 3–4 minutes. Season with kosher salt and freshly ground black pepper (usually about ½ tsp salt and ⅛ tsp pepper). Keep the sauce as warm as possible.

Cook the porcini gnocchi, in batches, as in the master recipe. When all are cooked and drained, reheat them gently in the cream sauce over medium heat. Spoon into warm bowls, sprinkle with the chopped parsley and remaining Parmesan, and then serve.

ASIAN NOODLES & DUMPLINGS

Chris Manfield

CHRISTINE MANFIELD

For the peoples of Asia, noodles and dumplings rival bread and rice as sources of energy, starch, and dietary fiber. From China to Indonesia, dishes are made with noodles or dumplings as their starting point. On Asian streets, noodles and dumplings dispensed from small carts, hole-in-the-wall counters, and restaurants sustain millions of locals daily, from sunrise to well into the night.

The variety of noodles Noodle types vary across the Asian continent. Those from northern China are tougher, made from wheat or barley and water; farther south, wheat noodles become more pliant with the use of egg; and in the wetter climes of Southeast Asia, the soft-textured rice noodle is more common. The Vietnamese and Cambodians have perfected the gorgeously soft and sensuous rice noodle; the Japanese are experts with soba and udon; and the Koreans have the unique dang myun, a translucent cellophane vermicelli made with vegetable starch, and a more textured version of the soba, naeng myun. In Malaysia and Singapore, where noodles were introduced by the Chinese, wheat, egg, and rice noodles weave their way into everything from soups to stir-fries.

In China, noodles are served on birthdays—symbolizing long life, they are considered as important as birthday cakes. Usually the e-fu, or long-life noodle, is used, and the noodles are never cut, because this would suggest shortening one's life. Another noodle, from China's Shandong province, is the la mian, or dragon's whisker. A work of art in itself, this noodle is hand-drawn and hand-thrown from a length of dough by specially trained master chefs.

Within the Taoist tradition of yin-yang, flavors and textures come together to create perfect harmony and balance—cold with hot, crunchy with soft, wet with dry, smooth with crisp. Noodles, whether steamed, boiled, braised, deep-fried, or stir-fried, make a vital contribution. When many dishes are to be shared at the table, the cook needs special knowledge of all the ingredients and skill in their assembly to achieve a true balance of yin and yang.

Dim sum and dumplings Dumplings have a slightly different role in the lives of Asians. The ritual of taking dim sum, traditionally served with jasmine tea, is practiced in the late morning and lunchtime in Chinese restaurants all over the world. Minuscule dumplings and pastry pillows are paraded before the customer—ingenious morsels with delicious centers, created daily by an army of cooks, and devoured within seconds. Vying for attention are deep-fried or boiled egg rolls or wontons, melt-in-the-mouth fried taro pastries called wu gok, and steamed har gau—translucent pastries with luscious shrimp, pork, or scallop centers. There are steamed siu mai, with their ground pork, shrimp, and water-chestnut filling; jai gau, glutinous rice wrappers stuffed with green leafy vegetables and ginger; and wondrous pot sticker dumplings, Chinese jiaozi, or Japanese gyoza, consisting of a special dough made with boiling water and usually filled with ground pork. Other components are the sublime duck pancakes—wafer-thin sheets cooked in a hot pan, steamed, and wrapped around crisp Peking duck, cucumber sticks, and green onions, seasoned with a hoisin or plum sauce.

The Vietnamese make an egg roll using rice-paper sheets for a light, crisp texture. The same rice-paper sheets are used to make cold rolls filled with shrimp, crab, pork, or vegetables, with fresh rice vermicelli usually added to enhance the soft textures. Malaysia has given us the popiah, another version of the fresh roll in which the pastry sheets are made paper-thin, in the same way as you would a crêpe, then filled with vegetables or ground pork and chili.

Dumplings can be made from glutinous rice flour, potato or water chestnut flour, eggs, wheat flour, duck fat, lard, rice paper, mung beans, or even green vegetable leaves, like screwpine or banana. Whatever the wrapper or pastry used to encase the filling, it should be paper-thin, with the texture and consistency of a floating cloud. It is important to consider the ratio of wrapper to filling, since the wrapper is there simply to hold the filling in place and shape, not to dominate the finished dumpling.

EGG NOODLES

Manufactured dried egg noodles produce good results, but there is a particular pleasure in making your own from fresh ingredients.

Serves 6

2 cups (250g) all-purpose flour
3 extra large eggs
1 tbsp olive oil
pinch of fine sea salt
rice flour for dusting

1 Blend all the ingredients, except the rice flour, in a food processor until a ball of dough is formed. Wrap the dough in plastic wrap and refrigerate for 1 hour.

2 Cut the dough into four pieces, then flatten each by hand or with a rolling pin. Pass each piece through the rollers of a pasta machine (dusting it each time with rice flour to prevent sticking). Work gradually through the settings until you reach the finest one. Hang the sheets over a broom handle or back of a chair to dry for 10 minutes. This makes the dough easier to cut.

3 Pass the dough through your pasta machine's spaghetti cutters. Hang the noodles over a broom handle or back of a chair for 30 minutes or until ready to cook.

4 Bring a large pot of water to a rolling boil. Add the noodles. When the water returns to a boil, cook for 2 minutes. Lift out the noodles with a strainer and then drain in a colander.

5 If not eating immediately, stop the cooking by running cold water over the noodles, then drain and toss lightly with oil to prevent them from sticking. To reheat, immerse the noodles in boiling water for 10 seconds, then drain.

BOILING NOODLES

All noodles, whether fresh or dried, need to be softened in hot or boiling water before use. Most are boiled for a few minutes. The exceptions are those noodles that would fall apart if boiled. To prepare fresh rice noodles, for instance, simply pour boiling water over them and immediately drain. Fine, dried cellophane noodles (bean threads) just need to be soaked in hot water.

1 To boil egg, wheat, or buckwheat noodles, bring a large saucepan of water to a rolling boil. Add the noodles. Let the water return to a boil, then cook until the noodles are softened and pliable, about 2 minutes.

2 Drain the noodles in a strainer. Refresh under cold running water to stop them from cooking further, then drain. Toss lightly with a little oil to keep them from sticking. Use immediately or set aside. To reheat for serving, immerse noodles in boiling water for 10 seconds, then drain.

UDON NOODLE SOUP

The thick, slippery Japanese udon noodle is ideal for soup and braising, and takes on big robust flavors with ease. It is used in this hearty broth, which is perfect during cold weather. Serve with chopsticks for the noodles and a spoon for the liquid.

1 knob of fresh ginger plus 2 slices of fresh ginger, shredded

1 tbsp water

¼ cup shiro (white) miso paste

3 tbsp mirin

2½ tbsp sake

5 tbsp light soy sauce

4oz (100g) dried udon noodles, boiled for 4–5 minutes, then drained

7oz (200g) salmon fillet, finely sliced

3oz (85g) fresh firm tofu, diced

8 shiitake mushrooms, sliced and sautéed until soft

4 scallions, finely sliced

1 tbsp snipped chives

For the dashi stock

2 quarts (2 liters) still mineral or spring water

1¼in (3in) piece of dried kombu

1¾oz (50g) dried bonito flakes

1 To make the dashi stock, place the water and kombu in a large pan and bring slowly to a boil over low heat. Once simmering, stir in the bonito flakes, then remove from the heat and let infuse for 30 minutes. Strain the stock through a fine-mesh strainer. Discard the solids.

2 Meanwhile, process the knob of ginger and the water in a blender to a paste, then press through a fine strainer to extract the juice. You need 1 tbsp (keep the rest in a jar, refrigerated).

3 Return the stock to the pan and bring to simmering point. Whisk in the miso, then season the soup with the mirin, sake, soy sauce, and ginger juice. Bring back to simmering point. Taste and adjust the flavorings, if necessary.

4 To serve the soup, divide the noodles, salmon, tofu, mushrooms, scallions, and shredded ginger equally among four bowls. Ladle in the hot soup and stir with a chopstick. Sprinkle with the chives and serve immediately.

Black pepper chicken tea, noodles & watercress

The chicken tea is made in the same way as consommé, providing a clear soup in which to float the solid ingredients. Enoki mushrooms are available in most supermarkets; if you cannot find cloud ear mushrooms (also called wood ear), leave them out—there is no substitute. I like to serve the soup in a cup on a saucer.

For the chicken tea

1 whole garlic bulb

4 tsp vegetable oil

1 onion, chopped

1 large, fresh red chili, sliced

1 tsp chopped fresh ginger

½ tsp black peppercorns, freshly cracked

1 tsp Sichuan peppercorns, freshly cracked

3 tbsp Shaoxing rice wine or dry sherry

2 kaffir lime leaves, shredded

2 scallions, chopped

6 cups chicken stock

3 tbsp light Chinese soy sauce

2 tbsp fish sauce

1 tbsp freshly squeezed lime juice, strained

For serving

1 cup cooked fresh egg noodles, made with 2 tsp freshly ground and sifted black pepper added to the basic recipe (p291)

10oz (300g) chicken breasts, cooked, boned, and meat finely shredded

4oz (120g) enoki mushrooms, trimmed

4 fresh cloud ear mushrooms, finely shredded

8 chives, finely snipped

½ cup tiny watercress leaves

2 tbsp chopped cilantro

To make the tea, preheat the oven to 350°F (180°C). Wrap the garlic in foil and roast until soft, about 30 minutes. Cool, then squeeze from the skins and slice thickly.

Heat the oil in a heavy pot and fry the onion, chili, and ginger until soft and starting to color. Stir in the peppercorns, then deglaze the pan with the rice wine. When the wine comes to a boil, remove from the heat.

Add the roasted garlic, lime leaves, scallions, chicken stock, and soy sauce. Slowly bring to a boil over gentle heat, then simmer for 1 hour, skimming the surface regularly with a slotted spoon. Do not allow to boil or the tea will become cloudy.

Strain the tea through a cheesecloth-lined strainer to ensure it is clear and free of sediment, pressing to extract the liquid. Discard the solids. Let cool, then refrigerate.

Remove any fat from the top of the chilled tea, then pour again through a cheesecloth-lined strainer into a clean saucepan, avoiding any sediment. Bring the tea to a simmer. Stir in the fish sauce and lime juice, and cook for 3 minutes. Taste and adjust the seasoning.

Divide the egg noodles, shredded chicken breast and mushrooms among four cups or bowls, then ladle in the hot tea. Swirl with a chopstick to combine, sprinkle with the chives, watercress and cilantro, and serve.

HONEY & SESAME BEEF WITH RICE STICKS

Once they have been softened in hot water, rice-flour noodles are ideal for braising or stir-frying in a sauce. You can also use fine egg noodles, boiled until soft and pliable. For a milder flavor, remove the chili seeds.

| s2 large garlic cloves, crushed |
| 2 tbsp light soy sauce |
| 1 tbsp fish sauce |
| 1 tsp toasted sesame oil |
| 2 tbsp light honey |
| 1 tsp freshly ground black pepper |
| 3 fresh, green Thai chilies, minced |
| 3 tbsp vegetable oil |
| 10oz (300g) beef tenderloin, thinly sliced |
| 7oz (200g) dried rice sticks, softened in hot water, then drained |
| 2 tsp white sesame seeds, lightly dry-roasted (p79) |
| bunch of watercress leaves or sprigs |
| ½ bunch (a large handful) of chives, snipped into 1in (2.5cm) lengths |

1 In a bowl, mix the garlic, soy sauce, fish sauce, sesame oil, honey, pepper, and chilies with half of the oil. Add the beef slices, mix well, and marinate for 10 minutes.

2 Heat a large wok and add 2 tsp oil. Add half the beef with half its marinade. Toss over a high heat to sear and cook quickly, separating the strips with chopsticks. Remove from the wok. Cook the remaining beef, using the rest of the oil.

3 Return all the seared beef to the wok with its juices and any remaining marinade. Add the rice sticks, and stir and toss to coat them with the sauce in the wok. Add the sesame seeds, watercress, and chives, and toss through to mix, then serve immediately.

SESAME CHICKEN & NOODLE SALAD

This recipe is a variation on the classic bang bang chicken. It uses thick and substantial Shanghai noodles. You can substitute rice sticks (thick-cut rice-flour noodles), but the texture and taste will be slightly different.

| 7oz (200g) fresh Shanghai noodles, boiled for 2–3 minutes, or until softened, then drained and refreshed |
| 10oz (300g) chicken breasts, cooked, boned, and meat shredded |
| 1 English cucumber, finely sliced |
| 1 cup bean sprouts |
| 1 tbsp white sesame seeds, dry-roasted (p79) |
| 4 scallions, finely sliced |
| **For the sesame dressing** |
| 3 tbsp Chinese toasted sesame paste |
| ¼ tsp Sichuan peppercorns, dry-roasted (p97) and ground |
| 4 garlic cloves |
| 2 tsp chopped fresh ginger |

| 1 small, fresh green chili, chopped |
| 1 tsp chili paste or sambal |
| 2 tbsp vegetable oil |
| 2 tbsp light soy sauce |
| 1 tbsp fish sauce |
| 1 tbsp Shaoxing rice wine or dry sherry |
| 1 tbsp Chinese black vinegar |
| 1 tbsp sugar |
| ½ cup chicken stock |

Arrange the noodles on a serving plate. Mix the other ingredients together and place on top. Process the dressing ingredients in a blender until smooth. Spoon the dressing over the salad and serve.

NOODLE-WRAPPED TIGER SHRIMP

Thin egg noodles wrapped around big juicy shrimp—or scallops or chunks of white fish —and then deep-fried until crisp make a perfect party snack for any occasion. Serve with a sweet chili dipping sauce.

16 raw tiger shrimp in shell
2 tsp fish sauce
½ tsp ground chili (hot chili powder)
8oz (250g) fresh, thin egg noodles, boiled for 2 minutes, or until softened, then drained and refreshed
vegetable oil for deep-frying

1 Peel the shrimp, leaving the last tail flange intact, then devein them (p126). Season the shrimp with the fish sauce and chili.

2 Divide the noodles into 16 bundles. Lay out each bundle of noodles in lengths and wrap around a shrimp.

3 Heat the vegetable oil in a large wok or deep-fryer to 350°F (180°C). Fry the shrimp, a few at a time, until they are pink and the noodles are crisp and golden, about 3 minutes.

4 Remove with a slotted spoon and drain on paper towels. Serve freshly fried, with sweet chili sauce for dipping.

SOMEN NOODLES WITH CLAMS & MUSSELS

This simple stir-fry is full of delicate, silky textures and fresh sea flavors. Instead of clams and mussels, you can use scallops or other mollusks— fresh abalone, steamed until softened and finely sliced, is fabulous.

2¼lb (1kg) mussels
2¼lb (1kg) hard-shell clams
¼ cup vegetable oil
6 scallions, cut into ⅜in (1cm) lengths
12 garlic cloves, crushed
4 large, dried chilies, crushed
3 tbsp Shaoxing rice wine
1 cup fish stock
3 tbsp mirin
2 tbsp Chinese black vinegar
2 tbsp fish sauce
7oz (200g) dried somen noodles, boiled for 2 minutes, then drained
6 Chinese cabbage leaves, shredded
large handful of Thai basil leaves

1 Steam the mussels and clams open, separately, in a covered pan over high heat; discard any that remain closed. Plunge into ice water, then remove from the shells. Reserve clam and mussel juices.

2 Heat the oil in a wok and stir-fry the scallions, garlic, and chilies briefly until softened. Add the rice wine and swirl to deglaze, then add the stock, mirin, vinegar, fish sauce, and reserved juices. Bring to a boil. Taste and adjust the seasoning, if necessary.

3 Add the clams and mussels to the wok, along with the noodles and cabbage. Stir over high heat until warmed through, about 1 minute. Add the Thai basil leaves and toss to mix, then ladle into deep bowls to serve.

THAI COOKING

DAVID THOMPSON

Thailand has produced one of the world's great cuisines. Developing over centuries from a rustic base, firmly rooted in the land, Thai cuisine came to reflect the sophistication and complexity of Thai society. In the palaces of the wealthy, elaborate methods prevailed—time, labor, and costs were barely considered, and days could be spent preparing dishes. By contrast, peasant food was always robust, but never coarse or tasteless. Refined or basic, Thai food is always eaten with rice. Curries, soups, salads, relishes, or stir-fries are merely savory accompaniments to this essential grain. Poorer households tend to consume more rice, and the accompanying dishes are usually spicier.

Agricultural self-sufficiency Rice-growing has sculpted the countryside. Small rivers and canals irrigate the fields and provide fresh fish, eels, frogs, and semi-aquatic greens. Slender jasmine rice is the preferred choice in the central plains and the south, while glutinous or sticky rice is consumed in the north and northeast. Groves of fruit trees ring the fields, which pass into forests where small game, wild herbs, and vegetables are gathered. Each house or compound has a small garden where vegetables and fruits, such as garlic, chilies, kaffir limes, cilantro, and basil, are grown, and where chickens, pigs, and ducks are raised. In Thailand, diet was always determined by availability—and to a large degree still is—since most Thais continue to live in the countryside, growing their own produce or purchasing food from traditional markets. What is constantly surprising is the quality and variety of ingredients to be found in even the dustiest of village markets.

Thailand is a geographically diverse country. In the northern forests, along the Mekong River, game, wild vegetables, and herbs abound. Away from the wilder areas, freshwater fish and pork may be found. Coconuts do not grow this far north, so pork fat—or now, more healthily, vegetable oil—is the cooking medium used instead of coconut cream. The remote northeast is poor and arid; here, sticky rice is preferred, and foods are whatever can be found: catfish, buffalo, vegetables—even insects are collected for the pot. Since the farmers are impoverished and food scarce, the cooking of this region is highly seasoned with chilies and often fermented fish, eaten whole or in a pungent sauce.

The central plains are cultivated with long-grain rice, and there is less wild food to be found. The Thai food most westerners are familiar with comes from this region. The south is monsoonal and here the diet depends on the sea. Fish and seafood are avidly consumed. Kapi (fermented shrimp paste) flavors most dishes, ample coconut cream enriches them, and hot chilies make them memorable.

Equipment determines culinary technique, no matter what the cuisine. Perhaps most indispensable in the Thai kitchen is the mortar and pestle, used in making relishes, curry pastes, and sauces. Knife work—chopping, fine slicing, and shredding—ensures that pungent ingredients are evenly distributed in the dish and do not overwhelm the palate.

Distinctive flavors Thai seasoning is a varying balance of four elements: salty, hot, sour, and sweet. The degree and sequence of the seasonings depends on the dish's style and region of origin. Northern food is primarily salty and not overly hot. Southern food is salty, sour, and hot, using chilies, sugar, and tamarind. The northeast is spicy and salty; the central plains combine all four seasonings.

Textures also play an important part in Thai cooking. Chilies sensitize the palate, heightening awareness of inherent textures in fruits and vegetables. The Thais also coax increased texture out of ingredients in their dish selections; for example, deep-fried shallots offer a crunchy contrast to soft stewed sweet pork and its spicy relish accompaniment.

When planning a meal, Thais avoid repeating the style of dishes, techniques used, and seasonings. This is because repetition indicates a lack of consideration on the part of the cook. A balanced meal comprises rice, a curry, a soup, a relish, a salad, and a stir-fried, deep-fried, or grilled dish, all working in concert with each other in their textures and seasonings.

MENU

■ Spicy relish of shrimp & pea
   eggplant with sweet pork

■ Stir-fried water spinach
   with yellow beans, garlic
   & chilies

■ Snake gourd, egg
   & crab soup

■ Green curry of beef with corn
   & Thai basil

SPICY RELISH OF SHRIMP & PEA EGGPLANT WITH SWEET PORK

The spicy relish called nahm prik should be thick, hot, salty, sour, and slightly sweet. Serve with sweet pork, green tomatoes, English cucumber, Belgian endive, and blanched green beans. You can buy the pea-sized eggplants in Asian markets.

For the spicy relish

2 cilantro roots, soaked in water for 5–10 minutes, scraped clean with a knife, and chopped

4 garlic cloves, chopped

9 fresh Thai chilies, or to taste, chopped

1½ tbsp ground dried shrimp

6 large raw shrimp, cooked in simmering water, peeled (heads reserved), and deveined

1 rounded tsp seasoned fresh shrimp paste (see opposite) (optional)

½ tsp roasted shrimp paste (kapi)

few tbsp chicken stock, or as needed

1½ tbsp palm sugar

tamarind water, made by dissolving 1½ tbsp tamarind pulp in 3 tbsp water and pressing through a strainer

2 tbsp lime juice

1½ tbsp mandarin juice (optional)

1½ tbsp fish sauce, or to taste

3 tbsp picked pea eggplants

3 sour fuzzy eggplants (maeuk), scraped and finely sliced (optional)

3 tbsp julienned green mango

pinch of julienned Asian citron or mandarin zest (optional)

For the sweet pork

8oz (225g) fresh pork belly (side)

chicken stock or water as needed

1 screwpine leaf (daun pandan)

1 cup palm sugar

¼ cup fish sauce or soy sauce

1 point of star anise (optional)

1 small piece of dried orange peel (optional)

3 deep-fried shallots (see opposite)

few cilantro leaves

1 Prepare the spicy relish (see opposite).

2 Place the pork in a saucepan. Cover with cold water and add a pinch of salt. Bring to a boil and simmer for 1 minute to remove excess blood and impurities. Drain.

3 Return the pork to the pan and cover with fresh water or chicken stock. Add a pinch of salt and the screwpine leaf. Bring to a boil, then cover and simmer until a skewer comes away clean from the meat, 20–30 minutes. Drain. When cool, cut into ½–¾in (1–2cm) cubes.

4 In a heavy saucepan, melt the sugar with a pinch of salt in chicken stock or water to cover. Add the pork, fish or soy sauce, and optional star anise and orange peel. Simmer, uncovered, until the sauce is thick and the pork is a rich amber, about 40 minutes. Add more stock as needed.

5 Present the pork sprinkled with the deep-fried shallots, white pepper, and cilantro leaves, and serve with the spicy relish.

SEASONED FRESH SHRIMP PASTE

This can be used to flavor soups, curries, salad dressing, or even fried rice, and will keep for several weeks in the refrigerator.

1 cilantro root, soaked in water for 5–10 minutes, scraped clean with a knife, and chopped

2 garlic cloves, chopped

5 white peppercorns

6 shrimp heads

1½ tbsp vegetable oil

1½–3 tbsp sugar, or to taste

1½ tbsp fish sauce

1 In a mortar with a pestle, pound the cilantro root with a pinch of salt, the garlic, and white peppercorns to make a fine paste. Squeeze the shrimp heads over a bowl to extract about 3–4 tbsp of the "butter." Discard the heads.

2 Heat the oil in a small wok or pan. Add the garlic paste and fry until golden, stirring often. Add the "butter" and simmer until it changes color. Season with sugar and fish sauce, and simmer for another minute or so. Let cool.

MAKING THE SPICY RELISH

This nahm prik can be served with deep-fried batter-coated breadfruit, fresh betel leaves (shown in the photograph opposite), or grilled fish. Traditionally this would be mackerel, but any oil-rich fish, such as sardines, herring, or tuna, can be used.

1 In a mortar with a pestle, pound the cilantro roots and garlic with a large pinch of salt into a paste. Add the chilies and continue to pound until quite fine. Add the dried shrimp, cooked shrimp, optional fresh shrimp paste, and roasted shrimp paste. Pound until puréed.

2 Moisten with stock. Season with the sugar, tamarind water, lime juice, and optional mandarin juice. Carefully add fish sauce to taste. (Do not add too much. There is already a lot of salt present.) Mix in the eggplants, green mango, and, if using, the Asian citron or mandarin zest.

DEEP-FRYING SHALLOTS

Deep-fried shallots are an important garnish in Thai cooking. Although you can buy them, it is much better to fry your own. They can burn easily, so fry at least a cup of shallots at a time in order to control their cooking, and take care when adding the shallots to the wok, because the oil will bubble up. Note that 2 cups fresh shallots will yield half that amount of deep-fried shallots, and for this quantity you need about 1¼ cups vegetable oil.

1 Peel the shallots and cut lengthwise into thin slices. Heat the oil in a wok until fairly hot, then turn up the heat and add the shallots. When the oil has recovered its heat and the shallots are frying, turn down the heat slightly. Deep-fry, stirring, until the shallots begin to color.

2 After about 5 minutes, when the shallots are golden, have lost their onionlike aroma, and begin to smell enticingly nutty, drain and spread out on paper towels to cool. The shallots will become crisp, retaining surprisingly little oil. They keep for 2 days in an airtight container.

STIR-FRIED WATER SPINACH
with yellow beans, garlic & chili

If you cannot find water spinach, use any other Asian green, such as gai lan (Chinese kale) or choy sum, or—in a pinch—spinach.

2 garlic cloves

3–4 tbsp vegetable oil

7oz (200g) water spinach or other greens

¼ cup yellow bean sauce

1 long, fresh, red chili, crushed (optional)

pinch of sugar

3 tbsp chicken stock

3 tbsp light soy sauce

Using a mortar and pestle, crush the garlic with a pinch of salt. Heat a wok, then add the oil. When hot, add the spinach, crushed garlic, yellow bean sauce, chili, if using, and sugar. When the spinach has wilted, add the stock and season with the soy sauce. Serve hot.

SNAKE GOURD, EGG & CRAB SOUP

This cooling soup is a perfect complement to any spicy dish. The best gourd to use is called a snake gourd because it is long, ribbed, and curvaceous.

1½ tbsp chopped garlic

1½ tbsp vegetable oil

4 cups Thai chicken stock (see opposite)

1½–3 tbsp light soy sauce

pinch of sugar

1 snake gourd or English cucumber, about 5oz (150g), prepared (see opposite)

1 egg, lightly beaten

1½ tbsp cooked fresh crab meat

1½ tbsp cilantro leaves

pinch of ground white pepper

1 Make a coarse paste by pounding the garlic with a pinch of salt in a mortar with a pestle. Heat the oil in a large pan and fry the garlic paste until golden. Drain off the excess oil, then pour in the stock and season with the soy sauce and sugar. Bring to a boil, then add the gourd or cucumber and simmer, uncovered, for a few minutes, skimming often.

2 When the gourd is tender, add the egg and continue to simmer until it is just scrambled. Remove the pan from the heat and transfer the soup to a tureen. Add the crab meat. Serve hot, sprinkled with a garnish of cilantro leaves and white pepper.

THAI CHICKEN STOCK

This stock can be made with chicken bones or with a whole chicken. Vegetables provide flavoring, but using too many can overwhelm the chicken flavor.

Makes 2–3 quarts (2–3 liters)

2¼lb (1kg) chicken bones, or a whole chicken without giblets

pinch of shredded fresh ginger

pinch of crushed garlic

7oz (200g) trimmings from vegetables such as scallions, cabbage, or cilantro stems

small piece of peeled daikon

6 shiitake mushroom stems (optional)

1 If using bones, rinse them well with water. Place in a stockpot or other large pot and add enough cold water to cover plus a pinch of salt. Bring to a boil to blanch the bones. Drain, then refresh under cold running water for a few minutes. Return to the pot.

2 If using a whole chicken, put it in the pot. Add water to cover plus a pinch of salt and bring to a boil. Simmer for 20 minutes. Add all the flavorings and vegetables. Continue to simmer for 2 hours. Strain the stock and let cool. The meat from the chicken can be used in another dish, if desired.

PREPARING SNAKE GOURD

1 Using a vegetable peeler, peel the skin from the snake gourd (or from an English cucumber, if you are using that instead).

2 With a chef's knife, trim off the ends from the gourd, then cut it into diagonal slices about 1in (2.5cm) thick.

COOKING RICE

To serve 4, measure 1 cup Thai or jasmine rice. Wash it (see right) only if it is imported. The cooked rice will stay warm in the covered pan for 30 minutes. Enhance by pushing a screwpine leaf (daun pandan) into the cooked rice and letting it infuse for a few minutes before serving. Do not add salt; the other dishes have enough seasoning.

1 Place the rice in a bowl of water. Wash it by combing your hands through the grains and rubbing your palms together to remove any husks or grit. Drain. Repeat the washing two to three times until the water is clear.

2 Drain the rice and transfer to a large saucepan. Add 2 cups water, cover, and bring rapidly to a boil. Then turn the heat right down and let cook for 10 minutes. Do not stir. Remove from the heat and let the rice rest, covered, for another 10 minutes.

GREEN CURRY PASTE

Curry paste made by hand in the traditional way has a vibrancy of flavor that commercial products cannot hope to achieve.

1½ tbsp chopped fresh Thai chilies
1½ tbsp seeded and chopped fresh, long, green chilies
1½ tbsp chopped galangal
¼ cup chopped lemon-grass
1 tsp kaffir lime zest
1½ tbsp chopped cilantro root
1 tsp chopped red turmeric (kamin leuang)
1 tsp chopped fingerroot (krachai)
¼ cup chopped shallots
3 tbsp chopped garlic
1 tsp roasted shrimp paste (kapi)
1 tsp white peppercorns
1 tsp coriander seeds, dry-roasted (p79)
⅛ tsp cumin seeds, dry-roasted
2–3 blades of mace, dry-roasted, or a large pinch of freshly grated nutmeg (optional)

1 Place a good pinch of salt in a mortar to act as an abrasive. Place each item in the mortar, one at a time in the order given, and pound with a pestle to make a fine paste. Stop when you have added and pounded in the shrimp paste.

2 Grind the peppercorns, coriander and cumin seeds, and optional mace, then sift before mixing into the paste. Put the finished paste into a sterilized jar and cover with wax paper or plastic wrap. The paste will last for a week or two if refrigerated.

PREPARING A COCONUT

When buying a coconut, choose one that feels heavy for its size, because there will be more flesh in the coconut and so it will yield more cream. Normally, one good coconut will yield about 1 cup cream. Shake the coconut: If there is water inside, the flesh is less likely to be fermented. Coconut water, when fresh, is the most thirst-quenching of liquids. However, it sours very quickly and is sometimes used to ferment vegetables or make vinegar.

1 Hold the coconut in a folded kitchen towel or thick cloth over a bowl. The coconut "eyes" should be near either your thumb or your little finger. Wallop the coconut crosswise through the middle a few times, turning the nut, until it is cleaved in half. The bowl will catch the coconut water.

2 Taking each coconut half in turn, score the flesh or cut it into segments. This makes it easier to prize the flesh away from the shell with a blunt knife.

3 Using a cleaver or sharp knife, peel away and discard the brown inner skin. Roughly chop the coconut flesh.

4 Blend the flesh in a food processor with 2 cups warm water until shredded. Use to make cream or milk (see opposite).

COCONUT CREAM & MILK

Fresh coconut cream is incomparably luscious, with a complexity and depth of flavor that justify the labor required to produce it.

1 To extract coconut cream and milk, squeeze the processed coconut flesh in two layers of cheesecloth or a very clean kitchen towel into a glass, china, or plastic bowl (metal taints the cream). Let sit for at least 20 minutes: It will separate into a thick, opaque liquid—the cream— floating on top of a thinner liquid, which is the milk.

2 Spoon off the cream into a separate bowl. Both the cream and milk are best used within a few hours. They can be refrigerated, but harden and become difficult to use. Coconut cream can begin to sour after a few hours and certainly within a day. Thai cooks bring the cream to a boil to delay its souring, although this does destroy some of its wonderful flavor.

CRACKED CREAM

Curries fried in coconut cream often call for the cream to be "cracked," or separated. The cream is simmered until most of the water evaporates.

Pour the cream into a wok or saucepan and simmer until the cream separates into thin oil and milk solids (the cracked cream). Cracked cream can be kept for a few weeks in the refrigerator. The oil can be used for deep-frying.

GREEN CURRY OF BEEF with corn & Thai basil

Green curries are hot, salty, and just a little sweet from the rich coconut cream used in the cooking. Kaffir lime leaves, cut chilies, and Thai basil leaves are customary garnishes.

¼ cup cracked coconut cream (see right)

¼ cup green curry paste (see opposite)

4oz (115g) boneless beef sirloin, with some fat attached, sliced into ¼in (5mm) pieces

3 tbsp fish sauce, or to taste

1 cup coconut milk (see above) or chicken stock

2oz (55g) baby corn, cut in half lengthwise

2 large kaffir lime leaves, torn

3 young, fresh, green or red chilies, diagonally cut from the center and seeded

handful of Thai basil leaves

large pinch of shredded fingerroot (krachai) (optional)

large pinch of shredded white turmeric (kamin kao) (optional)

1 Heat the cracked coconut cream in a wok or large saucepan. Add the curry paste and fry over medium heat, stirring regularly, until the cream is fragrant from the spices, 5–10 minutes.

2 Add the beef and simmer in the cream for a minute or so before seasoning with the fish sauce. Moisten with the coconut milk or stock. Bring to a boil, then add the corn and simmer for a few minutes, or until tender.

3 Add the remaining ingredients and simmer for a few seconds longer. Let rest, off the heat, for a minute before serving.

GRAINS & BEANS

PAUL GAYLER

Cereal grains have sustained humanity for centuries. In temperate climates, wheat, barley, rye, and oats are the staple grains, while rice, maize (corn), and millet grow in the tropics and subtropics. Grains are favored because they are economical and filling, and most of the world's population eat locally grown grains. Only in richer countries has meat overtaken cereals as the primary food.

Grains require some preparation before cooking. It is advisable to rinse them several times under cold running water to remove surface dust. Many milled rices have food additives tossed into the flour and added to the grains, so these should be washed under running water. Grains can be cooked dry, without presoaking, except for whole wheat, barley, brown and basmati rices, and rye.

Cooking grains To cook grains, all you need to know is how much water (or stock) to add to the quantity you are boiling, and how long you need to cook them. In addition to boiling, grains may also be steamed quite successfully. One tip I picked up in Asia is that if you run a little oil around the pan before cooking the grain, it not only prevents the grains from sticking, but also makes the pan easier to clean afterward. Whole grains tend to take longer to cook than processed grains. Some require stirring as they cool, but most do not. Some recipes call for the grain to be lightly fried in oil before water is added for boiling. Called toasting, this process is one of the steps in making pilaf rice and it enhances the flavor of grains dramatically.

The legume family Pulses, which are dried legumes, include beans, peas, and lentils. The lentil was reputedly the first plant ever to be domesticated by humans. Most legumes thrive in warm climates, but some grow better in temperate regions. They can be eaten fresh or dried and are found in many varieties, colors, flavors, and textures.

Today, the availability of dried legumes has never been better, ranging from deep maroon kidney beans and pale green limas to speckled cranberry and black beans. Europeans treat dried legumes (also referred to as beans) with reverence, but the English-speaking world has made only limited use of them. This may change with greater awareness of their value as a vegetarian source of protein and a complex carbohydrate—the body digests them slowly, ensuring a steady supply of energy.

All dried legumes, apart from soybeans, have a very similar content of protein, carbohydrate, vitamins, and minerals, especially iron. They provide protein in their own right, but eating them with grains or nuts also ensures a rich intake of essential amino acids. Except for soybeans, dried legumes are low in fat and packed with fiber, which helps to prevent fluctuations in blood-sugar levels. Recent research indicates that the fiber in beans helps to lower cholesterol. Dried legumes can also benefit diabetes-sufferers by helping to control their blood-glucose levels, appetite, and weight.

Some people avoid beans, because they can cause intestinal gas. This problem mostly arises when people follow a low-fiber eating pattern, then switch to a diet rich in beans. While the gases can produce discomfort, they are not harmful, and the problem lessens as the body adjusts to the diet. However, it is not safe to eat raw or undercooked beans, especially red kidney beans and soybeans, because their skins contain toxins. These beans are perfectly safe after thorough cooking.

Storing grains and beans While dried grains and beans last well if stored carefully, it is preferable to buy smaller quantities as you need them and so keep storage periods to a minimum. Buy from markets with a rapid and regular turnover. Grains should not be kept longer than six months because their oils can turn rancid. Dried beans become tough with age and take longer to cook.

Decant all grains and beans into airtight containers away from the light, preferably in a cool, dark cupboard, ideally at around 70°F (21°C). Never mix a new batch with an old one, since they may need different cooking times. Keeping grains and beans in glass jars is fine, as long as they are used rapidly and are not exposed to light, which impairs their flavor and nutrients.

RICE

There are over 2,000 varieties of rice, grown in more than 110 countries, and every culture has its own repertoire of rice dishes, from the paellas of Spain, the nasi goreng of Indonesia, and the congees served for breakfast throughout Asia to the famous pilavs of the Balkans and Middle East, and the risottos of Italy. Rice can generally be divided into two types—long-grain (which tends to stay separate when cooked) and round or short-grain (which sticks together, making it ideal for risottos and rice pudding).

Washing/rinsing

Packaged rice sold in the West is rigorously checked and thoroughly cleaned, so if you "wash" it (i.e. rinse it) all you are doing is washing away nutrients. In Asian countries, however, rice is normally washed several times before cooking to help keep the grains separate.

Soaking

With the exception of basmati, and sometimes wild rice (to reduce the cooking time), rice does not need to be soaked before use. Some people suggest soaking long-grain brown rice before cooking to make it softer; this will not shorten the cooking time. Follow recipe directions, and soak rice only if instructed to do so.

Toasting

When boiling or steaming rice, it can first be lightly toasted (i.e. fried) in oil or butter for 1–2 minutes before the water or other liquid is added. This greatly enhances the flavor.

Steaming

Steamed rice is cooked in a hot vapor, rather than directly in liquid, which significantly reduces the loss of nutrients. The rice in the upper section of a steamer cooks in the steam produced by the water or stock boiling in the lower section. A well-fitting lid is essential to keep the steam in, as is careful timing, since steamed rice is tasteless if even slightly overcooked. Rice can also be steamed very successfully in a pressure cooker.

Using leftover cooked rice

Once cooled, cooked rice can be kept in an airtight container in the refrigerator for up to 24 hours. It is great for rice salads and to use in stir-fries and soups.

When rice is reheated it tastes as good as it did when first prepared. Either reheat it in a tightly covered bowl in the microwave (see opposite) or put the rice in a saucepan with 2 tbsp water or stock, cover, and heat gently for 4–5 minutes. Fluff with a fork before serving.

THE ABSORPTION METHOD

This way of cooking rice is the most common method used throughout Asia. A pan with a tight-fitting lid is essential, and it is important to measure the water or stock accurately. You can cook the rice on the stovetop (as shown here) or in the oven, which is in fact the basic pilaf method (p312).

Brown rice (long-grain or basmati) can be cooked by this method, although it will need more liquid, or it can be boiled (see opposite). Whichever method is used, brown rice will take up to double the cooking time of white rice.

2 cups long-grain white rice

2 cups water or stock

1 Put the rice and water or stock into a large saucepan. Bring to a boil over medium heat. Stir once, then simmer, uncovered, until all liquid is absorbed, 10–12 minutes.

2 Remove from the heat. Cover the pan with a towel and a tight-fitting lid. Return to very low heat and leave undisturbed for 10 minutes.

3 Remove the pan from the heat and leave for 5 minutes with the towel and lid still in place, then uncover and serve.

TIPS FOR PERFECT RICE

■ Always buy good-quality rice.
■ Use a heavy-bottomed pan with a tight-fitting lid. Be sure the pan is big enough (rice will triple in volume).
■ To add extra flavor, use stock instead of water.
■ Do not add salt to the cooking water—it can cause the rice grains to rupture.

■ When cooking by the absorption method or boiling, never stir, prod, or even taste rice during the cooking process. Rice grains are delicate and can easily split, releasing their starch and becoming sticky.
■ As soon as it is cooked, remove the rice from the pan. If left in the pan it will become overcooked.

BOILING RICE

The usual way to boil rice is in twice its volume of liquid for 10–20 minutes, until all the water has been absorbed. But I have never been happy with the results, so I now cook rice in five to six times its volume of water at a rolling boil for 12–15 minutes. I believe the extra water used helps to dilute the starch from the rice during cooking and results in light, distinct grains. Never stir rice when boiling, because it ruptures the cells in the grain, making it sticky.

3 quarts (3 liters) water

2 cups long-grain white rice

OTHER WAYS TO COOK RICE

Electric rice cooker

This will cook glutinous rice, Japanese sushi rice, and brown rice very successfully and conveniently. Use the absorption method, opposite, with the same precise ratio of water to rice, and follow the manufacturer's directions for timings. When the rice is cooked the cooker will switch off automatically and keep the rice hot until needed. Although rice cookers can be expensive, it is important to buy a good-quality model —thermostats on cheaper models are not always accurate and you can end up with a sticky mass.

Microwave oven

You can cook good rice in a microwave, although, contrary to popular belief, you don't save any time by doing so. Use the absorption method ratio of water to rice, and choose a bowl large enough to ensure that the water doesn't boil over (I add a little oil to the water, which helps to prevent this). Microwave, covered, for 5 minutes on high, then on medium for 15 minutes. Do not stir during cooking. Cooked rice reheats well in a microwave—on high for about 2 minutes plus 2–3 minutes standing time.

1 Pour the water into a large saucepan and bring to a rolling boil. Add the rice and return to a boil. Reduce to a simmer and cook until tender but still firm, 12–15 minutes.

2 Pour the rice and water into a colander to drain, cover with a kitchen towel, and leave for 10 minutes. Fluff up with a fork and serve.

Preparation & cooking times for rice

The following chart gives basic guidelines for cooking rice. Wherever possible, it is advisable to check package directions, especially for Asian varieties of rice.

TYPE OF RICE	BEST FOR	SPECIAL PREPARATION	BEST COOKING METHODS AND APPROXIMATE COOKING TIMES
LONG-GRAIN White and brown	pilafs, salads, stuffings, stir-fries	can be toasted	absorption: 20 mins (white), 30–40 mins (brown); steam: 20 mins (white), 30–35 mins (brown)
Basmati (white and brown)	Indian pilaus, spicy Indian dishes	soak for 30 mins; can be toasted	absorption: 20–25 mins; boil: 20 mins (white), 40 mins (brown)
SHORT-GRAIN Risotto (arborio, carnaroli, vialone nano)	classic risottos	can be toasted	risotto: 20–25 mins
Paella (Valencia, calaspara, granza)	paella, other Spanish rice dishes	can be toasted	paella: 20–25 mins
ASIAN Chinese black	sweet and savory dishes, stuffings	soak overnight	boil: 30–40 mins
Glutinous (sticky)	sweet and savory dishes, rice dumplings	soak for 4 hours minimum	absorption (rice cooker): 20 mins; steam: 15–20 mins
Jasmine (Thai aromatic)	spicy Thai dishes, congees, stir-fries	wash	absorption (rice cooker): 25 mins; boil: 20–25 mins
Sushi	sushi, sweet dishes	wash	absorption (rice cooker): 20 mins; boil: 20–25 mins
SPECIALIST Red or Camargue, Himalayan red	stuffings, salads, pilafs, stir-fries	soak for 1 hour; can be toasted	boil: 40–60 mins
Wild	stuffings, pilafs, salads		boil: 40–60 mins

BASIC PILAF

A pilaf is cooked in different ways throughout the world, but what all the methods have in common is that the rice is not stirred during cooking so that the grains remain separate. The basic recipe here is cooked in the oven, which is indicative of the classic French style, although pilafs are also often cooked on the stovetop, as in Indian-style pilaus. For a Turkish pilav, the rice is first cooked with onions and other vegetables, topped with stock, and simmered for 30 minutes. It is then covered with a cloth and left to steam, off the heat, for 10 minutes, which results in a softer, fluffier pilaf.

3 tbsp unsalted butter or 2 tbsp olive oil

1 small onion, minced

1 cup long-grain rice

1½ cups well-flavored chicken or vegetable stock

PILAF ADDITIONS

Try these to vary the basic recipe:

■ Add 1 cup finely diced vegetables, such as red or yellow bell peppers, eggplant, or mushrooms, and cook with the onion.

■ Infuse the boiling stock with a pinch of saffron threads for 2–3 minutes before adding to the rice.

■ Add 2 tsp ground spice, such as cardamom, cinnamon, or cumin, to the softened onion and cook for 2 minutes longer before adding the rice.

■ Flavor with tomato by adding 1 tbsp tomato paste or a 16oz (450g) can of crushed tomatoes, drained, to the onions before stirring in the rice.

■ Fold ½ cup spiced cooked lentils into the cooked rice and add 1 tsp garam masala and 2 tbsp chopped cilantro with the salt and pepper.

■ Stir 2 tbsp chopped herbs into the finished pilaf.

1 Preheat the oven to 325°F (160°C). Heat half of the butter or oil in a Dutch oven or heavy pan. Add the onion and cook over medium heat until softened, about 5 minutes. Add the rice and stir with a wooden spoon to coat the grains well with the fat and onions.

2 Bring the stock to a boil in a separate pan. Add to the rice, stir once, and return to a boil. Cover with a tight-fitting lid, place in the oven, and cook until the rice is tender and all liquid has been absorbed, 18–20 minutes.

3 Fork in the remaining butter or oil, season to taste with salt and pepper, and serve.

PAELLA

The traditional Spanish dish paella takes its name from the pan in which it is cooked. The pan is in fact key to a good paella—it needs to be large and shallow with a flat base to ensure the rice cooks in a thin, even layer. Rice for paella is never washed first, as it is the starchy coating that keeps the grains separate during cooking. Nor is it stirred, as this would break up the grains. When the paella is ready, the pan is brought to the table and people help themselves.

6 cups fish stock

2 large pinches of saffron threads

3 garlic cloves, crushed

6 tbsp olive oil

2oz (50g) Spanish smoked chorizo sausage, thinly sliced (optional)

2 small bay leaves

1 onion, finely chopped

2 red bell peppers, halved, seeded, and cut into long strips

10oz (300g) monkfish fillet, cut into 1in (2.5cm) chunks

8oz (250g) small squid, cleaned and cut into pieces, including tentacles

6 tomatoes, peeled and chopped

1 tsp paprika

2½ cups Valencian paella rice or risotto rice

7oz (200g) fresh, small, hard-shell clams, scrubbed

12 raw tiger shrimp, heads removed but tails left on and deveined

8 raw langoustines (scampi)

8oz (250g) fresh mussels, scrubbed

2oz (50g) cooked, fine green beans, cut into 1in (2.5cm) lengths (about ½ cup)

⅓ cup cooked green peas

lemon wedges for serving

1 Pour the fish stock into a saucepan, add the saffron and one-third of the garlic, and bring to a boil. Simmer for 5 minutes. Meanwhile, heat half the oil in a paella pan, large skillet, or wok. Add the chorizo, if using, the remaining garlic, and the bay leaves, and cook over a gentle heat for 1 minute. Add the onion and red peppers and cook for 5 minutes. Add the monkfish and sauté until sealed all over, 2–3 minutes.

2 Increase the heat, add the squid, and fry until it is golden, 2–3 minutes. Stir in the tomatoes, paprika, and remaining oil, and fry for 4–5 minutes (this tomato mixture is known as a sofrito).

3 Scatter in the rice to distribute it evenly over the ingredients in the pan. Pour in the hot stock, then add the clams, tiger shrimp, langoustines, and mussels.

4 Reduce the heat and cook gently until the rice is tender but still slightly firm, 15–20 minutes (it may be necessary to add a little more stock or water). Shake the pan occasionally; do not stir.

5 The rice will form a golden crust on the bottom (called a soccarat). When all the liquid has been absorbed, gently fold in the beans and peas. Discard any clams or mussels that haven't opened.

Serve hot, garnished with lemon wedges

BASIC RISOTTO

Risotto, a dish from northern Italy, is simple food at its best. The basic recipe is made by gradually stirring hot stock into rice and softened onions until all the stock has been absorbed and the risotto is creamy with firm (al dente), separate rice grains. It is easy to prepare, the secrets being the choice of rice, the quality of the stock, and constant stirring. A basic risotto can be embellished with fish, shellfish, meat, chicken, or vegetables.

4 cups chicken or vegetable stock

1 tbsp olive oil

5 tbsp unsalted butter

1 onion or 2 shallots, minced

1½ cups risotto rice—vialone nano, arborio, or carnaroli

⅓ cup dry white wine

½ cup freshly grated Parmesan

1 Heat the stock in a saucepan to a gentle simmer. Meanwhile, heat the oil and half the butter in a wide, heavy pan. Add the onion and cook until softened, about 5 minutes. Add the rice and stir to coat the grains well with the fat.

2 Add the wine and boil, stirring, until absorbed. Add a ladleful of simmering stock and stir until absorbed. Continue adding stock by the ladleful, stirring, until the rice is tender but retains a bite. This will take 20–25 minutes in all.

3 Stir in the remaining butter and the Parmesan. Season to taste and remove from the heat. Cover the pan and let the risotto rest for 2 minutes before serving.

HOW TO EXCEL

■ Choose a wide, heavy-bottomed pan that will be large enough to hold the cooked rice as well as all of the other ingredients.

■ Only use risotto rice. The medium-short, stubby grains absorb liquid and swell up while retaining their individual shape.

■ Always use a good, well-flavored stock—chicken, fish, or vegetable, depending on the type of risotto.

■ Keep the stock at a gentle simmer, and the rice at a lively simmer.

■ Stir constantly throughout the cooking process to release the starch in the rice and give the risotto the desired creamy texture.

A basic risotto—creamy, but with separate grains of rice

Supplì al telefono

This is one of my favorite vegetarian dishes—moist, basil-flavored risotto patties filled with mozzarella and tomatoes. The dish gets its name because, when you cut into the patties, the melting mozzarella forms strings that look like telephone wires. A light supper dish for four with a crisp green salad, supplì can also be served as an appetizer for eight.

Makes 8

½ quantity basic risotto (see opposite), chilled

¼ cup pesto sauce (p42)

½ cup chopped oil-packed sun-dried tomatoes

8oz (225g) buffalo mozzarella, cut into 16 small cubes

2 cups fresh white bread crumbs

5 tbsp olive oil

Put the chilled risotto into a bowl and mix in the pesto with a fork. Divide the risotto into eight equal-sized balls. For each supplì, cup a ball in your hand and use your fingers to make a pocket about ½in (1cm) deep in the center.

Place about 1 tbsp tomatoes and 2 cubes of mozzarella in the pocket. Mold the rice over the filling to enclose it completely, then shape the ball into a small patty.

Put the bread crumbs into a shallow bowl and roll the patties around in them until they are well coated all over.

Heat the olive oil in a large frying pan over medium heat. Add the supplì and fry until golden brown and crisp, 4–5 minutes on each side. Drain on paper towels, then serve.

Fill the pocket in each risotto ball with sun-dried tomatoes and mozzarella

EGG FRIED RICE

When making any fried rice dish, it is important that the oil be hot before the rice is added. This will ensure the rice turns out crisp and light in texture rather than soggy and heavy. Cook the rice in advance and thoroughly cool before using.

2 tbsp vegetable oil

3 cups cold, steamed or boiled basmati or other long-grain rice

⅓ cup diced cooked ham

⅔ cup cooked green peas

¾ cup bean sprouts

⅓ head of iceberg lettuce, shredded

pinch of salt

2 extra large eggs, beaten

4 scallions, chopped (optional)

1 Heat a wok or heavy frying pan over high heat. Add the oil and swirl it around to coat the pan. When the oil is very hot, add the rice and stir-fry for 1 minute.

2 Add the ham, peas, bean sprouts, lettuce, and salt to the wok, and continue stir-frying over high heat for 1 minute.

3 Make a well in the ingredients and pour in the eggs. Stir in quickly, then cook for 2–3 minutes. Transfer to a dish, sprinkle with scallions, if using, and serve.

NASI GORENG

This is a well-loved Indonesian fried rice dish. Boil 1¾ cups basmati rice; cool. In a blender, mix 1 chopped onion, 2 crushed garlic cloves, 1 tsp dried shrimp paste, 1 seeded and chopped hot red chili, ¼ cup ketchup, and the juice of 1 lime to a paste (called a sambal). Heat ¼ cup vegetable oil in a wok or large frying pan. Add 1 thinly sliced onion and 1 seeded and shredded hot red chili, and stir-fry for 2–3 minutes. Stir in the sambal and cook for 2 minutes. Increase the heat to high, and add the rice and a pinch of salt. Stir well. Add 7oz (200g) thinly sliced cooked chicken breast, 5oz (150g) peeled cooked shrimp, 1 cup shredded bok choy, 2 tbsp soy sauce, and 2 tbsp peanuts. Stir-fry until hot, then serve, topped with fried eggs, deep-fried shallots (p301), and shredded cucumber.

CONGEE

Often eaten for breakfast throughout Asia, congee is rice poached until the grains swell and burst to form a kind of gruel. It can be made plain, simply with water, or using an aromatic broth and with the addition of various meats and fish or eggs. When enlivened with garlic, scallions, and cilantro leaves, it is delicious. My only reservation is the time of its serving—in the West we are not quite ready for such a heavy start to the day. For those who are like me, I suggest serving congee for lunch or dinner, or as an evening snack.

For the base broth and rice

4 cups chicken stock

3½oz (100g) cilantro roots or stalks, lightly smashed with the back of a knife

1 cup jasmine or white glutinous rice, rinsed under running water for 5 minutes

For the flavorings

2 tbsp groundnut oil

2 garlic cloves, thinly sliced

2in (5cm) piece of fresh ginger, peeled, and thinly shredded

1 tbsp light soy sauce

1 tbsp nam pla (fish sauce)

6 scallions, finely shredded

sprigs of cilantro, to garnish

1 Put the stock and cilantro roots in a large pot. Bring to a boil, then reduce the heat and simmer, uncovered, for 30 minutes. Strain into a clean pot, return to the heat, and bring to a simmer. Add the rice and let simmer gently, uncovered, until the grains are swollen and almost disintegrating, 1–1½ hours.

2 Meanwhile, heat the oil in a small pan. Add the garlic and ginger. Cook until golden and crisp, about 1 minute. Stir into the rice.

3 Stir in the soy and fish sauces. Spoon into individual soup bowls, sprinkle with the scallions, and top with cilantro sprigs.

CHICKEN DUMPLINGS

To make congee more substantial and interesting, add these little dumplings.

Combine 1 cup ground chicken, ¼ cup chopped cilantro, 2 garlic cloves, crushed, and 1 tbsp nam pla (fish sauce) in a bowl and season with ground white pepper. Using a teaspoon, form the mixture into small dumplings and drop into the strained stock, before the rice is added. Simmer for 8–10 minutes, then remove with a slotted spoon and keep warm while you make the congee. When serving the congee, place the dumplings on top.

RICE PAPER WRAPS

Delicate, thin rice paper sheets (banh trang) are used in Vietnam and Thailand to wrap all kinds of interesting fillings—fish, meat, or vegetable. Served uncooked, steamed, or fried, they make great pre-dinner snacks or appetizers. Rice paper is sold dried at Asian markets, and needs to be moistened before use. Prepare and fill one wrapper at a time.

1 Immerse the wrapper in a bowl filled with lukewarm water and leave for 30 seconds. Remove and place on a flat work surface.

2 Place the filling in the center of the wrapper. Fold the bottom half up over the filling.

3 Fold in the sides, then roll over to enclose the filling and make a square package. Repeat to moisten and fill the remaining wrappers.

STEAMED SEAFOOD WRAPS

Makes 12

12 rice paper wrappers

banana leaves or foil

2 scallions, shredded

2 hot red chilies, seeded and shredded

For the seafood filling

8oz (225g) fresh flaked white crab meat (about 2 cups)

⅔ cup chopped peeled, cooked shrimp

5 water chestnuts, chopped

½ cup bean sprouts

4 scallions, chopped

1in (2.5cm) piece of fresh ginger, peeled and minced

1 tbsp soy sauce

1 tbsp nam pla (fish sauce)

For the dipping sauce

2 tbsp rice vinegar

1 tbsp chopped pickled ginger

4 tbsp vegetable oil

1 tbsp soy sauce

3 tbsp chopped cilantro

1 tbsp sugar

1 small, hot red chili, seeded and chopped

1 tbsp chopped mint

1 Mix the ingredients for the filling in a bowl. Place 2 tbsp filling on a moistened rice paper wrapper and fold into a square package (see left). Repeat to make 12 packages.

2 Line a bamboo steamer with banana leaves or foil and brush with a little oil. Lay the prepared packages seam-side down on the leaves, spaced well apart. Cover, set over a pan of boiling water, and steam for 5–6 minutes.

3 Meanwhile, put all the sauce ingredients in a bowl and whisk to mix. Transfer the wraps to a plate, garnish with the scallions and chilies, and serve with the dipping sauce.

CORN (MAIZE)

Corn originates from Central and South America, where it was the staple grain of the Incas, Mayas, and Aztecs. There are several types of corn, and yellow, blue, red, and black varieties. In the kitchen, corn is used as hominy (dried and hulled whole kernels or ground grits), cornmeal or polenta, masa harina (a flour made from ground corn kernels cooked in limewater), and cornstarch (a fine white flour). Other types of corn yield sweet corn, which is eaten as a vegetable, and popping corn, which yields popcorn.

BUTTERMILK CORNBREAD

I always serve cornbread when I cook brunch and often add other ingredients to the batter, such as 3 crushed garlic cloves or diced chilies, or 1½ cups grated jalapeño Jack or Cheddar cheese, crumbled fried bacon, or sautéed diced mixed bell peppers. You can also use greased muffin pans and bake for 15–18 minutes.

Makes 16 squares

1 cup all-purpose flour
1¼ cups fine cornmeal
4 tsp baking powder
pinch of salt
¼ cup sugar
2 eggs, beaten
1 cup buttermilk or whole milk
2 tbsp melted unsalted butter

1 Preheat the oven to 375°F (190°C). Combine the flour, cornmeal, baking powder, salt, and sugar in a bowl, and make a well in the center. Pour in the eggs, buttermilk, and butter, and mix well to form a smooth batter.

2 Pour the batter into a lightly greased 8in (20cm) square cake pan. Place in the oven and bake until golden and firm to the touch, 25–30 minutes. Let the cornbread cool a little in the pan, then unmold it and cut into small squares. Serve warm.

MAKING SOFT POLENTA

Made from cornmeal, polenta is a staple food in northern Italy. Long associated with Italian peasant cooking, it now enjoys gourmet status and an international reputation. Whether served soft, or allowed to set and then broiled, pan-grilled, or fried, it is great with stews to soak up the juices, with grilled or roasted meats, or topped with cooked vegetables. Soft polenta can also be baked with a savory topping.

Instant or pre-cooked polenta can be cooked in just 5–8 minutes, but is not as good in quality as the traditional variety.

If polenta becomes lumpy during cooking, pour it into a blender and process until smooth, then return to the pan and continue to cook.

6 cups water
½ tbsp coarse sea salt
1¾ cups polenta meal or fine cornmeal
10 tbsp unsalted butter
1 cup freshly grated Parmesan

1 Pour the water and salt into a large, heavy-based pot and bring to a boil. Gradually sprinkle in the polenta meal, whisking constantly and rapidly to ensure that no lumps form and the mixture is smooth.

2 Reduce the heat to its lowest setting and cook until thick and creamy and coming away from the pan, 40–45 minutes. Whisk occasionally to prevent a skin from forming. Stir in the butter and cheese, and season well.

SOFT POLENTA IDEAS

You can enhance the basic soft polenta with many flavorings. Here are some to try.

■ Add 1 tsp saffron to the water with the salt.

■ Stir in 2 tbsp tapenade or ½ cup pesto sauce with the butter, cheese, and seasoning.

■ Add ⅔ cup red bell pepper purée or 1½ cups cooked ratatouille to the finished polenta.

■ Pour the soft polenta into a greased baking dish and top with a mixture of 3 cups browned ground pork seasoned with 1 crushed garlic clove, 2 tsp minced rosemary, and 1 tbsp freshly grated Parmesan. Bake in a preheated 350°F (180°C) oven for 15 minutes.

For a superb vegetarian dish, top the soft polenta with sautéed wild mushrooms garnished with parsley

SET POLENTA

1 Make soft polenta as opposite, but omit the butter and cheese. Pour onto an oiled baking pan and spread out evenly with a wet spatula to a ½–¾in (1–2cm) thickness. Let cool and set. (It can be kept in the refrigerator for up to 4 days.)

2 When ready to use, turn the set sheet of polenta out of the pan onto a board. Using a knife or pastry cutters, cut the polenta into triangles, rectangles, squares, or other shapes.

3 To toast, brush the polenta shapes with olive oil, then cook on a hot ridged grill pan or griddle, or under the broiler, until golden brown and crisp, 3–5 minutes on each side.

SET POLENTA IDEAS

■ Use toasted set polenta as a pizza base: Top with sliced tomatoes and mozzarella and basil leaves, then bake in a preheated 400°F (200°C) oven until lightly browned, 18–20 minutes.

■ Arrange slices or triangles of set polenta on top of a cooked meat or vegetable stew, drizzle with olive oil, and bake until golden and crisp, 15–18 minutes.

■ Cut set polenta into small squares, coat in beaten egg and bread crumbs, and deep-fry in hot oil until golden, 1–2 minutes.

■ Make a polenta-style lasagne: Layer slices of set polenta with 1 cup freshly grated Parmesan or Pecorino Romano, 2¼lb (1kg) spinach, cooked and drained, and 2½ cups tomato sauce (p40). Finish with another ½ cup grated cheese, then bake in a preheated 400°F (200°C) oven until bubbling and golden brown on top, 20–25 minutes.

Forms & uses of other grains

TYPE OF GRAIN	WHOLE GRAIN	REFINED GRAIN	FLAKES	FLOUR OR MEAL
Barley	(hulled barley) as brown rice, pilafs, soups, stews	(pearl barley) soups, casseroles, salads	granola, breakfast cereal	breads, in baking, thickening soups and casseroles
Buckwheat	(groats or kasha) as brown rice	–	breakfast cereal	blinis, pasta, soba noodles
Millet	as brown rice, stuffing vegetables	–	casseroles, soups, stews	soups, salads, as rice —in pilafs and risottos, stuffings for poultry and vegetables
Oats	(groats) as brown rice	–	(rolled oats) oatmeal, granola, in baking	breads, oatcakes, in baking
Quinoa	as brown rice	–	–	breads
Rye	(berries) as brown rice	(cracked rye) breads, pilafs	breakfast cereal	breads
Wheat	(berries) as brown rice	(cracked wheat, bulgur, couscous) salads, stuffings	breakfast cereal crisp toppings	breads, cakes, cookies, other baking

WHEAT

The most universally grown grain, wheat is also the most important of all the food grains. It is ground into flour for breadmaking and into semolina for gnocchi, pasta, and pudding-type desserts. In its other forms—"berries" (the whole grain), flakes, bulgur wheat, cracked wheat, and couscous—it needs only minimum preparation for use in pilafs, salads, stuffings, casserole toppings, and breakfast cereal. The pleasant, earthy flavor works well with a wide range of foods, most particularly fruit, vegetables, and nuts.

BULGUR WHEAT: Tabbouleh

Sold under various names (bulgar, burghul, pourgouri), bulgur is made by boiling wheat grains until they crack. As a result, it only needs to be rehydrated, by soaking or simmering. Cracked wheat, with which bulgur is often confused, is not pre-cooked.

Bulgur is a staple throughout the Middle East, where it is often combined with pounded lamb to make kibbeh. It is also the main ingredient in the Lebanese salad tabbouleh, which is often served as a mezze (appetizer) with lettuce leaves: A large spoonful of tabbouleh is rolled in a leaf and eaten with the fingers.

½ cup bulgur wheat, picked over to remove any grit

1 large bunch of flat-leaf parsley, stems removed and leaves coarsely chopped

4 tomatoes, peeled and chopped

6 scallions, chopped

4 tbsp chopped fresh mint or 1 tsp dried mint

½ tsp apple pie spice

juice of 2 lemons

4 tbsp olive oil

2 heads of lettuce, separated into leaves

1 Put the bulgur in a strainer and rinse well, then tip it into a bowl. Cover with hot water and let soak for 25 minutes. Drain well in the strainer and pat dry in a cloth. Put the bulgur into a clean bowl.

2 Add the parsley to the bulgur along with the tomatoes, scallions, mint, spice, lemon juice, and olive oil. Mix well together, and season with salt and pepper to taste. Spoon the tabbouleh into a wide serving bowl and garnish with the lettuce leaves.

Tabbouleh—a classic Lebanese salad

BULGUR PILAF

A bulgur pilaf is made in the same way as a rice pilaf (p312). Simply substitute bulgur wheat for rice, or combine equal quantities of white basmati rice and bulgur wheat. Either way, cook until the bulgur is tender to the bite, about 20 minutes.

Summer fruit tabbouleh

This unusual dessert—a variation of the classic tabbouleh—is light, fruity, and refreshing in warm weather. The choice of fruit can be varied depending on what is best in season.

½ cup bulgur wheat, picked over to remove any grit

1 cup blueberries

1 cup raspberries

1 cup halved strawberries

⅔ cup chopped pineapple

1 mango, peeled and chopped

1 cup chopped watermelon

1 cup red currants

For the syrup

6 tbsp sugar

⅔ cup water

4 passion fruits

small bunch of mint, stems removed

juice of 2 limes

Put the bulgur in a strainer and rinse well, then tip it into a bowl. Cover with hot water and let soak for 25 minutes. Drain well in the strainer and pat dry in a cloth. Put the bulgur into a large bowl. Add the fruit and fold together gently. Set aside in a cool place.

To make the syrup, put the sugar and water into a small pan and slowly bring to a boil. Cook to dissolve the sugar. Cut the passion fruits in half and, using a teaspoon, scoop out the seeds and juice. Add to the boiling syrup along with the fruit shells. Simmer gently for 10 minutes. Remove from the heat, discard the shells, and let cool.

Finely chop half the mint leaves. Stir into the cold syrup with the lime juice. Pour the syrup over the bulgur and fruit, and mix well. Cover and chill for 1 hour. Scatter the whole mint leaves over the tabbouleh before serving.

COUSCOUS

Couscous is a mixture of fine and coarse semolina, the finer flour binding itself around the coarser grain to form the couscous granules. Traditional couscous takes a long time to cook by steaming, whereas instant or quick-cooking couscous—the type most commonly available these days in supermarkets and Middle Eastern markets—has already been cooked and so cuts down on preparation time dramatically. Instant couscous only needs to be rehydrated with boiling water or a brief steaming.

Couscous can simply be enriched with oil or butter, but is also great when combined with other ingredients in salads and stuffings.

1⅔ cups instant couscous
1¾ cups boiling water
1 tbsp olive oil, or 3 tbsp unsalted butter, cut into cubes
1 tsp salt

Rehydrating instant couscous

1 Place the couscous in a large bowl and pour in the boiling water. Cover with plastic wrap to retain the heat and let stand for 5 minutes. Remove the plastic wrap and fluff up the couscous grains with a fork, then cover the bowl again and leave for 5 more minutes.

2 Remove the plastic wrap. Add the olive oil or butter and the salt, and fluff up the grains with a fork until they are light and separate. The couscous is now ready to serve.

Steaming instant couscous to serve hot

ADDING HERBS & SPICES

Couscous combines well with many flavorings and which ones you use depends largely on what you intend to serve with the couscous. Add 1 tsp spice, such as ground coriander seeds, cumin, or saffron, before you soak or steam the couscous. Or, stir 1 tbsp chopped herbs, such as cilantro, dill, parsley, or mint, into the rehydrated or steamed couscous.

Place the couscous in a bowl, sprinkle with boiling water, cover, and leave for 10 minutes.

Break up any lumps with your fingers, then transfer the couscous to a cheesecloth-lined steamer basket set over boiling water. Cover and steam until the grains are tender, 15–20 minutes. Add the olive oil or unsalted butter and salt as above, and fluff up the grains with a fork.

Roast squab chicken with couscous stuffing

This is one of my favorite chicken dishes, equally delicious served hot or cold.
The fruity couscous stuffing keeps the birds wonderfully moist.

4 squab chickens, 14–16oz (400–450g) each

For the marinade

3 tbsp chopped cilantro

3 tbsp chopped flat-leaf parsley

1 tbsp cumin seeds

1 tsp smoked sweet paprika

1 tsp ground turmeric

7 tbsp olive oil

juice of ½ lemon

1 tbsp harissa

For the stuffing

large pinch of saffron threads

1¼ cups boiling water

1 heaped cup instant couscous

6 tbsp chopped dried fruits, such as apricots, prunes, and figs

⅓ cup raisins, soaked in water until plump

3 tbsp pine nuts, toasted

2 tbsp chopped cilantro

Mix the ingredients for the marinade in a large, shallow dish. Place the chickens in the dish and coat generously with the marinade. Leave at cool room temperature for 2–3 hours, turning the birds occasionally.

Meanwhile, mix the saffron and boiling water in a cup, then use to rehydrate the couscous by soaking it (see opposite). Set aside to cool.

Preheat the oven to 400°F (200°C). Finish making the stuffing by stirring the rest of the ingredients into the cooled couscous.

Remove the chickens from the marinade and, using your fingers or a spoon, fill the body cavities loosely with the couscous stuffing. Tie the legs together with string.

Place the chickens in a large roasting pan and spoon any remaining marinade over them. Roast until golden and the juices run clear when one of the birds is pierced in the thigh with a skewer, 25–30 minutes. Remove the chickens from the oven and let stand in a warm place for 5 minutes before serving.

SEMOLINA: Gnocchi alla romana

Made from the endosperm of durum wheat, semolina is available in a range of grinds from fine to coarse (granular), and is primarily used to make pasta. Semolina pasta is firmer and more golden in color than that made from other wheat flours.

Semolina can also be used in hot milk puddings, cakes, breads, and to make gnocchi alla romana. Like gnocchi di patate (potato gnocchi, p286), these tiny dumplings are a staple of Italian cuisine. The semolina (preferably Italian semolina made from the best-quality durum wheat flour) is cooked in a similar way to soft polenta, but using milk rather than water, and the resulting paste is set and cut into shapes in the same way as polenta.

3 cups whole milk
1 small bay leaf
1 garlic clove, crushed
1 cup fine semolina flour
3 egg yolks
¾ cup freshly grated Parmesan
freshly grated nutmeg
3 tbsp unsalted butter plus extra for greasing

1 Put the milk, bay leaf, garlic, and a little salt into a heavy-based saucepan and bring to a boil. Remove the bay leaf, then slowly sprinkle in the semolina, whisking constantly to prevent any lumps from forming.

2 Lower the heat and cook gently, whisking occasionally, until the semolina mixture is thick and starts to pull away from the sides of the pan, 12–15 minutes.

5 When the gnocchi mixture is cold and set, cut into rounds with a 2in (5cm) cookie cutter. Reform the scraps with your hands and cut out more rounds. The mixture will make about 16 gnocchi rounds.

6 Melt the remaining butter in a frying pan over medium heat. When foaming, add the gnocchi and fry until golden and crisp, about 5 minutes on each side. Drain on paper towels, then finish with a sauce or another topping (see opposite) and serve.

3 Remove the pan from the heat and beat in the egg yolks, one at a time. Stir in the cheese and a little nutmeg, and season to taste with salt and pepper. Liberally butter a large jelly roll pan or other shallow pan.

4 Spoon the gnocchi mixture into the pan and spread it out evenly with a wet metal spatula to ½in (1cm) thickness. Melt half the butter and brush over the surface. Once cool, cover and refrigerate for 2–3 hours.

BAKING OR BROILING

Instead of frying in butter, gnocchi alla romana can be baked or broiled.

■ To bake, arrange the gnocchi rounds, in one layer, in a well-greased baking dish. Dot with 3 tbsp unsalted butter, cut into pieces, and sprinkle with ¾ cup freshly grated Parmesan. Bake on the top shelf of a preheated 450°F (230°C) oven until a light golden crust has formed and the gnocchi are heated through, about 15 minutes.

■ To grill, top the gnocchi rounds with ¾ cup freshly grated Parmesan and cook under a preheated hot broiler until golden, bubbling, and heated through.

FINISHING FRIED GNOCCHI

Once fried, place the gnocchi in a greased baking dish, in one layer, then add one of the following toppings. Bake in a preheated 450°F (230°C) oven for the timings given.

■ Top with 3 cups tomato sauce (p40) or cheese sauce (p33) and sprinkle evenly with ½ cup freshly grated Parmesan. Bake for 8–10 minutes.

■ Top with 10oz (300g) blanched broccoli florets, 1lb (450g) sliced, cooked spicy sausage, and ½ cup crumbled Gorgonzola cheese. Bake for 8–10 minutes.

■ Top with 2 thinly sliced buffalo mozzarella balls and 4 thinly sliced ripe tomatoes, drizzle with ½ cup pesto sauce (p42), and scatter on 12 black olives. Bake for 5 minutes.

BASIC PREPARATION OF DRIED LEGUMES

There is hardly a country or continent that does not have its own favorite dishes based on dried legumes, such as beans, peas, and lentils, whether it is refried beans from Mexico, hummus from the Middle East, the fragrant dals of the Indian subcontinent, or the grand meat and vegetable stew cocido from Spain. The basic preparation of dried legumes is simple—sort, rinse, soak if necessary, and then simmer, after which they are ready to use. See the chart opposite for individual soaking and cooking times.

Sorting & rinsing

This is the first step for all dried legumes, whether they are lentils or split peas you are about to cook, or beans or whole peas you intend to soak. Place them in a strainer or colander and pick them over carefully to remove any dirt or grit, tiny pebbles, or other foreign material. Then rinse the pulses well under cold running water.

USING CANNED BEANS

While I prefer freshly cooked beans, I recognize that canned beans are very convenient. I don't recommend them for salads, since they cannot absorb dressing easily and take on flavors, but the firmer beans—black and red kidney beans, for example—are fine added to stews and to make quick soups. Before using canned beans, drain and rinse them thoroughly in a strainer or colander.

Soaking

With the exception of lentils and split peas, dried legumes are soaked before cooking to ensure that they cook evenly and relatively quickly. Time permitting, I like to give them a long soak because I think they keep their shape better than pulses that have been quick-soaked (see below). Place the dried legumes in a large bowl and cover with three times their volume of cold water. Cover the bowl and let soak for 8 hours or overnight (I always refrigerate them, to avoid any chance of fermentation). The next day, drain them and discard the soaking water. They are now ready to cook.

Quick-soaking

This is a great shortcut when time is of the essence. Put the dried legumes in a large pan, cover with three times their volume of cold water, and bring quickly to a boil. Reduce the heat and simmer for 5 minutes. Remove from the heat, cover, and let soak for 1–2 hours. Drain. They are now ready to cook.

Adding flavor

Because dried legumes can be somewhat bland, when cooking them I often add an onion studded with a few cloves, or replace the water with a well-flavored chicken or beef stock. Spices such as coriander, cumin, caraway, anise, and chili can be added too, as can bay leaf, thyme, and rosemary. Vegetables such as carrots will add sweetness. Wait until toward the end of cooking to add salt, and be sure the dried legumes are completely cooked before mixing in acidic ingredients such as tomatoes, wine, and lemon. This is because salt and acidity will toughen their skins, preventing them from softening, and prolonging cooking time.

Cooking on the stovetop

I often start with a 10-minute period of rapid boiling (this is especially important for red kidney beans and soybeans, which have harmful toxins in their skins). Then I continue cooking, monitoring carefully—if dried legumes are overcooked, they will be soggy, with split skins.

1 Place the legumes in a large pan and cover with four times their volume of cold water. To stop them from sticking, add 1 tbsp vegetable oil for every 1lb (450g) soaked legumes. Bring quickly to a boil and boil over high heat for 10 minutes. Skim any scum from the surface.

2 Reduce the heat, partly cover with a lid, and simmer until tender (see right for timings), replenishing the boiling water if necessary. Add salt 15–20 minutes before the end of cooking.

Other cooking options

The stovetop method is a slow business, but it is hard to beat. Microwaves, slow cookers, and pressure cookers are other options, but the results are seldom as good: Microwaves can actually take longer to cook lentils and split peas, while the settings on slow cookers are often too high or too low. Pressure cookers do cut cooking times—by up to two-thirds—but they are not suitable if you want to add flavorings or cook more than 1lb (450g) at a time.

Soaking & cooking times for dried legumes

Soaking and cooking pulses can never be an exact science because much depends on the age and origin of the crop. The timings below are therefore approximate.

TYPE OF PULSE	SOAKING TIME	APPROXIMATE COOKING TIME	BEST FOR
Adzuki beans	overnight	40–45 minutes	pâtés, soups, sprouting
Black beans	overnight	1 hour	salads, soups, stews, refried beans
Black-eyed peas	overnight	1–1½ hours	casseroles, pâtés, salads, soups
Cannellini beans	overnight	1–1½ hours	Italian dishes, salads, soups
Chickpeas	overnight	2–3 hours	casseroles, hummus, Middle Eastern dishes, sprouting
Cranberry beans	overnight	1–1½ hours	Italian dishes, soups, stews
Fava beans (skinless)*	overnight	1½ hours	falafel, salads, soups, stews
Flageolet beans	overnight	1½ hours	casseroles, soups, salads
Ful medames	overnight	1–1½ hours	ful medames, bigilla
Lentils (split)	not required	25 minutes	casseroles, dals, pâtés, soups
Lentils (whole)	not required	45 minutes	casseroles, dals, pâtés, salads, soups, sprouting
Lima beans	overnight	1–1½ hours	pâtés, salads, soups
Mung beans (whole)	not required	¾–1 hour	salads, sprouting, stews
Navy beans	overnight	1–1½ hours	Boston baked beans, casseroles, cassoulet, salads, soups
Peas (whole)	overnight	1–1½ hours	casseroles, soups, pease pudding, purées
Peas (split)	not required	45 minutes	casseroles, dals, pease pudding, soups
Pinto beans	overnight	1–1½ hours	Mexican dishes, refried beans, soups, stews
Red kidney beans**	boil hard for 10 minutes, then soak for 4 hours	1–1½ hours	casseroles, chili con carne, salads, soups, stews
Soybeans**	boil hard for 10 minutes, then soak for 4 hours	3–4 hours	casseroles, fritters, pâtés, tofu

* fava beans with skins need to be soaked for 48 hours in several changes of water, then skinned before cooking; skinless fava beans require only an overnight soak

** to destroy toxins in their skins, red kidney beans and soybeans require a special soaking procedure. Follow the quick-soaking method, but boil the beans hard for 10 minutes. Remove from the heat, cover, and let soak for 4 hours, then drain and cook.

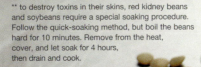

PURÉEING: Hummus

A blender or food processor take a lot of the hard work out of puréeing legumes, which would otherwise have to be done by working them through a food mill. The machines also give them a smooth, silky finish. For the Middle Eastern dip hummus, chickpeas are puréed to the consistency of wet mashed potatoes.

¾ cup dried chickpeas (garbanzo beans), soaked overnight, then drained

2½ cups water

2 large garlic cloves, crushed

juice of 2 lemons

5 tbsp olive oil

⅔ cup tahini (sesame seed paste)

cayenne pepper

For serving

2 tbsp olive oil

2 tbsp chopped flat-leaf parsley

pinch of cayenne pepper or paprika

1 Put the chickpeas and water in a large pan. Bring to a boil, then partly cover and simmer until tender, 2–3 hours. Drain, reserving the liquid. Set aside 2–3 tbsp chickpeas. Put the remainder in a blender with the garlic.

2 Add the lemon juice, olive oil, and ⅔ cup of the reserved cooking liquid. Process to a purée. Add the tahini and process again until smooth. Season with salt and cayenne pepper, then transfer to a bowl.

BIGILLA

Bigilla is a black bean paste eaten as a dip. To make it, soak 1lb (450g) dried ful medames overnight, then drain and put in a pan with 1 chopped onion and 2 peeled garlic cloves. Cover with water and bring to a boil. Boil for 10 minutes, then reduce the heat and simmer, partly covered, until the beans are soft, 1–1½ hours. Add 1 cup sun-dried tomatoes and cook for 15 minutes longer. Drain the bean mixture and let it cool, then put into a blender with 2 crushed garlic cloves, 3 tbsp chopped flat-leaf parsley, 2 seeded and minced hot red chilies, and salt and pepper to taste. Process, adding about ½ cup olive oil to form a smooth paste with the consistency of wet mashed potatoes. Refrigerate to chill, then serve the bigilla with slices of mature goat cheese liberally sprinkled with cracked black pepper and drizzled with olive oil, and plenty of bread.

Before serving, drizzle the olive oil over and garnish with the parsley, cayenne, and reserved chickpeas

PASTA E FAGIOLI

This is one of the all-time great soups, a hearty rustic dish made from cranberry beans, which are known as borlotti beans in Italy, flavored with pork, rosemary, and tomato, and finished with pasta and a drizzle of olive oil. There are many versions throughout Italy, but this is my favorite way to prepare it. I have to confess that on occasions of extreme hunger I have chopped up the ham hock and added it back to the soup. And why not?

Serve sprinkled with cracked black pepper and extra Parmesan, plus a little olive oil drizzled over the top

4 tbsp olive oil plus extra for drizzling

1 onion, finely chopped

2 carrots, finely diced

2 celery stalks, finely diced

7oz (200g) boned fresh ham hock, cut into large pieces

1½ cups dried cranberry beans, soaked overnight, then drained

16oz (450g) canned tomatoes, chopped with juice

1 tbsp tomato paste

2 sprigs of rosemary

4 cups beef or chicken stock

1 cup small tubular pasta, such as macaroni or maltagliati

½ cup freshly grated Parmesan plus extra for serving

1 Heat the oil in a large, heavy-based pan. Add the onion, carrots, and celery, and cook over medium heat until the onion is translucent, 5–10 minutes.

2 Add the ham, beans, tomatoes, tomato paste, rosemary, and stock. Bring to a boil. Reduce the heat, cover, and simmer until the beans are tender, 1–1¼ hours.

3 Remove the ham and discard the rosemary stems. Ladle one-third of the bean mixture into a blender and process to a purée, then return to the pan.

4 Bring back to a boil. Add the pasta and cook for 15 minutes, uncovered. Remove from heat, stir in the cheese, and season. Leave for a few minutes before serving.

Serves 4.

MASHING: Refried beans

For this dish (called Frijoles refritos in Mexico), black beans are cooked, then coarsely mashed and fried in lard with bacon and chilies. Also known as turtle beans, black beans are shiny and kidney-shaped with a white seam. They are popular in Latin America and the West Indies, where they are used in salads, soups, and stews.

2½ cups dried black beans, soaked overnight, then drained

7½ cups water

3 tbsp lard

1 onion, chopped

½ cup chopped bacon

2 small, hot red chilies, minced

1 sprig of epazote, or 2 tbsp chopped cilantro

For serving

⅓ cup crumbled queso fresco or feta cheese

4 scallions, chopped

2 tbsp chopped cilantro

fried tortilla triangles (see below)

1 Put the beans in a large pan with the water and bring to a boil. Boil for 10 minutes, then partly cover, reduce the heat, and simmer until tender, about 1 hour. Drain the beans, reserving the cooking liquid. Place in a mixing bowl with ½ cup of the reserved liquid. Mash with a potato masher until lightly crushed.

2 Heat the lard in a large frying pan. Add the onion, bacon, and chilies, and cook until soft and golden. Add the epazote and mashed beans. Cook, stirring, for 1–2 minutes to heat through. The mixture should be as thick as mashed potatoes; add 1 tbsp reserved liquid if too dry. Season and transfer to a serving bowl.

Serve topped with the cheese, scallions, and cilantro, and garnished with fried tortilla triangles

FRIED TORTILLA TRIANGLES

Cut 2 corn tortillas into equal-sized wedges using a sharp knife. Deep-fry in vegetable oil heated to 350°F (180°C) until golden and crisp, about 1 minute. Drain on paper towels.

STEWING: Dal

For this staple of Indian cuisine, split red lentils are gently stewed with chilies, then combined with tomatoes and a fried spice mixture. Dal can also be served with a little plain yogurt.

1 cup split red lentils, rinsed	
2 hot green chilies, seeded and minced	

1 tsp ground turmeric	
1 onion, finely chopped	
2 cups water	
16oz (450g) canned tomatoes, drained and chopped	
4 tbsp ghee or vegetable oil	
½ tsp mustard seeds	

½ tsp cumin seeds	
½ tsp grated fresh ginger	
1 garlic clove, crushed	
½ tsp ground coriander seed	
4 curry leaves (optional)	
½ tsp asafetida	

1 Put the lentils in a saucepan. Add the chilies, turmeric, onion, and water, and bring to a boil. Partly cover the pan and simmer, without stirring, until the lentils are soft, 30–35 minutes. Stir in the tomatoes.

2 Heat the ghee in a small pan. Add the rest of the ingredients and fry over medium heat for 2 minutes, stirring occasionally. Add to the lentils and cook, stirring, until thick. Season.

Serve with Indian bread to scoop up the dal

SLOW COOKING ON THE STOVETOP: Cocido español

Simmered gently with vegetables and meat, dried legumes make satisfying one-pot meals. Cocido, the national dish of Spain, is one of these, and there are as many variations of it as there are cooks. At its simplest, cocido is a peasant dish of potatoes or rice with vegetables, beans, and, sometimes, a piece of pork or a ham bone. Or, it may be rich with fatty meats like goose confit or spicy sausages. The slow, gentle cooking is considered to be the secret of its tastiness.

During cooking, keep the pan partly covered to stop the broth from evaporating too much, but with enough of a gap so that it will not boil over.

Following tradition, cocido is served in two parts: First the broth, then the boiled meat and vegetables. I like to finish the broth with rice instead of the traditional fine noodles.

Serves 8

5 quarts (4.75 liters) water
1lb 2oz (500g) flank steak
4 ham bones, about 1lb (450g)
8oz (250g) cured Serrano ham
7oz (200g) salt pork
1½ cups dried chickpeas (garbanzo beans), soaked overnight, then drained
5oz (150g) Spanish smoked chorizo sausage
4oz (125g) morcilla blood sausage (optional)
½ small chicken, cut up
4 potatoes, peeled and cut into large pieces
14oz (400g) turnips, cut into large wedges
14oz (400g) carrots, halved lengthwise
1¼lb (600g) cabbage, cut into thick wedges
3 tbsp olive oil
3 garlic cloves, crushed
¾ cup Valencian paella rice or risotto rice, or 5oz (150g) fine vermicelli noodles

1 Put the water in a large saucepan and add the flank steak, ham bones, Serrano ham, and salt pork. Bring to a boil, skimming off any impurities that rise to the surface. Add the chickpeas. Reduce the heat, partly cover the pan, and simmer for 1½ hours.

2 Add the sausages, chicken, potatoes, turnips, and carrots, and simmer, partly covered, for 30 minutes longer. Cook the cabbage in a pan of boiling water for 10–15 minutes; drain. Heat the oil and garlic in a frying pan and sauté the cabbage for 2–3 minutes to brown. Keep warm.

4 Arrange the chickpeas and vegetables on a warmed platter. Cut the sausage into thick slices and arrange with all the meats on another platter. Serve after the broth.

BREADS & BATTERS

DAN LEPARD

A table laid with simple things to eat is the kind of meal I most want for myself and to share with friends. Sometimes it might include a pot of meat and onions bobbing in a broth made with good stock, or perhaps a warm roast chicken stuffed with lemons, olives, and garlic; a little cheese, alongside a bowl of tender salad leaves; some good wine; and a whole loaf of bread, baked that day, but cool enough to be sliced. Perhaps it is to be expected that I should want to make bread whenever friends are due. But let me also tell you that every time I have the chance to bake some bread, I feel that I am the fortunate one.

Baking your first bread The perfect loaf is the result of care and practiced method. It doesn't come from an inherited knack for baking. If you have never baked before, be reassured that with simple ingredients and tools you can make a loaf to be proud of. The measured ingredients are mixed thoughtfully, kneaded carefully, nurtured through a gentle rise, and shaped; the baking itself just seals those good things in place. Avoid becoming overconcerned with perfection. In a working bakery we are obliged to sell what we make, and with that comes a pressure to make perfect bread, every day, without any dip in consistency—uniform loaves, day in and day out, and crusts that look perfect. That is what our customers demand. How is it that somewhere, during our transformation from hunter-gatherers to supermarket-gatherers, we lost our acceptance of variety?

I hope you will aspire to something less artificial and more human. Celebrate the odd tear that appears like a smile across the top of the loaf. Or the knobbly, crisp ends that make a homemade whole-wheat stick something earthborn and real. Bread-baking is not a ceramic art. It is, like all good cooking, about taste and the way that taste is affected by appearance, texture, and aroma.

Take a dusty, round loaf from the remarkable Poilâne bakery in Paris. Beneath its "P", cut with a razor-sharp blade into the surface of the dough, is an extraordinary texture and taste. Yet the ingredients are simple—flour, water, salt, and leaven—and the recipe is hardly complicated: Mix, shape, and bake. So how can a complex, elemental flavor grow from this simplicity? The secret lies in the interaction between ingredients, nature, and science. Just as an apple can reflect the care given to the orchard, so grain can reflect the region and its soil. Careful, slow milling can preserve much of the grain's taste. Slow mixing with good water and mineral-rich salt helps to enhance it. Layered over that foundation will be the complex flavors of the leaven—yeasts that multiply slowly in a doughy mixture alongside lactic acids and healthy bacteria. For some loaves, the smoky heat of a wood-fired oven will set the crust and add a little flavor, too.

Working with your ingredients The key to great bread-baking is care and consideration, from the purchase of ingredients through to the final bake. Wherever you live, in a city or town, your choice of ingredients will be the cornerstone of the final quality. It is a myth that excellent bread can be baked with poor ingredients, and it is equally untrue that you need the finest ingredients to bake well. But you do need to understand and work with the qualities of the ingredients you have at hand. You must believe that each ingredient in your kitchen will perform differently in accordance to your recipe and the way you use your hands, and oven. White wheat flours, each labeled "suitable for breadmaking," will not necessarily perform equally well. They will probably be similar, but each will need tweaking according to your taste and intention.

My hope is that you will attempt to understand the flour you use and make sure that your recipe, technique, and dough-handling serve to enhance the basic qualities of the grain. In the following chapter are recipes for breads and batters, some simple and others more demanding and complicated, to help you examine the ingredients you have and out of them create outstanding, nutritious foods that will give you pleasure and keep you baking for years to come.

MAKING YEAST BREADS

The single-celled fungus *Saccharomyces cerevisiae*—more commonly known as baker's yeast—is a fermentation machine, taking the natural sugars present in a mixture and releasing carbon dioxide as a result. Fermenting yeasts give beer its fizz, champagne its pop, and leavened bread its texture with a crumb full of bubbles.

When using commercial yeast in baking, I prefer compressed fresh yeast, as I think it gives a better result than active dry yeast. If you must use dry yeast because no fresh yeast is available, then follow this method. Use half the amount suggested for fresh yeast, and stir this into ¼ cup water or liquid taken from the total amount, but at a temperature of 95°F (35°C). Stir this with 1 tbsp flour, taken from the total amount of flour, then leave the mixture for 10 minutes. Add it to the dough with the rest of the liquids, and proceed according to the recipe.

Remember, though, that by changing from fresh to dry yeast you are tinkering with the heart of the loaf, and the result will not be as certain as the one I have written.

Read through the methods shown on the following pages for mixing, kneading, and shaping before making your first loaf, because the recipes will refer you to these techniques.

SIMPLE WHITE OR WHOLE-WHEAT BREAD

Once you have read the sections on mixing, kneading, and shaping, you will be ready to start baking. The whole-wheat loaf needs less rising time than the white—the husk and fiber in whole-wheat flour mean the percentage of gluten is lower; too long an initial rise might leave the dough exhausted. Both loaves are easier to slice the day after baking.

Makes 1 loaf

1½ tsp (10g) compressed fresh yeast

1½ cups (350g) water at 72°F (22°C)

4 cups (500g) unbleached white or whole-wheat high-gluten bread flour plus extra for shaping

1½ tsp (10g) fine sea salt

olive or sunflower oil for kneading

1 Mix the dough, then knead it (p346). Cover with a dish towel and let rise for 30 minutes before giving the dough a final knead. A whole-wheat dough is now ready to be shaped; let a white dough rise for another 30 minutes before shaping.

2 Oil and flour a deep 5 by 8in (12 by 19cm) loaf pan. Cut the dough into two equal pieces, round them, and tuck side by side into the pan (p346). Cover and let rise at room temperature (72°F/ 22°C) until almost doubled in height, 1–1½ hours.

3 Preheat the oven to 425°F (220°C). Uncover the loaf. Spray the top with a fine mist of water and dust lightly with flour.

4 Place the pan on the middle rack of the oven and bake for 15 minutes. Reduce the heat to 375°F (190°C) and continue baking until the bread is done, about 30 minutes longer.

5 Remove from the oven. After a few minutes, take the loaf out of the pan and let cool upright on a wire rack. When cool, wrap in wax or parchment paper and store in a bread box.

MIXING THE DOUGH

There is one commonly recommended step that I would remove from the baking lexicon: Do not throw handfuls of flour into a dough to keep it from sticking. Sticky dough is exactly what it will and should be at first.

Within wheat flour there are strands of protein that, after moistening, align to form the stretchy, resilient substance we know as gluten. Though it is important to make sure that the moisture is evenly incorporated through the dough for gluten to form, it is not kneading that determines whether gluten becomes elastic, since this is predetermined by the integral characteristics of the proteins. All that is required is patience: After the initial thorough mixing of the wet ingredients with the dry, let the dough sit for 10 minutes, covered with a dish towel to keep it moist.

WEIGHING INGREDIENTS

In this chapter, the metric equivalents for liquid quantities greater than ¼ cup are weighed in grams rather than measured in milliliters. This is because the ingredients used in my bread and batter recipes are calculated by reference to the flour weight. If you weigh all the ingredients using the metric system, then the recipe will stay true to the original. This will not be the case if you mix weights with volumes.

Digital kitchen scales—along with the metric system of measurement—are a great invention, and one I could not live without. It is true that skilled home bakers can create excellence while appearing to use less precise measurements, but it is their practiced eye that guides them, and they are still measuring while using their familiarity with the ingredients. In translating recipes for others to replicate, digital scales and the metric weighing of all ingredients enables me to convey to you exactly what I am measuring.

The only point where I would advise caution is that domestic scales often weigh in increments of 5 grams, and are therefore not always so good at measuring tiny amounts accurately. So even though the recipes show salt and yeast in grams, I have given teaspoons too, because I find it is better to use an accurate set of measuring spoons for these small but vitally important ingredients.

1 In a bowl, whisk the fresh yeast and water together with a fork until the yeast has completely dissolved.

2 Combine the flour and salt in a bowl. Mix the yeast liquid with the dry ingredients, stirring in with your hand.

3 Mix thoroughly, as quickly as possible, to make a soft, sticky dough. Dig right down to the bottom of the bowl, and squidge the dough through your fingers to be sure that all the flour is mixed with the liquid.

4 Scrape any dough from your fingers back into the bowl, then cover with a dish towel to keep the dough moist. Leave it for 10 minutes before starting to knead, because this will give you a more elastic dough with less effort.

KNEADING THE DOUGH

I use a lightly oiled rather than a floured surface for kneading. Instead of 10 minutes of constant working, I give the dough a series of brief kneads with rests in between. This produces an elastic result, avoids the damage caused by overzealous kneading, opens the texture by stretching the emerging gas pockets, and gives the flour time to fully absorb moisture. Forget about trying to "develop gluten." This will happen through hydration over time. What you need to do is concentrate on mixing the dough evenly.

1 Tip 1 tsp of oil onto the work surface and rub it out into a circle about 8in (20cm) in diameter. Also rub 2 tsp oil over the surface of the dough. Scrape the dough out onto the oiled surface and cover with a cloth.

2 Before starting to knead the dough, wash and dry the bowl, then rub the inside and your hands with a little oil. Set the bowl aside. Uncover the dough and fold it in half toward you. It will be very soft and sticky at this stage.

3 If you are right-handed, use your left thumb to hold the fold firmly in place, while with the heel of your right hand you gently press down and away through the middle of the dough to seal and stretch it.

WHICH OIL?

I like to use olive, corn, or sunflower oil for oiling the work surface, my hands, and the mixing bowl. The oil won't impart much flavor to the dough, as only a very small amount is needed to keep the dough moving smoothly as you knead it. Work surfaces made of laminate, marble, unvarnished wood, and stainless steel are all good for kneading dough.

4 Lift and rotate the dough a quarter turn. Repeat the folding, pressing, and rotating 10–12 times, stopping before the dough starts sticking to the surface. Then place the dough in the oiled bowl, seam-side down, cover, and leave for 10 minutes.

5 Repeat the kneading procedure twice at 10-minute intervals. Each kneading will require less oil. The dough will change from its lumpen start to a silken and elastic finish.

SHAPING THE DOUGH

After the initial rise, the dough is divided into smaller pieces according to the use you have in mind. You could simply chop the dough in half or fourths, not worrying about the exact weight of each piece. However, as larger loaves take longer to bake than smaller loaves, it is good practice to weigh your mass of dough and divide it accurately. For shaping, the work surface should be lightly floured. This will slightly dry the outside of the dough to encourage a good crust to form during baking. Once shaped, the dough is ready for its final rise.

Shaping a pan loaf

For a pan loaf, you can just press a short, stocky baton (see opposite) down into an oiled and floured loaf pan, or even roll up the dough neatly like a jelly roll to give an even rise. Here, though, I've cut the dough into two equal pieces, rounded the pieces, and tucked them side by side into the loaf pan.

Shaping a round loaf

1 If the dough has been cut in half, place a piece on the lightly floured work surface, smoothest side down. Pinch the edge of the dough and pull it into the center, holding it in place with the thumb of your other hand.

2 Continue the pinching and pulling, rotating the dough a little each time, until you have worked your way all around the dough in six or eight movements, and have shaped a rough ball. Flip the dough over.

3 Make sure that the work surface is only barely dusted with flour, then rotate and drag the ball of dough across it. As the underside of the dough catches slightly, the upper surface will be pulled taut, making a neat, round loaf.

Shaping a baton

1 Shape the dough into a ball (see above), then let rest, covered, for 10 minutes. Turn it over, seam-side up, and pat out into a flat oval.

2 Pinch the sides of the oval farthest from you and fold them both in toward the center, pressing them down to seal.

3 Fold the point you have made in toward the center and press down to seal. Turn the dough around 180°, then repeat steps 2 and 3.

A PROFESSIONAL FINISH

To get an extra fine finish to their loaves, bakers prefer to shape the dough on an unvarnished wooden surface. A cutting board with a lip along one side, to rest over the edge of the worktop and prevent slipping, is ideal for this purpose.

4 Turn the dough around 180° again and fold it lengthwise in half, sealing down with the heel of your hand. Avoid trapping pockets of air.

5 Roll the dough with your hands to taper the ends, giving the loaf a baton shape.

Shaping small, round dinner rolls

You can use simple white bread dough (p344) to make rolls. Put them on a baking sheet to rise, covered, until doubled in height, then bake in a preheated 410°F (210°C) oven until golden brown, about 20 minutes.

1 Divide the dough into pieces weighing 2–3oz (50–75g). Your flat hand holding the dough should be clean and your cupped hand floured. Place one piece of dough on your clean palm, then cup your floured hand over it so your fingers claw around the dough.

2 Quickly rotate your floured hand counterclockwise, spinning the ball of dough around but letting it catch a little on the clean hand (see right). This will pull the outer skin of the dough ball taut as it turns in your palm.

Shaping breadsticks

Make breadsticks from simple white bread dough (p344) or a dough enriched with oil and cheese. Once shaped, put them on a baking sheet sprinkled with semolina, cover, and let rise until barely doubled in height. Bake in a preheated 350°F (180°C) oven for 15–20 minutes, then leave in a warm place for a few hours to dry and crisp.

1 Roll out the dough on a lightly floured surface into a rectangle roughly ½in (1cm) thick. Cover and let rest for 5 minutes. Using a ruler or other straight edge as a guide, cut off thin, equal-sized strips with a pizza wheel or sharp knife.

2 Roll each strip back and forth on the lightly floured surface to make long, thin breadsticks.

THE FINAL RISE

Once the dough has been shaped, it is usually essential to protect its upper surface during the final rise by covering it with a dish towel or plastic wrap. This helps to preserve moisture and elasticity in the "skin" of the dough so that it won't crack as the dough rises before baking. It is impossible to give exact timings for the final rise, as so many variables in the dough can affect it—temperature, the amount of leavening, ingredients that can slow or hasten yeast fermentation, and the moisture content. The best guide is that the loaf should rise to at least one and a half times, but no more than double, its original volume before baking.

For a round loaf

1 Place the shaped dough, seam-side up, in a bowl lined with a floured dish towel. Fold the corners over to cover the dough.

2 Once risen, the ball of dough will be almost doubled in size.

For a baton

Set the shaped dough, seam-side up, on a floured dish towel. Pull the towel up in pleats along the sides of the dough, then twist the ends of the towel to tighten it. Place the wrapped loaf on a tray to rise: This will prevent the baton from spreading. For more than one baton, either wrap each one separately and set side by side on the tray, or use a larger dish towel with a fold sitting up between the two loaves and another to cover the upper surface.

GETTING THE LOAF READY FOR BAKING

Once the dough has risen, it needs to be baked without delay. With a naturally leavened loaf, the window in which the dough needs to be baked is quite large, perhaps an hour or more. But with many yeast breads, the time window is perhaps 15 minutes—the rapid production of CO_2 by the yeast might cause the dough to collapse upon itself. It is better to put the loaf into the oven a little too early, rather than a little too late.

Slashing the dough

1 To prevent the dough from tearing through the crust in an unexpected and unattractive way, popping out around the base rather than bustily through the top, slash it before you put it in the oven.

2 Very carefully tip the dough onto your outstretched hand, then slide it seam-side down onto a semolina-dusted baking sheet. Take care not to deflate the dough. Using a sharp blade, slash the upper surface, cutting at an angle and making the slashes about ¼in (5mm) deep.

Creating a humid environment

1 Creating a perfect crust is a surprisingly tricky balance between having the skin of the dough moist enough at the start of baking for the loaf to rise to its full expanse, yet dry within minutes so that it can then harden and crisp.

2 Spray the loaf with a fine mist of water before putting it into the oven. Alternatively—as long as you are not using a convection oven—spray water on the oven walls (avoiding internal lights), or throw a few ice cubes into a metal pan in the bottom of the oven.

CONTAINED RISE

If a shaped dough is set in a pan or in a basket or bowl lined with a floured dish towel, the loaf will be forced to rise upward. This is important for naturally leavened doughs that need a long final rise, and for doughs with a high moisture content that would have a tendency to spread if risen on a tray. If rising a round loaf in a bowl, choose one that is twice the size of the unrisen dough. The diameter of the bowl will affect the final shape— the wider the bowl, the flatter the final loaf will be. Containment will result in a loaf that is high and proud, with a light, aerated crumb.

CHECKING BREAD FOR DONENESS

When perfectly baked, most loaves will be golden brown. If baked in a pan, the sides of the loaf will have pulled in slightly, away from the pan.

To check if a loaf is baked through, tip it out of the pan or off the baking sheet and into a dish towel held in your other hand. The loaf should feel light and, when you rap the base with your knuckles, should sound hollow.

BAKING WITH A NATURAL LEAVEN

All artisan bakers nurture and use a natural or sourdough leaven. Kept chilled in the refrigerator, cool in a basement, or simply at the bakery temperature, this living mixture of flour and water is used to create richly flavored breads. Making a leaven is easy and doesn't require any special ingredients or equipment. The secret—if there is one—is to refresh the mixture with flour and water every day.

Adding 1 tbsp organic raisins to the initial mixture—and then straining them out after day four—appears to create a more vigorous fermentation, but is optional. After five days, visible fermentation will have begun, but the development of a complex, healthy leaven takes time. I suggest you try this as a two-week project, baking bread daily for the last five or six days.

A NATURAL LEAVEN

For the initial mixture

4 tsp unbleached white or whole-wheat high-gluten bread flour or rye flour

2 tsp live plain yogurt

3½ tbsp water at 65–68°F (18–20°C)

1 tbsp organic raisins (optional, see above)

For the daily refreshment

unbleached white or whole-wheat high-gluten bread flour or rye flour, depending on the bread you will make

STORING LEAVEN

You can keep the leaven between refreshments at cool room (kitchen) temperature, although that may fluctuate a little, or it can be kept in the refrigerator or a cellar. Wherever you keep it, just be sure to refresh it daily while you continue to use it. For long-term storage, place it in a sealed container and leave it undisturbed at the back of the refrigerator. After a week it may not look too pretty because, as the paste sinks to the bottom the liquid turns a gray-brown color. But it will be fine, just dormant.

To revive it, take 2 heaped tsp of the paste and stir it in a clean lidded jar with ¼ cup water and ½ cup (60g) high-gluten bread flour. The following day, remove three-fourths to four-fifths of the mixture and replace it with another ¼ cup water and ½ cup (60g) flour. Leave for one more day, then refresh once more. The leaven should now be active. If not, refresh again and check the following day. Nature will eventually allow fermentation to restart.

1 Measure all the ingredients for the initial mixture into a 1-pint jar with a lid and stir them together vigorously with a fork. Cover the jar with its lid, then leave for a day at room temperature.

2 The next day, both bacteria and yeasts will have begun to multiply, yet all you will see is a glassy layer of liquid over the solid matter. Measure 4 tsp of your chosen flour and 3½ tbsp water into the jar, stir vigorously, and replace the lid. Leave again until the following day.

3 On day 3, look for the odd tiny bubble on the surface of the mixture. This is the beginning of fermentation. Again, add 4 tsp flour and 3½ tbsp water to the jar, stir vigorously, and replace the lid. Leave until the following day.

4 By day 4, the mixture will be getting energetic and will benefit from a higher ratio of new ingredients to old leaven. Stir the mixture, then tip three-fourths to four-fifths out (throw this away). Add about ½ cup (100g) water to the jar. Stir vigorously, then add ¾ cup (100g) flour and stir vigorously again. The mixture will look like a thick batter. Replace the lid and leave until the following day.

5 On day 5, bubbles of fermentation will appear on the surface. Repeat the procedure followed on day 4, then put the lid back on and leave until the following day.

6 From day 6 on, the mixture will be able to raise a dough, but it will take more time for complex flavors to emerge. Repeat the day-4 procedure each day for the following 2–4 days. You will notice the aroma becoming sharper every day. After 8–10 days, you will have a healthy leaven that you can use in the recipe opposite and in the English leaven bread with potatoes and ale on p353.

SIMPLE LEAVEN BREAD

The secret to producing a good, naturally leavened loaf is in the initial rise. With a commercially yeasted loaf, recipes can be precise, but for a bread raised with a natural leaven, a baker must adapt the times and temperatures to suit the responsiveness of their dough.

Makes 1 loaf

4oz (120g) natural leaven (see opposite)

⅞ cup (200g) water at 22°C (72°F)

1 tsp (7g) fine sea salt

2½ cups (300g) unbleached high-gluten bread flour

olive or corn oil for kneading

1 Early in the morning, at around 8 a.m., combine the leaven and water, mixing it with your fingers. In a large bowl, mix the salt with the flour, stirring well with a spoon.

2 Tip the leaven mixture into the flour and, using your hands, mix it quickly and evenly to make a soft, sticky dough. Cover the bowl and leave for 10 minutes. The dough temperature should be about 68°F (20°C).

3 Spoon 1–2 tsp oil onto the top of the dough and rub it all over the surface. Turn the bowl over and scrape the dough onto an oiled surface. Knead the dough (p346), repeating after 10 and 20 minutes, then cover and leave it for 30 minutes at room temperature (68°F/20°C).

4 Fold the dough by thirds (p352), and repeat this every hour for 3–4 hours. Each time, return it either to a bowl or tray, seam-side down, and cover. At the 3-hour mark, cut a deep slash into the surface of the dough to check the aeration. If you can see a good network of air bubbles, it can be shaped.

5 Line a basket or bowl with a dish towel rubbed thickly with rye flour. Shape the dough into a round loaf or a baton (p347). Place it seam-side up in the towel, cover, and let rise until almost doubled in height. At 68°F (20°C), this will take 2–3 hours; rising time will be longer if the dough is cooler.

6 Preheat the oven to 425°F (220°C). Sprinkle a little semolina or flour on a baking sheet, then place the dough onto it, rounded side up. Slash the surface of the loaf, then lightly spray it with water. Bake for 20 minutes. Reduce the heat to 375°F (190°C) and continue baking until the loaf is a golden brown and feels light in weight, 15–20 minutes longer.

7 Let the bread cool on a wire rack. When cool, wrap in wax or parchment paper and store in the bread box.

FOLDING DURING THE INITIAL RISE

Though the procedure described here is particularly relevant to bread that relies on a natural leaven, it can successfully be applied to any dough that appears sluggish. By stretching and folding the dough during the initial rise, you can speed the fermentation and open the texture by elongating each pocket of gas produced by the yeast. Keep the dough cool, at 68–77°F (20–25°C), and try not to knock out the air. If a bread recipe contains a high proportion of water (more than 70 percent of the flour weight), this technique will make the dough more resilient and much easier to shape.

1 Put the dough on a lightly floured surface. (For some breads, like a focaccia, an oiled surface is used.) Pat out to a rectangle about 8 by 12in (20 by 30cm). Fold a short side in by one-third, then fold the other short side over it.

2 Fold the long sides in by one-third in the same way. Flip the dough over, cover with a dish towel, and let rest. Then repeat the patting out and folding into thirds at intervals, according to the particular recipe.

3 At the end of the rising period, cut through the surface of the dough to check the aeration that has formed. What you want to see is a lot of small bubbles, caused by the yeast as it ferments the natural sugars in the dough.

4 If bubbles have formed, you can proceed to shape the loaf and then give it its final rise prior to baking. If not, press the seam back together and leave the dough for 30–60 minutes, then check again. If the dough is very firm, just perform step 1 at each interval.

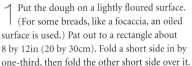

HELPING DOUGH TO RISE

Breads that rely on natural leavens—populated by a host of bacteria, enzymes, and yeasts that ferment the natural sugars slowly in a cool place—need to be nurtured until the point where they can be baked. The yeasts in a natural leaven produce carbon dioxide in much smaller quantities than commercial cultured yeasts, which is why rising times of 8 hours or more are not uncommon with naturally leavened loaves. Attempts to speed up the rising by putting the dough in a very warm place will fail to produce the flavor and crumb texture you want, and instead will make a heavy, leaden loaf. By manipulating the dough during the first long rise, and extending the period of that rise, you will achieve a light-textured loaf with a good, rounded appearance.

English leaven bread with potatoes & ale

The ale contributes both a hint of bitterness from the hops and a flavor of malt, to capture the best from England's breadmaking past. Traditionally, bakers steeped hops and mashed malt before adding flour to gelatinize the mixture (called a "barm"). Today's easier way uses imported bottle-conditioned ale.

Makes 2 loaves

For the barm

½ cup (125g) English bottle-conditioned ale or dark beer

3 tbsp (25g) unbleached high-gluten bread flour

scant 2oz (50g) natural leaven (p350)

For the dough

5oz (150g) firm, parboiled new potatoes, roughly diced (about 1 cup)

1 cup (225g) unsalted potato cooking water, cooled to 65–68°F (18–20°C)

1½ tsp (10g) fine sea salt

4 cups (500g) unbleached high-gluten bread flour

olive or corn oil for kneading

The morning before baking the bread, prepare the barm. Whisk the ale or beer with the flour in a saucepan. Heat, stirring often, until the mixture reaches 167°F (75°C) and thickens to a creamy paste. Transfer to a bowl and cool to about 68°F (20°C), then stir in the leaven. Cover and leave at room temperture until the following day, by which time the barm should be lively with fermentation.

Early on the day of baking, add the barm to the potato and its cooking water and mix well. In a large bowl, stir the salt with the flour. Tip the barm mixture into the flour and, using your hands, mix to a soft, sticky dough. Cover the bowl and leave for 10 minutes.

Spoon 2 tsp of oil onto the top of the dough and rub it all over the surface. Scrape the dough out onto an oiled surface and knead it thoroughly (p346). Return to the bowl, cover, and leave for 30 minutes.

Remove the dough from the bowl and fold it into thirds (see opposite). Repeat every hour for 4 hours. Each time, return it either to a bowl or tray, seam-side down, and cover. At the 4-hour mark, check the aeration. If the dough has risen enough you can shape it.

Divide the dough into two equal pieces and shape each into a baton (p347). Put each baton on a separate floured dish towel and place on trays. Cover and let rise until the loaves have doubled in height, 2–3 hours.

Preheat the oven to 425°F (220°C). Sprinkle a baking sheet with semolina or flour. Tip each baton onto your outstretched hand, then transfer, seam-side down, to the sheet, leaving 4in (10cm) space between the loaves. Slash them, then lightly spray them with water. Bake for 20 minutes. Reduce the heat to 375°F (190°C) and continue baking until the bread is done, 15–20 minutes longer.

Cool on a wire rack, then wrap in wax or parchment paper and store in the bread box.

MAKING RYE BREAD

When attempting to bake a good 100-percent rye loaf, you must first avoid any comparison with a wheat loaf. Although rye flour contains gluten, a rye dough handles as if the flour has been mixed with glue, and it lacks the stretchy, gas-holding properties that a wheat dough has. So there is no reason to give a rye loaf an extended first rise. And thus it is impossible for rye bread to have the crumb of a wheat bread. In countries where rye flour is the dominant milled grain, bakers have used various methods to work around these problems, like the two breads shown here and the crisp rye bread on p363.

SIMPLE RYE LOAF

Jan Hedh, Sweden's bread-maestro, gave me his method for making rye flour behave a little more like wheat flour. The flour is whisked into boiling water, then left overnight to cool. This batter becomes sweeter and almost elastic, which in turn makes the dough easier to shape. Note that the rye flour is sifted before use to remove the bran—if the bran is left in, the gluten it contains can make the loaf too sticky and harder to slice. Keep the bran to sprinkle over the baking sheet and the loaf before baking.

Makes 1 loaf

For the overnight batter

⅔ cup (150g) boiling water

¼ cup (25g) sifted light rye flour

For the dough

¾ tsp (5g) compressed fresh yeast

1 tbsp (20g) honey

⅓ cup (80g) water at 68°F (20°C)

3⅓ cups (300g) sifted light rye flour

1 tsp (7g) fine sea salt

1 For the overnight batter, measure the required amount of boiling water and pour it into a large bowl. Sift the flour into the water, whisking well as you do so. You should have a thickish gray liquid. Cover the bowl and leave at room temperature overnight.

2 Add the yeast, honey, and water to the batter and whisk together, then add the rye flour and salt. Squeeze through your fingers to make a soft, sticky dough. Cover and leave for 10 minutes.

3 Turn the dough onto an oiled surface and knead (p346). Cover the dough and leave for 30 minutes, then shape it into a baton (p347). Place, seam-side up, in a dish towel rubbed with rye flour for a contained rise. Let rise at 68°F (20°C) until risen by half its height again, 1½–2 hours.

4 Preheat the oven to 425°F (220°C). Sprinkle a little semolina (or sifted-out rye bran) onto a baking sheet. Transfer the baton, seam-side down, to the sheet. Gently brush off any excess flour, then spray the loaf with a fine mist of water and dust it lightly with rye bran. Bake for 20 minutes. Reduce the temperature to 375°F (190°C) and continue baking until the loaf is done, 30–35 minutes longer. Let the loaf cool on a wire rack.

WHOLE-GRAIN RYE BREAD

This is a heavy, dense loaf that needs to sit for a few days before it is sliced thinly. The secret for success is to get the rye or wheat berries plump and moist before they go into the dough. Finely milled and sifted rye flour is also essential—too much of the fiber and the result will be a bread that is too sticky to cut. To make the leaven, follow the instructions on p350, using equal quantities of water and fine sifted rye flour in the refreshments.

Makes 1 loaf

1½ cups (300g) whole rye or wheat berries
1¼ cups (300g) white wine, beer, or hard cider
7oz (200g) natural leaven, made with rye flour (see above)
¾ cup (175g) water at 68°F (20°C)
3⅓ cups (300g) sifted light rye flour
1 tsp (7g) fine sea salt
2 tbsp (40g) honey

1 The day before, simmer the berries in water to cover for 45 minutes. Drain and put in a large bowl. Cover with the white wine, beer, or cider and let to soak overnight at room temperature.

2 Drain the berries. Weigh about 1¼lb (600–650g) and return these to the bowl (discard the rest). Whisk in the rye leaven and water. Add the remaining ingredients and stir together with a spoon. The dough will be more like a paste than a dough, so don't try to knead it. Cover and leave it for 10 minutes. Then stir the dough and set aside again, covered.

3 Line a 12 by 4½ by 3in (30 by 11 by 7.5cm) loaf pan with brown paper or parchment paper rubbed with oil, taking care to fold the paper neatly so that you retain the sharp edges of the pan's corners.

4 Scrape the dough into the pan and smooth the surface. Cover the pan with a dish towel and let rise in a warm place until the dough has risen by almost one-third, 3–4 hours.

5 Preheat the oven to 400°F (200°C). Cover the pan with foil and bake in the middle of the oven for 30 minutes. Reduce the heat to 350°F (180°C) and bake for another 30 minutes. Then lower the heat to 300°F (150°C) and bake for 1½ hours longer, removing the foil for the last 30 minutes. The top of the bread should be dark brown.

6 Cool in the pan for a few minutes, then unmold the loaf. Peel off the paper and cool on a wire rack. Wrap in a fresh sheet of oiled paper and tie snugly with string. Leave the loaf for 2 days at room temperature before slicing.

MAKING PIZZA DOUGH

Pizza can be the simplest of flatbreads, or a complicated cheese-filled pie. I have a place in my heart for both. The quantity of yeast you use depends on when you want to bake. This recipe works best if the dough is at least 2 hours old, and it can be kept in a cool place for up to 4 hours. Reduce the yeast to ¼ tsp (1–2g) if you make the dough at noon, but want to bake with it that evening, and increase the yeast to 1 tsp (7g) if you are running late and want to use it almost immediately.

BASIC PIZZA DOUGH

Makes about 14oz (440g)

½ tsp (3–4g) compressed fresh yeast
⅔ cup (150g) water at 72°F (22°C)
2 tsp (10g) sugar
1½ tbsp olive oil plus more for kneading
1¼ cups (150g) Italian "00" flour
¾ cup (100g) unbleached high-gluten bread flour
¾ tsp (5g) fine sea salt

1 Whisk the yeast with the water, sugar, and oil. In another bowl, lightly toss the flours with the salt. Pour the liquid into the flour and stir together into a soft, sticky mass. Scrape any remaining dough from your hands, cover the bowl, and leave for 10 minutes.

2 Lightly knead the dough (p346). The series of light kneads and rising will take 1½ hours. Then round the dough into a ball, place in a bowl, and keep in a cool place until required.

ROLLING THE DOUGH

Roll out the dough into a circle or oval, then cover and let rest for 10 minutes. Uncover and roll it even thinner, as thin as you can—ideally about ⅛in (3mm) thick. Dust with flour so it doesn't stick.

PIZZA DI ACCIUGATA ALLA TORRESE

I adapted this from *Il Re Dei Cuochi*, edited by Giovanni Nelli, published in 1925 (mine is the revised edition). Anchovies, garlic, and parsley top a sheet of dough, which is then sprinkled with bread crumbs to give the surface a crunch.

Makes 2 pizzas, to serve 4–8

1 quantity of basic pizza dough (see left)
olive oil for brushing
6 tbsp (50g) cornmeal or polenta
8–10 salted anchovies, soaked and drained
1 garlic clove, finely chopped
2 good handfuls (25g) of chopped parsley
½ cup (50g) dry white bread crumbs, made from a good loaf

1 Divide the dough in half. Roll out each piece into a thin circle or oval (see left). Let rest for 10 minutes, covered with a dish towel.

2 Preheat the oven to 425°F (220°C), or as hot as it will go. Lightly brush two large baking sheets with olive oil, then sprinkle the surfaces lightly with the cornmeal or polenta.

3 Roll one of the dough circles even thinner (see left), then roll it around the rolling pin and unroll onto a baking sheet. Tuck back any edges of dough that hang over. Brush the dough with olive oil, then dust lightly with sea salt.

4 Tear half of the anchovies into strips and drop them randomly on top, along with dots of garlic. Finally, sprinkle with half of the parsley and bread crumbs.

5 Bake in the middle of the oven until the top is lightly browned and the edges are crisp, 12–15 minutes. Repeat with the other dough circle, rolling it out and topping it just before baking. Serve hot or warm.

HOT CHEESE & RADICCHIO PIZZA PIE

You will find that you have more pizza dough than this simple pie needs, but any attempt at being economical with the dough will make lining the pan difficult. Roll out any trimmed dough into a disk and freeze it unbaked to use as a pizza base another time.

Serves 6–8

1 tbsp olive oil plus more for the pan and brushing the pie
1 onion, thinly sliced
½ tsp dried red pepper flakes
1 small head of radicchio, thinly sliced
1 garlic clove, crushed
1 tsp red wine vinegar
1 quantity of basic pizza dough (see opposite)
10 thin slices of good ham
1 cup (250g) tomato sauce (p40)
5oz (150g) Fontina cheese, sliced
½ cup (50g) freshly grated Parmesan

1 First prepare the filling. In a saucepan, heat the olive oil with the onion and pepper flakes until they begin to sizzle. Reduce the heat, cover, and cook until the onion becomes somewhat translucent, 4–5 minutes. Add the radicchio and toss to mix. Add the garlic. Cook until the radicchio has wilted, 3–4 minutes. Remove from the heat, stir in the vinegar, and season to taste with salt and pepper. Let cool.

2 Mark the dough into thirds, then cut one-third off and place to one side, covered with a dish towel. Roll out the larger piece on a floured surface to a circle about 8in (20cm) in diameter. Cover it while you lightly grease an 8in (20cm) springform pan with olive oil.

3 Roll out the dough into an even larger, thinner circle, measuring 16in (40cm) in diameter. Cover again and let rest for a few minutes, then lift it up and lay it over the pan so that the center droops down to cover the bottom. Gently ease the dough into the corners and up the sides of the pan, leaving some hanging slightly over the rim.

4 Lay three-fourths of the ham evenly over the bottom. Cover with the drained radicchio, then with the tomato sauce. Finish with the Fontina layered with sprinkles of Parmesan and the remaining ham.

5 Roll out the smaller piece of dough to a circle 8in (20cm) in diameter. Place this on top of the pan. Use a knife or scissors to trim the edges of the dough lining the pan, so that they can be folded in over the top crust and overlap it slightly. Brush the top crust with a little olive oil, then let the pie rest at room temperature for 30–45 minutes.

6 Preheat the oven to 400°F (200°C). Place the pie in the middle of the oven and bake until the top is golden brown, about 40 minutes. Carefully remove the side of the pan and, with a metal spatula, ease the pie off the metal base onto a serving plate. Let cool for a moment, then serve the pie hot or warm.

MAKING LEAVENED FLATBREADS

For leavened flatbreads, a softer flour is good—the loss of height can mean a gain in taste, as there is less flavorless gluten in the loaf. The same soft dough can be used to make three Mediterranean-style breads: focaccia, pide, and paper-thin crispbread.

For Italian focaccia a little olive oil and malt are added to the dough, plus—if you can obtain it or like it—optional "strutto" (pork lard). Pide is the flatbread of Turkey, while paper-thin crispbread is inspired by the carta di musica of Italy.

Pocket breads such as pita and naan owe their appearance to the way heat is applied, rather than just to the dough used. In a Lebanese clay oven, the stone sole sits above a layer of salt, which helps to insulate it and keep it relatively cool. So most of the heat comes from above, to pull a pita dough upward. In a traditional tandoor oven used to bake a naan, the breads surround the central heat source. This creates a dryer heat, which blisters the outside of the bread while leaving it moist inside.

SIMPLE WHITE SOFT DOUGH

Use this dough to make pide (see below), focaccia (see opposite), or paper-thin crispbread (p363). As the dough is very soft, I fold and stretch it on an oiled surface, rather than knead it.

1¼ cups (150g) Italian "00" flour or all-purpose flour
⅞ cup (200g) water at 68°F (20°C)
1 tsp (7g) compressed fresh yeast
For the dough (2lb)
⅔ cup (150g) water at 68°F (20°C)
1 tbsp olive oil plus extra for folding
1½ tsp malt syrup for focaccia
3 cups (375g) Italian "00" flour or all-purpose flour
1½ tsp (10g) fine sea salt

1 In a medium bowl, mix together the flour, water, and yeast to make the ferment. Cover the bowl with a cloth and leave at warm room temperature (72°F/22°C) for about 2 hours, giving the mixture a stir after the first hour. At the end of this time the ferment should be bubbling and have risen to double its original height.

2 To make the dough, whisk the water and 1 tbsp oil into the ferment until combined. If you are going to use the dough to make focaccia, whisk in the malt syrup.

3 Mix the flour and salt into the ferment, and squeeze together in your hands to make a very soft, slightly lumpy, and very sticky dough. Scrape any remaining dough from your hands, then cover the bowl and leave for 10 minutes.

4 Rub 1 tbsp of oil all over the surface of the dough, then scrape it out onto an oiled work surface. Work the dough by patting and folding (p352) at 10-minute intervals for 30 minutes, then fold the dough every 40 minutes for the next 2 hours. The dough will then be ready to be shaped.

PIDE

These flatbreads are often topped with sesame seeds, nigella seeds, or fennel seeds. This is an Australian-inspired version of the popular Turkish bread—only much puffier and softer than the original.

Makes 6 breads

1 quantity of simple white soft dough (see above)
sesame seeds for the topping

1 Divide the dough into six equal pieces (about 5oz/150g each). Round on a floured surface into balls, then cover with a dish towel and leave for 15 minutes.

2 Roll out each ball into an oval shape about ½in (1cm) thick. Place on a floured dish towel and cover with another. Let rise for 30 minutes.

3 Preheat the oven to 425°F (220°C). Transfer the pides to a floured baking sheet. Brush lightly with water, then sprinkle with sesame seeds. Bake in the middle of the oven until golden, about 20 minutes. Serve warm.

FOCACCIA

Rubbing a mixture of water, oil, and salt over the dough before baking is the traditional method used by bakers in Italy to create a golden surface.

Makes 1 bread

good olive oil

1 quantity of simple white soft dough
(see opposite)

fine sea salt

rosemary leaves (optional)

1 Rub a 12 by 16in (30 by 40cm) baking sheet liberally with olive oil. Round the dough into a ball, then place it on the sheet.

2 Using a rolling pin and then prodding with your fingers, lightly flatten out the dough. Don't worry at this point if it springs back. Cover with a dish towel and leave in a warm place for 20–30 minutes.

3 Preheat the oven to 425°F (220°C). Pick up the corners of the dough and stretch them out until they reach up to the corners of the baking sheet. Sprinkle a little water, olive oil, and salt on the dough, and rub these together well all over the surface.

4 Lightly dimple the surface with your fingertips, pressing down without pushing too much gas out of the dough. Sprinkle with rosemary, if using. Bake in the middle of the oven for 15 minutes, then reduce the heat to 400°F (200°C) and bake for 15 minutes longer. Cool on a wire rack.

WORKING SOFT DOUGH

When working with this sort of soft dough, it is very important to keep the work surface and your hands well oiled. The dough will gradually absorb some of the oil, but when you are folding it, as soon as the dough starts to stick, put it back in the bowl, cover it with a dish towel, and let it rest.

Flatbread with pumpkin, green olives & shallots

I've always liked combinations of starchy foods—a particular favorite of mine is a focaccia topped with sliced potatoes and truffle oil. For this bread, pumpkin is baked, then sliced and tossed with shallots, garlic, green olives, and olive oil before being baked again on a sheet of white dough.

Scatter the pumpkin mixture over the dough

Makes 1 flatbread

8oz (250g) piece of pumpkin, seeds and fibers removed

4 shallots, finely sliced

⅔ cup sliced green olives

1 garlic clove, finely sliced

2 tbsp olive oil

one-quarter (250g) simple white soft dough, made with malt syrup (p358)

Preheat the oven to 400°F (200°C). Wrap the pumpkin in greased foil or parchment paper, place on a baking sheet, and bake until tender, 50–60 minutes. Let cool, then peel the pumpkin and slice the flesh thinly.

Mix the pumpkin with the shallots, olives, garlic, and olive oil. Set aside.

Roll out the dough on a lightly floured surface into a large oval about 12in (30cm) long and 6in (15cm) wide. Transfer to a lightly greased baking sheet.

Spread the pumpkin mixture evenly over the top of the dough, then season with salt and freshly ground black pepper. Bake until the top is golden and the edges are crisp, 25–30 minutes. Serve hot or warm.

PITA BREAD

Don't attempt to make these unless your oven can reach the required temperature. Bake another bread instead. The reason is that the dough needs to explode in the heat, causing the bread to puff like a balloon. Without a great heat, this just won't happen.

Makes 8 breads

For the ferment

½ tsp (3–4g) compressed fresh yeast

½ cup (125g) water at 86°F (30°C)

¾ cup (100g) unbleached high-gluten bread flour

For the dough

scant ⅞ cup (195g) water at 72°F (22°C)

1⅔ cups (200g) cake flour

2 cups (250g) unbleached high-gluten bread flour

3 tbsp (40g) sugar

1 tsp (7g) fine sea salt

1 To make the ferment, whisk the yeast with the water in a small bowl. Add the flour and stir until smooth. Cover and leave in a warm place (77°F/25°C) for 1½ hours.

2 For the dough, mix the water with the ferment. Put all the remaining ingredients in a large bowl and add the ferment mixture. Mix to a soft, sticky dough. Cover and leave for 10 minutes.

3 Knead the dough (p346), then leave it for 1 hour, giving it one more knead during that time.

4 Preheat the oven to at least 425°F (220°C). Place a clean baking sheet (or a baking stone) in the oven to heat. Meanwhile, on a lightly floured surface, divide the dough into eight equal pieces (about 3½oz/100g each). Round each piece into a ball and leave, covered, for 15 minutes.

5 Roll out each ball into a round roughly ¼in (5mm) thick. Let rest for 2 minutes.

6 Using a sheet of cardboard as a makeshift scoop, scoop up each pita and drop it onto the hot sheet (or stone). Bake, one or two at a time, until risen and barely colored, about 5 minutes. Remove with tongs and cool, covered.

PAPER-THIN CRISPBREAD

This thin, crisp bread can also be baked, covered, in an ungreased wok set over a heat-diffuser. Check after a few minutes to make sure that the bread has turned golden brown on the underside (lift it carefully with a spatula), then flip over and bake for a few minutes on the other side. Like cooking crêpes, this method requires some attention at the beginning to get the heat right.

Serves 6

1 quantity of simple white soft dough (p358)

olive oil for brushing

1 Divide the dough into six equal pieces (about 5oz/150g each) and roll out into ovals as for pides (p358). Cover the ovals and let rise for 30 minutes.

2 Preheat the oven to 425°F (220°C), or as hot as it will go. Just before baking, one at a time, roll and stretch each oval once more until it is thin and the length of your baking sheet.

3 Transfer to the oiled sheet and brush the dough with olive oil. Bake until lightly browned, 12–15 minutes. Cool on a wire rack, then wrap or freeze immediately. Break into pieces for serving.

NAAN BREAD

This is the quickest yeast-raised bread I make at home. The recipe uses soft flour, giving a very tender crust with almost no kneading, together with both fresh yeast and baking powder. I improvise on the traditional tandoor oven by using a wok with a lid (a rather nifty and easy solution). Failing that, use a nonstick skillet with a lid. The baked naan freeze very well. Reheat, wrapped in foil, in the oven.

Once it is made the dough must be used promptly. If you want to make the dough in the morning for use in the evening, reduce the amount of yeast to ¼ tsp, and keep the dough covered and chilled until required.

Makes 4 breads

⅔ cup (150g) water at 72°F (22°C)
¾ tsp (5g) compressed fresh yeast
2 cups (250g) cake flour
3½ tbsp plain low-fat yogurt
½ tsp (4g) fine sea salt
¾ tsp baking powder
sunflower oil, ghee, or melted butter for kneading
2 tbsp finely chopped cilantro or parsley (optional)

1 Pour the water into a bowl. Whisk in the yeast, then add half the flour. Mix together with a fork, then cover the bowl and leave in a warm place for 30 minutes.

2 Stir in the yogurt, then add the rest of the flour, the salt, and baking powder. Mix together with your hands (or a spoon if you find it easier) into a soft, sticky ball. Spoon 2 tsp oil, ghee, or melted butter into the bowl and rub it over the top of the dough, then pick the dough up out of the bowl and roughly squeeze it once or twice. Place the dough back in the bowl, cover, and leave for 15 minutes.

3 Pour another 1 tsp oil, ghee, or butter onto the dough and rub lightly all over, then turn the dough out onto a lightly oiled work surface. Knead the dough lightly for 30 seconds, then return it to the bowl. Cover and leave for another 15 minutes.

4 By this time the dough should be much smoother. Knead lightly on the oiled surface for a minute, then divide into fourths. Dust with flour and leave for 5 minutes. Meanwhile, heat a wok over medium heat.

5 Take one piece of dough and roll it out into a teardrop shape, dusting well with flour as you go. Try to get the dough quite thin, about ⅛in (3mm) if possible.

6 When the wok is very hot, gently lift the dough and lay it in the wok. Brush the surface of the dough with a little sunflower oil, ghee, or butter, mixed with the herbs, if using. Place the lid on the wok and leave for 1 minute, while you roll out another piece of dough.

7 Check the naan. It should have risen slightly and blisters of air should be forming on the top surface. With tongs, lift the bread carefully at one end and look to see whether it has browned lightly underneath. If so, flip the naan over and cook for 1 minute longer.

8 When the naan is cooked on both sides, remove it from the wok. Keep wrapped in a clean dish towel while you roll out and cook the remaining naan.

MAKING CRISP, WHEAT-FREE FLATBREADS

Though we now think of bread as soft and leavened, the earliest breads made by man were much simpler, and were made using the grain found through foraging. For example, some Australian Aboriginals use a type of wild millet, ground into flour and mixed with water, to make a basic flatbread. The recipe below is inspired by one of the great crispbreads of Scandinavia.

CRISP RYE BREAD

Makes 2

2 cups (200g) dark, whole rye flour plus extra for dredging

¾ tsp (5g) fine sea salt

¾ tsp (5g) compressed fresh yeast

¾ cup (175g) water at 68°F (20°C)

1 Combine the flour and salt in a large bowl. Whisk the yeast with the water, then add to the dry ingredients. Stir together until you have a smooth, sticky paste. Cover the bowl and leave until the paste is slightly puffy, about 3 hours.

2 You need two baking sheets about 8 by 12in (20 by 30cm). If they aren't nonstick, line them with parchment paper. Scrape half the paste onto each sheet and spread out to about ½in (1cm) thickness. If the paste starts to dry out as you are scraping, sprinkle it with water.

3 Dredge the surface liberally with additional rye flour, then, with a rolling pin and your fingers, roll and press out the paste to roughly ¼in (5mm) thick and smooth on the top. Cover with dish towels and leave in a warm place (77–83°F/25–28°C) until the sheets of paste are doubled in height, about 1 hour.

4 Preheat the oven to 400°F (200°C). Uncover the sheets. With the rounded end of a chopstick, make dimples all over the surface.

5 Using a round-bladed knife, cut out disks the size of an LP record (see left). In the middle score a smaller circle about 1½in (3–4cm) in diameter. Remove the paste from around the disks (the trimmings can be re-rolled to make another disk or other shapes). Alternatively, score the sheets of paste into squares or rectangles.

6 Bake in the middle of the oven until the crispbreads are dry and slightly crisp at the edges, about 40 minutes. Remove from the oven and, when cool enough to handle, break the breads into large pieces.

OATCAKES

Makes 12–15

1⅓ cups (200g) oat meal (finely ground rolled oats) plus extra for rolling and sprinkling

½ tsp (4g) baking soda

½ tsp (4g) fine sea salt

2 tbsp heavy cream

¼ cup milk

3 tbsp water

1 Mix together the oat meal, soda, and salt in a large bowl. Stir the cream, milk, and water together in a cup, then add to the dry ingredients. Stir to form a very thick paste that will stiffen as it rests. Cover and leave for 15 minutes to firm. (If it hardens too much, work in a little water.)

2 Preheat the oven to 350°F (180°C). Lightly dust the work surface with more oat meal. Roll out the dough carefully until it is ⅛–¼in (3–5mm) thick. To prevent the dough from sticking to the surface as you roll, keep sliding a metal spatula underneath.

3 Using a 3in (8cm) diameter cutter, cut disks from the dough. Use the spatula to transfer the disks to a clean, dry baking sheet. Re-roll the scraps and cut out more disks until you have finished the dough.

4 Sprinkle with extra oat meal, then bake until the oatcakes are dry and lightly tinged with brown around the edges, 15–20 minutes. Remove the oatcakes to a wire rack. When cool, store in an airtight container.

MAKING QUICK BREADS

In countries where the summertime temperatures often made it difficult to store yeast or dough before the advent of refrigeration, baking soda and baking powder were used as instant leavening agents for "quick" breads. These were a familiar part of home baking from America to Australia, and are now much loved everywhere.

CORNBREAD

I like cornbread made with a little sugar, plus butter to add a creamy taste. You can vary the proportions to suit your own preferences.

Serves 8

1⅔ cups (200g) cornmeal

⅔ cup (85g) all-purpose flour

½ cup (100g) sugar

2 tsp (15g) baking soda

1¼ cups (300g) low-fat milk

4 tbsp (60g) unsalted butter, cut into small dice

2 extra large eggs

1 heaping cup (275g) plain yogurt

4 long, hot, red chilies, seeded and thinly sliced lengthwise (optional)

1 Preheat the oven to 375°F (190°C). Line a deep, 8–10in (20–25cm) round baking pan with parchment paper.

2 Sift the cornmeal, flour, sugar, and baking soda into a bowl. In a saucepan, heat the milk until it simmers, then remove from the heat and add the butter. Let the butter melt and the mixture cool to lukewarm, then beat in the eggs and yogurt.

3 Pour the milk mixture into the dry ingredients in the bowl and whisk very lightly together. As soon as combined, pour the batter into the pan. Arrange the optional chilies on top (they will sink in during baking). Bake until a skewer inserted into the center comes out clean, 40–50 minutes. Serve warm.

CINNAMON & DATE COFFEE CAKE

Shaped into a big twist and curled in a ring mold, this coffee cake is very quick to make. Serve it torn up in a basket. It's perfect as part of a summer brunch, or—when the weather is a bit chilly—as part of an afternoon feast, with mugs of hot cocoa.

Makes 1 bread

2½ tbsp (40g) unsalted butter, softened, plus extra for the mold

1⅔ cups (250g) all-purpose flour

2 tbsp (25g) granulated sugar

2 tsp (14g) baking powder

1 extra large egg

5 tbsp (75g) milk

For layering the dough

6 tbsp (75g) brown sugar

½ heaped cup (100g) roughly chopped dates

3½ tbsp (50g) unsalted butter, softened

1 tsp (7g) ground cinnamon

1½ tbsp dark rum

1 Preheat the oven to 400°F (200°C). Thickly butter an 8½in (21cm) ring mold that is 2in (5cm) deep, or a cake pan of the same diameter. Line the bottom of the mold or pan with parchment peper.

2 Sift the flour, sugar, and baking powder into a bowl. Rub in the butter using your fingertips. Whisk the egg with the milk in a cup until well combined, then stir this into the dry ingredients in the bowl. Work the mixture together well with your hands until you have an evenly mixed, soft dough. Scrape the dough out onto a floured work surface and lightly knead it for 10–15 seconds.

3 Mix together the brown sugar, dates, butter, cinnamon, and rum in a small bowl; keep to one side. Roll out the dough to a rectangle that is roughly ¼in (5mm) thick, 14in (35cm) long, and 8in (20cm) wide.

4 Spread the date mixture evenly over the surface of the dough, then roll it up tightly like a jelly roll. With a sharp knife, cut the rolled dough in half lengthwise.

5 Twist the two pieces together, keeping the cut surfaces facing up, then curl into the mold. Bake in the middle of the oven for about 30 minutes. Let the coffee cake cool in the mold for 5 minutes, then unmold onto a wire rack. This is best served still warm.

MAKING BATTERS

A batter may be silky-smooth, with the consistency of thick cream, or slightly puffy, due to the action of yeast or the inclusion of an aerated mixture like beaten egg whites or whipped cream. Either way, a batter is perfect for cooking simply, in a heavy-based pan or on a griddle—one of the oldest ways of baking bread—as well as in a waffle iron or in the oven.

If the heavy-based frying pan or griddle you are going to use isn't nonstick, temper it by doing the following: Rub with vegetable oil, then heat until smoking hot. Remove from the heat and cool, then rub off any excess oil with a paper towel. Before cooking, lightly grease the pan with butter or oil. For all griddle-cooked cakes, cold batter onto a hot surface produces the best results.

CRÊPES

Before ovens were common, a griddle or pan placed over a fire would cook a mixture of grains and water into a flatbread—a "pan" cake. Today, pancakes may be thin and delicate, when they are called crêpes, or be fluffy and thick.

When making crêpes, the first few can be tricky to get right, as the heat needs to be adjusted so that the upper surface sets before the base of the crêpe gets too brown.

Makes 7–8

1 cup (125g) all-purpose flour
2 extra large eggs
1½ tbsp (20g) vanilla sugar (optional)
pinch of fine sea salt
1 cup (250g) cold milk
2½ tbsp (40g) butter, melted

1 Combine all the ingredients in a bowl and whisk to make a smooth batter. Cover and let rest in the refrigerator for 2 hours. The batter should be the consistency of light cream. Add a little more milk to thin it, if necessary.

Serve freshly made, simply sprinkled with sugar and lemon juice, or wrapped around a lavish sweet or savory filling

2 Heat a heavy-based nonstick crêpe pan (my pan is 10in/25cm diameter, but a pan smaller than this will be fine, too). Remove from the heat and ladle a small amount of batter into the pan.

PANCAKES

3 Swirl the batter around so that the bottom of the pan is evenly and lightly coated. Replace the pan on medium heat. Cook until the edges of the crêpe start to come away from the pan and are brown, 45–60 seconds.

4 Peel the crêpe loose and flip it over to cook the other side for 30–60 seconds. Then turn it out onto a plate. As the crêpes are made, pile them up and keep covered with a dish towel while you cook the remainder.

These can be made any diameter, although I like them king-size. Serve in a stack, with melted butter and plenty of maple syrup, a fruit syrup, or preserved ginger in syrup.

Makes 10–12 big pancakes

⅔ cup (150g) milk
2 extra large eggs plus 1 egg white
2½ tbsp (40g) butter, melted
1 tbsp (20g) golden or light corn syrup
2 tbsp (20g) sugar
1⅓ cups (200g) all-purpose flour
2 tsp (14g) baking powder

1 Combine the milk, whole eggs, melted butter, golden or corn syrup, sugar, flour, and baking powder in a bowl and whisk until smooth. The batter should pour from a ladle in a thick, soft ribbon. Cover the bowl and let the batter rest for 2 hours (or overnight in the refrigerator if you are going to make pancakes for breakfast or brunch).

2 Just before cooking, beat the egg white to soft peaks, then fold into the batter.

3 Heat a heavy-based, nonstick frying pan or griddle until hot. To test the heat of the pan, pour 1 tsp of the batter into the center. After a minute, the upper surface of the batter should be pitted with small holes.

4 With a pancake turner, flip the test pancake over. It should be an appetizing light brown on the cooked side. If it's too dark or burned, lower the heat and test again.

5 When you have the temperature right, make the pancakes. Ladle about 4 tbsp (60g) of batter into the pan and tilt it gently so the batter spreads evenly to a 6–8in (15–20cm) disk. After a minute, the upper surface should be pitted with small holes and have begun to set. Carefully lift up the pancake and flip it over to cook the other side for a minute or so.

6 Remove from the pan and keep warm while you cook the remaining pancakes. Serve the pancakes freshly made.

BLINIS

These little yeasted pancakes are perfect served freshly made with a little smoked fish, sour cream, or melted butter, and a mixture of grated raw beet and horseradish.

Makes 20

¾ cup (75g) light rye flour

¼ cup (25g) unbleached high-gluten bread flour

½ tsp (4g) fine sea salt

¼ cup (50g) warm, riced potato

½ tsp (3g) compressed fresh yeast

5 tbsp (75g) ale or dark beer

7 tbsp (100g) water

2½ tbsp (40g) butter, melted, plus extra for greasing the pan

1 extra large egg, separated

1 Sift the flours and salt into a bowl. In another bowl, whisk the riced potato with the yeast, ale, and water until smooth and combined. Stir in the flours, then cover and leave for 2 hours at room temperature, stirring once during this time.

2 Beat the melted butter and egg yolk into the yeast mixture. In a separate bowl, beat the egg white until it forms soft peaks. Fold the white gently through the batter.

3 Heat a large, heavy-based, nonstick frying pan or griddle. Using a large spoon or small ladle, pour two or three disks of batter into the pan. Let cook undisturbed over low heat until the edges of the disks start to matt and small bubbles open up on the surface.

4 With a spatula, lift up the blinis and flip over. Cook for a few more minutes, then remove. Keep covered while you cook the rest.

YORKSHIRE PUDDINGS

This recipe varies a little from traditional versions: The addition of a small amount of melted butter and a little baking powder produces a pudding that is less likely to fall after baking. Also, I prefer it made in individual molds. A dozen small Yorkshires are produced, which may be too many, but it is always a shame to have too few with roast beef.

Makes 12

1 cup (125g) all-purpose flour

¼ tsp (2g) fine sea salt

¼ tsp baking powder

2 extra large eggs

1¼ cups (275g) milk

2 tsp (10g) melted butter

lard or olive oil for the molds

CLAFOUTIS

Here, a batter enriched with eggs and cream is poured over ripe fruit and baked. You can also use drained, preserved fruit or soft dried fruit, such as plump prunes or apricots.

Serves 3–4

½ cup + 2 tbsp (125g) granulated sugar
7 tbsp (55g) all-purpose flour
⅞ cup (200g) whole milk
7 tbsp (100g) heavy cream
3 extra large eggs, separated
½ vanilla bean, split open
butter, flour, and superfine sugar for the dish
8oz (250g) ripe black cherries, pitted, or drained canned cherries (1½–2 cups)
sifted confectioners' sugar for dusting (optional)

1 Put the granulated sugar and flour in a bowl and slowly whisk in the milk, cream, and egg yolks to make a smooth batter. Scrape in the seeds from the vanilla bean and whisk to mix. Leave to one side for 2 hours.

2 Preheat the oven to 400°F (200°C). Rub an 8in (20cm) round baking dish liberally with butter and dust with a mixture of flour and superfine sugar. Spread the cherries in the dish.

3 In a clean bowl, beat the egg whites to soft peaks. Pour the batter through a strainer onto the egg whites and fold through until just combined. Pour this mixture over the cherries.

4 Bake 20–25 minutes, then reduce the heat to 350°F (180°C) and bake until the edges are puffed up and the center is just set. Serve warm.

1 Combine all the ingredients in a bowl and beat together to make a smooth batter. Transfer to a pitcher and let rest in the refrigerator for 2 hours.

2 Preheat the oven to 400°F (200°C). Put about 1 tsp of lard or oil in each of 12 small, cylindrical dariole molds. Set the molds on a baking sheet and put into the oven to heat.

3 Remove from the oven. Pour the batter evenly into the molds, half-filling them. Return to the oven and bake until well puffed and golden brown, 20–25 minutes. Turn out of the molds and serve immediately.

Dust with confectioners' sugar before serving, if desired

APPLE FRITTERS

Fresh fruit fritters, coated with cinnamon-sugar, are a traditional family dessert that deserves to see a revival in popularity.

¾ cup (175g) water at 68°F (20°C)
½ tsp (3–4g) compressed fresh yeast
1 tsp honey
6½ tbsp (50g) unbleached high-gluten bread flour
½ cup + 1 tbsp (50g) sifted rye flour
½ tsp (3g) fine sea salt
1 tbsp good olive oil
light vegetable oil for deep-frying
4 apples
1 extra large egg white
sugar mixed with ground cinnamon to finish

1 Pour the water into a bowl, then whisk in the yeast followed by the honey. Mix in both types of flour and the salt, then stir in the olive oil. Cover with a cloth and let the batter rise for 2 hours at room temperature.

2 Check the consistency of the batter. It should be like thick but pourable cream. Add more water, little by little, if necessary.

3 Heat the vegetable oil in a heavy pan. For safety's sake the oil should come no more than one-third the way up the side of the pan— say 2in (5cm) depth. When a cube of stale bread dropped into the hot oil turns golden in about 60 seconds, it is at the right temperature for frying the fritters.

4 Peel the apples, halve them lengthwise, and cut each half lengthwise into four pieces. Remove the cores from the apple pieces.

5 Beat the egg white to soft peaks and fold through the batter. One at a time, dip the apple pieces into the batter, using a fork, then lower them into the hot oil. Fry, a few at a time, until the batter is golden brown, 2–3 minutes. Remove with a slotted spoon and drain on paper towels. Serve freshly made, tossed in a little cinnamon-sugar.

WAFFLES

The most delicious waffles are made with rich ingredients. These are best eaten immediately after cooking, while they are still crisp and featherlight, topped with fruit, honey, or maple syrup, and whipped cream. For best results, use an electric waffle iron. Thicker waffles are easier to cook than thinner ones, but both will need to be watched carefully during cooking.

Makes 8–9 large, thick waffles

scant 1 cup (115g) all-purpose flour
¼ cup (50g) sugar
2 tsp (14g) baking powder
2 extra large eggs, separated
¾ cup (175g) milk
5 tbsp (75g) unsalted butter
½ tsp vanilla extract

1 Heat your waffle iron or pan according to the manufacturer's directions (mine makes 4in/10cm square waffles).

2 Sift the flour, sugar, and baking powder together into a large bowl. In another bowl, beat the egg yolks with the milk, then pour into the dry ingredients and stir until smooth.

3 In a small saucepan, melt the butter until liquid, but just warm rather than hot. Beat the butter into the batter along with the vanilla.

4 Beat the egg whites to soft peaks, then carefully fold into the batter. Once made, the batter can safely sit for up to 30–45 minutes at room temperature before using.

5 Lightly grease the waffle iron, if necessary, then, working quickly, spoon in enough of the batter just to cover the grid evenly. Close the lid and cook the waffle until risen and golden, 3–5 minutes or according to temperature and the manufacturer's directions.

6 Open the lid and ease the cooked waffle away from one corner, then quickly peel the waffle from the iron. Keep warm while the remaining waffles are cooked, then serve hot.

CRUMPETS

To make crumpets that stand tall, use greased metal rings (like egg rings). If you don't have rings, just pour the batter directly onto the griddle. They will be thinner, but just as good.

Makes 10–15

1 cup (125g) unbleached high-gluten bread flour
1 tbsp (15g) sugar
1 tsp (7g) compressed fresh yeast, crumbled
½ tsp (3g) fine sea salt
3½ tbsp warm water at 90°F (32°C)
7 tbsp (100g) lukewarm milk
¾ tsp (5g) baking soda, dissolved in 1 tsp boiling water

1 Combine the flour, sugar, yeast, salt, water, and milk in a bowl and beat together with a spoon to make a very smooth batter. Leave in a warm place until the batter has begun to bubble, about 45 minutes.

2 Very lightly grease a large, heavy-based frying pan or griddle. If you have 3–4in (8–10cm) metal crumpet rings, grease these, too, and place them on the pan to heat. When both the pan and rings are smoking hot, reduce the heat and place a heat-diffuser under the pan (or turn the heat down very low). Leave for a minute to cool down slightly.

Let crumpets cool completely before toasting and eating them

3 Pour the batter into a measuring jug and stir in the dissolved baking soda, stirring well to make sure that it is evenly combined. Pour a little of the batter into each of the rings to a depth of ½in (1cm). If not using rings, pour the batter directly onto the hot pan to make disks 3–4in (8–10cm) in diameter.

4 Let the crumpets cook until the surface is full of holes and the batter almost set, about 3 minutes. Flip the crumpets over and cook on the other side until lightly colored. (This is when you can tell if the heat is right—the base of the crumpets should be dark brown but not burned; if burned then reduce the heat.)

5 The crumpets may pop out of the rings on their own. If they don't, run a sharp knife around the inside of the rings to loosen them. Place the cooked crumpets on a wire rack to cool, then oil the rings once more and put back on the pan to heat. When the rings are hot, make another batch of crumpets.

PASTRY & SWEET DOUGHS

PIERRE HERMÉ

The art of pastrymaking can be traced back to the time of the Egyptians, who were the first to make yeast cakes. The Greeks baked confections of almonds, poppy seeds, honey, and black pepper, enclosed in a pastry made with flour, honey, and sesame seeds. Aristophanes, a Greek playwright of the 5th century B.C., wrote in the Archarnians of "sesame cakes and fruit pastries." Similar ingredients appear in classical Roman recipes, which survive in medieval transcriptions of the oldest surviving cookbook—the recipes of Apicius, a Roman epicure of the 1st century A.D.

The armies of Alexander the Great brought sugar cane to the Mediterranean; the Crusaders introduced the spices and nuts of the Orient; and chocolate was carried to Spain in the 16th century by the conquerors of Aztec Mexico. As a result the cooking of medieval Europe was greatly enriched.

Italian innovation Throughout the Middle East, cooks developed the art of making pastry and dough. The impact of this on Italian cooking was revealed when Bartolomeo Scappi, chef to two popes, published his cookbook, "Opera," in 1570. Scappi is to cooking what Michelangelo is to the fine arts. His cookbook was printed at a time when the arts of good living, manners, stylish clothes, furniture, and fine cooking were studied and enjoyed in Italy. Scappi was the first European cook to explore the Arabic art of pastrymaking, and he details several sophisticated methods for making sweet and savory doughs, which he uses in more than 200 recipes. One pastry, layered with melted lard and then folded and rolled, marks the beginnings of what was to become puff pastry.

These new ideas traveled to France, and some 85 years later the first French book devoted entirely to pastrymaking was published. François Pierre de la Varenne is the founder of French classical cooking. He is credited with the authorship of "Le Pâtissier François," the first comprehensive French work on pastrymaking. It was printed in 1655, and sadly few copies now survive. The book had step-by-step instructions, accurate measurements, and instructions for temperature control. Its methods for making pie pastry, puff pastry, macaroons, and waffles are very similar to those of today, and it is the first book to mention the small baking ovens known as "petits fours," a name now used for little cakes and pastries served with coffee.

Pastrymaking was now an established art, and thoughout the 18th century cooks created new confections. During this time, millers discovered that by sifting flour through finely woven silk they could extract most of the husk. Pastry cooks no longer relied on yeast to leaven their dough, and eggs alone were used to raise the now refined flour, giving light, airy doughs. In 1720, a Swiss pastry cook beat egg whites and sugar together to create the first meringues.

French excellence In the early 19th century, pâtisserie reached new heights of elaboration at the hands of Antonin Carême. Born in 1783 to poor parents, he was turned out onto the streets at the age of 10. He knocked on the door of a cookshop, was taken in, and began to serve a six-year apprenticeship. At 17, he went to work for Bailly, one of the most famous pâtissiers of the day. At the time the profession of pâtissier was very prestigious, because they were responsible for "pièces montées," the great decorative centerpieces that were the crowning glory of grand dinners. Carême excelled at these flights of fancy, and he produced two books in 1815 containing hundreds of designs for ornate creations in the shape of windmills, ruins, cascades, and temples.

Pastrymaking increased in status and came to be seen as a formal art. The unprecedented affluence of the period prompted thousands of pastry cooks throughout Europe to establish shops, and Vienna and Budapest vied with Paris for supremacy in cake and pastrymaking. Today, flamboyant displays are no longer fashionable, but happily the tradition of fine baking is thriving in bakeries and cafés. By reading this chapter you can benefit from centuries of sweetmeat-making expertise and learn how to bake delicious pastries, sweet doughs, and cookies.

PASTRY

The old adage that a good pastrymaker has "cold hands and a warm heart" is not far from the truth. Making melt-in-the-mouth pastry is not difficult, but it does require patience and attention to detail. Follow the instructions carefully and you will derive great pleasure from working with the ingredients and then producing wonderful pastries.

One of the most important things to remember when making pastry is to allow adequate time for resting and chilling. The times given in each recipe should be followed, since the resting time will make the pastry easier to handle and prevent any shrinkage.

Among pastry doughs, pâte brisée, and its sweet variations, is justly celebrated. It bakes to a crisp, compact pastry that makes a smooth container for tarts or a sturdy base for a layered confection. Pâte feuilletée has a complex texture, because the repeated rolling and folding creates layers which, on baking, rise up to form thin, buttery flakes. Choux pastry is a moist, airy paste that puffs up in the oven to form a crisp outer shell with a hollow inside. It can be piped and shaped, and makes a good container for creamy fillings.

PÂTE BRISÉE (SHORT PASTRY)

This amount of pastry is enough to make four 9½–10½in (24–26cm) tarts, six 8in (20cm) tarts, or sixteen 4in (10cm) tarts. The pastry can be used once it has rested, or it can be stored for up to 2 days in the refrigerator. It can also be frozen, tightly wrapped in portions; thaw slowly in the refrigerator before using. Do not knead again—if you do the pastry will lose its melting texture.

Makes 2¼lb (1kg) pastry

1⅔ cups (375g) unsalted butter, at room temperature and cut into pieces
2 scant tsp salt
1 egg yolk
2 scant tsp sugar

7 tbsp whole milk, at room temperature

4 cups (500g) pastry flour plus extra for dusting

Making pâte brisée by hand

This is not a classic pâte brisée, because it is made with milk and eggs instead of water, so the resulting dough is very crisp with a melting texture. Lightness of hand and speed are very important, and the whole process should not take longer than 4–5 minutes, or the pastry will be tough.

1 Place the butter in a bowl and beat with a wooden spoon to soften. Stir in the salt and egg yolk. Stir the sugar into the milk in a cup, then pour this onto the softened butter in a thin stream, stirring constantly.

2 Sift the flour into another bowl or onto a sheet of wax paper. Gradually stir the flour into the butter mixture.

3 Mix by stirring with a wooden spoon or gently bring the ingredients together by hand in the bowl.

4 Turn the mixture onto a floured work surface and, using the palm of your hand, knead just enough to form a soft, moist dough.

CHILLING TIME

Although the pastry dough is made in minutes, the recommended chilling time cannot be reduced. This is because the resting in the refrigerator gives the gluten in the flour a chance to relax. Effective chilling will prevent the dough from shrinking too much when it goes into the hot oven.

5 Shape the dough into a ball, flatten slightly, and wrap in plastic wrap. Let the dough rest in the refrigerator for at least 2 hours.

Using a food processor

This is the ideal way to make pâte brisée, because it is very fast. It is important to stop the machine the moment the dough gathers into a ball.

1 Fit the metal blade into the food processor. Put the butter, salt, egg yolk, sugar, and milk into the processor bowl, and process until you have a smooth cream. Sift the flour, then add to the food processor.

2 Process, using the pulse button, until the mixture just starts to come together. Stop as soon as a ball of dough has formed. Wrap in plastic wrap and refrigerate for at least 2 hours.

Rolling out & lining a tart pan

The dough for pâte brisée is very rich and so can be difficult to roll out. A well-floured work surface makes the job easier, but if you are new to pastrymaking you might want to roll the dough between two large sheets of parchment paper. If you do this, make sure to lift the top sheet of paper from time to time so that it does not crease into the dough.

1 Butter a flan ring (or a tart pan with a removable bottom). Place the ring on a baking sheet lined with parchment paper.

2 Dust the pastry dough with flour, then roll out evenly on a floured work surface to a ⅛–¼in (3–5mm) thickness.

6 Dust off the surplus flour again, then unroll the pastry dough over the flan ring.

7 Press the pastry dough into the bottom and up the sides of the ring.

8 Roll the rolling pin over the top of the ring to cut off the excess pastry dough.

3 Slip a metal spatula underneath now and again to prevent the pastry from sticking.

4 Carefully dust off the surplus flour using a dry pastry brush.

5 Drape the pastry over the rolling pin and roll up halfway so you can lift it.

CRACKING

If the dough cracks or splits as you work, simply patch the split with small scraps of dough. Moisten the edges to "glue" them into place and smooth gently with your finger, taking care not to stretch the pastry.

9 Using your fingertips, press the pastry dough into and up the sides of the ring.

10 Prick the bottom all over with a fork. Refrigerate for 30 minutes.

PEAR TART BOURDALOUE

A great classic of French pâtisserie, this delicious tart is named after a street in the 9th arrondissement in Paris. The optional caramel coating gives a lovely deep flavor to this fruit-filled tart and is well worth the extra effort needed to make it.

Makes an 8½in (22cm) tart

2½lb (1.1kg) ripe but firm Bartlett pears

4 cups water

6 tbsp lemon juice

½ vanilla bean, split lengthwise

scant ⅓ quantity (10oz/300g) pâte briseé (p500)

just over ⅓ quantity (280g) almond cream (p561)

½ cup (160g) apricot jam or quince jelly

1 Peel the pears, cut in half, and remove the cores. Place in a bowl and coat with half of the lemon juice. Put the water, remaining lemon juice, and the vanilla into a pot. Bring to a boil. Add the pears, place a cartouche (p207) on top, and simmer for 10–15 minutes. Remove from the heat, cover, and let infuse overnight.

2 The next day, roll out the pastry dough to ⅛in (3mm) thickness and use to line an 8½in (22cm) flan ring (p378). Trim the edge, then press the top between your thumb and index finger to ruffle the edge. Spread the almond cream evenly in the pastry shell. Arrange the drained pears on top, core-side down.

3 Preheat the oven to 350°F (180°C). Bake the tart for 30 minutes. Let it cool to lukewarm, then carefully remove the flan ring and slide the tart from the baking sheet onto a wire rack.

4 Warm the apricot jam in a pan to melt it, then purée with an immersion blender. Strain out bits of skin, if necessary. Brush the smooth apricot glaze evenly over the surface of the tart filling. Let the glaze cool and set before serving the tart.

CARAMEL COATING

For an optional caramel coating, make a dark golden caramel syrup with 2½ tbsp sugar and a little water (pp410–11). Remove the pan from the heat and add 2 tsp butter and 1½ tbsp crème fraîche. Just before serving, bring the caramel mixture to a boil, then immediately spread it over the tart.

Streusel tart with pistachios & cherries

This tart blends the classic flavors of pistachios and cherries, with a hint of cardamom in the streusel. The contrasting textures of crisp pastry, creamy filling, and crunchy topping make a mouthwatering dessert.

Makes a 10½in (26cm) tart

1lb 2oz (500g) fresh or thawed, frozen Morello cherries, pitted (about 3 cups)

6½ tbsp (80g) granulated sugar

scant ⅓ quantity (10oz/300g) pâte brisée (p376)

10oz (300g) fresh or thawed, frozen black cherries, pitted (about 2 cups)

For the almond pistachio cream

⅓ cup (50g) skinned pistachios

2 drops of bitter almond extract

½ cup + 1 tbsp (125g) butter, cut into pieces

1 cup (125g) confectioners' sugar

1⅓ cups (125g) ground almonds

1½ tbsp (12.5g) cornstarch

1 tbsp kirsch

2 eggs

2½ tbsp (25g) skinned pistachios, crushed

½ cup (150g) crème pâtissière (p418) or ⅔ cup crème fraîche

For the streusel

3½ tbsp (50g) butter, at room temperature

¼ cup (50g) granulated sugar

½ cup (50g) ground almonds

6½ tbsp (50g) pastry flour

pinch of ground green cardamom

pinch of salt (fleur de sel)

Toss the Morello cherries with the sugar in a bowl, then let macerate overnight. The next day, an hour before you are going to use them, drain the cherries.

For the almond pistachio cream, pound the pistachios with the almond extract in a mortar with a pestle to form a paste. Place the butter in a food processor and blend until creamy. Gradually add, one at a time, the pistachio paste, confectioners' sugar, ground almonds, cornstarch, kirsch, eggs, crushed pistachios, and crème pâtissière. Mix slowly. Place the pistachio cream in a shallow bowl and cover the surface closely with plastic wrap. Refrigerate while you make the streusel.

Combine the butter, sugar, ground almonds, flour, ground cardamom, and a pinch of salt in a bowl and rub together with your fingertips. Refrigerate until firm, about 2 hours. Then put the streusel on a wire rack and press through to make small pieces. Return to the refrigerator.

Preheat the oven to 350°F (180°C). Butter a 10½in (26cm) tart pan. Roll out the pastry dough on a floured surface and use to line the pan (p378). Spread a thin layer of almond pistachio cream over the bottom of the tart shell. Cover with the Morello cherries, then sprinkle over the black cherries. Cover with the remaining almond pistachio cream.

Press the streusel dough through a wire rack

Place the tart in the oven. After 10 minutes of baking, remove the tart and sprinkle the streusel over the top. Return the tart to the oven and bake for 15–30 minutes longer. Let cool, then dust with confectioners' sugar.

Prebaking a tart shell

Pastry shells may be prebaked unfilled ("baked blind") either partially or completely, depending on the filling to be used. If the filling is going to be moist—such as a custard—the shell is partially baked to prevent the moist filling from making the pastry soggy. The pastry shell has to be weighted down with dried beans to prevent it from losing its shape during the baking process.

PÂTE SUCRÉE

This amount of pastry dough is enough for three 10½–11in (26–28cm) tarts or five 9½in (24cm) tarts. The dough can be made and frozen, but divide it into portions first. Thaw in the refrigerator the day before you use it. Do not work or knead the dough again before rolling out.

Making pâte sucrée by hand

1 Cut out a disk of parchment paper slightly larger than the flan ring or tart pan. Fold the disk in half several times to make a triangular shape, then clip the outer edge with scissors. (Clipping the edge ensures a close fit against the rim when the paper is placed in the shell.)

2 Line the flan ring or tart pan with the pastry dough (pp378–79). Cover the bottom and sides of the pastry shell with the paper disk (the paper should extend above the sides of the shell). Fill with dried beans—metal pie weights are too heavy for delicate, brittle pastries.

1 Sift the flour onto a work surface. Sprinkle with salt and add the pieces of butter. Rub the flour and butter together between the palms of your hands until the mixture is the texture of fine crumbs and the butter has all disappeared.

3 Preheat the oven to 350°F (180°C). Place the tart shell in the oven and bake for 18–20 minutes; it will be partially baked. For a fully baked shell, remove the beans and lining paper, then return the tart shell to the oven.

4 Continue baking until the pastry is a rich golden color, 6–7 minutes longer. Let the pastry shell cool on a wire rack. Lift off the flan ring (or remove from the tart pan) before or after filling, according to recipe directions.

CHEF'S TIPS

■ When making pastry dough by hand, it is best to use a marble or wooden pastry board and to knead the dough as briefly as possible.
■ It is essential that the pastry dough rests for the time indicated. This allows it to relax and soften, and will prevent it from cracking when it is rolled out and from shrinking as it bakes.

Makes 2½lb (1.1kg) pastry

4 cups (500g) pastry flour

4 pinches of salt (fleur de sel)

1⅓ cups (300g) butter, at room temperature and cut up

¼ tsp vanilla powder or the seeds scraped from ½ vanilla bean (p420)

1½ cups (190g) confectioners' sugar

⅔ cup (60g) ground almonds

2 eggs

Using an electric mixer

When using an electric mixer, the ingredients will blend together quickly, so it is important to stop when the mixture just starts to cling together, or the dough will be overworked. The same applies if using a food processor.

1 Sift the flour and confectioners' sugar separately. Beat the eggs in a bowl. Place the butter in the bowl of the electric mixer. Using the paddle attachment, beat to soften the butter.

2 Mix the vanilla and confectioners' sugar together and add this to the flour mixture, along with the ground almonds.

3 Make a well in the center of the mixture. Pour the eggs into the well.

4 Using your fingertips, mix the ingredients together to form a soft dough, but do not overwork. Press the dough down with the palm of your hand, pushing it away from you, then bring it back toward you and shape into a ball. Wrap in plastic wrap and refrigerate until firm, at least 4 hours.

2 Add, in order, the confectioners' sugar, ground almonds, salt, vanilla, eggs, and, lastly, the flour. Mix slowly, or "pulse" in a food processor, until the mixture comes together in a ball. As soon as it does, stop mixing or the pastry will not have a delicate texture.

3 Wrap the dough in plastic wrap and flatten slightly. Let rest in the refrigerator until firm, at least 4 hours. The pastry dough can be kept in the refrigerator for 48 hours.

TARTE AU CITRON (LEMON TART)

A familiar sight in the windows of French
pâtisseries, tarte au citron is the ideal dessert.
With its crisp pastry and contrasting silky-
smooth filling, it is delicious alone, but equally
good served with red berries or a fruit coulis.

Makes a 10½in (26cm) tart

5 lemons
1¼ cups (240g) sugar
4 eggs
⅔ cup freshly squeezed lemon juice
1⅓ cups (300g) butter, at room temperature and cut into pieces
10½in (26cm) baked pâte sucrée pastry shell (p382)
apple or quince jelly (optional) for glazing

1 Zest the lemons over a large heatproof bowl.
Pour in the sugar. Using both hands, rub the
lemon zest into the sugar until the mixture is
damp and grainy. Add the eggs and whisk
everything together. Stir in the lemon juice.

2 Set the bowl over a pan of simmering water.
The base of the bowl must not touch the
water in the pan. Cook, stirring with a whisk,
until the mixture reaches 180–181°F (82–83°C)
—check with an instant-read thermometer.

LEMON CREAM

■ For a clean, sharp taste, use freshly squeezed
lemon juice. Nothing else will do.

■ There is a tricky moment when making the lemon
cream. This occurs when the butter is added to the
mixture of eggs, sugar, and lemon juice that has
been whisked over hot water. It is essential that the
egg mixture cools to 140°F (60°C) before the butter
is added. If it is hotter than this, the butter will melt
too much and the texture of the cream will be
irretrievably altered.

■ To make an airy lemon cream that is perfectly
smooth, beat with the immersion blender for the full
10 minutes. This is how long it takes for the butter
to be fully incorporated.

■ To intensify the lemon flavor, scatter little strips of
candied lemon peel or thin slices of fresh lemon over
the lemon cream filling.

3 Strain the mixture into a large bowl. Let
cool to 140°F (60°C), stirring from time to
time. Then add the butter pieces, one by one,
mixing them in with an immersion blender.
Whisk the lemon cream with the blender at full
speed until very smooth, about 10 minutes.

4 Pour the lemon cream filling into the baked
pastry shell. Smooth the surface with a
metal spatula. Slide the tart onto a serving plate,
then remove the flan ring.

Lemon tart is a
refreshing and tangy
dessert for any meal

5 To glaze the tart, melt some apple or quince
jelly in a small pan over low heat, or in a bowl
in the microwave. Drizzle the melted jelly evenly
over the lemon cream filling, then let cool and set.

CINNAMON PÂTE SABLÉE (SWEET CINNAMON PASTRY)

This recipe uses the yolks from hard-cooked eggs (p98). Once the peeled hard-cooked eggs have cooled, cut them in half and push the yolks through a fine-mesh strainer into a bowl. The amount of pastry dough made is enough for three 8½in (22cm) disks baked in flan rings or a 10½in (26cm) tart shell.

Makes 1lb 2oz (500g) pastry

¾ cup + 2 tbsp (200g) butter, at room temperature and cut into pieces

⅓ cup (40g) confectioners' sugar

⅓ heaped cup (35g) ground almonds

2 tsp ground cinnamon

2 hard-cooked egg yolks, strained (see left)

1 tbsp aged dark rum

pinch of salt (fleur de sel)

¼ tsp baking powder

1⅔ cups (200g) pastry flour

Making cinnamon pâte sablée by hand

1 Place the butter in a bowl and beat with a wooden spoon until creamy. Add the confectioners' sugar, ground almonds, ground cinnamon, egg yolks, rum, and salt, and mix them all into the butter.

2 Mix the baking powder with the flour, then add gradually to the butter mixture. Keep mixing until all the flour is blended in completely. The dough will be very soft.

3 Gather the dough into a ball. If you are making disks (see opposite), divide the dough into three pieces. Wrap each in plastic wrap. Let the dough rest in the refrigerator for at least 4 hours before using.

Using a food processor

1 Place the butter in the bowl of a food processor fitted with the metal blade and process at medium speed until the butter is creamy. Add the sugar, ground almonds, ground cinnamon, egg yolks, and salt.

2 Process on medium speed until the mixture is an even consistency. Add the rum. Mix the baking powder into the flour, then add to the butter mixture. Process, using the pulse button, until the flour is just mixed in.

3 The dough will be very soft. Shape into a ball, divide into three pieces if making disks, and wrap in plastic wrap. Let the dough rest in the refrigerator for 4 hours before using.

STORING PASTRY

■ The pastry dough can be kept in the refrigerator for up to 2 days before use.

■ The dough should be well chilled before rolling out. Any cracks can be patched with small pieces of leftover pastry dough.

Baking a pastry disk

If making more than one pastry disk, work with one piece of dough at a time and keep the remaining dough refrigerated until needed. Be sure that the work surface and the dough are well floured, because this pastry is very soft. Any trimmings can be chilled, then re-rolled, cut into small shapes, and baked to make cinnamon cookies.

1 Flour the work surface and the dough, then roll out the dough to a ⅛in (3mm) thickness. Dust off the excess flour with a dry pastry brush. Place a flan ring on top of the sheet of dough and press down firmly.

2 Cut cleanly around the inside edge of the flan ring using a small, sharp knife. Remove the ring and the excess dough.

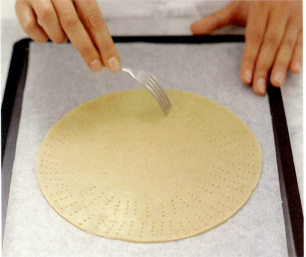

3 Slide the removable bottom of a tart pan or springform pan, or a piece of thin cardboard, underneath the pastry disk and transfer very carefully to a baking sheet lined with parchment paper.

4 Prick the pastry disk with a fork, then cover with plastic wrap and refrigerate for 30 minutes. Preheat the oven to 350°F (180°C) and bake the pastry disk for 18–20 minutes.

INVERTED PÂTE FEUILLETÉE ("INSIDE-OUT" PUFF PASTRY)

In classic puff pastry, a flour and water dough is used to encase a block of butter and then the whole is rolled and folded several times to make the many layers. This dough is different, since most of the butter is on the outside. A mixture of flour, water, and melted butter is made for the inside, resulting in a crisp yet melting pastry.

Makes about 2½lb (1.1kg) pastry

For stage 1

½ cup + 2 tbsp (75g) pastry flour

½ cup + 2 tbsp (75g) all-purpose flour

1⅔ cups (375g) unsalted butter, at room temperature

For stage 2 (the détrempe)

⅔ cup water

½ tsp white vinegar

2 tsp salt (fleur de sel)

1½ cups (175g) pastry flour

1½ cups (175g) all-purpose flour

½ cup (110g) unsalted butter, melted, then cooled

1 For stage 1, mix the flours with the butter in a bowl until the mixture comes together in a ball of dough. Flatten the dough into a disk ¾in (2cm) thick. Wrap it in plastic wrap and refrigerate for about 2 hours.

2 For stage 2, mix the water with the vinegar and salt. Combine the flours and butter in a bowl, gradually add the water, and mix well. Depending on how much water the flours absorb, you may not need to use all the water. The dough should be soft, but not too soft.

6 Pat the top of the wrapped dough all over with your fist to spread it out. Then, using a floured rolling pin, roll it out from the center into a rectangle three times as long as it is wide. Be careful not to squash the edges.

7 Fold the top fourth of the rectangle down to the middle, then fold the bottom fourth up to the middle, so they meet in the center.

3 Using a rolling pin, flatten the stage-2 dough (the détrempe) into a square that is ¾in (2cm) thick. Wrap it in plastic wrap and refrigerate for about 2 hours.

4 Dust the stage-1 dough with flour, then roll out on a sheet of floured parchment paper into a disk ½in (1cm) thick.

5 Place the square of détrempe in the center of the disk. Fold in all the sides of the disk, taking care that the seams meet and the square of détrempe is completely enclosed.

8 Fold the dough over in half. There will now be four layers of dough. This gives you a "tour portefeuille" which means a "double turn." Flatten slightly. Wrap in plastic wrap and refrigerate for 1 hour.

9 Place the dough on a floured work surface, with the main fold to the left. Flatten the dough again with your fist, then roll out to a rectangle three times as long as it is wide. Fold as before—another "tour portefeuille." Brush off any excess flour, then wrap in plastic wrap and refrigerate for 1 hour.

10 The last turn, called the "tour simple" or "single turn," is done just before using the dough. With the main fold on your left, roll out the dough into a rectangle as before. Fold into thirds this time, to make a square. Wrap in plastic wrap and refrigerate for 30 minutes.

Rolling out & baking pâte feuilletée

Make sure the pastry dough is very well chilled. When rolling out, use short, sharp strokes in the same direction. Firmly push the rolling pin away from yourself, in order to extend the pastry. Do not roll backward and forward haphazardly, or the layers in the pastry will not rise evenly.

1 Roll out the dough on a floured work surface to a ¹⁄₁₆–¹⁄₈in (2–3mm) thickness. From time to time, lift the sheet of dough off the work surface by sliding your hands underneath. It is essential to do this, as it will prevent the dough from being overstretched and then shrinking as it bakes. Brush off the excess flour.

CHEF'S TIPS

■ When you cut pâte feuilletée into a rectangle or a disk, there are always some trimmings left. Do not knead them together, but instead place one on top of the other and press them down firmly. Roll out the pastry and use to make sweet or savory mini bouchées ("puffs") or vol-au-vents.

■ The parchment paper is dampened when baking pâte feuilletée, because it helps to prevent the pastry from shrinking as it bakes.

2 Cover a shallow baking pan or sheet with dampened parchment paper, then slide the sheet of dough onto it. Prick all over with a fork. Let rest in the refrigerator for 1–2 hours. Preheat the oven to 400°F (200°C). Place the pastry in the oven and reduce the temperature to 375°F (190°C). Bake for 15–20 minutes.

CARAMELIZED INVERTED PÂTE FEUILLETÉE

This is ideal for small and large mille-feuilles, because the caramelization will prevent the cream filling from making the pastry soggy. Once the pastry sheet has cooled, cut it lengthwise in half. Spread one half with crème pâtissière (p418), crème Chantilly (p414), jam, or fruit purée and put the other piece of pastry on top.

scant ⅓ quantity (14oz/400g) inverted pâte feuilletée (p388), rolled out and pricked with a fork (see left), then left to rest in the refrigerator

3 tbsp (40g) granulated sugar

2½ tbsp (20g) confectioners' sugar

1 Preheat the oven to 450°F (230°C). Sprinkle the granulated sugar evenly all over the pastry sheet. Place in the oven and reduce the temperature immediately to 375°F (190°C). Bake for 8 minutes, then place a wire rack on top of the pastry sheet to prevent it from rising too much. Bake for 5 minutes longer.

2 Remove the pastry from the oven and turn up the oven temperature to 475°F (240°C). Remove the wire rack and cover the pastry with a sheet of parchment paper. Set another baking sheet, the same size as the first, on top. Turn the two sheets over, holding them firmly together. Set them down on the work surface.

3 Remove the baking sheet that is now on top and the parchment paper. Sprinkle the pastry sheet evenly with the confectioners' sugar. Return to the oven and bake until golden and caramelized, 5–7 minutes. Cool on a wire rack.

Arlettes

Light, delicate, spicy, and crunchy, these little cookies make a very good accompaniment for ice cream or they can be served as petit fours.

Makes 70–80

generous ¼ quantity (10oz/300g) inverted pâte feuilletée (p388)

For the spiced sugar

1 scant tsp vanilla powder

2 tsp ground allspice

4 cups (500g) confectioners' sugar

Flour the work surface, then roll out the pastry dough to a ⅛in (3mm) thickness. Cut out an 8 by 16in (20 by 40cm) rectangle. Place it so the long sides are at the top and bottom, then roll up very tightly. Cover with plastic wrap and freeze for 45 minutes. This will make the dough roll quite firm. Using a sharp knife, cut across into slices that are ⅛in (3mm) thick.

Line a baking sheet with parchment paper and set aside. Sift together the vanilla powder, allspice, and confectioners' sugar. Spoon some of the spiced sugar onto the work surface in a square about ¼in (5mm) deep.

Take two slices of pastry and place on the spiced sugar, with space between them. Roll out as thinly as possible, turning so both sides are sugared. Transfer to the baking sheet. Repeat the process with the remaining slices, adding more spiced sugar as required.

Preheat the oven to 450°F (230°C). Bake the cookies until caramelized, 5–6 minutes.

Remove from the oven and cool on a wire rack. Once cooled, place in an airtight container; the cookies will keep for up to a day.

Using a sharp knife, cut the rolled pastry into very thin slices

CROISSANTS

One of the more colorful accounts of the origin of the croissant is set in Vienna, Austria. In 1683, bakers were working overnight when they heard invading Turkish forces tunneling under the city walls. They alerted the authorities and the city was saved. To commemorate the event, the bakers created a pastry in a crescent shape—the emblem on the Turkish flag. In fact, the croissant was probably created in France after 1850.

Makes 24

½oz (12g) compressed fresh yeast or 1 envelope active dry yeast
scant 1 cup water at 68°F (20°C)
4¾ cups (600g) all-purpose flour
2 tsp salt (fleur de sel)
6 tbsp (75g) sugar
2½ tbsp (35g) very soft unsalted butter
2 tbsp (15g) dry whole milk
1½ cups (325g) unsalted butter, chilled

For the glaze

2 eggs
1 egg yolk
pinch of salt

FREEZING

It is best to make enough dough for 24 croissants and to shape all of them, then freeze what you do not need. Freeze the unbaked croissants on a tray, covered tightly with plastic wrap. Ideally they should be frozen for no more than 2–4 weeks. Let thaw in the refrigerator before baking.

1 Dissolve the yeast in two-thirds of the water. Sift the flour into a large bowl. Mix in the dissolved yeast, salt, sugar, very soft butter, and dry milk. Knead everything together quickly. If the dough is still a little stiff, add the rest of the water. Cover with plastic wrap and let rise at room temperature for 1–1½ hours.

2 When the dough has doubled in size, remove it from the bowl and punch it down, then return to the bowl. Cover with plastic again and refrigerate for 1–1¼ hours. Remove the dough from the bowl, punch down, cover with plastic wrap, and let rest in the freezer for 30 minutes longer.

6 Flour the work surface, then roll out the dough to a ⅛in (3mm) thickness. Using a sharp knife, cut out triangles that are 8in (20cm) tall and 5in (12cm) across the base.

7 To shape, place each triangle with the base nearest to you and roll up, then bring the ends around toward each other to make a crescent. Place the croissants 2in (5cm) apart on a baking sheet lined with parchment paper. Let rise at room temperature for 1½–2 hours.

3 Remove the dough from the freezer. Knead the cold butter until it is soft. On a floured surface, roll out the dough to a rectangle three times longer than it is wide. Place half of the butter at the bottom edge of the dough. With the palm of your hand, push the butter up to cover two-thirds of the rectangle of dough.

4 Fold the rectangle of dough into thirds, folding the unbuttered top third down first. Wrap the folded dough in plastic wrap. Let rest in the freezer for 30 minutes and then in the refrigerator for 1 hour.

5 Roll out the dough into a rectangle as before and spread with the remainder of the butter. Fold into thirds again and wrap in plastic wrap. Let rest in the freezer for 30 minutes and then in the refrigerator for 1 hour.

VARIATIONS

■ To make almond croissants, roll scant 2oz (50g) almond paste or pistachio-flavored paste into the dough. Sprinkle sliced almonds over the tops of the croissants after glazing.
■ For pains au chocolat, cut the dough into 5 by 2½in (12 by 6cm) rectangles. Place a small stick of bittersweet chocolate on each one and fold the dough into thirds, then brush with the glaze.

8 Preheat the oven to 450°F (230°C). Combine the eggs, egg yolk, and salt in a bowl and whisk together. Brush the croissants with this egg glaze, then place in the oven and reduce the temperature to 375°F (190°C). Bake for 20 minutes. Transfer the croissants to a wire rack and let cool.

BRIOCHE DOUGH

Brioche dough needs a lot of working and, because it is an extremely sticky dough, it is best made in an electric mixer. When baked, brioche is delicately savory and sweet at the same time— the ideal vehicle for jam as well as an excellent partner for foie gras and blue-veined cheeses.

Makes 3lb (1.3kg) dough

4 cups (500g) all-purpose flour

½oz (12.5g) compressed fresh yeast
or 1 envelope quick-rising active dry yeast

¼ cup (50g) sugar

7 eggs

2 scant tsp salt

1¾ cups (400g) unsalted butter, at room temperature and cut into pieces

1 Pour the flour into the bowl of an electric mixer fitted with the dough hook. Add the crumbled fresh yeast or the dry yeast and the sugar. Mix on medium speed, then add 4 of the eggs. Mix again, then add the remaining eggs, one by one, making sure that each is fully incorporated before adding the next.

2 Once the dough starts to come away from the sides of the bowl, add the salt and the butter pieces. Keep mixing on medium speed. The dough is ready when it comes away cleanly from the sides of the bowl and is silky in texture.

CHEF'S TIPS

■ The suggested warm room temperature for rising is around 72°F (22°C). Make sure that you cover the bowl, either with plastic wrap or a clean cloth. Do not leave the dough in a draft.

■ Unbaked brioche dough does not freeze well, although you can keep it in the refrigerator for a day before using.

4 Lift the sticky dough out of the bowl and place it on a lightly floured work surface.

5 Punch down the dough with your fist. This will deflate the dough and it will return to its original size. Put it back into the bowl and cover with plastic wrap again. Place in the refrigerator and let rise for 1¼ hours.

3 Transfer the dough to a large bowl. Cover with plastic wrap and let rise at warm room temperature until doubled in size, 2–3 hours. The risen dough will be very sticky.

6 Press down on the dough to check that it has risen again, then remove it to the work surface and punch down to deflate. The brioche dough is now ready to be shaped and baked.

RAISIN BRIOCHES

Makes 12

⅓ cup (50g) golden raisins

about ⅔ quantity (1lb 2oz/500g) brioche dough (see opposite)

1 egg

1 egg yolk

¼ tsp sugar

Mix the raisins into the brioche dough. Divide the dough into small balls, 1½oz (45g) each, and place 2in (5cm) apart on a baking sheet lined with parchment paper. Let them rise at room temperature until doubled in size. Preheat the oven to 425°F (220°C). Mix together the egg, egg yolk, and sugar, and brush this glaze over the brioches. Bake for 12–14 minutes. Cool for a short while on a wire rack.

Serve raisin brioches with tea or coffee mid-morning or afternoon

KUGELHOPF

A traditional cake from Alsace, this recipe for kugelhopf is from the repertoire of M. Hermé senior, who is a pâtissier in Colmar. The cake takes its name from the pan in which it is baked, whose shape has altered very little since the 16th century. A kugelhopf pan has sloping, furrowed, and molded sides and a central funnel. In the past the pans would have been made from tin, clay, and copper, but nowadays it is much easier to use one that has a nonstick lining.

Makes a 9in (23cm) kugelhopf

1⅔ cups (250g) golden raisins
3½ tbsp dark rum
1 quantity of brioche dough (p394)
scant ½ cup (40g) sliced almonds

For the syrup

1 cup water
1½ cups (300g) sugar
⅓ cup (30g) ground almonds
1 tbsp orange-flower water

To finish

6 tbsp (80g) butter
¼ cup (50g) sugar

1 Soak the raisins in the rum overnight. The next day, make the brioche dough, adding the soaked raisins 2 minutes before you finish kneading. Flour your fingers and flatten the dough into a disk.

2 Lift the edges up and over toward the center and shape the dough into a large ball. Roll the ball on the work surface, shaping it between the palms of your hands so that it will rise evenly during baking.

3 Make a hole in the center of the dough ball by pressing down with your fingertips.

4 Butter a 9in (23cm) kugelhopf pan and sprinkle evenly with the sliced almonds.

5 Transfer the dough to the pan and press it down onto the almonds. Cover the pan with a clean dish towel and let the dough rise at room temperature for about 1½ hours.

6 To make the syrup, pour the water and sugar into a pan. Bring to a boil. Remove from the heat and add the ground almonds and orange-flower water. Let cool, then refrigerate. Clarify the butter (p24).

7 Preheat the oven to 350°F (180°C). Bake the kugelhopf for 35 minutes. Remove the kugelhopf from the pan and place it on a wire rack. While it is still hot, brush with the clarified butter and then with the syrup.

8 Lightly sprinkle the sugar over the syrup-glazed kugelhopf, then let cool and set.

BRIOCHE NANTERRE

Brioche Nanterre is baked in a loaf pan, so is ideal for slicing. Try it toasted or, even better, brush untoasted slices with melted butter and toast under a hot broiler.

generous ¼ quantity (13oz/375g) brioche dough (p394)
1 egg plus 1 egg yolk
¼ tsp sugar

Slices of brioche Nanterre are great for breakfast or brunch or to accompany a rich foie gras terrine (p254)

1 Butter a 7 by 3½in (18 by 8.5cm) loaf pan. Divide the brioche dough into four equal portions. Roll each piece into a ball on an unfloured work surface, then press the ball out gently into an oval shape.

2 Set the ovals closely side by side in the pan. Let rise at room temperature until doubled in size. Preheat the oven to 350°F (180°C).

3 Beat the egg, yolk, and sugar together; brush over the loaf. Using scissors, snip a cross in each ball. Bake until well risen and golden brown, about 25 minutes. Cool on a wire rack.

SUGARED BRIOCHES

These are equally good served at breakfast or brunch.

Butter 2½in (6cm) fluted brioche molds. Divide the brioche dough into small balls, each weighing 1½oz (45g), and place in the molds. Let rise at room temperature until they have doubled in size.

Preheat the oven to 425°F (220°C). Brush with egg glaze (see opposite). Snip a cross in each ball, then sprinkle them generously with sugar. Bake for 12–14 minutes. Remove from the oven, shake the brioches out of the molds, and cool on a wire rack.

PÂTE À BRIOCHE FEUILLETÉE

This dough has the taste of brioche with the crispness and lightness of a croissant. It can be used in a similar way to croissant dough (see variations, p393).

Makes 4lb (1.7kg) dough

2oz (55g) compressed fresh yeast or 3 tbsp quick-rising active dry yeast
3 eggs, very cold
6 cups (750g) all-purpose flour
¼ cup (50g) sugar
2 tsp salt (fleur de sel)
5 tbsp (40g) dry whole milk
1⅓ cups very cold water
1⅓ cups (300g) unsalted butter, chilled

1 Place the crumbled fresh or dry yeast, eggs, flour, sugar, salt, dry milk, and water in the bowl of an electric mixer fitted with the dough hook. Mix together, stopping as soon as a smooth dough is formed. Wrap the dough in plastic wrap and put into the freezer to chill.

2 Meanwhile, cream the butter until soft. On a floured surface, roll out the chilled dough to a rectangle three times as long as it is wide. Place half the butter on the bottom edge of the rectangle. Using your palm, spread the butter evenly over two-thirds of the dough.

3 Fold the dough into thirds, folding the top, unbuttered third down first. Chill in the freezer for 30 minutes, then refrigerate for 1 hour. Roll out and spread with the remaining butter as before, then fold into thirds and chill in the freezer and refrigerator as before.

PAINS AUX RAISINS

For these pastries, a rich, sweet dough is rolled around an almond cream and plump raisins. The contrasting topping of slightly tart orange glaze is the perfect finishing touch.

Makes 24

1 quantity of pâte à brioche feuilletée (p399)

scant ¼ quantity (6oz/175g) almond cream (p419)

1⅔ cups (250g) golden raisins

For the orange glaze

1¼ cups (150g) confectioners' sugar

½ tsp (2.5g) gum arabic powder (available from specialty candymaking suppliers)

1 tsp (2.5g) dry whole milk

3 tbsp orange juice

1 tbsp Cointreau

1 The day before, make the orange glaze. Sift the confectioners' sugar into a pan. Add the gum arabic powder and the dry milk. Pour in the orange juice. Warm very slightly over a very low heat to dissolve the sugar and powders. Remove from the heat and stir in the Cointreau. Refrigerate until needed.

2 On a floured surface, roll out the dough into a rectangle 2ft (60cm) long and 1in (2.5cm) thick. Spread the almond cream over the dough, leaving a ¾in (2cm) border clear.

3 Sprinkle the raisins evenly over the almond cream. Roll up the dough like a jelly roll, starting from one of the long edges.

Flaky pains aux raisins are a richly flavored treat

FREEZING PASTRY

Shape all 24 pains aux raisins and store what you do not need in the freezer. Freeze unbaked on a tray, tightly wrapped with plastic. Do not freeze for more than a month, or the pastries will become covered in ice crystals. Let the pastries thaw properly in the refrigerator before baking.

CHOUX PASTRY

A great classic of French pâtisserie, choux pastry is used for making éclairs and profiteroles. The traditional cake for weddings and communions in France, the croquembouche is an elaborate cone-shaped confection of custard-filled choux puffs, caramel, spun sugar, and fresh flowers.

Makes 1lb 10oz (750g) dough

½ cup water
½ cup whole milk
1 scant tsp sugar
1 scant tsp salt
½ cup (110g) butter
1 cup (125g) all-purpose flour
5 eggs

4 Using a sharp knife, cut the roll across into slices about ¾in (2cm) thick. Tuck the end of each slice underneath to prevent the pastry from unrolling as it expands in the oven heat.

5 Place the pastries 2in (5cm) apart on baking sheets lined with parchment paper. Place in the freezer to chill for 30 minutes. Remove from the freezer and let rise at room temperature until doubled in size.

6 Preheat the oven to 350°F (180°C). Bake for 18 minutes. As soon as the pastries come out of the oven, brush them with the orange glaze. Eat freshly baked and warm.

2 Continue beating until the dough dries out and comes away from the sides of the pan in a ball, 2–3 minutes longer. Tip the dough into the bowl of an electric mixer.

1 Pour the water, milk, sugar, and salt into a pan. Add the butter. Bring to a boil. As soon as the liquid boils, add the flour all at once. Beat vigorously until the dough is smooth.

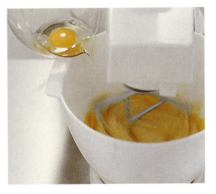

3 Add the eggs, one by one, beating well so that each egg is thoroughly incorporated before adding the next.

4 When the dough is smooth and shiny, and falls in a thick ribbon from the beaters, it is ready to be shaped and then baked.

CHEF'S TIPS

■ Choux pastry is made with equal amounts of water and milk. Using water alone results in rough pastry.

■ It is essential to transfer the dough to a bowl before adding the eggs in order to mix them in well and so make a light pastry.

COOKIES

The French word for cookie, "biscuit," comes from the words "bis," meaning twice, and "cuit," meaning baked. The name referred to twice-baked pieces of bread dough that were cooked until they had completely dried out and become hard. For centuries, no ship left port without a supply of these biscuits to last for the months, or even years, of a long voyage.

In medieval times, cooks in wealthy households experimented with honey, eggs, spices, cream, flour, butter, and bread crumbs, fashioning these ingredients into many kinds of sweetmeats. By the 17th century, sweet cookies were commonplace in prosperous households and street peddlers did a lively trade supplying cookies to those of more modest means. Today, there are many kinds of cookies available. Here, you will find recipes and variations for a few of the most popular: the buttery sablé, which is the French shortbread; delicately thin, crisp tuiles; and chocolate chip cookies. Any of these is ideal to serve with creamy desserts and ice creams.

SABLÉS DIAMANT VANILLE

The French name, "sablé" (sandy), for these crunchy, crisp, and crumbly shortbread cookies accurately describes their texture. They are especially good with tea or coffee.

Makes 50

1 cup (225g) unsalted butter, at room temperature and cut into pieces
½ cup (100g) sugar
½ tsp vanilla extract
¼ tsp salt (fleur de sel)
2½ cups (320g) cake or pastry flour

To finish

sugar crystals or Demerara sugar

CHEF'S TIPS

■ What makes these cookies special is that they are made without eggs, which are unnecessary because the dough contains a lot of butter. This makes the texture of the sablés very short.

■ To make the dough by hand, follow the same procedure as for making it in the food processor, taking care not to overwork the ingredients.

1 Place the pieces of butter in the bowl of a food processor fitted with the metal blade. Process until the butter is creamy, then add the sugar, vanilla extract, and salt, and process to blend. Sift the flour and add to the mixture. Process to make a smooth dough.

2 Remove the dough from the processor. Shape it into a ball, then divide into three. (Refrigerate for a while if you think the dough is too soft.) On a sheet of parchment paper, roll each portion of dough into a cylinder shape 2in (5cm) in diameter. Make sure that there are no bubbles of air in the dough.

3 Spread out the sugar crystals evenly on another sheet of parchment paper, then roll each cylinder in the sugar to coat on all sides. Preheat the oven to 350°F (180°C).

4 Using a sharp knife, cut each cylinder across into slices ¾in (2cm) thick.

5 Arrange the slices on a baking sheet lined with parchment paper. Bake the sablés until they are golden brown, 22–25 minutes. Transfer to a wire rack to cool.

TUILES AUX AMANDES EFFILÉES

This dough will keep for almost a week in the refrigerator. The baked tuiles can be stored for 2 days in an airtight container.

Makes 40 small or 25 large

1⅓ cups (125g) sliced almonds
½ cup + 2 tbsp (125g) sugar
2 drops of vanilla extract or 2 pinches of vanilla powder
drop of bitter almond extract
2 egg whites
2 tbsp (25g) butter
2½ tbsp (20g) cake or pastry flour

1 Using a rubber spatula, mix the almonds, sugar, vanilla extract or powder, bitter almond extract, and egg whites together in a bowl.

2 Melt the butter gently and, while it is still warm, pour it into the bowl. Mix thoroughly. Cover the bowl with plastic wrap and refrigerate overnight.

3 The next day, sift the flour into the bowl and mix in thoroughly. Place teaspoonfuls of the dough on a nonstick baking sheet, spaced well apart.

4 Preheat the oven to 300°F (150°C). Flatten each cookie with the back of a large spoon dipped in cold water, then bake for 15–18 minutes. The cookies should be an even golden color with no white in the center.

5 Remove the cookies from the baking sheet using a metal spatula and slide onto a sheet of parchment paper. Let cool.

ORANGE & NUT TUILES

Makes 25

grated zest of 1 orange

½ cup (100g) sugar

4 tsp orange juice

⅔ cup (100g) chopped almonds

6 tbsp (80g) clarified butter (p24)

2½ tbsp (20g) cake or pastry flour

1 Put the orange zest, sugar, orange juice, and almonds into a bowl and mix together. Stir in the melted clarified butter and mix well. Let rest for 24 hours.

2 The next day, preheat the oven to 300°F (150°C). Stir the flour into the almond mixture. Place teaspoonfuls of dough on a nonstick baking sheet, leaving a large space around each one.

3 Flatten each cookie with the back of a spoon dipped in cold water. Bake for 15–18 minutes. Cool on a wire rack.

SHAPED TUILES

For the traditional roof-tile shape (which is why these cookies are so-named), lift each cookie off the baking sheet with a metal spatula and, while still hot, drape it over a wine bottle or rolling pin. Let cool and set.

CHOCOLATE CHIP COOKIES

Chewy in the center and crunchy around the edges—and made with the best bittersweet chocolate—these cookies are irresistible.

Makes 30

⅔ cup (150g) butter, at room temperature and cut into pieces

1 tsp salt (fleur de sel)

1 rounded cup (240g) packed light brown sugar

1½ eggs

1⅔ cups (215g) all-purpose flour

1½ tsp baking powder

½ tsp baking soda

½ cup (120g) chopped pecans or macadamia nuts

8oz (240g) best-quality bittersweet chocolate (70% cocoa solids), cut into small pieces

1 Put the butter in the bowl of an electric mixer and beat until smooth and creamy. Add the salt and sugar, and beat well to mix.

2 Add the eggs and beat at low speed for 3 minutes, then add the flour, baking powder, and baking soda. Beat for 2–3 minutes longer. Finally, mix in the chopped nuts and chocolate.

3 Shape the dough into a ball. On a sheet of parchment paper, roll into a cylinder shape about 2½in (6cm) in diameter. Wrap the dough in plastic wrap and refrigerate for 2 hours.

4 Preheat the oven to 350°F (180°C). Cut into slices ½in (1cm) thick. Place on a baking sheet lined with parchment paper and bake for 12 minutes. Cool the cookies on a wire rack.

CAPPUCCINO COOKIES

Makes 25

½ cup (115g) softened butter

½ cup (125g) packed light brown sugar

scant 1 tbsp acacia honey

¼ tsp salt (fleur de sel)

1 egg

1 tbsp liquid coffee concentrate

2 tbsp instant coffee, dissolved in 1 tbsp hot water

1¼ cups (155g) all-purpose flour

1 tsp baking powder

½ tsp baking soda

¾ cup (85g) chopped macadamia nuts

5oz (140g) semisweet chocolate, chopped

1 Beat the butter in the bowl of an electric mixer until creamy. Beat in the sugar, honey, and salt. Add the egg, coffee concentrate, and dissolved coffee and beat at low speed for 3 minutes. Add the flour, baking powder, and soda, and beat for 3 minutes longer.

2 Mix in the chopped nuts and chocolate. Transfer the dough to a sheet of parchment paper and roll into a cylinder shape 2½in (6cm) in diameter. Wrap and refrigerate for 2 hours.

3 Preheat the oven to 350°F (180°C). Cut the dough into slices ½in (1cm) thick. Place on a baking sheet lined with parchment paper and bake for 14 minutes. Remove and cool on a wire rack.

DESSERTS

Pierre Hermé

PIERRE HERMÉ

Dessert is the last course of a meal, offered after all the other food has been "desservi," literally "unserved" (removed), which is where the word "dessert" comes from. Until the mid-19th century, it was usual to offer an array of sweets, such as crystallized fruits and nuts, before the actual dessert, which might be a cream, compote, fancy cake, or pastry. Nowadays, the habit is to offer one or other of these, not both—but the importance of the dessert course remains undiminished.

Fruit desserts At its simplest, dessert can consist of fresh fruit, but with just a little more effort that same fruit can be served in ways that turn it into something really special. For that reason, this chapter starts with instructions for making sugar syrups. From the basic ingredients of sugar and water, you can make the lightest of syrups to enhance the individual flavors in, for example, a fruit salad. Alternatively, you can cook that basic syrup until it begins to caramelize and take on its own distinctive character. Then, depending on its color and thickness, it can be used to glaze petits fours, coat molds, serve as a sauce, or flavor desserts, cakes, and pastries.

Continuing with the theme of simplicity, the recipes for apple and strawberry crisps really could not be easier. The finely sliced fruit is simply dried in a very low oven to preserve its color and flavor. The result is instantly familiar, yet surprisingly different—a light way of ending a rich meal. The same drying technique can be applied to any fruit that lends itself to being finely sliced, although for the best results you should use fruit that is in season and in peak condition.

Dairy classics Given France's long association with dairy farming, it is only natural that dairy products should have inspired so many wonderful desserts. Milk, cream, and crème fraîche (the last of these being cream sharpened but not soured by adding a special lactic culture in the form of sour cream or buttermilk) are important parts of numerous recipes. This section covers the four classic pastry creams—crème Chantilly, crème pâtissière, almond cream, and buttercream—that are used as accompaniments, fillings, or decoration, rather than being served on their own. Each of these creams may be flavored in a variety of ways and used in desserts ranging from parfaits and charlottes to mousses and tarts.

No dessert section would be complete without a recipe for the custard sauce, crème anglaise. Rich in egg yolks and delicately flavored with vanilla, it transforms a simple dessert of poached fruit into a sublime experience. Crème anglaise needs to be carefully monitored for temperature during cooking—if it overheats, it will curdle and be spoiled.

Meringue Another classic with an undeserved reputation for being difficult to make is meringue, that light-as-air mixture of stiffly beaten egg whites and sugar. Various countries have claimed the credit for this wonderful invention, but it was the great French pâtissier, Antonin Carême, who exploited its versatility to make desserts of architectural splendor as well as breathtaking flavor. The method for making meringue in Carême's classic style is given, and also a recipe for Italian meringue, which is made with a hot sugar syrup and used to top trifle and tarts, make frosting, and fold into soufflés.

The selection of desserts also includes some excitingly flavored sorbets (water ices) and ice creams. Since the advent of refrigeration, both can be made easily at home, and more than repay the time involved. The key thing is to beat them at least twice during the freezing process so that the mixture becomes smooth and free of ice.

We hope you will see that the recipes in this section have been carefully chosen to link to each other in subtle but important ways. The techniques of one recipe can be applied or adapted elsewhere, and the ideas build upon each other rather than exist in isolation. Applying and combining techniques is a skill that every good cook needs to acquire, and we hope the desserts in this section will give you a good grounding in the most delicious ways possible.

MAKING SUGAR SYRUPS

Sugar syrups form the basis of a range of delicious desserts—from fruit salads and sweet fruit chips to ice creams and meringues—as well as being the foundation of candymaking. The basic sugar and water syrup is cooked to different temperatures to produce varying concentrations of sugar that make the syrup suitable for different pâtisseries, chocolate confections, and other preparations.

Sugar syrup stages

The best way to test the rising temperature of a sugar syrup is with a candy thermometer, although you can also use an ice-water test up to the hard crack stage (see below). For the ice-water test, place a bowl of ice water beside the pan; dip your fingers in the water, then dip them very quickly into the sugar syrup and straight back into the ice water. Lift your fingers up and separate them to check the consistency of the syrup. Once the syrup reaches the hard crack stage, it will be too hot, so test by dropping a little syrup into the ice water.

SYRUP STAGE	TEMPERATURE	DESCRIPTION
Coating syrup	212°F (100°C)	Slowly bring the water and sugar to a boil over low heat. If you dip a spoon in very quickly, the sugar syrup will spread and cover the back of the spoon. At this stage, the syrup is used for babas, savarins, and fruit in syrup.
Small thread or small gloss	217°–221°F (103°–105°C)	The sugar syrup begins to thicken. If you take it between your wet fingers, it will make a very thin thread about $\frac{1}{16}$–$\frac{1}{8}$in (2–3mm) thick that will break very easily. This syrup is used for making glacé and candied fruits.
Large thread or large gloss	223°–230°F (106°–110°C)	When picked up between wet fingers, the syrup forms a thicker, stronger thread at this stage, about $\frac{1}{4}$in (5mm) thick. This syrup is used for glazing.
Small pearl	230°–234°F (110°–112°C)	The syrup produces small bubbles on the surface and a thick, solid thread between wet fingers. It is used for making marshmallows.
Large pearl	235°–239°F (113°–115°C)	If you pull the syrup out with your wet fingers, it will make a long thread up to $\frac{3}{4}$in (2cm) long. It is used for making marrons glacés.
Small or soft ball	241°–257°F (116°–125°C)	If you take a little syrup between wet fingers, it will form a soft, flat ball. At this stage it is used for making classic buttercream, macaroons, Italian meringue, and nougat.
Hard ball	259°–275°F (126°–135°C)	When a little syrup is dropped into ice water, the ball that forms does not collapse, as it is harder. Used for making caramel and sugar decorations.
Soft crack	277°–284°F (136°–140°C)	At this stage it is not used, as it sticks to the teeth.
Hard crack	295°–311°F (146°–155°C)	Drop a little syrup into ice water; when the ball that forms is flattened between wet fingers it is hard and brittle, but not sticky. It breaks easily. The syrup will have turned to a pale straw-yellow color. This is used for hard candies, sugar flowers, and spun sugar decorations.
Light caramel	313°–329°F (156°–165°C)	The syrup now contains hardly any water, and it is at this stage that it becomes caramel, turning light brown in color. It is used for lining molds and flavoring desserts.
Brown or dark caramel	331°–347°F (166°–175°C)	At this point the syrup takes on an intense caramel flavor as it turns a darker brown and loses its sweetening power. This is used for flavoring creams, mousses, and ice creams.

Coating syrup

Small thread or small gloss

Light caramel

Dark caramel

CARAMEL SYRUP

If you want to make caramel successfully, it is best to add some liquid glucose or light corn syrup to the sugar to prevent crystallization. This recipe makes a coating caramel syrup that is suitable for dipping baked choux puffs, lining molds, and making caramel decorations.

Makes 2 cups

⅔ cup water

1½ cups + 2½ tbsp (330g) sugar

6 tbsp liquid glucose or light corn syrup

1 Combine the water, sugar, and glucose in a heavy-based pan and stir over low heat until the sugar has dissolved. Use a wet pastry brush to wipe down the side of the pan to prevent grains of sugar from sticking, as this might make the syrup crystallize. Bring to a boil.

2 When the caramel is a light golden color and coats the back of a spoon, remove from the heat and plunge the base of the pan into a shallow bowl filled with ice water. This will stop the syrup from cooking any further.

CARAMEL SAUCE

For an intense flavor, this sauce needs to be caramelized to a good, rich color.

Makes about 1¼ cups

scant ½ cup liquid glucose or light corn syrup

scant ¾ cup (130g) sugar

2 tbsp (25g) slightly salted butter

1 cup heavy cream, softly whipped

1 Place the glucose in a heavy-based pan and warm over a low heat; do not let the glucose boil, otherwise it will become sticky. Add the sugar and stir to dissolve, then cook until the caramel is a lovely amber color.

2 Remove the pan from the heat and whisk in the butter and the whipped cream. Place the pan back on a low heat and bring gently to a boil (217°F/103°C). Set aside and let the caramel sauce cool before serving.

CHEF'S TIPS

■ Always ensure the sugar has completely dissolved before bringing the syrup to a boil.

■ Do not stir the syrup once it has started boiling.

■ You can use crème fraîche instead of whipped cream in the caramel sauce, although the caramel will spatter more onto the sides of the pan.

■ Use a candy thermometer to determine the exact temperature of the caramel.

EXOTIC FRUIT SALAD

Fruit salad always makes a light and refreshing end to a meal. As spirits and liqueurs tend to change the taste of the fruit, I have created a fresh, flavorsome syrup for this recipe.

Serves 8

For the exotic syrup

2 cups water

½ cup (100g) sugar

2 strips of lemon peel, 2½in (6cm) long

2 strips of orange peel, 2½in (6cm) long

1 vanilla bean, split lengthwise

14 mint leaves

For the fruit salad

1 ruby red grapefruit

3 oranges

1 small pineapple

3 mangoes

6 peaches

6 apricots

10oz (300g) mixed red and black berries, such as strawberries, raspberries, red currants, blackberries, and blueberries (about 2 heaped cups)

1 Pour the water and sugar into a heavy-based pan. Add the lemon and orange peel. Scrape the seeds from the vanilla bean and add both pod and seeds to the pan. Dissolve the sugar over a low heat, stirring, then bring to a boil. Remove from the heat and add the mint. Cover and let infuse for 30 minutes. Strain and chill.

2 Meanwhile, remove the peel and pith from the grapefruit and oranges, then section them. Peel the pineapple, cut lengthwise into quarters, and slice thinly. Peel the mangoes and cut the flesh from the pit. Cut the peaches and apricots in half and remove the pits. Thinly slice the mangoes, peaches, and apricots.

3 Mix the fruits together, then divide among shallow serving dishes. Sprinkle with the berries. Spoon the very cold syrup over the fruit and serve immediately.

FRUIT FOR THE SALAD

■ To retain the full flavor and freshness of the fruit, prepare it just before serving.

■ I never include melon or bananas in a fruit salad, as their flavors are too strong.

■ When they are in season, quartered figs and thin slices of peeled kiwi fruit can be added to the salad.

CANDIED FRUIT & NUTS

It is very easy to prepare these syrup-dipped fresh fruits and nuts. You can serve them as sweetmeats after dinner, or use them to decorate cakes and special desserts.

Serves 6–8

1½lb (675g) mixed fruits and nuts, such as kumquats, cape gooseberries (with their papery husks opened out), black or white grapes, strawberries, blueberries, and shelled almonds

⅔ cup water

2½ cups (500g) sugar

⅔ cup liquid glucose or light corn syrup

Fresh fruits dipped in a sugar syrup make a refreshing alternative to dessert

CHOOSE THE BEST

- Use only very high quality fruit for candying.
- Wash the fruit before use and make sure it is well dried—the syrup will not stick to the surface of the fruit if it is at all damp.
- Candied fresh fruits and nuts will not keep for more than 5–6 hours.

1 Spear each piece of fruit and the nuts onto a wooden toothpick.

2 Place the water, sugar, and glucose in a heavy-based pan. Dissolve the sugar over a low heat, then bring to a boil and cook until the syrup reaches 311°F (155°C)—the hard crack stage (p410). Immediately rem ove the pan from the heat and immerse the base in ice water.

3 Dip the fruits and nuts into the syrup, one piece at a time, then spear them into whole oranges or grapefruit to set. When the syrup in the pan starts to cool and thicken, warm it for a few minutes over very low heat until it has become liquid again.

CRÈME CHANTILLY

This simple sweetened whipped cream is a classic accompaniment for desserts and is used in many recipes, such as mousses and charlottes.

Makes about 4 cups

2 cups very cold crème fraîche or heavy cream

2½ tbsp (30g) sugar

CHEF'S TIP

Use pasteurized crème fraîche, if available. The cream must be very cold before you whip it, so always use it straight from the refrigerator. It will whip up faster and more easily if you place the bowl in a larger, shallow bowl filled with ice cubes.

1 Pour the cream into a shallow bowl set in another, larger bowl filled with ice cubes. Whip with a balloon whisk, or a hand-held electric mixer on medium speed, until the cream thickens a little. Slowly add the sugar, whipping as you go.

2 Keep whipping until the cream is nearly firm but still fluffy. Chill until ready to use.

Chantilly ideas

Crème Chantilly can be flavored in many different ways, to create a pleasing harmony or contrast of flavors with the desserts the cream is to accompany.

Coffee Chantilly

Bring 2 cups crème fraîche or heavy cream to a boil and add 6 tbsp (30g) ground coffee. Let infuse for 15 minutes. Strain, then chill. Whip with the sugar as in the basic recipe.

Cinnamon Chantilly

Bring 2 cups crème fraîche or heavy cream to a boil and add a cinnamon stick. Let infuse off the heat until cool, then chill. Remove the cinnamon stick and whip the cream with the sugar as in the basic recipe. This is delicious served with muscat grapes.

Star anise Chantilly

Bring 2 cups crème fraîche or heavy cream to a boil and add 1½ whole star anise. Let infuse off the heat until cool, then chill. Remove the star anise and whip the cream with the sugar as in the basic recipe. Serve with pineapple or figs, decorated with raspberries.

Vanilla Chantilly

Bring 2 cups crème fraîche or heavy cream to a boil. Split 2 vanilla beans lengthwise and scrape out the seeds (p420); add both empty pods and seeds to the cream. Let infuse off the heat for 30 minutes, then chill. Strain and whip with the sugar as in the basic recipe.

Mint Chantilly

Bring 2 cups crème fraîche or heavy cream to a boil and stir in ½ cup chopped mint. Let infuse off the heat for 15 minutes, then strain and chill. Whip with the sugar as in the basic recipe.

Other flavorings

The basic Chantilly can also be flavored with a few drops of bitter almond extract or the finely grated zest of an orange or lemon. Add with the sugar when whipping the cream.

CHOCOLATE CRÈME CHANTILLY

This silky chocolate cream is luscious served as a dip for fresh fruit. It can also be used to fill pairs of meringue shells (p472) or cookie cups.

Makes about 4 cups

scant 4oz (100g) best-quality bitter chocolate (70–75% cocoa solids)

2 cups crème fraîche or heavy cream

¼ cup (50g) sugar

1 Chop the chocolate very finely with a serrated-edge knife.

2 Combine the crème fraîche and sugar in a pan and bring to a boil. Remove the pan from the heat and add the chocolate, whisking vigorously. Pour the chocolate cream into a bowl and set aside to cool completely. Then cover with plastic wrap and chill for 6–8 hours.

3 Set the bowl of chocolate cream in another, larger bowl filled with ice cubes. Whip the chocolate cream with a balloon whisk, or with a hand-held electric mixer on medium speed, until it is just firm and fluffy.

Milk chocolate Chantilly

Whisk 7oz (210g) very finely chopped good-quality milk chocolate into 1¼ cups boiling crème fraîche or heavy cream. Let cool and chill, then whip as in the basic recipe.

TIP FOR SUCCESS

Good-quality chocolate is essential for making the best chocolate crème Chantilly. If possible, use Guanaja dark bitter chocolate, and Valrhona milk chocolate for the milk chocolate version.

CHANTILLY TUILE BASKETS

Crisp little cookie baskets make perfect containers for smooth creams. Slightly tart berries, such as raspberries or even tiny wild strawberries, are the finishing touch. Serve with coffee or for afternoon tea.

Makes 8

8 tuiles aux amandes effilées (p404), freshly baked and still hot

1 quantity of crème Chantilly or chocolate crème Chantilly (see left)

2 cups raspberries

Shape the baskets by placing each tuile in an individual fluted brioche mold. Let the tuile baskets cool and set, then remove them from the molds. Fill with the crème Chantilly and top with raspberries.

Crème Chantilly and fresh berries are lovely in crisp cookie cups

HOT APPLE SABAYON

This recipe follows the general principle of a traditional sabayon, but uses spiced apple juice rather than white wine or liqueur, and it is whisked in a pan over direct heat rather than in a bowl set over a pan of hot water. To serve, the sabayon is spooned over a sautéed apple and gingerbread mixture and glazed under a hot broiler. If you prefer, the sabayon can be simply served alongside the apple mixture.

Serves 6

⅔ cup apple juice

grated zest of ½ orange

3 tbsp lemon juice

small pinch of ground cardamom

½ cinnamon stick

½ tsp grated fresh ginger

3 grindings of black pepper

small pinch of salt (fleur de sel)

5 egg yolks

⅓ cup (65g) sugar

For the apple mixture

1¾lb (800g) Granny Smith apples, peeled, cored, and diced

3 tbsp lemon juice

5 tbsp (60g) sugar

few drops of vanilla extract

6½ tbsp (90g) butter

scant 3oz (80g) moist pain d'épices or gingerbread, cut into ¼in (5mm) cubes

scant ¼ cup (20g) sliced almonds, lightly dry-roasted (p480)

2½ tbsp (20g) pine nuts

1 Combine the apple juice, orange zest, lemon juice, cardamom, cinnamon, ginger, pepper, and salt in a heavy pan. Bring to a boil, then strain. Whisk the egg yolks with the sugar in a bowl for 2 minutes. Add one-fourth of the apple juice and whisk vigorously until frothy.

2 Pour the egg mixture and the remaining strained apple juice back into the pan and place over medium heat. Start whisking with a balloon whisk.

3 Keep whisking vigorously until the mixture thickens and becomes light and frothy. To test if the sabayon is done, lift out the whisk: The sabayon falling from the whisk onto the surface should leave a ribbon trail. Remove the pan from the heat and set aside. Preheat the broiler.

4 In a bowl, toss the apples with the lemon juice, sugar, and vanilla. Melt half the butter in a frying pan, add the pain d'épices, and brown lightly. Remove and keep warm. Heat the remaining butter in the pan. Add the apple mixture and sauté over high heat until golden. Mix in the almonds, pine nuts, and pain d'épices.

5 Spoon the apple mixture into individual flameproof dishes or gratin dishes. Spoon the sabayon over. Place the dishes under the hot broiler, close to the heat, for a few moments to caramelize the top. Serve immediately.

Sabayon turns golden under the broiler heat

CRÈME PÂTISSIÈRE

Crème pâtissière, or pastry cream, is the classic custard-style filling for many desserts, including profiteroles, éclairs, and the famous Gâteau St. Honoré. It is also often used as a filling for Danish pastries. Crème pâtissière is best made just before you are going to serve it.

Makes about 1¼ cups

1 cup whole milk
3 tbsp cornstarch
5 tbsp (62.5g) sugar
1 vanilla bean
3 egg yolks
2 tbsp (25g) butter at room temperature and cut into cubes

1 Whisk the milk, cornstarch, and 2 tbsp of the sugar in a heavy-based pan. Split the vanilla bean in half lengthwise and scrape out the seeds with the point of a sharp knife (p420). Add the vanilla seeds and empty pod to the pan. Bring to a boil, whisking all the time.

2 In a bowl, whisk the egg yolks with the remaining sugar. Pour the hot milk onto the egg mixture in a thin stream, whisking all the time. Pour the mixture back into the pan and bring just to a boil, whisking constantly. Immediately remove the pan from the heat.

4 When the custard has cooled a little, to about 140°F (60°C), add the pieces of butter and whisk vigorously until they have melted and the sauce is smooth and shiny.

VARIATIONS

Chocolate crème pâtissière
Add 4½oz (125g) finely grated bittersweet or semisweet chocolate to the warm custard in three batches, after the butter, stirring until smooth.

Coffee crème pâtissière
Dissolve ½ tsp instant coffee in 1 tsp hot water and add 2 drops of coffee concentrate. Stir this mixture into the custard after the butter.

Alcoholic flavors
Stir 1 tbsp Cointreau, Grand Marnier, kirsch, or dark rum into the finished crème pâtissière.

The finished crème pâtissière is smooth and glossy

3 Immere the base of the pan in a shallow bowl filled with ice water. This will keep the custard from cooking any further. Remove the empty vanilla pod and discard.

ALMOND CREAM

Like crème pâtissière, almond cream is often used to fill cakes and pastries, including brioches and small tarts. It may also be baked, as in the classic Gâteau Pithiviers.

Makes about 1¾lb (800g)

½ cup + 2 tbsp (135g) butter, at room temperature
1⅓ cups (165g) confectioners' sugar
4 tsp cornstarch
1¾ cups (165g) ground almonds
2 eggs
1 tbsp dark rum
1 cup crème fraîche

1 Cut the butter into pieces and place in a bowl. Work with a rubber spatula or wooden spoon to cream and soften it.

2 Combine the confectioners' sugar, cornstarch, and ground almonds in another bowl. Sift the mixture into the softened butter and mix well. Add the eggs, one at a time, blending with the spatula or spoon.

3 Pour in the rum, followed by the crème fraîche, and mix until perfectly smooth. Cover with plastic wrap and refrigerate. The almond cream will keep for 36–48 hours in the refrigerator or it can be frozen.

CREAMING BUTTER

It is important to work the butter without making it fluffy. If air is beaten in, the almond cream will rise during baking, but will collapse and lose its shape when it comes out of the oven and starts to cool.

CRÈME ANGLAISE (EGG CUSTARD SAUCE)

This rich egg custard is a wonderful sauce. It can be served warm or cold with so many desserts. For the best result, flavor the milk the day before, then chill the finished sauce overnight to allow the flavors to blend together.

Serves 10

2 vanilla beans

2 cups whole milk

2 cups crème fraîche

12 egg yolks

1 cup (200g) sugar

1 Using a sharp knife, split the vanilla beans in half lengthwise. Scrape the tiny, sticky seeds from the pod with a teaspoon.

2 Pour the milk and crème fraîche into a heavy pan and whisk to combine. Add the empty vanilla pods and seeds to the pan. Bring to a boil, then remove from the heat. Cover and let cool completely, then put the pan in the refrigerator to infuse overnight.

VANILLA ICE CREAM

Crème anglaise is often used as the base for a homemade ice cream. To make vanilla ice cream, pour the well-chilled crème anglaise into your ice cream maker and churn until frozen, following the manufacturer's directions. If you do not have an ice cream maker, see p423.

3 The next day, remove the pan from the refrigerator and discard the vanilla pods. Bring the flavored milk to a boil. Combine the egg yolks and sugar in a bowl and whisk for 3 minutes. Pour the hot milk onto the egg mixture in a thin stream, whisking all the time.

4 Pour the mixture back into the pan and continue to whisk over medium heat until the custard reaches a temperature of 185°F (85°C)—test with an instant-read thermometer.

5 The custard will now be thick enough to coat the back of a wooden spoon. Remove the pan from the heat and stir the custard slowly and gently for 4–5 minutes, until it is completely smooth.

6 Set a large bowl in a larger, shallow bowl containing ice water. Strain the custard into the large bowl. Let the custard cool, stirring from time to time, then cover and chill overnight.

Aromatic vanilla
crème anglaise pours
like a thin cream

CHEF'S TIPS

■ If you are short of time, you can infuse the vanilla in the milk mixture for just 10 minutes rather than overnight; however, the flavor won't be as strong.
■ Use only fresh whole milk; low-fat varieties simply don't give a rich enough result.
■ Cook the custard slowly or it will taste eggy.
■ In French, crème anglaise is deemed to be perfectly cooked when it is "à la rose"—if you blow gently on the custard-coated wooden spoon, a perfect rosette should be formed.
■ Stirring the custard slowly for 4–5 minutes after removing it from the heat will give the sauce a superbly smooth texture.

CARAMEL ICE CREAM

There is nothing like homemade ice cream, especially when it has the superb flavor and texture of this recipe. It makes the perfect light dessert to finish an elegant dinner party. The use of salted butter balances the sweetness of the caramel, while bringing out its flavor. Serve the ice cream drizzled with caramel sauce (p411).

Makes 2 quarts (2 liters)

4 cups whole milk

1¼ cups crème fraîche

5 egg yolks

2½ cups (500g) sugar

5 tbsp (70g) slightly salted butter

1 The day before, combine the milk and ½ cup of the crème fraîche in a pan and bring to a boil. Remove from the heat, cover, and set aside. Whip the remaining crème fraîche to soft peaks in a bowl. In a large, heavy pan, whisk the egg yolks with ¾ cup (150g) of the sugar.

5 Pour the caramel-cream mixture into the hot milk, whisking vigorously.

2 Put scant 3 tbsp of the remaining sugar in a smaller heavy pan. Melt the sugar gently over low heat, then add another 3 tbsp sugar and melt it. Repeat this process until all of the sugar has been added to the pan. Bring to a boil and cook to a dark amber caramel.

3 Remove the pan from the heat and add the butter, stirring it into the hot caramel with a balloon whisk or wooden spoon in a figure-eight motion. The mixture will be frothy.

4 Add the whipped crème fraîche to the pan and whisk well to mix with the caramel.

ICE CREAM TIPS

■ It is possible to make good ice cream without an ice cream maker. Follow the steps given here up to the end of step 6. Then pour the caramel custard into a shallow freezerproof container and freeze until mushy. Turn the mixture into a cold bowl and whisk to break up the ice crystals. Return to the container and freeze again until mushy. Repeat the whisking and freezing once more.

■ For a delicious dessert, serve scoops of caramel ice cream layered with scoops of dark chocolate mousse (p431).

6 Pour the caramel milk over the egg yolk and sugar mixture, stirring it all together. Cook over medium heat, stirring well, until the custard is thick enough to coat the back of a wooden spoon. Cool the caramel custard over ice (see crème anglaise, p420). Chill overnight.

7 The following day, transfer the caramel custard to an ice cream maker and churn to freeze, following the manufacturer's directions. If you do not have a machine, see right. Serve the finished ice cream in scoops, drizzled with caramel sauce.

ROSE ICE CREAM

This pretty, pale pink, delicately flavored ice cream is the perfect dessert to finish a meal on a warm summer's day.

Makes 1 quart (1 liter)

3 cups whole milk

1 cup crème fraîche

12 egg yolks

1 cup (200g) sugar

7 tbsp rose-hip syrup

3 tbsp rose water

1 Bring the milk and crème fraîche to a boil in a heavy pan, then remove from the heat. Whisk the egg yolks and sugar in a bowl. Pour the hot milk onto the yolks in a thin stream, whisking, then pour back into the pan. Cook over medium heat, stirring, until thick enough to coat the back of a wooden spoon. Cool over ice (see crème anglaise, p421).

2 Stir in the rose-hip syrup and rose water. Chill overnight, then freeze as for caramel ice cream (p422).

EXTRA SPECIAL DESSERTS

■ This is my favorite dessert. Arrange 12 fresh figs in a small baking dish, dredge with sugar, and sprinkle with a few drops of lemon juice, 6 tbsp (85g) butter cut in small cubes, and 3 tbsp water. Tuck in a vanilla bean, split lengthwise, and a small cinnamon stick. Bake in a preheated 450°F (230°C) oven for about 20 minutes. Divide the figs among four plates. Coat the figs with the juices in the baking dish, then add a scoop of rose ice cream to each plate and surround the figs with fresh, crushed raspberries.

■ For a sundae, layer scoops of rose ice cream with caramel ice cream (p422) and litchi sorbet.

Serve the ice cream in scoops, with "fairy's fingers" (p427)

MINT ICE CREAM

This is a very refreshing ice cream. Don't be tempted to use dried mint—only fresh mint will give the desired flavor.

Makes 1 quart (1 liter)

1 bunch of mint, about 2oz (55g)

2 cups whole milk

½ cup crème fraîche

6 egg yolks

½ cup + 2 tbsp (120g) sugar

3–4 grindings of black pepper

1 Remove the mint leaves from the stems. Set one-fourth of the leaves aside and roughly chop the rest. Whisk the milk and crème fraîche together in a pan, then bring to a boil. Remove from the heat. Stir in the chopped mint, cover, and let infuse for 5–6 minutes. Strain and discard the chopped mint.

2 Place the egg yolks and sugar in another heavy-based pan. Beat for 3 minutes, then pour in the hot milk in a thin stream, whisking constantly. Set the pan over medium heat and cook the custard, stirring constantly, until it reaches 185°F (85°C). Season with the black pepper. Remove from the heat and stir slowly and gently for 3–4 minutes.

3 Set the pan in a shallow bowl filled with ice cubes. Coarsely chop half of the mint leaves and add to the custard. Mix with an immersion blender. Cover and refrigerate overnight.

4 The following day, transfer the mixture to an ice cream maker and churn until frozen, following the manufacturer's directions. (If you do not have a machine, see p423.) Once the ice cream starts to become firm, add the remaining coarsely chopped mint leaves.

CHEF'S TIPS

■ Do not infuse with the mint for longer than indicated, because it will affect the flavor and color.

■ Fresh mint ice cream is best eaten on the day it is made, when its flavor is at its most intense. However, it can be kept in the freezer for up to a week.

RASPBERRY SORBET

Refreshing and fruity, this sorbet makes a melt-in-the-mouth treat on a hot day. Since the fruit content in this recipe is very high, it is essential to use only the very best quality raspberries to ensure a wonderful flavor.

Makes 1 quart (1 liter)

¾ cup (150g) sugar

3 tbsp mineral water

2lb (900g) raspberries (about 8 cups)

1 tbsp lemon juice

1 Pour the sugar and water into a heavy-based pan and place over low heat. When the sugar has dissolved, bring to a boil. Let cool. Once the syrup is cold, add the raspberries and lemon juice. Purée the mixture in a food processor.

2 Press the puréed raspberries through a fine-mesh strainer. Pour into an ice cream maker and freeze, following the manufacturer's directions. To make without a machine, see p423. Serve the sorbet in scoops on the day of making.

BITTER CHOCOLATE SORBET

I prefer to use bitter chocolate for this sorbet instead of cocoa powder, because it has a cleaner flavor.

Serves 6–8

7oz (200g) best-quality dark bitter chocolate (70–75% cocoa solids)

¾ cup (160g) sugar

2 cups mineral water

chocolate curls for decoration

1 Chop the chocolate coarsely using a serrated-edge knife. Dissolve the sugar in the water in a large pan over low heat. Bring to a boil. Add the chocolate and stir for 2 minutes. The mixture will become very frothy.

2 Set the pan in a shallow bowl of ice water and let cool, stirring from time to time.

3 Transfer the mixture to an ice cream maker and freeze, following the manufacturer's directions. To make without a machine, see p423. Serve in scoops, topped with chocolate curls.

MAKING FRENCH MERINGUE

This egg white and sugar mixture, lightly flavored with vanilla, is sometimes called simple meringue. It makes crisp, light-as-air meringue disks that can be used as a base for all kinds of desserts, as well as meringue shells and fingers to serve with fresh fruit and whipped cream.

Makes enough for about four 8in (20cm) disks, or 30 fingers or small shells

8 egg whites

2½ cups (500g) superfine sugar

seeds from 2–3 vanilla beans (p420)

EGG WHITES

Before making the meringue, it is best to leave the egg whites in a covered bowl for 2–3 days at cool room temperature. This will allow them to liquefy a little, so they will be easier to whisk to a peak and then less likely to collapse during baking.

1 Place the egg whites in the bowl of an electric mixer and beat on medium speed, gradually adding half of the sugar and the vanilla seeds as you go.

2 Continue beating until the egg whites are shiny and smooth, and will hold a peak.

3 Using a rubber spatula, gradually fold in the rest of the sugar, lifting the egg whites up from the bottom and over, taking care not to deflate them.

Piping and baking meringue shapes

Pipe the meringue shapes onto a baking sheet lined with parchment paper and bake in a preheated 225°F (120°C) oven. Then turn off the oven, prop open the oven door slightly with a wooden spoon, and let the meringue shapes dry for at least 8 hours or overnight.

Disks or layers

Use a pastry bag fitted with a No. 9 star tip. Pipe the meringue in a spiral, starting in the center, to make a disk about 8in (20cm) in diameter. Bake for 1 hour and 20 minutes, then let dry.

Shells

Use a pastry bag fitted with a No. 14/16 round tip. Pipe the meringue in dollops about 3in (7.5cm) in diameter. Bake for 1 hour and 10 minutes (when a shell is broken open, the center should be slightly golden), then let dry.

Fingers

Use a pastry bag fitted with a No. 10 round tip. Pipe the meringue in thin sticks about 3in (7.5cm) long. Dust lightly with confectioners' sugar. Bake for 30–35 minutes, then let dry. I call these "fairy's fingers."

Perfectly cooked meringues are slightly golden in the center

MERINGUE TIPS

■ To make sure egg whites have been beaten to the right peaked consistency—described in French as "blancs au bec d'oiseau" or "bird's beak whites"—use this traditional trick of the trade. Dip a fingertip into the whites and remove it: The whites should hang off your fingertip in the hooked shape resembling an eagle's beak.

■ Meringue shapes can be "pearled" by sprinkling them with a fine coating of confectioners' sugar during baking. Put them into the oven and bake until they develop a light crust, about 15 minutes, then dust with confectioners' sugar. Return to the oven to finish baking. When cooked, the meringues will be covered with tiny golden balls.

DARK CHOCOLATE TRUFFLES WITH LIME & HONEY

Surprisingly simple to prepare, these delicious truffles are made from a slightly bitter ganache, which is a richly flavored chocolate cream that is also used to fill cakes and decorate desserts.

Makes about 50

1lb (440g) best-quality bitter chocolate (60–70% cocoa solids)
7 tbsp (95g) butter
¾ cup crème fraîche
2–3 limes
2½ tbsp (50g) acacia honey
For the coating
finely grated zest of ½ lime
½ cup + 2 tbsp (120g) sugar
1⅓ cups (120g) unsweetened cocoa powder

1 Prepare the coating the day before needed. Mix the lime zest with the sugar and rub between the palms of your hands. Spread in a thin layer on a nonstick baking sheet and let dry overnight at room temperature. Before mixing with the cocoa powder in step 8, check to be sure that the sugar is completely dry.

2 The following day, chop the chocolate into small pieces with a serrated-edge knife and place in a large heatproof bowl. Cut the butter into walnut-sized pieces, place in a bowl, and let soften to room temperature.

3 Pour the crème fraîche into a pan and bring to a boil. Finely grate the zest from 1 lime into the crème fraîche. Remove the pan from the heat, cover, and let infuse for 10 minutes. Return to the heat and bring back just to a boil. Remove from the heat again.

4 While the crème fraîche is infusing, squeeze the limes to yield 3½ tbsp of juice. Put the lime juice and honey into another small pan. Warm without boiling.

CHEF'S TIPS

■ Truffles that have not been rolled in cocoa powder can be stored in the refrigerator, in an airtight container, for 2 weeks. Remove from the refrigerator and from the container 2 hours before serving.
■ This ganache can also be used as the basis of a chocolate sauce to be drizzled over desserts, such as poached fruits and ice cream.

6 Once the chocolate mixture is smooth, add the pieces of butter, a few at a time, stirring them in gently. Chill until the ganache has thickened, at least 30 minutes.

7 Stir the ganache gently before pouring it into a pastry bag fitted with a No. 9 round tip. Pipe balls of ganache onto a baking sheet lined with parchment paper. Chill for 2 hours.

5 Pour half of the hot crème fraîche over the chocolate and stir with a wooden spoon, starting at the center with small circles and moving outward. Add the rest of the crème fraîche and repeat the stirring process. Add the lime juice and honey mixture.

8 Mix the cocoa powder with the dry lime-flavored sugar and spread over a tray. Using a fork, roll the balls of ganache in the coating mixture. Remove with a slotted spoon, then shake gently in a strainer to remove any excess coating. Store in an airtight container.

Milk chocolate truffles with passion fruit

An intriguing combination of flavors makes these truffles sweet with just a hint of acidity from the passion fruit.

Makes about 70

1lb 9oz (700g) good-quality milk chocolate

7 tbsp (100g) butter

20 passion fruits

2 tbsp (40g) acacia, flower, or plain honey

unsweetened cocoa powder for coating

Shake off excess cocoa powder in a strainer

Chop the chocolate finely with a serrated-edge knife. Cut the butter into walnut-sized pieces, place in a shallow bowl, and let soften to room temperature.

Line the bottom and sides of a large rectangular dish with parchment paper.

Cut the passion fruits in half. Remove the flesh and seeds with a teaspoon and press in a strainer set over a bowl. Pour the strained juice and the honey into a pan and bring to a boil. Add the chopped chocolate, a handful at a time, and stir gently with a wooden spoon, starting from the center and gradually working outward.

Once the chocolate mixture is well combined, add the butter, a few pieces at a time, stirring as before. Pour the ganache into the prepared dish. Chill until set, about 2 hours.

Place a sheet of parchment paper on the work surface. Lift the ganache from the dish by lifting the paper, then turn it over onto the paper on the work surface. Cut the ganache into small rectangles about 1 by ½in (2.5 by 1cm).

Sift the cocoa powder onto a baking sheet. Coat the truffles in the cocoa powder, one by one, turning them with a fork. Remove with a slotted spoon and shake gently in a strainer to remove excess cocoa powder.

DARK CHOCOLATE MOUSSE

This simple-to-make mousse has a smooth, silky texture and rich chocolate flavor. The lightness is achieved by adding the egg whites in two stages. If serving the mousse in small cups, you can spoon or pipe it in. Decorate the mousse with flakes or curls of dark chocolate, whole or lightly crushed raspberries, finely shredded mint, or crushed caramelized hazelnuts.

6oz (170g) best-quality bitter chocolate (67–70% cocoa solids)
⅓ cup whole milk
1 egg yolk
4 egg whites
1½ tbsp (20g) sugar

1 Chop the chocolate with a serrated-edge knife. Place the chocolate in a heatproof bowl set over a pan of simmering water and let it melt. Remove the bowl from the pan.

2 Bring the milk to a boil. Pour onto the melted chocolate, stirring with a whisk to mix. Add the egg yolk and mix in thoroughly. The temperature of the mixture should be 104°F (40°C). You can check by dipping in a fingertip: The mixture should feel hot to the touch but not uncomfortably hot. Let cool.

3 Beat the egg whites to firm peaks, adding the sugar bit by bit. Add one-third of the whites to the chocolate mixture and whisk briskly, then carefully fold in the rest of the whites, lifting the mousse from the center bottom of the bowl up and out, and turning the bowl around as you fold.

4 Spoon or pipe the mousse into individual cups or dishes, or one large serving bowl. Chill for 1 hour before serving. Decorate the mousse with chocolate curls, if desired.

CHEF'S TIPS

■ It's important to use the very best quality chocolate, with a high percentage of cocoa solids.
■ The egg whites should be very fresh. Use them cold, not at room temperature.
■ For an exotic mousse, you can flavor the milk by infusing it with a pinch of orange zest, 1 tsp ground Ceylon cinnamon, a pinch of ground cardamom, or a few twists of freshly ground Sichuan pepper.

STEPHAN FRANZ

Sweet-tasting foods have always been among life's pleasures. While not indispensable for man's survival, they have, in the truest sense, sweetened our existence. While our forebears were familiar with the sweetness of honey and fruits, they could not have dreamed of the baked pleasures to come. In 15th-century Germany, the word "torte" was already in use for round, salted, savory pastries, such as meat torte and oil cake, but sweet "torten" did not appear there until the 19th century. The word itself stems from the Latin "tortus," meaning "turned" or "wound."

Offerings to impress Sweet pastries were popularized by the newly prosperous burghers of the German industrial age, who were able to afford the expensive and luxurious ingredients. Wanting to show off their new-found wealth, the burghers emulated the royal households by ordering fine pastries and confections from the same bakers that served the nobility. Indeed, entertaining friends at "Kaffee Kränzchen," or coffee gatherings, became so popular that hostesses would vie with each other to offer their guests increasingly elaborate and fine fare. Even today in Germany, a home-baked cake is a highly appreciated gift for loved ones, and a special treat for oneself.

Austria gained a fine reputation for its bakery at an earlier time. Influences from eastern European countries, Arabia, and France were strongly reflected in Austrian culture and folk history, and the traditions of foreign kitchens were also evident in Austrian cuisine, particularly in cakes and pastries. The art of baking was held in such high esteem that a head pastry chef at one of the royal courts was actually decorated as a general. The first known recipe for a chocolate cake originated in Austria, in 1778. Later, at the court of Chancellor Lothar Metternich in 1832, a chef's apprentice, Franz Sacher, created Europe's most famous chocolate cake, the Sachertorte. This complicated and inspired creation, consisting of flavored sponge-cake layers filled with a thin layer of apricot jam and covered by a shiny glaze of rich, dark chocolate, is now baked in professional Viennese kitchens and dispatched around the world. The recipe features in the following chapter.

The more formal "afternoon tea" that Lady Bedford devised in England, in 1840, gave renewed impetus to cakemaking. Lady Bedford's social circle, finding the interval between lunch and dinner to be too long, were craving some refreshment, especially something sweet, in the late afternoon. Lady Bedford's innovation, also known as the "five o'clock tea," was to become the essence of English tea culture. It was an excuse for friends to meet each afternoon and share a cup of tea with pastry or shortbread. The upper classes celebrated this repast between luncheon and dinner in grand style. Fine table linen, a silver tea service, and expensive porcelain decorated the table. Cucumber sandwiches and small cakes were served and scones became increasingly popular.

Modern-day cakes The cost of ingredients and basic foodstuffs is not such an important consideration today, and baked confections have been adapted to meet the demands of our diet-conscious society. The elaborately prepared, multilayered, buttercream-filled cakes of earlier times very often have been replaced by lighter concoctions of cream and fruit, and small, delicate creations are preferred to larger and richer fare. Baking at home has become popular again, and the arts of our ancestors are appreciated once more. Children are meeting their parents and grandparents to exchange recipes, and grandmothers are explaining the detail of great-grandmothers' recipes. In North America and Europe, baking has customarily helped to celebrate Christmas, Easter, and birthdays, and the preparations for the forthcoming feast are just as important as the event itself.

Baking certainly has its history and traditions, but it also reflects the spirit of our time. While some new confections pay homage to the preferences and styles of past times, they are often lighter than the old classics. In the recipes that follow, we have adapted some of the traditional techniques so that the final products benefit from simpler, more contemporary baking methods.

SPONGE CAKES

All sponge batters are rich in egg content, but the texture of the finished cake depends on the method and other ingredients used. Fatless sponges, used for jelly rolls, are light and fluffy, ideal to hold a simple cream or jam filling. But when a firmer structure is needed, capable of soaking up flavored syrups or supporting fresh seasonal fruits without collapsing, then a génoise batter, made with butter and whisked over heat, is most suitable. Heavier, richer batters have more than 20 percent butter content.

GÉNOISE

This light sponge cake is the base for many layer cakes, such as Frankfurter kranz (p446) and Stephan's cheesecake (p603). When beating over heat, the temperature of the mixture should be about 113°F (45°C). It must never exceed 122°F (50°C), otherwise the texture of the baked cake will be like straw rather than moist. An instant-read thermometer can be used to check the temperature. Or, test by putting a finger into the egg mixture: it should feel just hotter than bath water. There is no need to grease the sides of the pan—the dry surface will prevent the cake from shrinking and losing shape as it cools.

Makes a 10in (25cm) cake

¾ cup + 2 tbsp (110g) cake flour
⅔ cup (90g) potato flour
6 medium eggs, precise shelled weight 10oz (300g)
scant 1 cup (180g) sugar
1 tbsp acacia or clear honey
grated zest of ½ lemon
4 tbsp (60g) unsalted butter, melted and cooled to lukewarm

1 Preheat the oven to 375°F (190°C). Line the bottom of a 10in (25cm) springform pan with parchment paper. Sift together the cake and potato flours twice, then sift onto a sheet of wax paper. Set aside.

CHOCOLATE GÉNOISE

To prepare a chocolate génoise, replace half of the potato flour with ½ cup (45g) unsweetened cocoa powder. Reduce the amount of butter to 3½ tbsp (50g) and add 1 tbsp water to the eggs before beating. Use grated orange zest instead of lemon.

2 Put the eggs into a heatproof bowl and add the sugar, honey, and a pinch of salt. Set the bowl over a pan of barely simmering water and beat until the mixture is more than double in volume, and is thick, pale, and creamy. Be sure that the base of the bowl does not touch the water, or the eggs will overcook.

3 Lift the bowl off the pan and place on the worktop. Continue beating at high speed until the mixture has cooled and falls from the beaters in a thick ribbon. Add the grated lemon zest and beat at half speed for 15 more minutes. The long beating helps to stabilize the eggs so they keep their volume.

4 Using a spatula, gently fold the sifted flours into the egg mixture in large spoonfuls until well blended. Stir 2–3 tbsp of the mixture into the butter. Then, working quickly and taking care not to lose any volume, fold the two mixtures together until combined.

5 Pour the batter into the prepared pan and lightly smooth the surface. Place in the oven and reduce the temperature to 350°F (175°C). Bake until golden brown and light and springy to the touch, 30–40 minutes.

6 Remove from the oven and let cool for 10 minutes. Slide a knife around the inside of the pan to loosen the cake. Pull back the clamp of the springform to release the side, then lift it away. Remove the cake from the base and peel off the lining paper. Cool on a wire rack.

CUTTING & FILLING

An unfilled génoise will keep fresh in the refrigerator for 3–4 days; it also freezes very well. Once filled or topped, it is best eaten on the day it is made. The plainness of a génoise lends itself to the contrast of rich, creamy, or fruity fillings. To serve very simply, just spread a topping over the cake and cut into wedges. Génoise is delicious when moistened with a flavored syrup as in Frankfurter kranz (p446).

1 Place the cake on a firm, level surface. For a simple filled cake, cut into two layers: Using a sharp, long-bladed, serrated-edge knife, first score a guideline all around the side, then slice through the cake, carefully following the marked guideline. Place your hand lightly on top of the cake to hold it steady as you cut.

2 Using a spatula or the springform base to help you, carefully lift off the top layer and place it on a flat surface while you fill the cake. You can also slice the cake into three or four layers, depending on its depth. If the cake is chilled, the skin on top may become soft. This should be removed before cutting into layers.

EASY FILLINGS & FINISHES

■ Sweetened whipped cream with fresh fruit, such as red berries, grapes, and sliced kiwi fruit.
■ A thick layer of homemade or good-quality jam or lemon curd is simple but mouthwatering.
■ Flavored buttercream.
■ For a quick finish, place thin strips of parchment paper at an angle across the top of the cake. Dredge liberally with confectioners' sugar, then carefully remove the strips to reveal a pattern.

Place a thin strip of parchment paper along the top of the roll, sift confectioners' sugar on top, and then carefully remove the paper strip

JELLY ROLL

I think a fatless sponge cake is best for a jelly roll or roulade. Fillings such as strawberry, cherry, or apricot jam are delicious, as are sweet whipped and flavored creams. The cake is made using separated eggs. It keeps fresh for a day.

A jelly roll is less likely to tear if filled and rolled up while it is still warm and flexible. Alternatively, roll up the cake with a sheet of parchment paper inside, then let cool before unrolling, removing the paper, and filling.

For a chocolate jelly roll, replace 1 tbsp of the potato flour with unsweetened cocoa powder and sift this with the cake flour.

Makes a 15½ by 11in (40 by 28cm) sheet cake

6½ tbsp (50g) cake flour

7 tbsp (55g) potato flour, sifted

5 extra large egg yolks, precise weight 3½oz (100g)

2 tsp vanilla sugar (p634)

grated zest of ½ lemon

3 extra large egg whites, precise weight 4oz (115g)

6 tbsp (75g) granulated sugar

confectioners' sugar for dusting

For the filling

5 tbsp raspberry jam, strained and warmed

GRATING LEMON ZEST

Lay a sheet of parchment paper on the cutting surface of the grater. Rub the lemon across it and the zest will fall straight off without getting trapped in the grater.

1 Preheat the oven to 400°F (200°C). Line a 15½ by 11in (40 by 28cm) jelly roll pan with parchment paper. Sift the cake flour and 3 tbsp (25g) of the potato flour together twice onto a sheet of wax paper. Set aside.

2 Using a balloon whisk or hand-held electric mixer, beat the egg yolks with the vanilla sugar until the mixture is pale and creamy, and falls in a thick ribbon. Stir in the lemon zest.

3 Place the egg whites, granulated sugar, remaining potato flour, and a pinch of salt in another, very clean bowl. Beat with an electric mixer at medium speed until the mixture is white and creamy, forms soft peaks, and has at least doubled in volume. This creates a foam with a strong structure that will not collapse when the egg yolks and flours are folded in.

4 Using a rubber spatula, fold one-third of the egg-white mixture into the yolk mixture, gently mixing them together. Then add this mixture to the remaining egg whites and fold together very gently, taking care not to lose any air. Again taking care not to lose any air, gently fold in the sifted flours.

5 Transfer the batter to the pan and spread lightly to within ¾in (2cm) of the edge. Bake until golden, light, and springy to the touch, 12–15 minutes. Remove from the oven and sprinkle with granulated sugar, then cover with a clean sheet of parchment paper. Carefully turn the sheet cake over onto a clean towel.

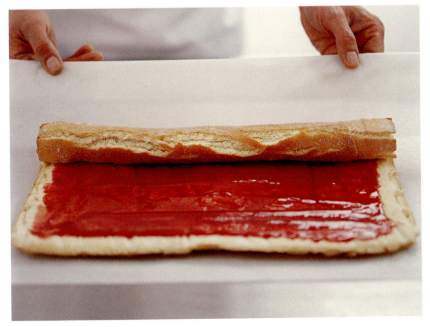

6 Gently peel away the lining paper, pressing down onto it with a ruler to avoid tearing the cake. Spread the warm jam evenly over the cake to within ¾in (2cm) of the edge. Lifting the cake with the help of the new sheet of parchment paper underneath, roll up with gentle pressure.

7 Lay the roll on another sheet of paper and drape one end of the paper over it. Hold the other end of the paper with your left hand and push a ruler against the roll with your free hand. The paper will wrap tightly around the roll to give a good even shape. Remove the paper, cover the cake, and refrigerate for 2 hours. Trim the ends.

2 Preheat the oven to 325°F (160°C). Sift the cake flour again onto a sheet of wax paper. Beat together the butter, potato flour, vanilla sugar, and lemon zest until thick and creamy.

3 Put the eggs, granulated sugar, honey, and a pinch of salt into a large heatproof bowl and set over a pan of simmering water. Using a hand-held electric mixer, beat until pale and creamy. Lift the bowl off the pan and beat for 5 more minutes, on the highest speed, until cooled. Turn the speed to low and beat for 10–15 minutes longer.

4 Stir one-third of the egg mixture into the creamed butter to lighten it, then gently fold in the remaining egg mixture, using a large rubber spatula. Finally, fold in the cake flour.

5 Spoon the batter into the prepared pan and bake until risen and golden brown, about 50 minutes. Test with a skewer: It should come out clean. Remove from the oven and leave for 10 minutes before unmolding onto a wire rack. Dust with confectioners' sugar before serving.

POUND CAKE

This cake is so-named because it was originally made using equal weights of flour, butter, sugar, and eggs. It is a firm favorite in the baker's repertoire. The texture is delicate, short, and crumbly, and the sweet buttery taste is good plain or with added fruits, nuts, or chocolate.

Makes a 9in (23cm) kugelhopf or a large loaf cake

3 tbsp toasted fine bread crumbs
1 cup + 2 tbsp (140g) cake flour, sifted twice
¾ cup (175g) unsalted butter, softened
¼ cup (35g) potato flour, sifted
4 tsp vanilla sugar (p482)
grated zest of ½ lemon
3 large eggs, precise shelled weight 6oz (175g)
½ cup + 3 tbsp (140g) granulated sugar
2 tsp clear honey
confectioners' sugar for dusting

1 Prepare a 9in (23cm) kugelhopf pan by brushing it with melted butter to within ½in (1cm) of the top edge, then dusting it evenly with the toasted bread crumbs (or with flour). Alternatively, use a large loaf pan and line it with parchment paper.

VARIATIONS

Try adding any of the following:
- 6½ tbsp raisins, steeped overnight in 2 tbsp rum.
- 2oz (60g) finely chopped best-quality bittersweet or semisweet chocolate.
- ½ cup chopped walnuts, toasted hazelnuts, or macadamia nuts.

Lightly fold any of the above into the prepared cake batter before spooning into the pan for baking.

APRICOT STREUSEL CRUMBLE CAKE

A rich cake batter and fresh fruit taste delicious baked together, especially with a marzipan and almond streusel topping. Other fresh fruits you could use are cherries, apples, and pears.

Makes a 9 by 11in (23 by 28cm) cake

1½lb (750g) fresh apricots, halved and pitted

sprig of thyme

1 juniper berry

2 cups water

1½ cups (300g) granulated sugar

½ cup (50g) sliced almonds

confectioners' sugar to dust

For the streusel

½ cup +2 tbsp (140g) chilled unsalted butter, diced

½ cup (100g) granulated sugar

2oz (50g) marzipan, finely chopped

grated zest of ½ lemon

seeds from ½ vanilla bean (p89)

pinch of ground cinnamon

2 cups (250g) all-purpose flour, sifted

For the cake batter

2½ cups (300g) cake flour

1 heaped tsp baking powder

3oz (80g) marzipan, finely chopped

6 medium eggs, precise shelled weight 10oz (300g)

1 cup (225g) unsalted butter, diced and softened

1 cup + 2 tbsp (225g) granulated sugar

1½ tbsp liquid glucose or light corn syrup

seeds from ½ vanilla bean (p89)

grated zest of ½ orange

grated zest of ½ lemon

1 The day before, place the apricots, thyme, and juniper berry in a bowl. Bring the water and sugar slowly to a boil, stirring until the sugar is dissolved. Pour this over the fruit and leave for 24 hours. Drain the fruit and remove the loosened skins. Pat dry with paper towels.

2 Butter a baking or roasting pan that is about 9 by 11in (23 by 28cm) and 1¾in (4cm) deep. Line the bottom with parchment paper.

3 For the streusel, combine the butter, sugar, marzipan, lemon zest, vanilla seeds, and cinnamon in a bowl. Add a pinch of salt and mix together until smooth. Sift the flour over and rub in with your fingertips (do not knead), to make a light, crumbly mixture.

4 Preheat the oven to 425°F (220°C). To make the cake batter, sift together twice the flour, baking powder, and a pinch of salt onto a sheet of wax paper. Set aside.

5 Put the marzipan and one of the eggs in the bowl of an electric mixer (or use a hand-held electric mixer). Beat well to form a smooth paste. Add the butter and sugar, and beat until lump-free. Beat in the glucose or corn syrup.

6 Add the remaining eggs, one at a time. Beat the mixture very thoroughly after each egg is added so that it will be completely absorbed and the mixture remains smooth and shiny. Mix in the vanilla seeds and orange and lemon zests. Carefully fold in the flour using a rubber spatula.

7 With a metal spatula, spread the batter evenly in the prepared pan. Arrange the apricots halves on top, close together and cut-side up. Sprinkle the streusel mixture over and finish with the almonds.

8 Place in the oven and reduce the temperature to 350°F (175°C). Bake for 45 minutes. Remove from the oven and let cool in the pan. Dust with confectioners' sugar before serving.

RICH FRUIT LOAF

This unusual fruitcake is finished by coating it with jam and wrapping it in a layer of sponge cake, giving a pleasing contrast in textures. If you do not want to wrap the fruit loaf in sponge cake, you can use marzipan instead, or just leave it plain. The cake will keep for 1 week.

Makes a large fruit loaf

⅓ cup (40g) chopped almonds, lightly dry-roasted (p480)

½ cup (80g) golden raisins

½ cup (80g) dark raisins

⅓ cup (60g) finely chopped candied orange peel

⅓ cup (60g) finely chopped candied lemon peel

¾ cup (120g) halved candied cherries

3 tbsp dark rum

2oz (50g) hard nougat, finely chopped

2oz (50g) bittersweet cooking chocolate (70% cocoa solids), finely chopped

⅓ cup (40g) cake flour

For the cake batter

1⅔ cups (200g) cake flour

1 heaped tsp baking powder

3oz (80g) marzipan, finely chopped

5 medium eggs, precise shelled weight 8½oz (250g)

¾ cup + 2 tbsp (200g) unsalted butter, diced and softened

½ cup + 2 tbsp (120g) sugar

3 tbsp golden syrup or light corn syrup

seeds from 1 vanilla bean (p89)

grated zest of 1 lemon

5 drops of bitter almond extract

To finish (optional)

⅔ cup apricot brandy or Cognac

½ cup (150g) apricot jam, boiled and strained

½ sheet cake for jelly roll (p438) or 1lb 2oz (500g) marzipan

¾ cup (80g) sliced almonds, lightly dry-roasted (p480)

LINING THE PAN

Brush a large (2¼lb/1kg) loaf pan with melted butter and dust with flour. Turn the pan over and cut a piece of parchment paper the same size as the base. Turn the pan over again and place the paper in the bottom.

1 The day before, stir together the almonds, dried fruits, candied peels, candied cherries, and rum in a bowl. Cover and leave overnight at room temperature. Place the nougat and chocolate in another bowl, cover, and refrigerate.

2 To make the cake batter, sift the flour and baking powder together twice, then sift again onto a sheet of wax paper. Set aside. Using a hand-held electric mixer, beat the marzipan with 1 of the eggs until smooth. Add the butter, sugar, and golden or light corn syrup, and beat well together.

3 Lightly beat the remaining eggs. Add them, a little at a time, to the batter, beating well after each addition. Mix in the vanilla seeds, lemon zest, and almond extract. Gently fold in the flour in three batches. Preheat the oven to 425°F (220°C).

4 Mix together the fruit and nut mixture and the chocolate mixture, and coat with the flour. Fold into the batter. Pour into the pan (see left), smooth the top, and place in the oven. Reduce the temperature to 325°F (170°C).

5 After 15 minutes of baking, gently open the oven door. Dip the tip of a knife in oil and use to make a shallow cut along the top of the cake to prevent it from peaking.

6 After 50 minutes, insert a skewer into the center of the cake; if it comes out with no batter sticking to it, then the cake is done. Remove the cake from the oven and unmold onto a wire rack. To serve plain, simply wrap in foil and keep for a few days before slicing.

7 If you want to wrap the cake, lightly warm the apricot brandy in a pan, then set alight and spoon the flaming spirit over the warm cake, letting it soak in.

8 Trim the sides of the cake to neaten them, then brush with the warm apricot glaze. Wrap the sheet cake or rolled-out marzipan around the loaf. Brush the top with the remaining glaze and decorate with the sliced almonds.

MARBLE CAKE

An attractive and easy cake, this is made from ingredients you are likely to have on hand. Popular in Europe and North America, it is sometimes called tiger cake.

Makes a large loaf cake

2 tbsp unsweetened cocoa powder
2 tbsp milk
1 cup (110g) cake flour
5 tbsp (40g) potato flour
½ tsp baking powder
6 tbsp clarified butter (p24)
6 tbsp corn oil
1 cup + 3 tbsp (140g) confectioners' sugar, sifted, plus extra for dusting
2 tsp vanilla sugar (p482)
grated zest of ½ lemon
3 large eggs, precise shelled weight 6oz (175g)

1 Prepare a large (2¼lb/1kg) loaf pan by brushing the bottom and two-thirds up the sides with melted butter, then dusting with flour. (Leaving the top edge ungreased prevents the batter from overflowing.)

2 Mix together the cocoa powder and milk to make a smooth paste. Set aside. Sift the flours, a pinch of salt, and the baking powder together twice, then sift onto a sheet of wax paper. Preheat the oven to 425°F (220°C).

LEMON CAKE

To make a lemon-flavored cake, omit the cocoa powder, and add 1 tbsp grated lemon zest and 2 tbsp chopped candied peel to the batter. Mix 1 cup (125g) confectioners' sugar with 4 tsp powdered milk and 5 tsp lemon juice, and drizzle this over the baked cake.

3 Heat the butter and oil very gently in a pan until warm. In a large bowl, combine the sugars with the lemon zest. Add the butter and oil, and mix well with a hand-held electric mixer.

4 Add the eggs one at a time, beating to incorporate, then add the flour mixture in large spoonfuls, beating well between additions. Beat for 5 minutes longer at maximum speed.

5 Spoon one-third of the batter into another bowl. Add the cocoa paste to this and, with a balloon whisk, blend the mixtures together until smooth.

6 Spread a layer of pale batter in the loaf pan, then add alternate spoonfuls of dark and pale batters. Finish with a pale layer. Drag a fork through the dark and pale batters in a zigzag movement to create the marbled effect.

7 Place in the oven and reduce the temperature to 400°F (200°C). After 15–20 minutes of baking, dip the tip of a knife in oil and use to make a shallow cut along the top of the cake. Lower the heat to 350°F (175°C) and bake for 35 minutes longer.

8 Test with a skewer: If it comes out clean, the cake is done. Run a knife around the inside of the pan, then unmold the cake onto a wire rack to cool. Before serving, dust with confectioners' sugar.

HAZELNUT CAKE WITH CHERRIES

This is a cross between a cake and a tart, and is equally delicious at teatime or served with cream as a dessert. To ensure a crisp pastry base, it is part-baked before the sides of the pan are lined with pastry. Then the filling is added and the cake is baked.

Makes a 10in (25cm) cake

½ quantity (1lb/450g) pâte brisée, chilled (p376)

confectioners' sugar for dusting

For the vanilla cream

1¼ cups milk

7 medium egg yolks, precise weight 3½oz (100g)

6 tbsp (75g) granulated sugar

2 tbsp (15g) cornstarch

½ cup heavy cream

seeds from ½ vanilla bean (p89)

For the filling

1⅔ cups (500g) black cherry jam (pits removed)

For the hazelnut mixture

1 cup (100g) dry cake crumbs or toasted bread crumbs, finely ground

⅔ cup (90g) shelled hazelnuts, skinned (p480) and finely ground

pinch of ground cinnamon

7 tbsp (100g) unsalted butter, diced and softened

½ cup (100g) granulated sugar

2oz (60g) egg yolks, about 4 medium

seeds from ½ vanilla bean (p89)

grated zest of ½ lemon

4 medium egg whites, precise weight 4oz (120g)

1 Preheat the oven to 400°F (200°C). Lightly butter a 10in (25cm) deep-dish pie pan or a springform pan.

2 Roll out half of the pastry to a ⅛in (3mm) thickness and cut out a circle to fit the bottom of the pan. Lay the pastry circle in the pan and prick all over with a fork so that no air bubbles will occur during baking. Bake for 10 minutes. The pastry should be set and only very slightly colored.

3 Remove the pan from the oven and set aside to let the pastry base cool. Lower the oven temperature to 350°F (175°C).

4 Roll out the remaining pastry to the same thickness and cut into two equal strips that are as wide as the depth of the pan and half the circumference. Use these to line the sides of the pan. With the back of a knife, carefully trim off the excess pastry without tearing. Set aside.

5 For the vanilla cream, pour 6 tbsp of the milk into a bowl and mix in the egg yolks, half of the sugar, and the cornstarch. Pour the rest of the milk into a pan and add the cream, remaining sugar, and vanilla seeds. Bring just to a boil, then pour onto the egg yolk mixture, stirring well. Tip the mixture back into the pan.

6 Stirring constantly, bring to a boil. Remove from the heat immediately. Press the cream through a fine-mesh strainer, then spread evenly in the pastry shell.

7 Put the cherry jam into a large pastry bag (without a tip) and pipe in a swirl onto the surface of the vanilla cream.

8 To make the hazelnut mixture, lightly stir together the cake or bread crumbs, the hazelnuts, and cinnamon. In a large bowl, beat the butter with 2½ tbsp (30g) of the sugar until pale and creamy. Beat in the egg yolks one at a time. Add the vanilla seeds and lemon zest, and combine well.

9 In a clean bowl, beat the egg whites with the remaining sugar and a pinch of salt to stiff peaks. Add one-third of the egg whites to the butter mixture and stir to combine. Carefully fold in the remaining whites using a large rubber spatula. Fold in the hazelnut mixture in batches.

10 Fit a clean pastry bag with a large, plain tip and spoon in the hazelnut mixture. Pipe in a spiral over the top of the jam layer to cover the cake completely (see left). Place in the oven and bake for 45 minutes.

11 Remove from the oven and run a small knife around the inside of the pan to release the cake. Hold a cookie sheet over the pan and turn them over together so that the cake drops out onto the sheet. Lift off the pan. Hold a wire rack, upside-down, over the cake and turn over again so it is the right way up on the rack. When cool, dust with confectioners' sugar or cover with a fondant glaze (see below).

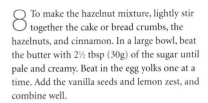

FONDANT GLAZE

Simmer together ⅓ cup (100g) strained apricot jam, 4 tsp water, and 3½ tbsp (45g) sugar. Brush evenly over the top of the cake. Work 5oz (150g) fondant with 2 tbsp poire Williams eau-de-vie until smooth. When the apricot glaze has set, heat the fondant glaze to 104°F (40°C) and spread over the cake. Alternatively, mix 1¼ cups (150g) confectioners' sugar with a little poire Williams eau-de-vie, and spread evenly over the cake.

FRANKFURTER KRANZ

This irresistible German confection is drenched with kirsch syrup and layered with a classic buttercream and cherries.

Makes a 10in (25cm) cake

For the buttercream

8 medium egg yolks, precise weight 4oz (120g)

½ cup water

¾ cup (150g) sugar

1½ cups (360g) unsalted butter, at room temperature

seeds from ½ vanilla bean (p89)

4 tsp kirsch

For the croquant

2¼ cups (450g) sugar

3 tbsp water

1lb 2oz (500g) hazelnuts, shelled, skinned (p480), and chopped (about 4 cups)

For the kirsch syrup

½ heaped cup (115g) sugar

½ cup water

2 tbsp kirsch

For the cake batter

6½ tbsp (50g) cake flour, sifted

2¼ cups (285g) potato flour

6 medium eggs, precise shelled weight 10oz (300g)

1 cup + 2 tbsp (225g) sugar

4 tsp water

grated zest of 1 lemon

¾ cup (165g) unsalted butter, melted and cooled to lukewarm

For the filling

1⅔ cups (500g) sour cherry jam (pits removed)

11–12 candied cherries

1 To make the buttercream, beat the egg yolks with a pinch of salt until pale and creamy. Set aside. Put the water in a small, heavy pan, add the sugar, and set over medium heat. Stir until the sugar dissolves, then bring to a boil. As the syrup starts to foam, use a fine-mesh strainer to skim off any impurities.

2 Raise the heat and continue boiling the syrup until it reaches 248°F (120°C) on a candy thermometer. Two or three times during boiling, dip a pastry brush in cold water and wash down the sugar crystals from the side of the pan. Do not stir the syrup. Remove from the heat and immediately plunge the base of the pan into cold water to stop the syrup cooking.

3 Quickly pour the hot syrup in a thin, steady stream onto the egg yolk mixture, beating with a hand-held electric mixer. Continue beating at a lower speed until the mixture has cooled to room temperature. Set aside.

4 In a separate bowl, beat the softened butter until pale and creamy. Add the vanilla seeds and mix well. Beat the butter mixture, 1 tbsp at a time, into the egg yolk and syrup mixture. Fold in the kirsch. Cover and set aside.

5 To make the croquant, pour the sugar and water into a heavy-based pan. Heat slowly at first to dissolve the sugar, then raise the heat and bring to a boil. Add the hazelnuts and stir well to coat with syrup. Continue boiling, without stirring, until it turns a golden caramel color.

6 Pour the mixture onto a marble slab or stone and spread out with an oiled spoon. Let cool. To use, first carefully break up the croquant with a rolling pin.

7 To make the kirsch syrup, bring the sugar and water to a rolling boil, skimming off any froth and impurities. Remove from the heat and let cool. Measure ½ cup of the syrup and add the kirsch. (Store the rest of the syrup in the refrigerator for future use.)

8 Preheat the oven to 375°F (190°C). Grease and flour a 10in (25cm) savarin mold. Make the batter as for a génoise (p436). Pour into the mold. Reduce the oven heat to 350°F (175°C) and bake for 40 minutes. Leave for 10 minutes, then unmold onto a wire rack. When cold, cut the cake into four layers.

9 Spread just over one-third of the cherry jam on the bottom layer, up to ½in (1cm) of the inner and outer edges. Fit a large pastry bag with a plain tip, then fill with three-fourths of the buttercream. Pipe a ring around the inner and outer edges. Cover with the second cake layer and press down lightly. Use half the kirsch syrup to lightly moisten the cake surface, then spread with jam and pipe buttercream as before. Finish the third layer in the same way. Set the final layer on top.

10 Spread the remaining buttercream all over the cake, including the inside of the ring. Take a strip of wax paper and use it to smooth the surface of the buttercream. Sprinkle the crushed croquant all over the cake and decorate with the candied cherries. The cake will keep fresh for up to 2 days in the refrigerator.

CHEESECAKES

Cheesecakes are traditionally baked from fresh, soft cheeses, cream, eggs, sugar, and spices on a pastry, cake, or crumb base. They have been made in Europe and many other places around the world since the 15th century. Ranging from light and fluffy to dense and very rich, they usually use a local dairy product, such as ricotta, mascarpone, quark, cottage, or cream cheese.

APPLE CHEESECAKE

The base of pastry topped with sponge cake can be made a day ahead. The water content of cottage cheese is high; baking in three stages prevents the surface of the cake from cracking.

Makes a 10in (25cm) cheesecake

1 thin pâte brisée disk (p376), part-baked in a 10in (25cm) springform pan

1½ tbsp apricot jam, boiled and strained

half quantity jam roulade batter (p438), baked in a 10in (25cm) springform pan

For the apple filling

2 tbsp (30g) unsalted butter

1⅓ cups (60g) fresh bread crumbs, lightly toasted

1⅓lb (600g) tart apples, peeled and thickly sliced

¼ cup (50g) granulated sugar

grated zest and juice of ½ lemon

grated zest and juice of ½ orange

⅓ cup (40g) finely chopped walnuts

pinch of ground cinnamon

3 tbsp (30g) raisins

1 tbsp rum

For the cheese mixture

6 tbsp (75g) vanilla sugar (p482)

¼ heaped cup (35g) custard powder or vanilla pudding mix

pinch of ground cinnamon

3½ cups (800g) cottage cheese, strained

⅔ cup whole milk

⅔ cup heavy cream

5 extra large egg yolks, precise weight 3½oz (100g)

grated zest of 1 lemon

2 tbsp lemon juice, strained

4 tsp kirsch

3½ tbsp (50g) unsalted butter, melted

4 extra large egg whites, precise weight 5½oz (150g)

½ heaped cup (110g) granulated sugar

¼ cup (30g) potato flour

1 Preheat the oven to 375°F (190°C). Place the baked pastry disk in the springform pan and brush with apricot jam. Slide in the cake layer, using the base of another springform pan as a support. Set aside.

2 For the apple filling, melt the butter in a pan, stir in the bread crumbs, and brown lightly. Add one-third of the apple slices and coat well with the buttered crumbs. Add the sugar, citrus zests and juice, walnuts, cinnamon, raisins, and rum. Stir together, then mix with the remaining apples. Set aside.

3 For the cheese mixture, mix together the vanilla sugar, custard powder or pudding mix, and cinnamon. Set aside. In a separate bowl, combine the cottage cheese, milk, cream, and egg yolks, blending thoroughly.

4 Add the lemon zest and juice and kirsch, and mix well. Fold in the vanilla sugar mixture. Add 2 tbsp of the cheese mixture with the melted butter, then fold this into the rest of the cheese mixture. Avoid stirring, otherwise the cheese cream might separate. Set aside.

A light fruit cheesecake for any occasion

5 Beat the egg whites with a pinch of salt, 2½ tbsp (30g) of the sugar, and the potato flour until pale and creamy. Gradually add the remaining sugar and beat to a firm and creamy snow. Using a whisk, stir one-third of the egg whites into the cheese cream. Gently fold in the remaining egg whites using a rubber spatula.

6 Spread the apple mixture evenly over the cake layer in the pan. Pour the cheese mixture onto the apples and spread out gently with a rubber spatula.

7 Place the cheesecake in the oven and bake until the top starts to set (only a short time). Then open the oven door carefully and slide an oiled knife around the inside edge of the pan to release the cheesecake mixture. Close the oven door and continue baking.

8 When the cake has risen, remove it from the oven and reduce the temperature to 325°F (170°C). Let the surface sink to level with the top of the pan, then put the cheesecake back into the oven. Repeat this twice more. The overall baking time is 50–60 minutes.

9 Remove the cheesecake from the oven and run a knife around the edge to loosen the sides. Let cool in the pan, then unclamp the side and remove it. Slide the cheesecake off the base onto a serving plate. The cheesecake will usually keep fresh for 2 days.

NEW YORK CHEESECAKE

This version of a classic cheesecake is unbaked and made with white chocolate. Its rich, creamy filling contrasts well with the crunchy almond-flavored base. It is easy to make and you can vary the toppings: Try red berries or orange or banana slices, or simply spread sour cream over the top.

Makes an 11in (28cm) cheesecake

For the base

½ cup (120g) unsalted butter

8oz (250g) amaretti cookies, crushed

For the filling

13oz (380g) white chocolate, finely chopped

1⅔ cups whole milk

3 cups (750g) cream cheese, at room temperature

seeds from 1 vanilla bean (p89)

½ cup (60g) confectioners' sugar, sifted

bittersweet and white chocolate scrolls for decoration

LINING THE PAN

Use a springform pan about 11in (28cm) in diameter. To line the pan, place a large sheet of parchment paper on the base, position the pan's side, and clamp it in place. Trim off the excess paper with scissors .

1 Preheat the oven to 350°F (180°C). Melt the butter in a small pan and mix in the amaretti crumbs. Press evenly over the bottom of the prepared pan (see left). Bake for 12 minutes. Set aside to cool.

2 To make the filling, place the chocolate and milk in a heatproof bowl set over a pan of barely simmering water. When melted, gently stir using an immersion blender, avoiding beating in any air. Let cool, stirring now and then to prevent a skin from forming.

3 Meanwhile, beat together the cream cheese, vanilla seeds, and confectioners' sugar until creamy. Stir in half of the white chocolate mixture, then fold in the remainder. Pour into the cake pan and spread level. Cover and chill for at least 6 hours.

4 Run a sharp knife carefully around the inside of the pan to release the cheesecake, then unclamp the side and lift off. Transfer the cheesecake to a serving plate and then decorate with chocolate scrolls.

Stephan's cheesecake

This is my own recipe for a very special occasion. Use the ring (the side) of a 10in (25cm) springform pan (no base needed), lightly brushed with unflavored oil and lined with strips of foil. The cheesecake stays fresh for 1–2 days.

Makes a 10in (25cm) cheesecake

For the cake

1 baked 10in (25cm) pâte brisée disk (p376)

1½ tbsp (30g) apricot jam, boiled and strained

1 baked génoise (p436), cut into 2 layers

12 bottled or canned peach halves, drained and dried on paper towels

confectioners' sugar for dusting

For the cheese cream filling

1½ cups (340g) farmer cheese, pressed through a strainer

⅓ cup (75g) sour cream

6 tbsp whole milk

½ cup + 3 tbsp (140g) granulated sugar

6 large egg yolks, precise weight 3½oz (100g)

4 tsp lemon juice

seeds from ½ vanilla bean (p89)

grated zest of ½ lemon

8 sheets of gelatin

2½ cups heavy cream, lightly whipped

Place the pastry disk on a baking sheet. Brush with apricot jam, then cover with the bottom génoise layer. Arrange the peaches, cut-side down, on the surface. Set the prepared pan side (see above) around the cake layers. Set aside.

For the filling, combine the cheese, sour cream, milk, sugar, egg yolks, and a pinch of salt in a large heatproof bowl set over a pan of barely simmering water. Beat the mixture until light and airy, and doubled in volume. Mix in the lemon juice. Remove from the heat and stir in the vanilla seeds and lemon zest.

Soften the gelatin sheets in a large bowl of cold water for 2 minutes, then remove and squeeze gently. Add to the warm cheese mixture and stir very gently until melted.

Set the bowl in another bowl of crushed ice and stir until the mixture starts to thicken to the consistency of raw egg white. At this point,

the mixture is beginning to set, so remove from the bowl of ice and beat in one-third of the whipped cream. Use a rubber spatula to fold in the remainder.

Reserve one-fourth of the filling; keep, covered, in a cool place. Carefully spoon the remaining filling over the peaches, spreading evenly and filling all the gaps. Smooth the top. Chill for at least 4 hours. Remove the cake ring and finish the cake shortly before serving.

To finish the cheesecake, cut the other (top) génoise layer into 12 triangles. Fit a pastry bag with a large, plain tip and fill with the reserved filling. Pipe 12 rosettes on the cake top, then arrange the génoise triangles at an angle, with points to the center. Dust with confectioners' sugar.

YEAST CAKES

If compressed fresh yeast is unavailable, you can substitute active dry yeast for the buttercake below and the stollen on p454. A fresh-yeast cake batter takes about 20 minutes to rise; a batter made with dry yeast will take 40 minutes. The general rule for testing the rise in either is to push a finger into the batter—it should spring apart and then shrink back in on itself.

BUTTERCAKE

This is a simple version of one of the most traditional German cakes. As yeast works better in a large mixture, the batter quantity is enough for two cakes. If baking just one of the cakes, wrap the leftoever batter in foil and a freezer bag. Freeze for up to one month. The topping and finishing ingredients are for one cake only.

Makes 2 large cakes

For the yeast sponge

1¼oz (35g) compressed fresh yeast or 5 tsp active dry yeast

½ cup milk, warmed to lukewarm

1 cup + 3 tbsp (150g) all-purpose flour

For the yeast batter

2¾ cups (350g) all-purpose flour

1 tsp salt

5 extra large egg yolks, precise weight 3¼oz (90g)

5 tbsp milk

5 tbsp (60g) granulated sugar

¼ cup (50g) quark or farmer cheese, pressed through a strainer

grated zest of 1 lemon

seeds from 1 vanilla bean (p89)

7 tbsp (100g) unsalted butter, softened

2 tsp dark rum

scant ½ cup (100g) sour cream

For the butter topping (1 cake only)

¾ cup + 2 tbsp (200g) unsalted butter, diced and softened

¾ cup (200g) crème pâtissière (p418)

1 extra large egg yolk, precise weight ¾oz (20g)

To finish (1 cake only)

¾ cup + 2 tbsp (175g) granulated sugar

2 tbsp (25g) vanilla sugar (p482)

¾ cup (80g) sliced almonds

2½ tbsp (50g) honey

½ cup heavy cream

1 For the yeast sponge, crumble the fresh yeast, or sprinkle the dry yeast, onto the warm milk in the mixing bowl of an electric mixer fitted with the dough hook. Sift the flour twice, then sift into the bowl.

2 Set the machine at slow speed and knead until the mixture is smooth and rolls off the sides of the bowl. Remove to another bowl, cover with a dish towel, and let rise in a warm place for 20 minutes.

3 To make the yeast batter, sift the flour and salt together twice, then sift into the clean bowl of the electric mixer.

4 Lightly beat the egg yolks together in another small bowl; reserve 2 tsp (10g) of the yolks and add the rest to the mixer bowl, along with the milk, sugar, cheese, lemon zest, and vanilla seeds. With the dough hook, slowly knead until firm and smooth.

5 Add the risen yeast sponge to the bowl and continue kneading with the dough hook until the batter has large air bubbles. Mix in the softened butter and rum. Transfer the batter to a large bowl. Cover with a dish towel and let rise in a cool place for 20 minutes.

6 Grease a 12 by 8in (30 by 20cm) baking pan and line with parchment paper. Divide the batter in half. Roll out half the batter to fit the prepared pan. (Freeze the remaining batter for later use.) Cover with a dish towel and set aside to rise again for 20 minutes.

7 Using a large metal spatula, spread the sour cream evenly over the risen batter. Do this as gently as possible so as not to deflate it.

8 Lightly press your fingertips into the batter, at regular intervals over the whole surface. Preheat the oven to 400°F (200°C).

9 For the butter topping, beat together the butter, crème pâtissière, and egg yolk. Put into a large pastry bag fitted with a plain tip, and pipe diagonal lines across the surface.

10 To finish, fork the sugars and reserved egg yolk together, and sprinkle over the top along with the almonds. Place in the oven and reduce the temperature to 350°F (175°C).

11 Bake for 40 minutes, then switch off the oven and turn on the broiler (or turn the oven to top heat only and increase the temperature to 425°F/220°C). Toast the top of the cake for 5 minutes. Remove from the oven. Bring the honey and cream to a boil, and brush over the hot cake. Cut into squares before the topping hardens, then let cool in the pan for 30 minutes. This is best eaten freshly made.

Dresden stollen

Christmas stollen first appeared as a festive bread in 1427, in the court of Saxony. This recipe is a modern version, buttery and spicy, and full of nuts, marzipan, and candied fruits. Stollen should be left to mature for 2–3 days before being eaten.

Makes 2

For the fruits

3¼ cups (480g) golden raisins

⅓ cup (60g) chopped candied lemon peel

¾ cup (120g) chopped candied orange peel

1 tbsp dark rum

1 cup (120g) slivered or sliced almonds

2 tsp vanilla extract

3 tbsp water

grated zest of 1 lemon

For the yeast sponge

1⅔ cups (200g) all-purpose flour

1½oz (40g) compressed fresh yeast or 2 envelopes active dry yeast

⅔ cup milk

4 tsp sugar

For the dough

2 cups (250g) all-purpose flour

1 tsp salt

1 medium egg, precise shelled weight 1¾oz (50g)

5½ medium or 5 large egg yolks, precise weight 3oz (80g)

6 tbsp milk

5 tsp sugar

1 tsp apple pie spice

1½ tbsp (20g) cream cheese

5oz (140g) marzipan, diced

½ cup + 2 tbsp (150g) unsalted butter, chilled and diced

pinch of grated lemon zest

few drops of vanilla extract

2 tbsp minced candied orange peel

To finish

1 cup (250g) unsalted butter, clarified (p24)

2 cups confectioners' sugar

Start the day before. Place all the ingredients for the fruits in a bowl. Stir well, then cover and leave at room temperature overnight.

For the yeast sponge, have all the ingredients at room temperature. Sift the flour into the bowl of an electric mixer fitted with the dough hook. Crumble in the fresh yeast, or sprinkle over the dry yeast, and add the milk and sugar. Knead for 15 minutes at slow speed. Cover with a dish towel and let rise in a cool place for at least 30 minutes.

For the dough, sift the flour and salt into a bowl. Add the whole egg and yolks, milk, sugar, spice, and cream cheese. Knead to a very soft dough. Incorporate the yeast sponge and continue kneading for 5 minutes.

Add the marzipan pieces and knead until the mixture rolls off the sides of the bowl. Add the butter, piece by piece, and knead until the mixture is elastic and smooth. Add the lemon zest, vanilla, and orange peel. Knead well.

Turn the dough out onto a floured surface and, with floured hands, knead in the drained, dried fruit mixture. Cover with a dish towel and let rest for 20 minutes. Gently shape the dough into a ball, cover, and leave for 10 minutes longer.

Preheat the oven to 400°F (200°C). Grease a large baking sheet and line with parchment paper. Divide the dough into two pieces. On a floured surface, using a rolling pin, roll out one piece into a rectangle and gently press flat. Fold both long sides into the middle. Then fold in one of the long sides to the middle, curling it over slightly on the top. Repeat this process with the second piece of dough.

Lay the stollen, flat side down, on the prepared baking sheet. Let rest for 5 minutes, then place in the oven. Reduce the temperature to 350°F (175°C) and bake for 50–60 minutes. Transfer the stollen to a wire rack and immediately brush them with clarified butter and dredge with sifted confectioners' sugar.

SMALL CAKES

This section includes some all-time favorites, such as scones, doughnuts, and chocolate-covered oat bars. These small cakes may be less grand than their elaborately decorated sisters, but they make up for this by being some of the most addictive to eat. Who hasn't found it hard to resist yet another chocolate brownie or warm-from-the-oven muffin?

SCONES WITH RAISINS

As traditional as cucumber sandwiches on the tea table, scones originated in Scotland. They taste best filled with strawberry jam and rich clotted cream. Failing that, whipped cream or mascarpone blended with cream also taste good. The raw dough freezes well for up to a month.

Makes 10

¾ cup (115g) raisins
1 cup strong tea, cold
1 tbsp dark rum
2¼ cups (270g) cake flour
¾ cup (90g) all-purpose flour
4 tsp baking powder
7 tbsp (100g) unsalted butter, softened
7 tbsp (85g) sugar
grated zest of ½ lemon
1½ large eggs, lightly beaten together, precise shelled weight 3oz (85g)
7 tbsp milk
1–2 tbsp heavy cream

1 The day before, put the raisins in the tea and rum, and let soak overnight.

2 Sift the two flours and the baking powder together twice, then sift onto a sheet of wax paper. Set aside.

3 In a large mixing bowl, beat together the butter, sugar, and lemon zest until thick and creamy. Mix in the eggs in three stages, then add the milk a little at a time. Stir well until the mixture is smooth and lump-free.

4 Add the sifted flour in stages and knead lightly until smooth and elastic in texture. Mix in the drained raisins. Shape into a ball, wrap in plastic wrap, and refrigerate overnight.

5 The next day, grease a large baking sheet and line it with parchment paper. Roll out the chilled scone dough on a lightly floured surface to a ¾in (2cm) thickness. Preheat the oven to 400°F (210°C).

6 Using a 2½in (6cm) round cutter, stamp out circles. Place them slightly apart on the baking sheet. Lightly beat the cream with a pinch each of salt and sugar. Use this to glaze the tops of the scones. Bake for 15–18 minutes. Cool on a wire rack.

OAT-CRANBERRY BARS

If preferred, you can omit the white chocolate coating. Kept in an airtight tin, the oat bars will keep fresh for 4–5 days.

Makes 16

1 cup (250g) unsalted butter, cut into pieces
⅔ cup (200g) golden syrup
½ cup packed (100g) light brown sugar
3 cups (250g) rolled oats
¾ cup (100g) cake flour, sifted twice
1 cup (150g) dried cranberries
3½oz (100g) white couverture chocolate, finely chopped

1 Grease a deep 9in (23cm) square baking pan and line the bottom with parchment paper. Preheat the oven to 350°F (170°C).

2 Combine the butter, golden syrup, and brown sugar in a small pan and melt gently over low heat until foaming.

3 In a mixing bowl, stir together the oats, flour, and cranberries. Add the warm butter and sugar mixture and blend well. Press the mixture into the lined pan and bake for 25–30 minutes. Let cool. Cut into small rectangles.

4 Melt the chocolate pieces in a heatproof bowl set over a pan of barely simmering water. Pour half of the melted chocolate onto a clean marble slab or stone surface. Cool it down by tempering it (moving the chocolate back and forth using a scraper until it firms up.

5 Before it hardens, scrape the chocolate back into the pan (off the heat) and gently stir to combine; the chocolate should be no warmer than 84°F (29°C). Repeat the tempering process. When ready to use, if the chocolate has cooled too much, put the bowl back over the hot water.

6 Dip each oat bar diagonally into the chocolate, then let set on a wire rack covered with parchment paper.

SOUR CREAM DOUGHNUTS

Purists argue whether a true doughnut is raised with yeast or baking powder. The yeasted version comes from 18th-century Austria. This recipe, made with baking powder, takes much less time to prepare. Eat the doughnuts on the day they are made.

Makes 28

3½ cups (440g) all-purpose flour

1 tsp salt

pinch of grated nutmeg

1 tbsp baking powder

2 medium eggs, precise shelled weight 3½oz (100g)

1¼ cups (250g) granulated sugar

scant 1 cup (200g) sour cream

3 tbsp whole milk

3 tbsp (45g) unsalted butter, melted

1 tbsp orange marmalade, strained

2 tsp grated orange zest

peanut oil for deep-frying

confectioners' sugar for dusting

VARIATION

The doughnuts are also good coated with shredded coconut. Alternatively, brush them with strained apricot jam and coat with glacé icing or melted semisweet chocolate.

Dust the warm doughnuts with confectioners' sugar

1 Sift together the flour, salt, nutmeg, and baking powder twice, then sift again onto a sheet of wax paper. Set aside.

2 Beat the eggs in a large bowl, then beat in the sugar, 1 tbsp at a time, until pale, thick, and creamy. Stir in the sour cream, milk, butter, marmalade, and grated orange zest. Blend well.

3 Carefully fold in spoonfuls of the flour mixture until just combined. With lightly floured hands, shape the dough into a ball, cover with a dish towel, and let rest in a cool place for 20 minutes.

4 Roll out the dough to a 2in (5cm) thickness. Using a 2½in (6cm) cutter, cut out large circles, then stamp out the centers with a ⅝in (1.5cm) cutter. Gather up the scraps, knead together, roll out, and cut out more rings.

5 Heat oil for deep-frying to 350°F (180°C). Gently add the doughnuts to the hot oil, two or three at a time. They must not touch each other in the pan. Fry until they are golden brown, about 1½ minutes on each side. Lift out and drain on paper towels.

BROWNIES WITH CHEESECAKE FILLING

Who created brownies? Folklore suggests that a Miss Brown, a librarian in Maine, forgot to add baking powder to her chocolate cake batter. It came out of the oven completely flat. Despite this, she served it to her friends, who loved it. The test of time and the huge popularity of brownies have overcome all professional criticism. These will keep fresh for one week.

Makes 24

For the cheese filling

1 cup (250g) cream cheese, at room temperature

½ cup (140g) farmer cheese, pressed through a strainer

5 tbsp (60g) sugar

2 tbsp (15g) cake flour

1 medium egg, precise shelled weight 1¾oz (50g)

2½ medium egg yolks, beaten together, precise weight 1½oz (40g)

For the brownie batter

1¾ cups (200g) dry-roasted (p480) and coarsely chopped pecans

1⅔ cups (200g) cake flour, sifted twice and then into a bowl

6 medium eggs, precise shelled weight 10oz (300g)

2¼ cups (450g) sugar

7oz (200g) best-quality bittersweet chocolate (70% cocoa solids), finely chopped

1⅓ cups (300g) unsalted butter

For the glaze

6 tbsp (85g) unsalted butter, diced

½ cup water

8oz (250g) best-quality bittersweet chocolate, finely chopped

1 Grease an 11 by 9 by 1⅜in (28 by 23 by 4cm) cake or baking pan with butter and line the bottom with parchment paper. Preheat the oven to 350°F (170°C).

2 For the cheese filling, stir all ingredients together in a large bowl. Cover and set aside.

3 For the brownie batter, stir the nuts into the flour. Put the eggs in a separate large bowl with a pinch of salt and 1 cup (200g) of the sugar. Beat together until pale and foamy, then gradually beat in the rest of the sugar.

4 Melt the chocolate pieces in a heatproof bowl set over a pan of barely simmering water. Heat the butter until foaming, then stir in the melted chocolate and stir until the temperature has dropped to 104°F (40°C). Let cool.

5 Stir 2–3 tbsp of the egg mixture into the chocolate mixture to lighten it, then fold in the remaining egg mixture with a rubber spatula, taking care not to lose air. Fold in the flour and pecan mixture a spoonful at a time. Pour into the prepared pan.

6 Put the cheese filling into a large pastry bag fitted with a plain tip. Pipe blobs, ¾in (2cm) deep, into the chocolate mixture, close together, at regular intervals.

7 Bake until the center of the cake starts to thicken and set, 35–40 minutes. Remove from the oven and let cool in the pan.

8 To make the glaze, put the butter and water into a pan and bring just to a boil. Spoon the chopped chocolate pieces into the center, remove from the heat, and leave for a few moments.

9 Using a rubber spatula and working from the middle, start stirring, gradually drawing the liquid into the chocolate. Always work from the center out. Stir until well blended, taking care not to beat in air while stirring. The glaze will develop a slight sheen.

10 Spread in a smooth layer on the surface of the brownie cake, then drag a decorating comb or a fork across it in a wavy line. To serve, cut in squares using a knife dipped in hot water.

APRICOT MUFFINS

Muffins made with yeast originated in England, where they were very popular during the 19th century. American muffins, which are much more like cakes than their English cousins, are occasionally yeast-raised, but are more likely to be leavened with baking powder.

Makes 10

2 cups (250g) dried apricots, finely chopped

½ cup fresh orange juice, strained

3 cups (375g) all-purpose flour

4 tsp baking powder

½ cup (125g) unsalted butter, diced and softened

½ cup + 2 tbsp (125g) sugar

2 large eggs, beaten together, precise shelled weight 4oz (110g)

1 cup plain yogurt

grated zest of 1 orange

1 Put the apricots and orange juice in a bowl and let soak for at least 3 hours.

2 Preheat the oven to 400°F (200°C). Grease a standard 12-muffin pan with butter. Sift the flour and baking powder twice, then sift again onto a sheet of wax paper. Set aside.

3 In a large bowl, beat together the butter, sugar, and a pinch of salt until light and fluffy. Add the eggs to the mixture in three stages, beating well between each addition. If the mixture curdles, stir in a small amount of flour to bind. Add the yogurt, orange zest, and drained apricots, and stir lightly together until just mixed.

4 Gently mix in the flour until just blended. Avoid overmixing, because it will make the batter heavy. Spoon into 10 of the muffin cups and pour a little water into the two empty cups.

5 Reduce the oven temperature to 350°F (180°C) and bake the muffins until well risen and golden, about 25 minutes.

PERFECT MUFFINS

■ Butter the muffin pan, then place it in the freezer briefly. Having the pan very cold and the butter set before the batter is poured in will make the baked muffins pop out of the cups more easily.
■ Steam from the water in the empty cups makes the baked muffins soft, light, and moist.

6 To test if the muffins are done, stick a toothpick into the center of one of them: It should come out completely clean and dry.

7 Remove the pan from the oven and leave on a damp cloth for 5 minutes. (This makes it easier to unmold the muffins from the pan.) Eat on the day of baking.

FRUIT & NUTS

SHAUN HILL

Today, fruit has a healthy aura, but it was not always so. In Roman times, fruits, especially soft fruit, were regarded with some disdain. The great physician Galen saw moist fruits as little better than a laxative, claiming that their nutrients are easily leeched away. In fact, fruits are among the few foodstuffs that evolved to attract the hungry, their perfume and sweetness being nature's way of enticing those creatures able to eat them and distribute their seeds. Before Adam's unfortunate episode with the apple, fruits were the nourishment of the Garden of Eden.

Seasonal fare Fruits and nuts are emblems of their seasons. Just as the first strawberries represent all the freshness and vitality of early summer, apples are as much wedded in the mind with Halloween as pumpkins and ghosts, and nuts, tangerines, dates, and figs with Christmas. The recipes and dishes that have developed around specific fruits reflect the seasonal desire for appropriate fare. Most apple and pear dishes are served hot rather than cold, whereas fresh drupe fruits and berries are associated more with light desserts and refreshing ice creams.

Dried fruits such as figs, dates, apricots, raisins, and currants are pantry items, ingredients for winter cakes and desserts. Candied and preserved drupe fruits such as cherries are also welcome by-products of the pre-freezer era, ingredients that brighten up a range of winter dishes and closely linked in most people's minds with Christmas feasting.

All-year availability Fruits have their seasons, but many of us expect to eat all kinds of fruits and nuts year round. While most fruits naturally ripen on the bush or tree, imported fruit has to be gathered under-ripe to survive the long journey from grower to kitchen. Of course, these fruits continue to ripen after purchase and, if kept too long or in overly warm conditions, will overripen and spoil. This process can be slowed by chilling the fruit and by isolating it from other fruits, since gases given off by ripening fruit help to ripen the fruit around them. Conversely, you can speed up the ripening process by placing ripe fruits with unripe ones.

While it is convenient to buy fruits according to whim, the shopper has to be alert to practices that favor those supplying fruit, rather than those buying and eating it. Irradiation of soft fruit in countries where this is permitted encourages lazy handling and storage. Excessive spraying with pesticides is a menace in foodstuffs that are likely to be eaten raw. Even the standard treatment of citrus fruits makes it necessary for organic or unwaxed fruit to be specified if the peel is to be used in the recipe. Genetic engineering and changes in horticultural technique have extended the season for most soft fruits and, while the result has been cheaper fruits and better availability, there is a danger of less prolific fruit varieties becoming rare, as we select newer strains that crop more heavily or store better, but possibly have inferior flavor and character.

The value of nuts Unlike fruits, nuts are more often used as ingredients than served as a separate course in a meal. In the past, some nuts played a much more significant part in the diet—even the humble acorn was ground and used as a flour substitute when food was short. Acorn flour is rarely on offer now, but you can buy chestnut flour in Italian shops for making into fritters and cakes.

Many nuts are now cultivated primarily for their oil. For a long time peanut oil was a staple kitchen ingredient, but the burgeoning sensitivity of many people to nut products has reduced its importance. Walnut oil is second only to olive oil as a salad dressing ingredient, and hazelnut, coconut, and almond oils are all used to flavor both sweet and savory dishes.

Nuts are high in oil and vitamin B, and, like anything oily, turn rancid if stored badly or for too long. The best way to keep nuts is to refrigerate them in their shells, sealed in glass or plastic containers to avoid being tainted by other odors. Almonds and cashews are among the most hardy; walnuts and pecans are most prone to deterioration in storage.

PREPARING FRESH FRUIT

Fruit has evolved to be eaten. When it is ripe, it is at its best and little of the chef's art is called for to improve matters. The citrus family forms segments and all members are easily tackled in the same way as oranges. Fruit that is difficult to peel, such as peaches, can be dropped into boiling water for a few moments to blanch and loosen the skin for easy removal.

SECTIONING AN ORANGE

1 With a sharp knife, cut a small piece of peel from the top and base of the orange. Hold the orange firmly with a fork, or your other hand, and slice down and around the flesh. Try to take off as much pith as possible. Use a small knife to cut away any left clinging to the fruit.

2 The orange will now show the contours of each section, separated from the next by a membrane. Cut into and along the edge of a section. Cut the section back along its outer edge, leaving behind the membrane, so that it is freed. Repeat this process with all the sections.

CUTTING PINEAPPLE RINGS & CHUNKS

1 Cut off the stalky top and then the base of the pineapple. Stand the fruit upright on the cutting board, then slice off the skin in long strips, cutting from top to bottom. Follow the contour of the pineapple so that no flesh is cut off where the fruit bulges toward the middle.

2 For pineapple rings, turn the fruit on its side and cut into slices of the desired thickness. Take a small, round cutter and cut out the hard center of each slice. For pineapple chunks, cut the fruit into thicker slices, remove the hard centers, and cut into sections.

PREPARING A MANGO

Mangoes must be ripe and sweet, unless they are an ingredient in a savory stew or chutney. It is not necessary to peel them to get at the flesh—I think the best way to prepare cubes of mango is the one shown below. In Britain, we call this making a mango "hedgehog."

1 Stand the fruit on its side and slice down and into the middle, until you meet the large, flat pit. Continue cutting around the pit and down to the cutting board. Repeat to cut away the flesh from the other side of the pit.

2 Place each mango "half" flesh-side up. Cut the flesh lengthwise into strips, then cut across the strips. Do not cut through the skin. Press the skin side of the mango half so that the fruit bursts upward into cubes.

REMOVING POMEGRANATE SEEDS

Cut the fruit in half and carefully scoop out the seeds with a teaspoon. The pithy membrane is bitter, so discard this.

PEELING PEACHES OR NECTARINES

1 With a small, sharp knife, cut a small cross in the skin on the base of the fruit.

2 Immerse the fruit in boiling water for 30 seconds. Remove from the water and pull off the skin with your fingers.

PREPARING GOOSEBERRIES

With a sharp knife or scissors, cut off both ends. Frozen gooseberries are already "topped and tailed," but you still need to remove any stalky pieces for a smooth dessert like gooseberry fool.

PURÉEING FRUIT

Soft fruits like raspberries and strawberries need no cooking before being puréed. Most other fruits need to be braised or poached first, to soften them. This gives an opportunity for judicious spicing and for the sweetness of the fruit to be altered to suit the treatment —ice creams need more sugar than a mousse that is served at room temperature, and ripe fruit needs little sweetening.

GOOSEBERRY FOOL

There are differing degrees of smoothness desirable in a fruit purée, from the completely smooth and homogenous result of a blender to mashing in a food mill or pressing the cooked fruit through a coarse strainer. Gooseberry fool is best made with the latter method, because the texture and specks of fruit still remaining are part of the dessert's appeal.

Most gooseberries need to be cooked with sugar. They turn yellow during the process and their firm texture softens—not an aesthetic improvement, but essential to a successful fool. Gooseberries have an affinity with elderflowers, which blossom at the same time, so a few drops of elderflower syrup work well in this or any other gooseberry dish. Rhubarb makes an excellent alternative to gooseberries.

Serves 4–6

1lb 2oz (500g) gooseberries
4 tsp unsalted butter
1 cup sugar
few drops of elderflower syrup (optional)
1¼ cups heavy cream

1 Prepare the gooseberries (p465). In a heavy-based saucepan, heat them gently with the butter and sugar. Once the gooseberries start to cook, they produce plenty of liquid. If they or the sugar catch on the bottom of the pan before softening, they will caramelize to produce a different flavor from that wanted, so keep the heat low. Cook until soft, 10–15 minutes.

2 Mash the cooked fruit or press through a coarse strainer, then let cool. Add a few drops of elderflower syrup, if using.

3 Whip the cream until it is thick but not fully whipped. Fold in the fruit purée. Check for sweetness—a tart-sweet, refreshing flavor is the objective—then spoon or pipe into glasses and refrigerate until needed.

BANANA MOUSSE

The smooth purée achieved by a blender is called for here, and also the use of gelatin to set the mousse properly (most mousses are set with gelatin). Use as little as possible so that the finished mousse is soft and delicate rather than rubbery. For a more complex dish with varying textures, you could combine a fruit mousse with a layer of the same fruit in jelled form (p468).

Serves 4–6

8oz (250g) ripe bananas

juice of 1 lemon

juice of 1 orange

½ cup + 2 tbsp sugar

2 tbsp crème de banane liqueur

1 tbsp water

3 sheets of gelatin, soaked for 10 minutes, then squeezed dry

1½ cups heavy cream

1 Peel the bananas and cut into pieces. Purée in a blender with the fruit juices and sugar.

2 Warm the water and crème de banane, then, off the heat, stir in the soaked gelatin. When the gelatin has completely melted, stir the mixture into the puréed fruit. Whip the cream until thick but not fully whipped, then fold it into the fruit purée. Spoon the mousse into individual ramekins or dishes of your choice and refrigerate until set.

USING GELATIN

Unflavored gelatin comes in two forms: clear, paper-thin sheets or leaves and granules or powder. Whichever kind you use, it needs the same treatment: It must be softened in a little cold liquid before being dissolved in warm, but not boiling, liquid. Gelatin is added to warm liquid so that it will melt and disperse evenly before the dessert is chilled and set.

Sheet gelatin is less easy to find than powdered, but it produces smoother, clearer results. Look for sheet gelatin in gourmet and specialty food or baking stores.

Sheet gelatin

1 Soak the sheets of gelatin in cold water to cover for at least 10 minutes. Then gently squeeze out as much water as possible.

2 Warm water or a flavored liquid in a small pan. Remove from the heat and add the gelatin. Stir until completely melted.

Powdered gelatin

A ¼-oz envelope of powdered unflavored gelatin, which contains 1 scant tbsp, is equivalent to 4 sheets of gelatin. Sprinkle powdered gelatin over cold liquid (about ¼ cup for 1 envelope) and let soften for 3–5 minutes.

JELLED FRUIT DESSERTS

For success, you need just enough liquid, at a high enough temperature, to melt the gelatin. Too much gelatin and the dessert will set like rubber; too little and it may not set at all. In the past, jelled or gelatin desserts were made too hard in order to produce molded shapes for buffets or table decoration, and it may be memories of these chewy and wildly colored confections that lowered their popularity. The vegetable counterpart—aspic—has suffered a fall from grace for the same reasons. The best advice is to err on the side of softness and refrigerate the dessert until it is to be eaten, rather than trying to display it.

ROSÉ WINE GELATIN WITH BERRIES

All rosé wines will work in this recipe, but the style and weight of the finished dish will be affected by your choice. I have used hefty Californian blush wines as well as fruity Anjou and Australian rosés. The wine need not be extra sweet—in fact, it is its tartness balanced by sugar that produces the right effect. The fragile nature of berries are well served by this treatment.

The recipe makes enough for six 5oz (150ml) dishes, and the gelatin can be eaten from the dishes or unmolded onto serving plates.

Serves 6

3 cups rosé wine

3 cups sugar

8 sheets of gelatin, soaked for 10 minutes, then squeezed dry

6 heaped tbsp mixed blueberries, raspberries, and blackberries

1 Heat the wine and sugar in a pan to boiling point. Remove from the heat and stir in the gelatin until melted. Let the wine syrup cool to lukewarm, then pour a ⅛in (3mm) layer into each dish. Refrigerate until this starts to set.

2 Spoon the fruit on top of the layer of set gelatin. Pour on the remaining cool wine syrup and refrigerate overnight. Serve with cream or ice cream, if desired.

POACHING FRUIT

Poaching is an extension of the ripening process, with the fruit intensifying in flavor but deteriorating in texture. It also gives an opportunity to add complementary flavors, such as vanilla to pears or sweet wine to plums. There are two main categories of poached fruit. In compotes, the fruit retains its shape, while in dishes like summer pudding and rote grütze, any loss of texture is more than compensated for by the juices and extra flavor. Larger fruits are suited to poaching as compote: apples, pears, and quinces in the fall; apricots, peaches, and plums in summer. The sweeter the syrup used to cook the fruit, the better it will retain its shape.

SUMMER PUDDING

The essence of summer, this dessert contains whatever summer fruits are at their best and transforms them by first poaching, then pressing in white bread. The bread becomes saturated with the warm fruit juices and, when chilled, tastes completely of these fruits, lending just texture and body to the finished dish. My own fruit preference is to add pitted cherries to the mixture—berries soften completely, losing all texture, and currants can feel almost gritty if used to excess. The objectives are a deep red color, fruitiness, and a touch of tartness to balance the sweetness of the sugar and ripe fruit.

2¼lb (1kg) fruit, such as raspberries, pitted cherries, and red currants; peaches, plums, black currants, and strawberries can also be used

1¼ cups sugar

1 loaf of white bread, sliced and crusts removed

2 Cut a disk of white bread to fit in the bottom of a steamed-pudding basin or other mold. Cut the remaining bread into triangles. Dip these in the fruit juice, then use to line the basin evenly. Pour in the fruit and remaining juice. Cover the basin with more slices of bread.

3 Place a small plate on top of the pudding and weight down. Set in a dish to catch any drips of juice. Once cool, refrigerate the pudding. Leave at least overnight, or preferably for a few days, before unmolding and serving in wedges with whipped cream.

POINTS TO WATCH

■ The fruit must produce enough juice to soak the bread completely. Should you be short of juice at the crucial moment, heat a few more raspberries in sugar and water to produce the extra juice needed.

■ The pudding shouldn't be overly sweet. Err on the side of less sugar and adjust while the poached fruits are still hot enough to dissolve any additional sugar required.

■ The flavor of summer pudding develops over a few days, as the bread and juices combine, so it is best made well in advance.

1 Toss the fruit with the sugar in a pot, then gently bring to a boil, stirring to prevent burning. Simmer gently until plenty of juice is produced, about 2 minutes. Add more sugar, if necessary, or a few drops of lemon juice if too sweet.

ROTE GRÜTZE (RASPBERRY PUDDING)

This German name translates as "red grits" or "red gruel." Not the marketing man's ideal title, is it the stuff of nostalgia for many nonetheless. Throughout Germany, Austria, and Denmark, there are many variations, some thickened with sago starch, some with gelatin, and some with cornstarch. This recipe uses potato flour, sometimes sold by its French name "fécule de pommes de terre." Raspberries are the only essential ingredient, with whatever else you want to keep them company. The objective is a slightly thickened pudding with a consistency almost like oatmeal.

2 tbsp potato flour

1¼ cups water

2 cups raspberries

1½ cups red currants

¾ cup sugar

squeeze of lemon juice

few drops of vanilla extract

1 Combine the potato flour and ¾ cup of the water in a small bowl and whisk to dissolve. Bring the fruit, sugar, and remaining water to a boil in a medium saucepan.

2 Whisk the flour solution again, then stir into the fruit. Bring back to a boil to thicken. Add the lemon juice and vanilla extract. Decant into a serving dish and cool.

FIG COMPOTE

If fruit is to be kept for any time, they have to be preserved to stay in perfect condition. For this compote of figs, use heat-resistant canning jars that have a rubber seal, and wash and sterilize the jars before use. Most fruits with a reasonably firm texture can be substituted for the figs. Pears and peaches work very well. Like figs, they need to be poached until tender. Cherries can be made into compote without poaching. The flavor of the syrup can be tailored to your own taste by adding, say, preserved ginger to syrup for pears or vanilla to syrup for cherries.

4 cups water

2½ cups sugar

1 tsp lemon juice

3 cinnamon sticks

6½lb (3kg) figs, stems removed and poached in water to cover until tender, 10–15 minutes, then drained

1 Bring the water, sugar, lemon, and cinnamon to a boil. Fill the sterilized jars with the poached figs, then pour in the hot syrup.

2 Seal the jars and place in a pan half-full of water. Bring to a boil, then cover and reduce the heat. Simmer for 5 minutes. Let cool.

Poached pears with cinnamon ice cream

The choice of pear variety is important for this dessert: Bartlett pears are the best suited to poaching. The recipe works equally well made with red wine, but produces a slightly different dish—not just darker, but with the wine dominating the delicate pear flavor. The ice cream recipe produces about 1 quart (1 liter). It may be more than needed, but it is really not worth making less. If you do not have an ice cream machine, whisk periodically while the ice cream is freezing, to break up the ice crystals. Made this way it will have the texture of a parfait rather than ice cream.

Be sure the pears are covered with poaching syrup so they don't discolor

4 small or 2 large, firm or under-ripe pears

2 cups white wine

6 tbsp sugar

strip of lemon peel

For the ice cream

2½ cups whole milk

1¼ cups heavy cream

1¼ cups sugar

4 cinnamon sticks, broken into pieces

1 vanilla bean, halved lengthwise

6 egg yolks

Peel the pears. If they are large enough to make two portions apiece, then core and halve them. Place the pears in a saucepan and add the wine, sugar, lemon peel, and enough water to cover the fruit. Bring to a boil, then immediately reduce the heat to a simmer. Cover and poach until soft, 15–20 minutes—the timing will vary with the size, variety, and ripeness of the pears. Let the pears cool in the poaching liquid.

For the ice cream, heat the milk and cream with 3 tbsp of the sugar, the cinnamon, and vanilla. Bring to just below boiling point, then cover and let infuse off the heat for about 20 minutes.

Whisk the remaining sugar with the egg yolks in a bowl. Reheat the milk mixture to near boiling point, then whisk slowly into the egg and sugar mixture. Return the mixture to a clean saucepan, preferably one with rounded edges so that the custard does not coagulate in the corners. Stir slowly over a low heat until the custard thickens perceptibly, 5–8 minutes. The custard must not come to a boil or it will curdle.

Strain the custard into a bowl and let cool, then chill, preferably overnight. When very cold, churn in an ice cream machine.

Serve each pear next to or fanned across a scoop of the ice cream, with the poaching liquid as a sauce.

BAKING FRUIT

Peaches and nectarines are well suited to baking (or roasting with a coating of oil or butter to caramelize the outside), but the star baking performer is the apple. The finest cooking apple variety in Britain is the Bramley. It is the fruit equivalent of a floury baking potato—the flesh disintegrates into a soft, tart mush during baking and takes on the flavor of whatever sugars, dried fruit, and spices with it. In North America, for baking choose a variety of apple that is firm, tart, and characterful, such as Rome Beauty or McIntosh.

BAKED APPLES

4 firm, tart apples
¼ cup sugar
1 tsp ground cinnamon
1 tbsp golden raisins

1 Preheat the oven to 375°F (190°C). Core the apples, stopping just short of the base, but do not peel them. Mix the sugar, cinnamon, and raisins together and use to fill each core cavity.

2 Make a small incision around the middle of each apple to prevent it from bursting. Place in a baking dish or pan and bake for 1 hour. Serve with whipped cream or ice cream.

BAKED PEACHES WITH AMARETTI

In Italy, roasting and baking are regular treatments for peaches. This recipe fills peach halves with ground amaretti cookies, which are usually sold attractively wrapped in pairs, like candy.

4 ripe peaches

8 amaretti cookies

¼ cup sugar

seeds from 1 vanilla bean (p89)

1 egg yolk

2 tbsp unsalted butter

1 Preheat the oven to 375°F (190°C). Cut the peaches in half and remove the pits. Enlarge the space left by the pits by removing 1 tsp of peach flesh from each half; reserve this. Grind the cookies to the consistency of fine crumbs in a food processor. Take care not to overprocess.

2 Mix the peach pulp, sugar, vanilla seeds, and egg yolk with the amaretti crumbs. Butter a baking dish and place the peaches cut-side up in the dish. Spoon the amaretti mixture into the cavities in the peach halves and dot with the butter. Bake until the peaches are soft and the filling crusty, about 40 minutes. Serve hot.

FRYING FRUIT

Banana and pineapple are often served as fritters, but apples, pears, peaches, rhubarb, and oranges work just as well. A light batter is essential to success, and the fritters should be dry and crisp with no hint of greasiness. A bland oil, such as sunflower or corn oil, works best for frying fritters, as it provides no additional flavor. These oils also have high smoke points—they survive high temperatures before burning. Heat the oil to about 375°F (190°C). When the oil is hot, its surface should be still and not giving off any sign of smoke. If the oil becomes too hot, correct it by adding a little more oil.

BANANA OR PINEAPPLE FRITTERS

Fritters rarely suit an accompanying sauce—certainly never a custard—and are best just dusted with granulated or confectioners' sugar before serving. This still leaves scope for vanilla or cinnamon sugar, if that partners the fruit in question to its advantage.

6 bananas or 12 pineapple rings

¼ cup granulated sugar

2 tbsp kirsch (optional)

oil for deep-frying

For the batter

⅔ cup low-fat milk or water

1 cup self-rising flour

1 tbsp olive oil

2 egg whites

1 tsp superfine sugar

1 For the batter, mix the milk or water, flour, and oil together until smooth. In a separate bowl, beat the egg whites until stiff. Add a pinch of salt and the sugar to the egg whites at the final stages of beating. Fold the egg whites into the milk, flour, and oil mixture.

2 Sprinkle the fruit with the sugar and the kirsch (if using), then dip into the batter. Fry in hot oil until golden brown, 3–5 minutes. Drain.

STEAMED & BOILED PUDDINGS

Steamed puddings and dumplings are made from similar mixtures of flour and fat as puddings that are baked. But steaming is a slower process, and you will need to check water levels in the pan or steamer regularly to be sure that it hasn't boiled dry. The size of the pudding and its content will decide cooking times—a family-sized Christmas or plum pudding will need 6 hours or more.

PLUM DUMPLINGS

This is a Hungarian dish in which the plums are covered in a potato dough and then boiled. In Hungary, they roll the dumplings in fried bread crumbs, but for me this is too hefty.

8 plums

¼ cup granulated sugar

1 tsp ground cinnamon

1lb 2oz (500g) potatoes, peeled and boiled

2 tbsp butter, softened

1 egg

¾ cup all-purpose flour

1 tbsp ground poppy seeds

1 tbsp confectioners' sugar, sifted

1 Dig out the plum pits with a sharp knife and fill the plums with the sugar and cinnamon. Rice the potatoes into a bowl. Using a fork, mix in the butter, egg, and a pinch of salt.

2 Add as much flour as needed to form a firm dough, then roll it out as thinly as possible and cut into eight squares. Wrap each plum in a dough square and seal all the edges. Drop the dumplings into a pan of boiling water and cook until they rise to the top, about 5 minutes.

3 Lift out the dumplings with a slotted spoon and dust with a mixture of ground poppy seeds and confectioners' sugar.

STICKY TOFFEE PUDDING

This dessert comes from the late Francis Coulson of Sharrow Bay in England's Lake District. He may have invented the recipe or collected it locally. However it originated, it is now standard in the UK.

Serves 6

For the sponge cake batter

5 tbsp unsalted butter

1 cup sugar

3 eggs

1½ cups self-rising flour, sifted

1½ cups water

1 heaped cup coarsely chopped dates

1½ tsp baking powder

For the sauce

⅓ cup packed dark brown or Demerara sugar

1¼ cups heavy cream or condensed milk

4 tbsp unsalted butter

1 Preheat the oven to 400°F (200°C). To make the batter, cream together the butter and sugar until fluffy. Beat in the eggs, then fold in the flour. Bring the water to a boil in a small pan. Add the chopped dates and simmer for 2 minutes, until soft. Remove from the heat and add the baking powder.

2 Stir the date mixture into the batter, then pour into a deep, 9in (23cm) square baking dish. Bake until set, about 30 minutes.

3 Stir all the sauce ingredients together in a pan and bring to a boil. Pour half of the sauce onto the cake, then put it back into the oven for 2 minutes so the sauce can soak in. Cut into squares and serve with the remaining sauce.

Steamed orange pudding

This traditional British steamed pudding is usually made with suet (hard kidney fat), but a softer, lighter texture can be obtained with butter. This recipe calls for individual molds, of a size and type sometimes known as dariole molds. Alternatively, the batter can be steamed in a larger steamed-pudding basin, then divided into portions for serving. In a larger mold it will need longer cooking, about 1½ hours. If you don't have a steamer, or your steamer is too small, place the molds in a roasting pan half-filled with boiling water and bake in a preheated 400°F (200°C) oven for 40 minutes.

Spoon the batter on top of the syrup

7 tbsp unsalted butter, softened

½ cup sugar

⅔ cup self-rising flour

½ tsp baking powder

2 eggs

2 tbsp low-fat milk

grated zest and juice of 2 oranges

4 tbsp golden syrup or light corn syrup

cream or crème anglaise (p420) for serving

Cream the butter and sugar together until fluffy, then mix in the flour and baking powder. Beat in the eggs, one at a time, then add the milk and orange zest and juice.

Butter the inside of four dariole molds or ramekin dishes. Put 1 tbsp of golden syrup in each mold, then pour in the batter. Cover the molds with foil.

Place the molds on the rack of a steamer over boiling water and steam for 40 minutes. Unmold the puddings into warmed bowls. Serve with cream or crème anglaise, if desired.

NUTS FOR SWEET USE

The most versatile nuts for candies and deserts are almonds—sweetened almond preparations are a cornerstone of every classic pastry and confectionery kitchen. Both almonds and walnuts can be made into a "milk" by finely grinding the nuts and steeping in boiling water, then straining (see below). Vegans and those with dairy allergies can use a nut milk like soymilk.

PREPARING ALMONDS

You can buy almonds already blanched and skinned, sliced, chopped, and ground, but it is easy to prepare them yourself. Dry-roasting (p480) intensifies their flavor and adds crunch.

Blanching

1 Place the almonds in a bowl and cover with boiling water. Leave them for 2–3 minutes, then drain in a colander. Set aside until the almonds are cool enough to handle.

2 Pinch each almond between your thumbs and index fingers to slip the nut out of the skin. Alternatively, rub the nuts in a kitchen towel (p478) to remove the skins.

Slicing

Use a large, sharp knife and hold each nut flat on the cutting board. Cut into slices of the required thickness. To sliver almonds, cut each slice lengthwise into fine sticks.

Chopping

Using a large, sharp knife, chop the nuts into pieces of the required size—coarse or fine—guiding the knife with your knuckles. Other nuts can be chopped in the same way.

Grinding

Grind almonds (and other nuts) in a rotary nut mill or food processor to the consistency of fine bread crumbs. If using a food processor, take care not to overprocess, as nuts release their natural oils during grinding and you could end up with a nut butter.

Making almond milk

Put ground almonds in a bowl and cover with double their volume of boiling water. Let steep, covered, for 30 minutes. Pour the mixture into a fine-mesh strainer held over a bowl. Press the ground nuts in the strainer to extract all of the milk, then discard the nuts.

PRALINE

As in any specialized craft, there is a jargon used in pastrymaking. A mixture of caramelized sugar and almonds is known as croquant or nougat, and is used for petits fours (small fancy cookies) and to make baskets to serve them in. Once crushed or ground into a paste, croquant changes its name to praline, which flavors tarts, soufflés, and ice cream.

2½ cups sugar

juice of ½ lemon

4 cups sliced almonds or 2 cups chopped almonds

1 Stir the sugar and lemon juice in a pot over a gentle heat until the sugar melts into syrup. (A few drops of water may make this easier, but slows the process, as the water has to evaporate before the sugar will caramelize.) Bring the melted sugar to a boil, then cook until pale amber in color, about 20 minutes.

2 Warm the almonds, then add them to the sugar and cook for a moment. Pour the mixture into an oiled pan, and let cool and set.

3 Grind the croquant in a food processor or mill. The resulting paste is praline.

BAKED ALMOND PUDDING

Bitter almonds, which have a stronger flavor than sweet almonds, are not available for sale in the U.S. and Canada. However, bitter almond extract can be found, and this can add depth to a sweet almond preparation. If you can track down bitter almond extract, add a few drops to the batter for this dessert.

½ cup + 1 tbsp unsalted butter, melted
3 cups ground almonds
2 tbsp heavy cream
1 tbsp Cognac
grated zest of ½ lemon
⅓ cup sugar plus extra for sprinkling
2 eggs
2 egg yolks

1 Preheat the oven to 375°F (190°C). In a mixing bowl, stir together the melted butter, almonds, cream, Cognac, lemon zest, and sugar. Stir in the whole eggs and yolks.

2 Oil or butter a shallow baking dish and pour in the batter. Bake for 40 minutes. Sprinkle with sugar before serving.

NOUGAT MONTELIMAR

In my childhood, this confection was sold in candy stores everywhere. It has improved its status in the meantime and can now be found gracing the petits fours selection in grand restaurants. The recipe calls for pistachio nuts. The unsalted variety—which is what you need—comes shelled, but with a pale outer skin that has to be removed (see below). Use the bright green nuts whole. You need edible rice paper (or plastic wrap) to line the pan.

Makes about 2¼lb (1kg)

2 cups sugar
½ cup water
⅓ cup clear honey
1 tbsp liquid glucose or light corn syrup
1½ egg whites, precise weight 1½oz (45g)
⅓ cup coarsely chopped candied cherries
½ cup shelled unsalted pistachio nuts
⅓ cup sliced almonds
¼ cup coarsely chopped almonds

SKINNING PISTACHIOS

Blanch as for almonds (p476), then rub the skins off between sheets of paper towel or a dish towel.

1 Dissolve the sugar in the water in a pot, then bring rapidly to a boil. Boil until the syrup reaches 224°F (107°C). The water will have evaporated by this stage, and the hot, liquid sugar will have begun a series of changes that thicken and eventually color it. At this point it should not show any sign of caramelization.

2 Add the honey and glucose, and boil until the syrup reaches 275°F (135°C). Beat the egg white to stiff peaks. Remove the syrup from the heat and spoon the egg white on top, beating constantly. This is best done with a portable electric mixer at maximum speed.

3 Warm the cherries and nuts, then stir into the mixture. Line a shallow pan with rice paper. Pour the nougat into the pan and spread evenly, then cover with more rice paper. Press the surface with a weighted flat board and let cool overnight. To serve, cut the nougat into small rectangles with a knife dipped in hot water.

Serve nougat with the rice paper attached

NUTS FOR USE IN SAVORY DISHES

Many nuts can be used in savory dishes as well as sweet ones. Hazelnuts, for instance, can be toasted and then tossed with Brussels sprouts to partner game or poultry, or ground and used to flavor meringues. Nuts can also be used as a flour substitute or in stuffings. Bear in mind when substituting ground nuts for any dry ingredient that their natural oils will soften the texture of the dish.

CRACKING HARD-SHELLED NUTS

You need a nutcracker to crack the hard shells of nuts such as pecans, walnuts, and Brazil nuts. Use a small hammer for macadamias.

DRY-ROASTING OR TOASTING NUTS

Browning nuts enriches their flavor and makes them more crunchy. This method is also used for removing the papery skins from hazelnuts, walnuts, and peanuts. Spread the nuts in a baking pan and dry-roast in a preheated 350°F (180°C) oven, or under the broiler, until golden, 7–12 minutes. Shake the pan frequently to turn the nuts. To remove skins, wrap the nuts in a coarse kitchen cloth and rub vigorously.

PARSLEY & SCALLION TART WITH WALNUT PASTRY

Substituting ground walnuts for some of the flour in this pastry imparts an interesting taste and texture. The pastry is easier to handle if made in advance, then rested in the refrigerator for an hour or so, plus another hour's resting after lining the pan. Grind the walnuts in the same way as almonds (p476), pulsing the nuts to avoid overworking them. Also, be sure that the food processor is completely dry before putting in the nuts to grind.

For the pastry

1½ cups (170g) unsalted butter, at room temperature
1 medium egg
1 cup (150g) all-purpose flour
1¼ cups (100 g) ground walnuts

For the filling

3 eggs and 1 egg yolk
1¼ cups heavy cream
3 tbsp low-fat milk
1 heaping tbsp chopped parsley
6 scallions, chopped
¼ cup grated Cheddar cheese
pinch of freshly grated nutmeg

1 Mix the butter with the egg and a pinch of salt. Add the flour and walnuts, and knead once or twice to combine the ingredients evenly. Refrigerate for at least 1 hour.

2 Roll out the pastry and line a 10in (25cm) tart pan. Refrigerate for 1 hour. Preheat the oven to 400°F (200°C), then bake the pastry shell for 15 minutes. If the side of the shell has slid down a bit, repair any gaps with pieces of leftover pastry. Let the shell cool for 10 minutes. Turn the oven down to 350°F (180°C).

3 Whisk all the filling ingredients together and season. Place the pastry shell on a baking sheet on the lower shelf of the oven and pour in the filling. Bake until the filling is set but still soft and lightly browned on top, about 30 minutes.

PREPARING FRESH CHESTNUTS

Chestnuts are available fresh, as well as canned whole, in pieces, or as a purée. To shell and skin fresh chestnuts, you first need to roast them—by heating them under the broiler, on a griddle, in an open fire, or in the oven—or you can blanch them in boiling water.

1 Before roasting or blanching, pierce the top of each chestnut with the point of a sharp knife to prevent it from exploding when hot.

2 Broil the chestnuts until the shells split, about 3 minutes. When cool enough to handle, peel off the shell and the inner skin. Alternatively, blanch the chestnuts by bringing them to a boil in a pan of water. Remove a few at a time and peel before they cool down.

3 To use in the stuffing (right), coarsely chop the chestnuts with a sharp knife.

CHESTNUT STUFFING

The stuffings that partner the Thanksgiving or Christmas bird are often more interesting than the birds themselves. This stuffing goes well with both goose and turkey, but is fine with chicken or any white game bird, too. If you do not want to use fresh chestnuts, you can substitute canned whole chestnuts (unsweetened).

Serves 6

2 tbsp butter
1 shallot, finely chopped
14oz (400g) fresh pork sausage meat
2 cups fresh bread crumbs
2 apples, peeled, cored, and diced
1 pear, peeled, cored, and diced
1¼ cups coarsely chopped chestnuts (see left)

1 Preheat the oven to 400°F (200°C). Heat the butter in a medium pan, add the shallot, and sweat until soft but not colored. Remove from the heat. Stir in all the remaining ingredients and add salt and pepper to taste.

2 Roll the stuffing in a sheet of well-buttered foil into the shape of a thick sausage. Bake for 1 hour. Serve cut in thick slices.

GLOSSARY

Acidulate To add an acid such as lemon juice or vinegar to cooking or soaking water to prevent vegetables or fruit from discoloring.

Al dente Literally "to the tooth." Pasta, rice, and vegetables may be cooked until al dente, which is until just tender yet still offering a slight resistance when you bite into them.

Amaretti Small, crisp almond cookies, which are sometimes sold in attractively wrapped in pairs.

Annatto and annatto oil Orange-red seeds from a small tropical tree, used to give color to Asian and Latin American cooking. Fat or oil in which the seeds have been fried turns deep orange.

Armagnac A brandy from southwestern France, sometimes used to flavor desserts or pâtés.

Aspic Savory jelly made from meat, fish, or vegetable stock, usually set with *gelatin*.

Bake blind To prebake a pastry shell without the filling, either partially or completely. The pastry shell is lined with paper and weighted down with beans to prevent it from losing its shape.

Baste To spoon fat or a liquid over food as it cooks to prevent it from drying out and to enhance the flavor.

Beurre manié Meaning "kneaded butter," this paste of butter and flour is added at the end of cooking to thicken a sauce.

Bhuna An Indian sautéing technique that lightly toasts spices, releasing their essential oils to flavor meat, fish, or vegetable dishes.

Bitter almond extract A flavoring made from bitter almonds that can add depth and balance when used with sweet almonds.

Blanch To immerse in boiling water for a very short time. Blanching is done to set color (vegetables); to eliminate strong flavors (some vegetables, sweetbreads); and to loosen skins before peeling (tomatoes, drupe fruit such as peaches, some nuts).

Brioche A lightly sweetened, butter-rich yeast bread, served plain or toasted, with jam for breakfast or with *foie gras* and strong cheeses for lunch or dinner.

Brunoise Very finely diced vegetables.

Buckwheat A grain used to make flour for pasta, dumplings, blini, and Japanese soba noodles.

Bulgur wheat Also burghul and bulgar, wheat grains that are boiled until they crack. Bulgur is a staple in the Middle East and used to make kibbeh and tabbouleh.

Butterfly To remove the backbone from a bird and then flatten it; to bone a leg of lamb and flatten it; and to split open a shrimp.

Buttermilk Originally a by-product of butter-making, today it is made by adding bacteria to milk to thicken and sour it.

Caramel Sugar syrup heated above 313ºF (156°C) until it contains very little water and takes on a darker color. Caramel is used as a topping for desserts and to make candy.

Caramelize To heat a food until its surface sugars break down and turn brown. Both savory and sweet foods can be caramelized.

Cartouche A disk of parchment paper cut to fit a pan and laid directly on the surface of food, to prevent evaporation and to keep it from drying out during cooking.

Cassava A root vegetable that is a staple in Africa and Central and South America.

Ceviche A South American and Caribbean technique of "cooking" seafood without heat. A lime juice marinade partially cooks thinly sliced raw fish, which is served cold, sometimes accompanied by boiled vegetables or salad.

Chiffonade Shredded herbs or leafy vegetables. The leaves are piled on top of each other, rolled up tightly, and cut across into strips.

Clarify To skim or filter a liquid, such as a consommé or melted butter, until it is clear and free of impurities. Egg whites are sometimes used to clarify consommé because they can entrap particulate matter. To clarify butter it is gently heated until the milk solids separate from the clear liquid fat, which can then be poured off.

Compote Fruits poached gently in a *sugar syrup* so they keep their shape.

Confit Meat or poultry cooked in its own fat to preserve it.

Coral The eggs of *crustaceans* such as scallops and lobster.

Cornichons The French name for gherkins, these are small, crisp, tart pickles.

Cornmeal Fine, medium, or coarse meal ground from dried corn. In North America, it is used to make cornbread and other breads; in northern Italy, it is known as polenta and cooked to make a dish of the same name.

Cornstarch A fine, white powder obtained from corn that is used to thicken sauces. It needs to be mixed with cold water before being heated.

Court bouillon A poaching stock, most commonly used for cooking fish.

Couscous A mixture of fine and coarse *semolina*, in which the finer flour binds itself around the coarser grains to form granules. Traditional couscous takes a long time to cook, but instant couscous is pre-cooked and needs only to be rehydrated.

Couverture A high-quality chocolate that melts and coats easily to give a glossy finish.

Crème anglaise A thin, vanilla-flavored egg-custard sauce, served warm or cold with many desserts; also used as a base for ice cream.

Crème fraîche A fermented, thickened cream with a tangy flavor.

Croquant Sugar and nuts, usually almonds, caramelized together and used to make *petits fours* and sweet baskets. Once crushed or milled into a paste, it is known as *praline*.

Croûtons Small cubes of bread fried until crisp.

Crustaceans Shellfish, such as lobsters, shrimp, and crabs, which have an exterior skeleton, segmented body, and jointed limbs.

Cure To add flavor and to preserve fish, poultry, and meat by drying, salting, and smoking or by marinating in an *escabeche* or *ceviche*.

Cutlet A thin cut of meat, often chicken or veal, flattened to tenderize it and to help the meat cook evenly.

Dashi A tuna and seaweed-based fish stock used in Japanese cooking.

Deglaze To use the caramelized juices released by roasted or fried meat, or vegetables, to make a sauce or gravy. A pan is deglazed by adding stock, water, or wine and scraping it to loosen the juices and sediment that stick to the bottom.

Devein To remove the dark vein from shrimp.

Durum wheat The hardest of all wheat grains with a high proportion of gluten, durum wheat is mostly used to make dried pasta.

Duxelles A classic mixture of cooked chopped mushrooms and shallots.

Egg wash A glaze made from egg or egg yolk and water or milk, brushed on foods before baking to encourage browning.

Emulsion A suspension of droplets of fat, such as oil or melted butter, in liquids such as water, vinegar, or lemon juice. Emulsified sauces include mayonnaise and hollandaise.

En papillote To cook foods by sealing them in a package (a "papillote") so as to retain texture, flavor, and aroma.

Escabeche Fried or poached fish pickled in a spicy warm vinegar and served cold as an appetizer. Vegetables and chilies may also be pickled in this way.

Fillet A boneless piece of fish or meat.
Fingerroot (krachai) A lemon-flavored rhizome used in Southeast Asian cooking.

Flour All-purpose flour, used for most cooking, contains a blend of high-gluten hard wheat and low-gluten soft wheat. Cake and pastry flours, which are used for many cakes and pastries, are soft-wheat flours. Italian "00," or "doppio zero," flour is used mainly for pasta. Bread flour has a high proportion of gluten, which makes it ideal for yeast doughs. Rye flour comes in light or dark varieties.

Foie gras The fattened liver of a duck or goose. Goose liver is the more expensive and more pronounced in flavor.

Fumet Concentrated fish stock.

Galangal A rhizome with a spicy-hot flavor, used in Southeast Asian cooking. It is prepared in a similar way to raw ginger root.

Ganache A rich chocolate cream that is used to fill cakes, decorate desserts and pastries, and make truffles.

Garam masala Meaning "hot mixture," this spice blend from northern India is usually added at the end of cooking.

Gelatin A setting agent available in sheet or granulated form; it must be soaked in cold water before being dissolved in a warm liquid.

Ghee A *clarified* butter used in Indian cooking and capable of being heated to a high temperature without burning.

Glucose A thick liquid added to *sugar syrups* to reduce the risk of crystallization. Corn syrup is a form of glucose made from *cornstarch*.

Gum arabic A powdered, tasteless gum that is used to thicken and *emulsify* foods, and prevents sugar from crystallizing. Available from specialist candymaking suppliers.

Gut To remove the viscera (everything in the stomach cavity) of a whole fish before cooking.

Hang To let meat hang after slaughter to disperse the lactic acid present in muscles, maximize tenderness, and enhance flavor.

Heritage varieties Vegetables and fruit that have not been hybridized to "improve" them. They often have a more natural, less-than-perfect appearance.

Jicama A bulb-shaped root vegetable native to Mexico, and also used in Southeast Asian cooking. It has crunchy flesh with a sweet flavor.

Jus French term for a light sauce produced by reducing a well-flavored stock. If thickened, it is called a jus lié.

Kadhai An Indian wok. Kadhai cooking combines stir-frying and sautéing, and uses specific spices.

Kaffir lime A knobbly citrus fruit, the leaves and zest of which are used in Southeast Asian cooking, particularly the cuisine of Thailand.

Kirsch A clear "eau-de-vie" (colorless brandy or spirit) made from black cherries.

Leaven (natural leaven) A living mixture of flour and water that causes breads to rise without the use of commercial yeast. It is also called a sourdough starter.

Legumes An excellent source of protein, vitamins, and fiber, the legume family includes peas and lentils as well as beans.

Lemon-grass A thick grass used in Thai cooking to add a lemon flavor and aroma.

Liaison A thickening agent, most often a mixture of eggs and cream, that is added to soups or sauces at the end of cooking.

Malt syrup Also called malt extract, a thick, sweet liquid made from barley that, when added to bread, gives extra flavor and a good texture.

Marinade A liquid for soaking or basting that adds flavor to food and protects it from drying out. If the marinade has an acid component, it can also have a tenderizing effect on meat, poultry, and fish.

Masa harina A finely ground powder made from corn that has been simmered with mineral lime, then dehydrated. Masa harina is used throughout Mexico, Central America, and South America to make *tortillas*.

Matzo Unleavened Jewish flat bread that resembles a cracker and is traditionally eaten during Passover. Matzo is also ground into a meal and used to make matzo balls, called "kneidlach" in Yiddish.

Meringue A light-as-air mixture of stiffly beaten egg whites and sugar, baked for a dessert or used as a topping for tarts.

Mirepoix A mixture of diced or chopped aromatic vegetables, usually carrots, onions, and celery, used as a flavoring.

Miso A paste made from fermented soybeans used in Japanese cooking as a flavoring and as a condiment.

Mole A smooth, rich, dark Mexican sauce of which there are many variations. Most moles contain a small amount of chocolate.

Mollusk A soft-bodied creature that usually has a hard shell. Mollusks include single-shell univalves, such as conch; two-shell bivalves, such as mussels; and cephalopods, such as octopus and squid, which don't have a shell.

Morels Stubby, short wild mushrooms that resemble sponges.

Mount To *emulsify* a sauce and make it richer and more glossy by whisking in small pieces of butter. Also, adding volume to egg whites or cream by beating in air.

Mousseline A very light, delicate mixture of puréed seafood, meat, or *foie gras* and cream, often shaped into *quenelles* and poached. Also, any sauce lightened with whipped cream or stiffly beaten egg whites.

Nam pla (fish sauce) A strong flavoring made from salted, fermented fish, used in Southeast Asian cooking.

Palm sugar A sugar obtained from the sap of sugar palm trees and used in Southeast Asian cooking. It is usually sold in a block, and is added to sweet and savory dishes. There are pale and dark versions of palm sugar.

Pancetta Italian cured pork belly, similar to bacon but not smoked. It is used to flavor pasta sauces and vegetable and meat dishes.

Parboil To partially cook in boiling water.

Parfait In French cooking, a dessert similar to ice cream made from custard enriched with cream and flavorings such as fruit purée.

Parmigiano Reggiano The true Italian Parmesan cheese, which is often aged for 2 years and sometimes longer. Available in specialty cheese stores and Italian supermarkets.

Pâte French for paste or pastry (also batter or dough). Pâte brisée is basic short pastry; pâte sucrée is sweet pastry.

Pâtisserie The art of pastrymaking and a collective name for the cakes and pastries sold in a shop that is also called a pâtisserie.

Pea eggplant A small, grapelike variety of eggplant with a rather bitter taste, often used in Thai cooking.

Petits fours Small, fancy cookies or cakes served at the end of a meal.

Pickle To preserve or cure foods, especially firm vegetables, in a brine or acid to give a sweet-and-sour taste.

Pilaf A method of cooking rice so that every grain remains separate, and also the name of the resulting dish. Pilafs can be plain or flavored with meat or vegetables.

Porcini Also known by their French name cèpes, porcini are an excellent species of boletus fungi. They are used fresh or dried to give a rich flavor to a variety of dishes.

Praline Nuts, especially almonds, that have been *caramelized* in boiling sugar and then crushed to a paste. See also *Croquant*.

Prosciutto The Italian word for ham, prosciutto normally refers to salt-cured and air-dried ham. That from Parma is the true prosciutto.

Purge To prepare mollusks such as clams for cooking by putting them in a large bowl of cold water with some cornmeal and letting them soak overnight in the refrigerator. The mollusks eat the meal and expel the sand.

Quick bread A bread raised with a leavening agent such as baking soda or baking powder instead of yeast.

Radicchio Italian red-leafed chicory, which can be eaten raw in salads, or braised or sautéed.

RAW A style of vegetable preparation where nothing is heated above 118°F (48°C) to prevent enzymes from being destroyed and food from losing its nutritional value. Techniques include sprouting nuts and beans, and marinating vegetables to break down their undesirable starchy complexity.

Reduce To boil rapidly in order to evaporate excess liquid. Reducing intensifies flavor.

Refresh To cool in cold or ice water. This stops the cooking process and cools food quickly.

Rehydrate To add water to a food that has been dried, such as mushrooms, to reconstitute it.

Render To gently melt fat from birds such as duck and goose or from bacon (bacon grease). Once strained, the rendered fat can be used for frying and roasting.

Rest To allow food to stand. Meat is rested after roasting to relax the muscles so juices are retained within the meat. If meat is rested, the taste and texture are better, and carving is easier. Pastry dough is rested before rolling out so the flour gluten can relax. A batter is rested before cooking so the flour particles can expand in the liquid.

Rice vinegar Usually mildly acidic and sweet, varieties include Chinese red, black, and white vinegars and Japanese kinds based on *mirin*.

Risotto A rice dish from northern Italy in which hot stock is stirred gradually into short-grain risotto rice until the grains are creamy, but still firm and separate.

Roasted shrimp paste (kapi) A strong-flavored paste made from salted and fermented dried shrimp; used in Southeast Asian cooking.

Roe Fish eggs, which may be hard (from the female) or soft (from the male, also called milt). If roe is salted it becomes caviar.

Roux A cooked mixture of butter and flour used to thicken sauces such as béchamel.

Saffron threads The dried red stigmas of the saffron crocus. One of the most expensive spices in the world, saffron adds color and a warm, musky flavor to food.

Salsify A long, slim root vegetable with a waxy texture. The variety with grayish skin is also known as oyster plant; the black-skinned variety is also called scorzonera.

Screwpine leaf A long green leaf, also called pandanus, used in Southeast Asian cooking to wrap food and to flavor rice dishes and sweets.

Semolina The endosperm of durum wheat, available in a variety of grinds and primarily used to make pasta. See also *Couscous*.

Shiitake Brown cap mushrooms that can be bought fresh or dried and are often used in Southeast Asian cooking.

Shuck To remove the outer covering, such as the shells of oysters or scallops, or the husks and silk from ears of corn.

Skim To remove fats and impurities from the surface of a sauce or other liquid using a perforated skimmer.

Smoke point The temperature at which an oil starts to burn and color. Oils with a low smoke point, such as olive oil, are unsuited to cooking at high temperatures.

Smoked sweet paprika Also called "pimentón," this is a mild Spanish paprika ground from aromatic sweet red peppers.

Soft-shell crab A blue crab that has molted its shell and is in the process of hardening its skin to form a new shell. The entire crab is eaten.

Spaetzle Squiggly dumplings made from a batterlike dough pressed through the holes of a special strainer into simmering water.

Squab A young domesticated pigeon that has dark, tender meat with a delicate flavor. Do not confuse with squab chicken.

Star anise A star-shaped, anise-flavored spice that is used in Asian cooking.

Stewing hen An older chicken, also called a boiling fowl, with good flavor but tough meat. Best used for stocks and soups.

Streusel A crumbly topping sprinkled over tarts, cakes, and muffins.

Suet The hard white fat that surrounds sheep or beef kidneys. Finely chopped fresh suet is used to make pastry, mincemeat, and stuffings.

Sugar syrup Sugar and water cooked together to different temperatures to produce varying concentrations of syrup for *pâtisserie*, confectionery, and chocolate products.

Tadka An Indian cooking technique in which foods, such as lentils, are prepared with few spices, then spiced just before serving.

Tamarind Sour pulp from the pod of a tropical tree; used in curries, chutneys, and sweets.

Temper To mix something until it reaches the correct consistency. Chocolate is tempered by heating and cooling until its fat stabilizes and it becomes glossy and malleable.

Tofu Also called bean curd, tofu is made from soybeans in a similar way to the preparation of curd cheeses. Tofu absorbs flavors easily and is used widely in Southeast Asian cooking.

Tomatillo A green husk tomato that is a distant relative of the tomato. Its citrus flavor is often combined with cilantro in Mexican cooking.

Tortilla Corn or wheat flat bread that forms an essential part of Mexican cooking. Also, in Spain, an unfolded omelet that traditionally contains potatoes and onions.

Tourner A cutting technique that involves shaving pieces of vegetable into seven-sided oval shapes. Often used for roots and tubers.

Turmeric A rhizome that is an important spice and food coloring, particularly in Indian cooking. In Thailand, the red (yellow) variety is added to curry pastes, while a white variety is eaten raw as a vegetable.

Vanilla sugar Granulated or confectioners' sugar flavored by leaving a vanilla bean in it.

Water bath A shallow pan of water, also called a bain marie, in which a container of food is set for cooking—in the oven or on the stovetop—or to keep the food warm.

Yeast A living organism that uses the natural sugars in a mixture to create alcohol and carbon dioxide. This process makes bread rise and gives beer and champagne their fizz. Yeast can be bought as compressed fresh yeast or active dry yeast (regular or quick-rising) and needs to be activated by mixing with a liquid before use.

Yuzu A citrus fruit with an agreeable sour taste. The bottled, salted juice and the zest are used a great deal in Japanese cooking.

Zest The colored, outer skin of a citrus fruit.

INDEX

Roasting temperatures & times

When you do not have a recipe for roasting a joint of meat, this chart will provide you with a foolproof formula for working out the roasting time. To calculate the time accurately, you need to know the precise weight of the roast, after stuffing if applicable. To test for doneness, you can pierce the meat in its thickest part (away from any bones) with a metal skewer. Leave the skewer in the meat for 30 seconds, then withdraw it: It should feel warm for rare meat; fairly hot for medium; and very hot for well done. For greater accuracy, use a thermometer.

SUITABLE CUTS, ON OR OFF THE BONE	ROAST AT 425°F (220°C) FOR THE FIRST 15 MINUTES, THEN AT 350°F (180°C)	
BEEF rib, rump, sirloin	rare medium well done	15 mins per 1lb (450g) + 15 mins 20 mins per 1lb (450g) + 20 mins 25 mins per 1lb (450g) + 25 mins
tenderloin (châteaubriand) weighing 3lb 3oz (1.5kg)	all at 425°F (220°C) rare medium	 25 mins 30 mins
VEAL breast, loin, round, shoulder	well done	25 mins per 1lb (450g) + 25 mins
LAMB breast, leg, rib (rack), saddle, shoulder	rare medium well done	15 mins per 1lb (450g) + 15 mins 20 mins per 1lb (450g) + 20 mins 25 mins per 1lb (450g) + 25 mins
PORK belly, leg, loin, shoulder	medium well done	25 mins per 1lb (450g) + 25 mins 30 mins per 1lb (450g) + 30 mins
VENISON leg, saddle	medium	20 mins per 1lb (450g) + 20 mins

Grilling & broiling times

The timings below are for meat that is cut about 1½in (4cm) thick, cooked on the grill, in a ridged cast-iron grill pan, or under the broiler. Timings given are the total time, and will vary depending on the type of pan, the exact degree of heat used, and the quality and thickness of the meat.

CUT	RARE	MEDIUM	WELL DONE
BEEF STEAKS Filet mignon	4 minutes	5–7 minutes	–
Rump, top round	6–8 minutes	10–12 minutes	12–14 minutes
Sirloin/entrecôte (rib)/ porterhouse	6–8 minutes	10–12 minutes	12–14 minutes
T-bone	6–8 minutes	10–12 minutes	12–14 minutes
VEAL Chops	–	12–14 minutes	–
LAMB Boneless loin, cubed en brochette	6–8 minutes	8–10 minutes	10–12 minutes
Butterflied leg	–	30 minutes	–
Leg steaks	6–8 minutes	8–10 minutes	–
Loin chops	8–10 minutes	10–12 minutes	12–14 minutes
Rib chops	4–6 minutes	8–10 minutes	10–12 minutes
Sirloin chops	6–8 minutes	10–12 minutes	12–14 minutes
PORK Belly slices (thin)	–	–	6–8 minutes
Leg steaks	–	12–14 minutes	–
Loin chops	–	12–14 minutes	–
Shoulder chops	–	12–14 minutes	–
Sirloin chops	–	12–14 minutes	–

PUBLISHER'S ACKNOWLEDGEMENTS

Dorling Kindersley would like to thank the following:

Hugh Thompson, for his initial planning and management of the project.

Bridget Sargeson, food stylist, for her unfailing professionalism and good humour in preparing and presenting for the camera over half of the techniques and recipes in this book.

All of the chefs who generously made available their facilities and materials for photography.

Editorial assistance
Valerie Barrett, Shannon Beatty, Stuart Cooper, Roz Denny, Barbara Dixon, Anna Fischel, Kay Halsey, Karola Handwerker, Eleanor Holme, Katie John, Bridget Jones, Jenny Lane, Beverly le Blanc, Irene Lyford, Marie-Pierre Moine, Connie Novis, Gary Werner, Fiona Wild, Jeni Wright.

Design assistance
Maggie Aldred, Briony Chappell, Murdo Culver, Jo Grey, Toni Kay, Elly King, Luis Peral-Aranda, Judith Robertson, Liz Sephton, Alison Shackleton, Penny Stock, Sue Storey, Ann Thompson.

DTP design assistance
Alistair Richardson, Louise Waller.

Editorial consultation
Rosie Adams, Henja Schneider, Margaret Thomason, Jill van Cleave, Kate Whiteman.

Translation
Janine Broom, Cristina Garcia, Barbara Mayer.

Index
Valerie Chandler & Dorothy Frame.

Chefs' liaison
Marion Franz (for Stephan Franz); Rosie Gayler (for Paul Gayler); Barbara Maher (for Stephan Franz); Anne Roche-Nöel (for Pierre Hermé); Rochelle Smith (for Charlie Trotter); Jane Wareing (for Marcus Wareing); David Whitehouse (for Dan Lepard).

On behalf of the contributing chefs
The following chefs prepared and styled food and demonstrated cooking techniques for photography: Sébastien Bauer (for Pierre Hermé), Julien Tessier (for David Thompson), Guiseppe Tentori (for Charlie Trotter).

Food stylists
Stephana Bottom, Angela Nilsen, Lucinda Rushbrooke, Nicole Szabason, Linda Tubby, Kirsten West, Sari Zernich. Susanna Tee for recipe testing.

Hand models
Virpi Davies, Harriet Eastwood, Saliha Fellache, Caroline Green, Jane Hornby, Olivia King, Emma McIntosh, Carlyn van Niekerk, Brittany Williams, Bethan Woodyatt, Tanongsak Yordwai (for David Thompson).

Props stylists
Victoria Allen, John Bentham, Bette Blau, Andrea Kuhn, Hendrik Schaulin, Helen Trent.

Photographic studio production
Carol Myers and Alex Grant at Divine Studio/Piquant Productions, New York; Sid Kelly at Code Management Inc, Miami; Oliver Beuvre-Méry at Blanc Loft, Gentilly, Paris; Nicole Werth and Stefan Richter at Lightclub Photographic, Hamburg.

Administrative assistance
Laura Dixon, Alex Farrell, Zoe Moore, Jolyon Rubinstein.